# Round the Tea *Totum*

*When Sri Lanka was Ceylon*

# David L Ebbels

authorHOUSE®

*AuthorHouse™ UK*
*1663 Liberty Drive*
*Bloomington, IN 47403 USA*
*www.authorhouse.co.uk*
*Phone: 0800.197.4150*

*Published by AuthorHouse  08/24/2015*

*ISBN: 978-1-4259-2174-3 (sc)*

*Library of Congress Control Number:  2006902303*

*View north over Lahugalla Tank to the ancient rock fortress of Govindahella ("Westminster Abbey"). Situated 10 miles from the east coast, inland from Arugam Bay, this was a favourite spot for watching birds and elephants. Floating vegetation covers most of the water.*

Valerie Jones, 1959, oil on canvas, 76 x 64 cm.

In memory of my sister

Valla;

for Shirley, to remember the early days,

and for

Suzie, Catherine and Tim

to explain how it was.

# Contents

# Illustrations

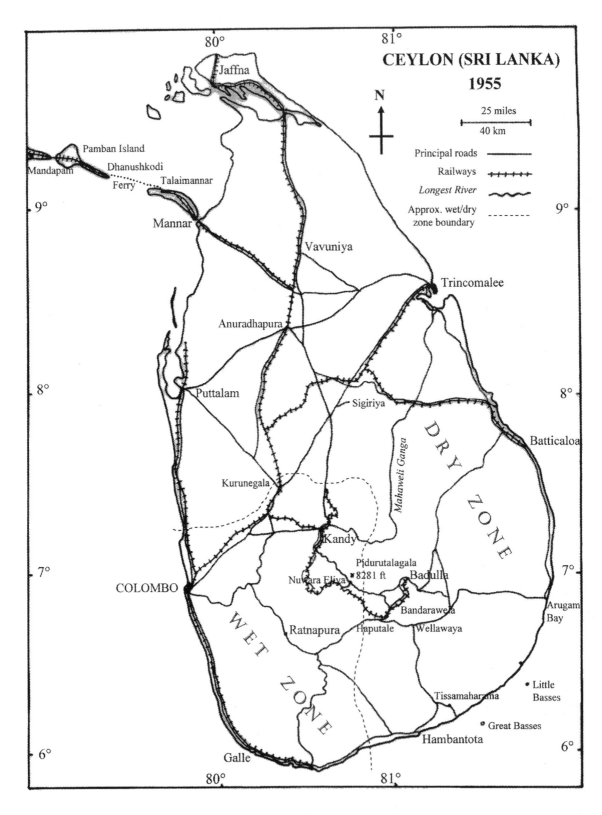

*Map 1. Sketch map of Ceylon (Sri Lanka), 1955. The eastern hill country around Badulla, Bandarawela and Haputale lies within the dry zone.*

x

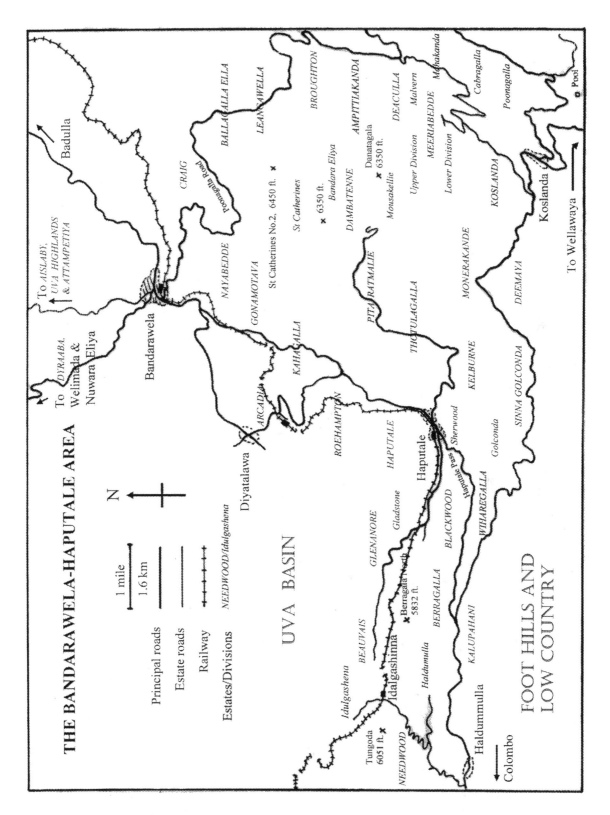

Map 2. Sketch map of the Bandarawela-Haputale area, showing the location of the principal estates and the highest peaks.

# Preface

This is the story of six years which I spent on tea estates in the green hills of Ceylon, now Sri Lanka, some 50 years ago. Ceylon became independent from Britain on 4th February 1948 so, by the time my story starts, independence was already nearly eight years old. But things had not really changed very much since pre-war times and I encountered many of the old attitudes and prejudices of the colonial era. However, beyond giving my personal reaction to events and circumstances, I do not attempt to criticise or condone any policy or attitude, either pre- or post-colonial, and I merely try to paint a picture of what life was like for a young tea planter in Ceylon during the last years of European participation in this industry.

The distinguished writer, Elspeth Huxley, remarked that, if one lived long enough, one would be surprised to find that one had lived through a part of history. This, of course, is particularly so if one has experienced major events or has participated in something which no longer exists. In the same way that the young and middle-aged people of today regard those who lived through the Second World War as part of history, so those who lived in Britain's long-relinquished colonies become, *ipso facto*, a part of colonial history. In this way, although they survived for a couple of decades after independence, the European tea planter of Ceylon has also become a part of history and has thus acquired some additional interest which was absent in former times.

Ceylon adopted the Sinhala name of Sri Lanka with the revised constitution in 1972. The Island has had many names over the past three thousand years and 'Lanka' is one of them. Nevertheless, at the time the events I describe took place, the name was Ceylon (which is still used in the tea industry), so it is appropriate to use this name here for most narrative purposes, reserving the name Sri Lanka for matters which are current today. Likewise, although Sri Lanka has adopted the metric system for most measurements, I have used Imperial units for the same reason. Those not familiar with these may like to know that 1 mile is approximately 1.6 km, 1,000 ft is equivalent to 305 m, 1 acre to 0.4 ha, and 1 lb to 0.45 kg.

My grandfather was the first of our family to work in the colonies, going first to British Guiana in the 1880s to escape the high unemployment in Devon. He became a sugar planter and later moved to Mauritius, where my father and both his brothers were born. My father went out to Ceylon in 1924 and eventually retired to the UK in 1965 after 41 years as a tea planter. So it was not very surprising that I should follow in his footsteps: it was a lifestyle I knew, the Country and climate were wonderful and, best of all, there was plenty of opportunity to enjoy the magnificent natural history.

This book was started about 15 years ago, but has only recently taken its final shape. I am most grateful to Nicola Seymour, Rothamsted Research, Harpenden, for help in preparing the front cover. I thank Garry Fry, Central Science Laboratory, York, for the portrait on the back cover. All illustrations which are not attributed to others are the work of the author except for one for which attribution could not be determined. I am also grateful to Karl Ludvigsen for elucidating the significance of the Uva Goose emblem shown on the players' jerseys in the photo of the rugby match.

Many centuries ago, a Chinese poet apparently remarked that to re-create something in words is like being alive twice. Perhaps it is easier to do this in the medium of poetry, but I have enjoyed a similar feeling while writing this book. If I have successfully conveyed something of this to the reader, I shall be well satisfied.

David Ebbels

Harpenden
January 2006

# Arrival 1

---

Railway authorities often seem impelled to give their rolling stock grandiose or fanciful names and the Ceylon Railways in 1955 were no exception. The *Uda-Rata Menike* or *Up-Country Maiden* was the name of the up-country mail train which each morning and each evening departed from Maradana Station in Colombo to run the 180 miles to the upcountry terminus at Badulla. It progressed from the coastal plain by way of the Kaduganawa Pass to Perideniya Junction, diverged briefly to call at the ancient Sinhalese capital of Kandy, and then continued on through Gampola and Narwalapitiya, climbing all the way up through the various planting districts to Nanuoya and eventually, near Pattipola, crossed the shoulder of the Horton Plains at over 6,200 ft. From there it gradually descended on the eastern side of the mountains to Haputale, Bandarawela and finally to Badulla, the capital of Uva Province which, at about 1,600 ft, was at a comparatively low elevation. The line had severely challenged the engineering skills of the time and was built in stages with lengthy periods of wrangling about funding and routes between each bout of construction. Starting from Colombo in 1858, it had arrived at Kandy by 1867, but it was another 57 years before it reached Badulla in 1924. The whole journey took about 12 hours, as there were stops at every station from Kandy onwards and, even with diesel engines both pulling from the front and pushing from the rear, the gradients and tortuous course of the line prevented very rapid progress. Like many maidens, however, the Uda-Rata Menike was a little unpredictable in behaviour. Indeed, there was always some degree of doubt as to whether she would arrive at all, for there were many possible hazards, ranging from floods and landslips (during the monsoons) to mechanical failures or even suicides on the line, which could upset the carefully published schedule.

It had been arranged that on 1st December 1955 I should take up appointment as a trainee tea planter with a firm named The Gibson Estates Ltd. This firm owned four tea estates, three of which (Needwood, Meeriabedde and Kahagalla) were in the Uva Province and it was on Needwood that I was to start my training. In my case this was not such an unusual choice of employment as it might seem. My father had been a planter in Ceylon since 1924 and I had been brought up on tea estates and amongst the tea planting fraternity from a very early age, with spells away at school in England and Australia. It seemed quite natural, therefore, especially for someone so interested in the outdoors and natural history as I was, that I should take up a tea planting career. It was quite common for planters' sons to follow their fathers into the planting business, and many could quote grandfathers or even great grandfathers who had been planters before them. Appointments were frequently arranged through the 'old boy' network. I believe that this was so in my case and, as far as I can remember, the post was found for me by one of my father's numerous ex-rugby-playing friends. At any rate, I do not recall any but the most perfunctory of interviews; scarcely more than an introduction to my new employers and of them to me. In fact they seemed a good deal more interested in the cricket and rugby results of the day than in their newest recruit and I was virtually ignored while rounds of pink gins and John Collinses lubricated their pompous gossip. It seemed to be confidently assumed by all concerned that the son of such a jolly good chap as my father, especially one who was the product of a well-known public school (even if it was Australian), must be eminently suitable to make a reliable estate superintendent.

In fact the people I met on this occasion were the directors, not of The Gibson Estates Ltd. (which was a firm based in London), but of their agents in Ceylon, the well-known Colombo firm of George Steuart & Co. Ltd. The George Steuart who gave his name to the firm was the youngest of three brothers, all of whom started out as mariners of one kind or another. Back in 1843, commercial activity had actually been started by the eldest of the brothers, James Steuart, but the firm was established in the name of his younger brothe,r George, to avoid apparent conflicts of interest with James' duties as a civil servant and to comply with civil service regulations. The UK civil service regulations have not changed in this respect. By the time I arrived on the scene, George Steuart had become the oldest-established and the largest of the Colombo agency houses.

On the appointed day I was driven by my parents from the estate where my father was superintendent to catch the train at Narwalapitiya. This was about an hour's drive along the narrow and twisting but tarmac-surfaced roads through the steep, tea-covered hills of mid-country Ceylon. At this elevation and in this area the tea estates did not completely cover the hillsides and the tops of the hills were normally left in untouched forest as a soil and water conservation measure. This was a left-over from one of the more enlightened policies of colonial days which had restricted development of land above 5,000 ft., so that the upper boundaries of estates opened after this edict could often be seen to follow this contour. Sometimes the hill tops and upper slopes would be covered by patana grassland which was maintained by occasional burning to produce grazeable new growth. It was composed of coarse, tussocky grasses, mostly the tall *maana* grass (*Cymbopogon confertiflorus*) commonly used locally for thatching, and was usually dotted with a few fire-resistant trees and shrubs. Crags and rocky outcrops of granite were frequent and the sides of the valleys usually sloped steeply to the boulder-strewn bed of a gushing stream or river running between grassy banks with occasional clumps of bamboo and scrub.

The small town of Narwalapitiya consisted of little more than the main street, lined with *caddies* - small, open-fronted shops which all seemed to be selling the same wares: dry and tinned foodstuffs, some vegetables, a few items of household hardware, and bananas hanging in bunches from the eaves. Although popularly known amongst the planting community as the 'arsehole of Ceylon' on account of its lack of amenities and high rainfall, on this day the weather was kind and the town almost picturesque. The small station was busy preparing for the main event of the day and the platform was crowded with waiting travellers accompanied by relatives and friends come to see them depart. On this occasion the train was more or less on time, it's approach being heralded while still some distance down the line by the drumming of its diesels straining at the gradient, and a few anticipatory whistles.

I was soon installed in a first class compartment and presently waved to my parents as the train pulled out of the station. There was no-one else in my compartment, although the second and third class carriages were crowded. However, it would then have been considered inappropriate for a European or a Ceylonese member of the 'professional classes' to travel in any but first class accommodation. Although this was eight years after independence, Ceylon society was still stratified rather sharply into social classes which echoed colonial times, with European and well-to-do Ceylonese at the top and the villagers and estate labourers at the bottom of the heap, with a myriad of employees such as post-office clerks, shop workers and civil servants occupying the middle ranks. In fact the Europeans themselves were divided into several sub-classes, with diplomats, planters and administrative types at the top and engineers and retail sales commercial people, who were regarded as 'trade', at the bottom. Although this hidebound and snobbish attitude was disappearing, it could still be found in many of the older planters and their wives, who retained views which had been much more prevalent between the wars.

The countryside moved slowly past the window as the train climbed higher into the hills. Gradually the scenery changed. The hillsides became increasingly covered with tea and less with patana, village gardens or rice paddies. We wound through estates where the tea bushes jostled ever closer to their neighbours, carpeting the contours in undulating waves of greenery and sprinkled with dadap or grevillea shade trees. Terraced paths converged and diverged from gravelled cart roads leading to tea factories clad in silver-painted corrugated iron gleaming in the afternoon sun. By the time the train halted at Hatton, tea had completely monopolised the landscape for some time, only the graceful outlines of the mountains giving relief from the 'green desert'. From Hatton the train continued to climb, giving brief vignettes of life on the estates through which it passed. A group of tea pluckers in bright saris beneath their dark head cloths chattered like mynah birds as their hands flew over the bushes and cast handfuls of leaf into the baskets on their backs. At the side of a road a lone kangani (foreman) in jacket and sarong was allotting them to the rows of bushes, his umbrella hooked neatly into his collar and hanging down his back. On another slope a gang of men were cleaning out the ditches and silt pits, some grunting as their mamoties bit into the soil and some leaning on their mamoty handles, gauging to a nicety the maximum possible period of inactivity possible without provoking the kangani's sharp tongue. Nearby, the low dadap and glyricidia shade trees were being lopped, the long and leafy branches seeming suddenly to detach themselves unaided and fall to reveal a climbing figure with glinting blade trimming the cut stump. Other men cleared the fallen branches from the tops of the tea bushes and chopped them to pieces between the rows to rot down into a mulch.

All this seemed comfortably familiar. I had seen it all a thousand times since childhood and the sights of a working tea estate seemed no more unusual to me than the activities on a building site would be to a city dweller. Yet I could not help a tinge of unease. It was all very well to be familiar with the sights, but how about being responsible for the smooth running of an estate? Would I be able to cope with the labour? My Tamil wasn't yet very good, although I had been doing my best to learn the language for the past eight months. How would I get on with my new boss? I was not used to dealing with bosses - except in the shape of schoolmasters - and I wondered what sort of person he would be: irascible and difficult or easy-going and friendly? Perhaps neither. Anyway, I thought, with 18-year-old optimism, it was no use getting worried; no doubt I would cope in much the same way as I had done during my boarding school days so very recently past.

The train continued to halt regularly at small stations through the tea planting districts, their signboards announcing well-remembered names which somehow had an evocative ring about them: Kotagala, Talawakelle, Watagoda, Great Western, Nanuoya. There was no doubt why the latter was familiar. Nanuoya was the station serving the hill resort town of Nuwara Eliya (pronounced 'Newrailiya') where I had had various spells at school. Situated high on a shelf of land amongst the highest hills at over 6,000 ft, Nuwara Eliya was the Simla of Ceylon, although it was never used as a seat of government. A boarding preparatory school had been established there for the children of planters and other Europeans so that parents did not have to send their offspring back to Britain as soon as they reached school age (as used to be the case), but could keep them in Ceylon following a British school curriculum geared to getting them through the Public Schools Common Entrance examination. It was confidently assumed that the normal goal was to move on at the age of 12 or 13 to one or other of the British public schools, of which so many of the planters were products (my father among them). At the beginning of each of the four terms during the year a convoy of children would travel up by train from Colombo to Nanuoya, the nucleus of children of commercial people in Colombo being augmented by planters' children as the train moved through the planting districts. The school bus would be waiting to collect us at Nanuoya station and up we would grind, round the twists and bends of the road until at Nuwara Eliya we were reunited with the smells of boiled milk and floor polish in the school buildings by the lake shore.

After Nanuoya the railway soon left the tea estates behind and below, continuing to climb higher through the dense and dark green highland jungle which had once covered all these hills. The deep valleys and ravines contained tumbling streams cascading down rocky beds, and at one point the white waters of the Elgin Falls appeared through the trees on the opposite side of a valley where the crystal clear waters of the Maskeliya Oya poured off the high plateau of the Horton Plains. Tunnels became more frequent and the weather more overcast, with some mist and light drizzle obscuring the mountain tops. The gradient eventually moderated and between the stations of Ambawela and Pattipola the line ran almost level. At Pattipola the rain increased and the few dark figures on the wet and glistening platform pulled coats and kumblies (dark, blanket-like cloaks) over their heads. At this elevation it was also cold and the dripping vegetation covering the sides of the embankments and cuttings looked depressing and rather forbidding.

Soon after pulling out of Pattipola we entered a lengthy tunnel from which, after some time, we emerged into completely changed countryside. Bright sunshine came through the carriage windows, glinting on the remaining drops drying on their grimy exterior. To the north a great vista opened across undulating hills and I realised we had passed the Summit Tunnel, highest point on the railway, and in doing so had passed from the wet hill zone (which receives both the south-west and north-east monsoons) to the dry hill zone (receiving only the north-east monsoon). At some times of the year the difference in weather between the entrance and exit of this tunnel can be even more dramatic than it was on this occasion, with hot sunshine replacing impenetrable fog and rain. I had never been on this side of the hills before and it seemed that I had now left behind not only the weather of the wetter hills but also the countryside that I knew. From now on I was entering unknown territory and I eagerly watched the hills and valleys roll by.

The view to the north was over the Uva Basin, a great depression in the hills some 20 miles across. The central area, at an average elevation of about 4,000 ft., consists of dry, rounded hills reminiscent of chalk downs and covered with patana grassland, small cultivations and eucalyptus plantations. The surrounding mountains forming the rim of the Basin are between 5,000 and 6,000 ft in height, but rise above this in the pyramid of Namunukula mountain to the east, the hills of Kandapola and Uda Pussellawa to the north, and in the west to the bastions of the Horton Plains where the jungle-clad slopes of Mt. Thotupolakanda peak at 7,733 ft. Tea estates form a broken band around the mountains of the Basin rim: there is less tea on the western side, and there are a few estates on the central hills (which during the dry months of July and August produce the much prized flavour teas which command high prices at the Colombo and London auctions). The railway line runs along the ridge forming the southern rim of the Basin, circling the perimeter towards the east and turning north at Haputale before descending gradually to the town of Bandarawela and on to the terminus at Badulla. At the highest elevations, after emerging from the Summit Tunnel, the line is cut sharply into the steep, jungle-covered hillsides, interspersed with short tunnels and cuttings and with magnificent northerly views. There was little life visible by the side of the track. A few blackbirds and bulbuls skulked in the undergrowth and a hawk-eagle circled over the deep ravines.

Presently the jungle covering the slopes below the railway gave way to tea, glowing golden green in the evening sunshine. A bungalow with a red roof appeared amidst the tea below, set in gardens which were obviously well tended with splashes of colour from flower borders clearly visible. I wondered who lived there. It was obviously quite remote, yet looked homely and well-kept. I knew my destination was the next station, which I thought must now be quite near, and perhaps the bungalow and its surrounding tea was in some way connected with the estate where I was to spend my apprenticeship.

A tea factory came into view below, with a cart road winding up towards the railway past a few small houses set in little gardens with grass fences. As the train rattled over a level crossing the dark hillside above the line suddenly fell away and the train was bathed in bright evening sunlight as it ran onto the saddle of the mountain and slowed to a halt at a small station. A signboard read 'Idalgashinna' successively in Roman, Sinhala, and Tamil characters. Gathering up my suitcase, I opened the carriage door and stepped down onto the platform.

Idalgashinna railway station must surely be one of the most spectacular in the world. The line, the narrow platform and one small siding occupy the summit of a knife-edge ridge at 5,200 ft. This is the Idalgashinna Pass (or Gap, as such features are usually called in Sri Lanka), bounded on the western side by the peak of Tungoda, which rises another 800 ft, and to the east by a lower hump which then gives way to a smaller 'gap' before the range rises again to the peak of Berragala North. To the north the land fell steeply away from the railway line in tea-covered slopes and the small room which served for both ticket sales and as the station master's office looked out over the undulating hills and valleys of the Uva Basin to the mountains of Uda Pussellawa and Namunukula to the north and north-east. However, the view to the south was even more spectacular. At the back of the platform a rickety fence guarded a drop to steep slopes, again covered with tea, which descended precipitously to the lowlands far below. Looking straight out, one could see a patterned and runched carpet of wooded foothills flattening out into forested plains which were dotted here and there with a few small 'tanks' (ancient irrigation reservoirs), the sheets of water winking and gleaming like discarded pewter salvers in the evening light. Far off on the horizon the sea showed as a pale band between land and sky, some 60 miles distant.

*View east over the Idalgashinna Gap to the peak of Beragalla North (5,832 ft.), showing the railway line and Idalgashinna Station. Some labour lines on Needwood Division are in the foreground, while Kahagalla Estate lies on the slopes of the distant mountains. On the southern side of the Gap the land falls away to the coastal plains.*

Not many passengers alighted. Looking round I became aware of a European walking towards me, dressed in navy-blue shorts, a cream-coloured short-sleeved shirt and long white stockings reaching to just below the knee. As he drew closer I saw he was rather heavily built, considerably shorter than myself, with iron-grey hair and what seemed to be an unusually florid complexion. He was accompanied by a small but solid-looking brownish dog who's appearance and demeanour gave just a hint that Aberdeen Terrier might have featured amongst his decidedly mixed antecedents. Busily investigating the numerous local smells wafted over the platform by the departing train, he came up to greet me with furiously wagging tail. His master and I were now within communication distance, so I decided to make the opening move.

'Mr Meikle?' I ventured, feeling much as Stanley must have done when he unthinkingly blurted his famously idiotic greeting to Livingstone.

'Aye. You must be Ebbels.' he replied, extending a hand, 'Good journey? The Landrover's over here.'

I patted the waggling dog. 'That's Haggis, - refers to his mixed ancestry, y'see.' he explained.

I followed him to a green, canvas-topped Landrover parked near the level crossing. Having deposited both Haggis and my case in the back, we set off along the narrow but tarmac-surfaced cart road cut into the southern slopes of the mountainside, which here was covered with tea to several hundred feet above the road. We soon came to the first of what proved to be more than 20 hairpin bends around which the road looped its way down to the lower areas of the estate. These were now darkening in the evening shadows as the sun descended behind the ramparts of the Horton Plains which rose as a continuation of the range to the west, above the winking lights of the small town of Belihuloya. A few lights had appeared elsewhere, but most of the vast landscape showed scant evidence of human habitation. Mr Meikle concentrated for a while on his driving as we seemed almost aerially suspended above the darkening view and then turned to me.

'How's your father?' he enquired. 'Used to play rugby with him long ago, but haven't seen him for years. A bit out of my class, though; captain of Ceylon, wasn't he?'

'He's fine, thank you, Sir' said I, groping in my memory along the endless cricket and rugby team photographs which hung in the corridors of my parents' bungalow, 'but I don't think he was actually captain, although he was in the Ceylon team; - captain of Uva, I think.'

He paused to consider this while he reversed back to get round a particularly sharp bend. 'Hm', he said, obviously prefacing a remark of some consideration and importance, 'I shall call you David in future.'

Evidently he considered the rugby connection sufficiently strong to overcome conventional protocol.

'Thank you, Sir' I said.

After descending for what seemed a considerable time but could only have been about 20 minutes, we passed Needwood tea factory, which occupied a site on a spur of the mountainside, and about a mile farther on we came to a barrier gate across the road, close by Needwood bungalow. Many estates had such barriers to control traffic and make it more difficult for stolen tea to be carted away or for undesirable people to enter the estate. Usually they consisted of a stout galvanised steel pipe, counterbalanced at one end and with provision for a padlock at the other. Normally they would be locked only at night and would be sited where a watchman could attend if anyone wished to pass through. Here the bungalow watchman did the job. In later years I found that, like many watchmen, he was a sound sleeper and when in the small hours it sometimes took a lot of hooting to wake him, I hoped that Mr Meikle would not be aware that I was the cause of the disturbance. On this occasion the watchman was ostentatiously alert, raising the barrier and salaaming loudly as we passed through and turned up the bungalow drive.

The Landrover came to a stop outside the garage, where I found the household staff assembled to greet me. This comprised the appu, or cook, who was always the head of the domestic staff, the kitchen coolie (who acted as assistant to the appu and also performed duties which would have fallen to the house boy in larger households) and Mr Meikle's driver, Muliniandy, who had not accompanied him to the station to fetch me but had occupied himself in cleaning and polishing Mr Meikle's large black Vauxhall Cresta car, of which he was obviously very proud. I returned the greeting salaams of the assembled group in the customary way, with my hands together in prayer-like formation and a slight bowing of my head. The kitchen coolie was detailed to take my case to my room while Mr Meikle showed me the bungalow. Planters' residences are always known as bungalows, although they are not invariably without an upper floor. Needwood Bungalow was typical, however, and was on one level, with a high pitched roof covered (unusually) with wooden shingles. A flight of granite steps led up to a spacious veranda which ran across the entire front of the bungalow and onto which opened the windows of the sitting room and dining room, with the front door leading to a passageway between them. The walls were covered in roughcast cement plaster which had been whitewashed and now supported a multitude of climbing plants. Against the rear wall of the veranda were stepped flower pot racks made of green-painted wood and these displayed a tremendous collection of different varieties of pelargonium. In resplendent bloom, these carried frothy heads of white and every shade of pink and scarlet, while the trailing varieties cascaded down the racks in waves of mauve and salmon. The open veranda looked out over a wide lawn bordered by flower beds with a large mango tree at one side and, at the end, the stupendous view over the lowlands to the distant coast.

It was immediately apparent that Mr Meikle was a keen gardener, although he did not do much actual gardening, and he could not resist leading me round the garden to point out choice plants and features. Everything seemed to be bursting with vigour.

'Aye', he said, when I complimented him on this, 'Shit, that's the secret. When I came here I found the labour lines piled high with shit - great heaps of the stuff - so I had the whole lot cleaned out and put in here. Did wonders. Dogs are good too.'

'Dogs?', I enquired, feeling I had lost the thread of the conversation.

'Yes. Shit and dogs. Lines were full of 'em. So one day I told the coolies to keep all their dogs indoors or tied up and had the rest shot. Then I buried two or three dogs under each tree, - and look at them now, especially those cypresses.' He indicated several dark and pencil-thin Italian cypress trees, apparently grown from seed which he had collected from a Tuscan monastery during one of his home leaves and which were now about 12 ft high.

My bedroom was at the back of the bungalow, near the kitchen. It was huge and dark, with a window much too small for the size of the room, giving onto a patch of lawn. The floor was of dark polished cement and, apart from the bed and mosquito net, the only furniture consisted of an upright chair, a small table, a dressing table, and an almirah (wardrobe) made of dark brown jak wood. In the far corner of the room a door led into the bathroom, which contained a huge cast iron bath set on sturdy legs and an equally massive porcelain basin and toilet. A bath mat stand of portcullis proportions, also made of jak wood, was pushed under the bath. On the wall adjacent to the WC there hung a small plywood holder which contained a packet of Bromo lavatory paper. This was generally considered to be a superior brand and was popular among the planting community. As one frequently had the opportunity to read on the packet, it had evidently won numerous prises and medals at such illustrious events as the Paris Exposition in the 1890s. These were conspicuously illustrated on the packet in graphic detail and it seemed that quality competitions for lavatory paper had been a common feature of such trade fairs. Bromo came as separate, individual sheets with the consistency of tracing paper, for which in fact it was often used as an effective substitute. Soft lavatory paper was unknown in Ceylon at that time.

After a bath I changed into a long-sleeved shirt and flannel trousers before going along the passage to join Mr Meikle in the sitting room. Like all the rooms, this was also large. The cement floor here was covered with rush matting and a well-filled book case stood against one wall. There were also two armchairs and a comfortable settee, but the outstanding feature was the huge, dark and highly polished Bechstein piano, a concert grand, part of which extended into the bay window. Mr Meikle was seated on a low pouffe, dressed in his pyjamas and dressing gown. In front of him, on the seat of an armchair, was a copy of the *Illustrated London News*, which he was reading by the light of a standard lamp. A half-empty bottle of Johnnie Walker, a soda siphon, and a single glass occupied a tray on the floor beside him.

'Ah, come in, David', he said, as I hesitated. 'I always dress like this in the evenings when I'm not expecting visitors. Saves the bother of changing twice. Do the same in future, if you like.'

'Thank you, Sir.'

'And I always sit here', he added, 'Got used to reading like this when the lights weren't so good. Use the books, if you want to.' With this, he helped himself to another tot of whisky and ignored me for the next half hour.

I was rather glad I did not have to make conversation and, not being a whisky drinker, I did not hanker after the Johnnie Walker. At first I found this kind of 'dressing for dinner' somewhat disconcerting and hardly the sort of thing of which the early empire-builders would have approved. It is said that King George V was much pained by rumours of similar slovenly habits amongst his white subjects in the wilds of East Africa, so perhaps it was just as well that he apparently remained unaware that such degeneration was to be found even in the respectable and esteemed colony of Ceylon. However, it was certainly convenient and in fact I adopted the habit myself when eventually I moved into a bungalow on my own.

Admiring the piano, I asked ingenuously if he was a pianist (it would certainly have been very curious if he wasn't).

'Well, hardly an expert performer', he replied, 'but I enjoy it and the piano has come everywhere with me, - sometimes with considerable difficulty. When I became SD on Idulgashena there was no cart road up to the division and it had to be manhandled all the way up the mountain along the paths through the tea. Took about 50 coolies two days to do it, and we had to cover it with a tarpaulin overnight. Luckily it didn't rain.'

'That's amazing', I exclaimed, wondering how he would react if I requested 50 labourers for two days when the time came for my own move. 'It looks in excellent condition after all that; - how do you keep it in tune?'

'Actually it seems to keep in tune pretty well, and occasionally I get a chap up from Colombo to check it over', he said. 'The only time I've had any trouble with it was on one occasion when several notes stopped sounding. When I had a look, I found some blasted creeper had grown through the window, under the lid, and into the strings - curled right round inside - so now I keep a sharp watch on the vegetation and Parkin polishes it every day.'

Turning my attention to the bookcase, I found that the books consisted almost entirely of volumes produced by the Gardening Book Club with titles like *Roses for everyone* and *Gardening on chalk and limestone*. On a lower shelf there were several photo albums with photographs showing Mr Meikle as a young man in various rather adventurous situations: climbing Mt Cook in the Southern Alps of New Zealand, sailing in a schooner in what looked like the South Seas, and various tropical scenes with palms and sea. There were also numerous papers and magazines, which evidently arrived on subscription as their successive issues were neatly arranged in serried ranks on a long table at one side of the room. Besides the *Illustrated London News*, there was *The Scotsman*, the *Economist*, the *Journal of the Royal Horticultural Society*, and the airmail edition of *The Daily Telegraph*.

At 7.30 Mr Meikle rose and rang the bell for the appu. 'Parkin', he shouted, '*Teeni condava*' (bring dinner).

'Yessah', replied the appu (whose name I discovered later was actually Paikiam), 'Dinner ready, Sah'. He had evidently been expecting the summons as he had already donned the customary high-collared white jacket which he reserved for waiting at table.

I followed Mr Meikle across the passage into the dining room, where two places were set, on opposite sides of the table. The room was in darkness except for a heavily shaded light hanging low over the centre of the table. An electric bell-push also hung from the ceiling on a long wire and with this Mr Meikle summoned the appu at the end of each course.

Dinner, which hardly ever varied, always started with either baked eggs or soup, both violently peppered. Not content with this, Mr Meikle added liberal quantities of chilli sherry from a bottle fitted with a top which emitted a few drops at each shake. This was a powerful condiment much favoured by Ceylon planters and also, I believe, by the Portuguese. Since it was they who brought chillies from the New World to Ceylon 500 years ago, and sherry from their homeland, chilli sherry is perhaps a legacy from Ceylon's days of Portuguese rule. It is made by soaking the small, red and exceedingly hot 'bird's-eye' chillies in sherry for several weeks, and a couple of drops are guaranteed to ignite the innards of anyone not inured to it.

After a meat course (also well peppered) Paikiam appeared with the sweet. This consisted of custard glasses filled with what appeared to be excellent junket.

'Hope you like junket', observed Mr Meikle, tackling his enthusiastically with a teaspoon.

'Yes, I do very much', I replied truthfully, 'but I didn't know it could be made with boiled milk'.

'Oh, Parkin seems to manage', he said, scraping the last vestiges from the glass, 'I have it every day'.

This caused me considerable doubt. I had been thoroughly drilled from childhood never to drink unboiled milk in tropical countries. My mother in fact made quite a ceremony of milk boiling, never entrusting it to the appu, but always doing it herself on a small paraffin cooker in the dining room. First she would strain the milk carefully through muslin to remove any foreign bodies (and usually there would be several bits of grass, various drowned insects and some unidentifiable black bits left in the muslin, even if there was nothing worse). Then she would pour the milk into an enamel saucepan specially reserved for the purpose, bring it to the boil, and simmer it for 20 minutes before allowing it to cool in a large jug sheltered from the attentions of interested flies by a circular net cover weighted at the edges with large glass beads. She religiously observed the 20 minutes boiling time, having read somewhere that nothing less would kill the numerous nasties which might be lurking in the milky depths. This was quite a tedious job, relieved only by the necessity of deftly juggling with the primitive cooker controls to prevent the milk boiling over, which was an almost daily occurrence.

I was quite sure that Paikiam and his kitchen coolie assistant had not done all this unsupervised and in truth I was also sure that junket could not be made with boiled milk, since my parents often bemoaned this fact. However, despite the fact that I knew tuberculosis, brucellosis, and many other unpleasant milk-borne diseases were common in estate cattle, I felt quite unable to make any demur on the occasion of my first dinner at Needwood. So I consumed the junket with relish, consoling myself with the thought that Mr Meikle had evidently been eating the stuff for upwards of 30 years and was still apparently hale and hearty. I ate it nearly every day for the next eight months without any ill effects.

After dinner we returned to the sitting room, where Mr Meikle continued to read his magazines and to partake of several more tots of whisky, while I resumed my perusal of the products of the Gardeners' Book Club. Eventually he put down *The Scotsman* and turned to me.

'Well, David', he said, 'its time we turned in. As its your first day tomorrow, I'll take you along to muster at 6.30 and introduce you to the Conductor. I've told Parkin to wake you at six'.

Slowly, I unpacked my case and put my clothes in the almirah. The single shaded bulb hanging from the centre of the ceiling had little effect in dispelling the gloom and the room seemed even more cavernous than it had done earlier. However, at this elevation it was not cold and the mosquitoes were lively. I could hear their high-pitched whines rising and falling as they patrolled the room, although it was too gloomy actually to see them. I crawled quickly into bed and tucked in the skimpy mosquito net, wondering if I really would make a success of planting and what might be the first symptoms of brucellosis.

# The lowest form of life　　　　　　　　　　　　**2**

---

The usual way for a European to become a tea planter in Ceylon was to be taken on in Britain by one of the British tea companies, or in Ceylon by their agents in Colombo, and placed with an experienced manager for about six months. After this one would be appointed as an Assistant Superintendent or 'SD' The manager or superintendent of an estate was always known as the 'PD', which stood for *Peria Dorai* or 'Senior Master', while 'SD' denoted *Sinna Dorai*, meaning 'Junior Master'. During the six months' apprenticeship the experienced PD was expected to impart to the new trainee (often straight out from an English public school) the essential elements of tea planting and give him the fruits of his experience, such as they might be. All this included basic agricultural principles, agronomy of the tea plant, the routine management of an estate and its labour force, including the rudiments of accounting and correspondence with the agents in Colombo, simple building construction, road making, and tea manufacture. In addition, and most importantly, the trainee had to learn the Tamil language as spoken by the Tamil labourers.

Tamil is a Dravidian language and is one of the major Indian languages, being spoken by millions in the large south Indian state of Tamil Nadu and by the related Tamil people who form the majority of the indigenous population of northern and eastern Sri Lanka. However, most of the tea and rubber plantations originally drew their labour force as indentured peasants from small villages in south India. Therefore, although Tamil is a highly sophisticated language, the plantation labourers spoke a peasant dialect with a much simplified grammar. The script is syllabic, with 247 characters, but it was not really necessary to be able to read and write Tamil so long as one could speak it reasonably fluently. Very few European planters were literate in Tamil or, indeed, had the inclination and ability to become so, as it was necessary to master the complications of the grammar before being able to write the language properly.

It was usual for European planting families to employ an *ayah* (nanny) for their children. Some ayahs did not speak very good English and so spoke to their charges mostly in their native tongue. Sometimes the parents took little part in looking after their children, who consequently grew up speaking Tamil or Sinhala (depending on whether the ayah was Tamil or Sinhalese) almost better than they did English. In some cases the ayah might be a burgher, an English-speaking Eurasian community descending from the Dutch and Portuguese colonists and perpetuating many common Dutch and Portuguese names, such as Muller, Van Rooyen, Van der Wall, De Silva and Perera. Many burghers occupied the top ranks of the professions and spoke English as their mother tongue, but the less well educated could be found in more menial positions. In this case the ayah might impart the sing-song 'chi-chi' accent to her charges, much to the horror of their parents. At that time, as Bernard Shaw maintained, one's accent was still regarded as defining one's social status and the development of a chi-chi accent would be regarded as a major disaster by the unhappy British parents, who would go to almost any lengths to get it eliminated.

My own parents, although they did employ a motherly and much-loved Sinhalese lady named Louise Podiharmini (known affectionately as Lou) as ayah for my sister and myself for a few years, felt very strongly that they did not want to relinquish the responsibilities of parenthood, and so we were rarely left in Lou's capable care. Although this was admirable in cementing our bonds with our parents, it also meant that we never acquired either Tamil or Sinhala as children and so, unlike many other planters' sons, I came to planting with virtually no knowledge of either language. I hate learning languages (although it seems to have been my fate through life to have had to learn something of several) and I found learning Tamil very hard going. Before I joined The Gibson Estates Company I had had several months' tuition from the local schoolmaster on the estate where my father was manager. Mr Vijayanathan was earnest and diligent and attempted to teach me the elements of the written language as well as the spoken. Although I was a poor pupil, he was successful in the limited time available in teaching me the script and enough spoken Tamil for rudimentary conversation. This was lucky for me, as I received no help from Mr Meikle, who made no attempt to teach me anything, either linguistic or agricultural. He seemed to assume that either I had received all necessary instruction from my father or that I would pick it up as I went along. Perhaps he felt too senior actually to spend time instructing a trainee and that the fee he drew from the agents on my account barely compensated him for the inconvenience and irritation of having me in the bungalow. In former times trainees had received no remuneration but, on the contrary, had had to pay their PD for instruction and their board and lodging. In the 1930s and earlier, PDs often used this system as an extra source of income, sometimes having five or six hopeful planters under training at a time, but without any guarantee of future employment. So Mr Meikle probably felt I was getting a good deal anyway.

Tea planting apprentices were universally known as 'creepers' and the term was also used as a verb. One often heard planters saying they had 'crept' with old so-and-so, usually to the accompaniment of some scandalous or scurrilous anecdote depicting the boss as hilariously eccentric or parsimonious. I am not sure of the derivation, but I was confidently informed by everybody that the reason was that 'creepers' had metaphorically only just crawled out of the primeval planting slime and were generally agreed to be the lowest form of life on any tea estate.

Very many of the tea estates in Ceylon were originally opened during the nineteenth century for growing coffee and were replanted with tea in the 1870s and 1880s as the coffee rust disease swept through the plantations, reducing the coffee crop to uneconomic levels. Later on, estates were opened from the mountain jungles directly into tea, and the hillsides became much more extensively cloaked with tea than ever they had been with coffee. To clear the land, the trick was partially to cut the trunks of all the main trees so as to leave them weakened but still standing. The cuts were made on the down-hill side of the trunks. Later, when the trees at the top of the slope were then felled, they fell on and collapsed those below them, like a pack of dominoes. When the wood had dried sufficiently, the fallen trees and brushwood were burnt to leave the slopes covered in nutritious ash and clear for the final removal of the stumps, cutting of paths, and planting of seedlings. In those pioneering days estates tended to be small, a couple of hundred acres or so; small enough to be closely supervised personally by the owner or his manager. As time went on, amalgamations began to take place and larger units emerged combining several of the original holdings into one estate and later combining several estates into Groups (as they were then known). The original holdings and estates often retained their identity and names as Divisions of the amalgamated estate or Group.

The early pioneers lived very rough lives in shacks and wooden huts constructed from the timber felled in clearing the land. They would have well fitted the wag's definition of bungalow construction as 'just put up four walls and bung a low roof on'. However, when the estates were sufficiently well established and had started to generate some money, the owner-occupiers usually built themselves substantial bungalows which, after the estates had been acquired by tea estate companies, were occupied by their superintendents and assistant superintendents. The vast majority had only one floor, but a few were two-storied, although all were invariably known as 'bungalows'. Some bungalows, indeed, were more than substantial, bordering on the palatial. These might have six or seven bedrooms, several bathrooms, and were often surrounded by gardens and views which were nothing short of spectacular. Although in pioneering days the first bungalows were usually constructed of timber or wattle-and-daub with thatched roofs, these later bungalows were often built of dressed stone blocks, as there was always a plentiful supply of granite on the rocky hillsides. They were usually roofed with corrugated iron, which experience showed to be the best material to keep out the torrential monsoon rains.

Needwood Group occupied 1452 acres, of which 1123 were tea in bearing. The rest was composed of timber plantations, upland jungle, patana grassland and rocky scree. There were three divisions: Needwood Division, which lay on the southern slopes of the mountain range and extended from the village of Haldummulla at 3,000 ft up to the jungles bordering the railway at 5,200 ft; Haldumulla Division, which also lay on the southern slopes, but to the east of Needwood Division, and Idulgashena Division, which lay on the northern slopes of the range, the other side of the railway, tucked away into the head of a valley reaching up to nearly 6000 ft.

Nearly all tea estates had their own factories, unless they were very small indeed. Groups and large estates usually had more than one, often retaining the factories which had originally served their constituent estates before they had been amalgamated. The main Needwood factory was on Needwood Division, but there was another, smaller, factory on Idulgashena, the one I had seen on my arrival, situated at a much higher altitude, just below Idalgashinna railway station. This received leaf from the higher elevations of all divisions and produced rather better quality teas than was possible at Needwood factory. Needwood 'Big Bungalow', in which Mr Meikle lived, was rather less than half way up the mountain between Haldummulla village and the railway, at about the same elevation as Needwood factory.

A Ceylonese 'conductor' was responsible for Needwood Division (theoretically under Mr Meikle's guidance), but on each of the other two divisions there were SDs. Wimal Wickremasinghe was in charge of Haldumulla and lived with his wife, young family, and a large German Shepherd dog, in the Haldumulla Bungalow, which was also at about the same elevation as that at Needwood and enjoyed the same view southwards over the jungle-clad plains to the coast. The SD on Idulgashena was 'Dinky' de Fonseka, a young bachelor, who lived in the red-roofed bungalow I had seen from the train on the day I arrived. Wimal was a pleasant and intelligent person and, although I did not see much of him, he was always very friendly towards me. He did not hold a high opinion of Mr Meikle, who he found difficult to deal with and to avoid confrontation he usually took the line of least resistance.

'David', he would say, 'that man is totally out of his mind. You simply cannot have a rational discussion with him. If he tells me to plant bushes upside down, I will do it - but I will not guarantee they will grow.'

It was still quite dark when Paikiam woke me with a knock on my door and a cup of tea. However, Mr Meikle was evidently already up as the notes of a Chopin nocturne being played quite competently floated down the passage from the sitting room. Chopin was evidently a favourite with him and for the following eight months I often awoke to a nocturne, prélude or polonaise. I dressed hurriedly and shaved using the jug of hot water Paikiam had thoughtfully brought along with the tea. In fact at this time shaving was still quite a novelty to me and it did not take long to remove my rather slight growth, but I thought I had better look as smart as possible on my first day. Dressing also did not take long as one did not need more than shorts and shirt, with a short-sleeved jumper for the chill of the early mornings and evenings.

There was a very definite planting 'uniform', although I did not then recognise it as such as it had been normal dress for my father for as long as I could remember. Basically, the outfit consisted of khaki shorts and a short-sleeved shirt, both usually made locally from Indian or Ceylonese cotton cloth by one of the innumerable tailors in every town and village. However, these were no ordinary shorts, having long and voluminously wide legs which kept one cool and also shaded the backs of one's knees from the sun. Today, they would provoke most people to hysterics, but in those days they were just considered normal attire and were certainly practical and comfortable. Another peculiarity, which sometimes could also be found on locally made trousers, was that the size of the waist was adjusted on each side by straps and little buckles with sharply pointed prongs which had to be removed each time they were washed. Shirts tended to be of a rather military pattern and often had button-down flaps over breast pockets on either side. Of course they were always tucked in and were never worn outside shorts or trousers, which would have been regarded as dangerously slovenly even if it was not thought to cast doubts on one's character. Below the shorts the traditional planter wore long khaki cotton stockings, reaching to just below the knee, and locally made stout shoes soled with crepe rubber of local manufacture. These sometimes had canvas leggings attached to ward off the leeches. In my own case, as one of the younger generation, I demonstrated my independence of habit by dispensing with the stockings in favour of ankle socks, and on Needwood leeches were not such a pest as to necessitate leech leggings. Quite a variety of hats were worn, but the old-fashioned solar topee and double Terai had long since disappeared, killed off during the second world war by the self-evident fact that service personnel who did not wear them did not promptly die of sun stroke. Many planters, myself included, favoured khaki cotton hats in a vaguely Homburg style which were manufactured in Colombo.

I found Mr Meikle already at the wheel of the Landrover and, as the eastern sky brightened, we soon covered the mile between the bungalow and the muster ground near Needwood factory. Here Mr Meikle briefly introduced me to Mr Premadasa, the conductor, and disappeared back to the bungalow, leaving me to observe the proceedings. The post of conductor was the most senior in the hierarchy of estate field staff and ranked approximately equal to the Head Clerk (who was in charge of the estate office) and the Head Teamaker (who was the factory manager and was responsible for tea manufacture). Below him, depending on the size of the estate or division, there came the overseer or *kanakapullay* (KP for short) and assistant KPs, whose job it was to allot the daily tasks (*kanaks*) and see that they were done properly, to weigh-in the picked leaf, issue tools and rations, and sort out minor problems. Conductors were usually well educated and tri-lingual in English, Tamil and Sinhala. Some were very superior personages indeed and could hope eventually to make the transition to senior management by gaining appointment as an SD. This was similar to making the transition between NCO and commissioned officer and was just as difficult.

Muster was held at 6.30 a.m. six days a week, Sunday normally being a holiday. Like many aspects of estate life, it was operated in military style and for the many ex-army planters muster took on all the ceremony of a parade ground. One difference, however, was in the dress of the participants, the working clothes of the labourers being considerably less than smart and some garments seemed to have greater areas occupied by holes than by fabric. The men normally wore a sarong and a short-sleeved shirt, although the younger ones sometimes wore vests and shorts, and all were barefooted. The older ones normally wore a loose turban while youngsters were bare-headed. They paraded in line, each gang headed by a *kangany* or headman who in former times would have been the headman who had arranged the recruitment of his followers from their village in India and to whom they would have been responsible. In these modern times, however, a kangany seldom had this status and relationship and might have been appointed by reason of his reliability and force of character.

Usually he would also have come from a high caste family and often was related to former kanganys and headmen.

Mr Premadasa was busy allotting tasks for the day. One field was being pruned and the regular pruners were not at muster. As befitted those skilled in this estate task of highest status, they were allowed to go straight to the field and to keep their pruning knives with them at home. However, a few extra hands were needed and these men were carefully selected and sent to the tool store for the KP to issue them with the distinctively-shaped pruning knives used for all cutting and trimming jobs on tea estates. Rather like a slim billhook with a short handle, the blade was straight for 4 or 5 inches and then curved sharply almost into a semi-circle, with a sharp point. Next a gang was allotted to continue applying fertiliser according to the estate's manuring programme and they marched off to the fertiliser store to be issued with the necessary measures - little tin scoops on the ends of sticks - which held the dose of fertiliser for one tea bush and *shundus* for measuring out the fertiliser from the sacks. These shundus were cigarette tins of the cylindrical, 50-cigarette size, and were used universally for measuring all kinds of dry foodstuffs and other goods. The heavy bags of fertiliser were not issued to the labourers at muster but would be transported by the estate lorry to the point on the cart road nearest to the area to be treated. As was usual, there was then assembled a gang for cleaning out the field drains and they went off to be issued with mamoties (the large, flat-bladed hoes used throughout the tropics) and alavangoes. The latter were a sort of crowbar which seem peculiarly popular in Sri Lanka (although usually bearing the words 'Made in England'), being a stout and straight steel bar about 5 ft long with a sharpened point at one end and a flattened blade at the other. Mr Premadasa went on methodically allotting various kinds of work for the day until finally the remaining odds and sods were herded together to form a weeding gang and were dispatched to one of the farthest fields clutching their *surrandys* - small, angled, weed scrapers on a short handle. Mr Premadasa entered the number of labourers against each task on a printed list, added in the figures brought to him by the assistant KP for the pruners and pluckers (who also did not attend muster), and made a total for the day of all labourers who had turned out for work. Entering this at the foot of the list, he signed it with a flourish, tore it off the block and handed it to me for delivery to Mr Meikle.

As I walked back to the bungalow in the bright early morning sunshine the air was delightfully cool. At this point the spur of the mountain on which Needwood factory was built more or less obscured the distant view to the coast, but the midday haze had not yet developed and I admired the long ridge of the Rakwana hills, standing clear to the south-west. At one point on my way there were some labour lines near the road and I found myself the object of sensational interest. Innumerable scantily-clad children of various sizes crowded the compound, almost falling over one another in their efforts to get the best view of me, and a chorus of '*Salaam, Dorai*' was repeated to beyond the point of impudence. Some of the older ones showed off their scholastic prowess with 'Good morning, Sah'. Not wishing to encourage too much of this, yet feeling obliged to make some response, I gave them a suitably dignified wave, wondering how long it would be before the novelty of my presence wore off. However, my regular appearance each morning on the way back from muster never seemed to be less than the most exciting event of their day all the time I was on Needwood.

Back at the bungalow, I found that Mr Meikle had already left for the estate office, adjacent to Needwood factory, and so I breakfasted alone. The sun came streaming in at the dining room window, gleaming on the well-polished knobs and corners of the furniture and glinting on the pieces of silver and brass on the sideboard. Being a bachelor, Mr Meikle had relatively few of these, presumably inherited from relatives, but in many planters' bungalows the dining room housed considerable collections of silver and brass pieces, many of which would have been locally made wedding presents, as Sri Lanka is famous for its brass and silverware and such items were favourite gifts. Such displays were often the pride of the planter's wife (always addressed by the household servants as 'Lady' or *Dorasani*) and keeping them polished provided almost continuous employment for the most junior houseboy or *podian*.

Paikiam did a good breakfast, often starting with a grapefruit and including porridge, bacon and eggs (well peppered, needless to say), toast and, of course, tea. In fact tea estate superintendents and their assistants did not enjoy unlimited supplies of tea, although they usually had a free allowance of several pounds of loose tea per month (tea bags had yet to be invented). This was generous enough for personal needs and to give as a perk to the bungalow staff, but it did not always cover the occasional present to friends and visitors, for which extra sometimes had to be bought at the prevailing market price if enough had not been saved from one's allowance.

My morning task was always to make a tour of the Division on foot, visiting every item of work going on that day. First and foremost there would be the fields being plucked (usually two or three) and then any fields which were being pruned. Special works, such as planting up a new area, nursery operations, or repairs to a bridge or culvert, also required special attention. Other works, such as cleaning out the road and field drains, lopping shade trees, or weeding were visited en route. It took quite a lot of planning to visit all the works being done by the most direct path and I walked many extra miles along the inspection paths through the tea before I knew the Division well enough to pick the best route. It also took me several weeks before I got to know the fields into which the Division was divided. I think there were 15 or 16 of these and their boundaries were usually anything but clear except where they followed a ravine, a road, or where they bordered non-tea land. Otherwise field boundaries followed drainage ditches (often completely hidden by the bushes meeting over them), minor footpaths, lines of steps, or even simply an imaginary line between one bend in the road and another. Also, unless they had recently been pruned or were at very different stages of growth, to my inexperienced eye the tea in all fields tended to look much the same: a continuous, thigh-high shrubby green carpet smoothly following the contours of the hillside.

The tea plant, if left to its own devices, grows into quite a handsome small tree up to about 20 or 30 feet high. For tea production, however, it is pruned and shaped (sometimes by pegging down the branches) to form a flat-topped bush. Once established, it is deep rooted and quite tough, living and producing for upwards of 100 years if given reasonable conditions. As its scientific name (*Camellia sinensis*) implies, it is a close relative of the ornamental camellias. It is also very variable in its botanical characteristicss. The two main types are the China teas (slow growing with small leaves and mild flavours) and the Assam teas, which normally grow faster, have larger leaves and give stronger infusions. Indian teas are of the Assam type and it was this type which was introduced to Ceylon. However, because in the early days all tea was grown from seed and not from cuttings, the individual bushes in older fields varied enormously in size of leaf, growth habit, ease of flowering, resistance to disease, and in almost every other conceivable way. In its native habitat in the upland forests of Assam and Burma tea is part of the under-storey vegetation beneath the canopy of the taller forest trees and it was generally assumed that it would grow best in shaded or semi-shaded conditions. Tea plantations were therefore quite intensively planted with shade trees dotted amongst the tea bushes. Many different kinds of shade trees were used, according to the density of shade intended and the altitude of the land, and these made a very pleasant landscape as well as providing shade for humans and being good for birds. Some shade trees were huge, like the giant albizzias (*Albizzia gigantea*) which grew to 100 ft in height with a wide crown of feathery leaves spreading to about the same distance in diameter, supported by a massive trunk and framework of branches. Others were smaller and often of leguminous species, such as the dadap (*Erythrina lithosperma*) and glyricidia (*Glyricidia maculata*) which it was hoped would benefit the tea by adding nitrogen to the soil and having foliage which could be lopped to provide green manure. Other commonly planted shade trees were mimosas of various kinds (at the higher elevations) and the Australian silky oak (*Grevillea robusta*). The latter formed a tall tree and provided estates with good timber and firewood.

Some time before I arrived on Needwood it had been shown by the Ceylon Tea Research Institute at St Coombs Estate, up at Talawakele, that shade, especially heavy shade, was not essential to the wellbeing of the tea bush. In fact, if the shade was removed and the application of fertiliser increased, the yields could be substantially improved. This piece of information percolated down to the estates through the reports of Visiting Agents and the T.R.I. journal (which was read by some of the more progressive planters) and was being put into practice on Needwood in so far as the giant albizzias were being removed. One could not simply cut them down as they would each have destroyed a sizeable area of tea in their fall. Instead, a couple of years previously they had been killed by ring-barking (removal of a band of bark from around the main trunk) and were now being felled in each field shortly before it was due to be pruned. However, in most fields the dead trees were still standing, white, gaunt and leafless, having shed most of their bark, smaller twigs and

branches. In fact the wood (which was rather light and brittle anyway) was now becoming quite rotten, and the crack and crash as another branch was shed could be heard quite frequently on my perambulations. But although they did not improve the landscape and were becoming something of a hazard to those working beneath them, the dead albizzias were a paradise for every kind of wood boring bug and bird, which were many and various.

The large black carpenter bees with their steel-blue bodies rasped their way into the wood, making large, deep, and beautifully circular nest holes which looked just as though they had been cut with a joiner's brace and bit. One usually saw them devoting their attentions to the exposed ends of rafters around the eaves of bungalows and other buildings, but here they could exercise their talents to the full. These heavy-bodied carpenter bees zoomed around at high speed with the drone of model aeroplanes and were commonly known as 'borer beetles'. Wood-boring types of true beetles also abounded, but their tunnels did not compare in size with those of the carpenter bees.

The birds which benefited most from this abundance of dead wood were the woodpeckers. Sri Lanka is a good place for woodpeckers and nine different species occur on the Island. Of these, no less than seven were present on Needwood and their populations had exploded to exploit the food and nesting sites which the dead albizzias provided. The drumming noise which the birds produce by rapidly hammering their closed bills on the tree trunks could be heard everywhere and flashes of green, red and yellow showed amongst the white branches as the birds swooped from the top of one tree to the base of another with their characteristic undulating flight. The woodpeckers varied a lot in size, from the tiny, sparrow-sized Pigmy Woodpecker to the large Red-backed Woodpecker, the size of a pigeon with red wings and a fiery crest. Judging by the size of the entrance, one could usually make a good guess as to which species was the owner of any particular nest hole and, not being restricted by cold or lack of food, there were nearly always some birds nesting. Occasionally, however, one would be surprised by a different bird emerging from woodpeckers' nest holes. Barbets and parakeets especially were quick to move in when woodpeckers of similar size moved out. These were consequently also numerous and greatly enhanced the bird population with their brilliant colours and varied calls. Except for their drumming, woodpeckers are usually rather silent birds, but the barbets and parakeets were anything but silent. The latter flew fast and straight in tight little flocks like clusters of green arrows, screeching as they went, while the barbets were more sedentary and could usually be seen perched on top of a bare tree making their mellow, fruity and resonant, but rather monotonous 'wok, wok, wok' calls, which echoed around the estate during the heat of the day.

After breakfast I collected my hat and stick and set off on my round of the estate works. My first call was to the gang of pluckers in a field not far from the bungalow. As I approached, the nearest kangany salaamed respectfully, making a kind of salute by raising his hand in front of his face to touch his forehead. I returned his greeting (but without the salute) and could hear a sudden increase in the babble of chatter as the women pluckers moved through the tea. My arrival was obviously the talking point of the day, if not the week.

Plucking tea leaves seems a simple task, but in fact there was quite a lot to it. Firstly, the objective was to take only the apical bud and the top two leaves from each shoot. If the shoot was at just the right stage of growth since the last plucking, it would carry three full leaves above the small 'fish' leaf on the new growth from the axillary bud below the last plucking point. The plucking rounds

*A tea plucker in a typical tea field.  Photo: Catherine Ebbels.*

on the estate were supposed to be arranged so that each field was plucked when most shoots were at this stage which, on Needwood, varied from about 8 days at the lower elevations during the monsoon, when growth was lush and rapid, to about 14 days or more at the highest elevations, especially in the dry months and in fields which were several years from their last pruning.  However, all kinds of events would interrupt this schedule, including festival holidays, lack of sufficient labour and bad weather, let alone labour disputes, which could result in go-slows or even strikes.  Any of these (or a combination) could result in the plucking rounds becoming too long, resulting in too much shoot growth on the bushes.  Constant vigilance would then be needed to try to ensure that the pluckers still kept to two-leaves-and-a-bud and did not succumb to the temptation to take more of the shoot, including the tough lower stalk and fibrous lower leaves, which had to be broken off and discarded.  Such temptation was in fact extremely strong because pluckers were paid extra for every pound of leaf above the daily norm or 'kanak', set each day by the KP according to the amount of growth on the bushes and also taking into account other factors, such as the steepness of the terrain.  In fact the KP and the kanganys needed to watch like hawks to keep the plucked leaf of good quality.  Every kind of ruse was used by the pluckers to evade supervision and to increase their weighed total for the day including, on wet days, dipping their baskets in the nearest stream when the KP wasn't looking.  On the other hand, when growth was slow, there was less leaf to pluck and then one would find that the shoots were being plucked right down to the 'fish' leaf, or even below, which deprived the bush of young photosynthetic tissue and delayed the new growth coming on.

There were about 80 women in the plucking gang on this day, each dressed in a less-than-pristine 'working' sari and tight, brightly coloured bodice.  Most of them had wrapped hessian sacks or sacking around their waists as protection against the stiff branches of the bushes and in an attempt to ward off the worst of the morning dew with which the lower leaves were loaded (plastic sheeting had not yet made its appearance).  All had large cylindrical plucking baskets made of split bamboo

17

slung on their backs and supported by a rope or strap coming up over their foreheads. Hands flashed over the surface of the bushes, gathering handfuls of leaf shoot by shoot and throwing each handful over the shoulder into the baskets without pause in either plucking or chatter. The best used each hand independently, like a skilled pianist, and seemed to take no more note of what they were doing than an experienced knitter. The tea bushes were planted in rows running more or less up and down the hillside, as was usual for plantations established before the need for soil conservation was realised, and these, being large bushes several years from pruning, had mostly met both within and between the rows to form a continuous cover, making it quite difficult for the pluckers to push their way along. Parts of the field were extremely steep and in these places the pluckers had to haul themselves and their heavy baskets from bush to bush, up the slope or down, and the next bush could be level either with her head or feet. One group of pluckers had come to the end of their rows and were being allotted to new rows by one of the kanganys, who was walking along the path counting the bushes and whacking each allocated row with his stick. I climbed up the bank with them and pushed my way across the rows to see the work of each plucker. Besides gathering the proper parts of the shoots, pluckers were also expected to maintain and improve the 'plucking table' - the flat top of the bushes parallel to the slope of the ground. All shoots above the level of the 'table' had to be snapped off together with any shoots which had stopped producing new leaves and had either ceased growth altogether (gone 'banji', as was said) or had gone into the flowering phase. Some pluckers carried thin straight sticks which they placed across the tops of the bushes to help in judging the level, whilst others relied on eye alone. In my presence the kangany became exaggeratedly animated, calling to the pluckers to take only the young shoots, to remember to remove the 'banjies', and to keep to their own rows, - all of which they knew perfectly well and I knew that he would subside into a more apathetic mode as soon as I had disappeared around the hillside.

I asked him how many pluckers there were in this field and quickly checked his figure by counting. I would later have to compare this with the total recorded on the Conductor's muster chit to make sure neither he nor anyone else was falsely charging pluckers to the payroll while in fact he was getting them to do work for him at his house, or even perhaps favouring a woman with a day's pay for other motives.

After half an hour with the pluckers I left them and made my way up the steep hillside along one of the many inspection paths zig-zagging across the slopes towards the field which was being pruned. It was counter-productive to stay with any work gang for too long: their initial increase in work rate on my appearance would gradually subside and too close supervision would only generate irritation and annoyance. Besides, I should seem to be unduly suspicious and, in the end, also to accept the final slower rate of work as the norm. So, having checked that nothing seemed seriously amiss, I moved on and left them to their routine.

The pruning field was easy to spot. After pruning had been going on for several days, the areas cut first would show at a distance as grey and brown in contrast to the usual green, as the cut branches littering the slopes dried out and their leaves withered brown and fell. Newly pruned areas presented a chaotic appearance, with the cut stumps of stems covered in jumbled drifts of prunings, sometimes up to waist height. However, usually the prunings were quite quickly disposed of, as fuel was always scarce on tea estates and the labourers welcomed the chance to stock up with firewood from this plentiful source. Small groups of children were busy collecting the dry prunings, brushing them together to knock off the remaining leaves, and tying them into bundles as big as themselves for carrying back on their heads to the lines.

Pruning tea is strenuous work as well as requiring skill and dexterity. In Sri Lanka it is usual to prune the bushes quite severely, cutting right down to the thicker stems, whereas in some other tea-growing areas where it is done more frequently, the pruning is much lighter. The gang of pruners and their kangany had little breath for talk and only occasional questions or shouted instructions could be heard above the rustle and crash of branches being cut and rolled aside and the thud of knives biting into the wood. Tea wood is hard, pale and close-grained, rather like boxwood, and the knives had to be kept razor sharp. This was usually done with a simple method which I often used myself for sharpening all manner of knives. As I approached, one of the men straightened himself and stepped down onto the path. Selecting a branch about the thickness of my wrist which had been lopped from one of the soft-wooded shade trees, he deftly shaved a short length flat on one side and propped the branch up against the bank. Squatting down on his haunches, he held the base steady with his feet. Taking two pieces of milky quartz (of which there was plenty on every hillside) he tapped them together so that a fine quartz powder descended onto the flat cut surface of the branch. Spreading this evenly with a stroke of the back of the knife, he then began to strop the blade on this surface until, testing it with his thumb, he was satisfied with the edge he had given it. The fine and hard particles of quartz were held and became ingrained amongst the soft fibres of the wood, making this a surprisingly effective improvised whetstone which could give a very keen edge to knife or axe, as was only too evident by the numerous strips of bloody cloth bandage which covered cuts and nicks on the hands or legs of most pruners. In fact pruning knives were not the only hazards in the pruning field. The sharp, obliquely cut ends of stems could cause ugly wounds on legs and ankles and were often hidden from view by the piles of cut branches heaped over them. These also obscured the sometimes deep drains running through the field which could then act as effective man traps for the unwary, as I found to my cost. Wounds, especially deep jabs from cut tea stems, could often become septic in these tropical conditions and some time previously I had had a severe dose of blood poisoning in this way, recovering only after the administration of large doses of penicillin to which, fortunately, I react with miraculous rapidity.

I again asked the kangany how many there were working in the pruning field and checked his reply. I then spent some time watching carefully how the pruning was done, as I felt very much a novice amongst these men, most of whom had many years experience of the work. The kangany seemed to sense this (knowing full well that I was a 'creeper') and kindly gave me a demonstration, attacking a large and overgrown old bush with swift and sure strokes to leave the frame of pruned stems cut level, with dead and rotten wood removed and each cut end neatly finished, without splits or torn bark. The idea seemed to be to encourage the bush to spread out as much as possible and to leave a good number of healthy stems from which the new shoots would grow to form the plucking 'table'. There were quite a number of different styles of pruning, some hard (as here), some rather less severe, and some in which a few uncut branches or 'lungs' were left on the bush to draw the sap and provide some sustenance for the bush until it had formed new leafy shoots. These 'lungs' would be removed later on, usually at the time when the new young shoots were tipped to make them produce more branches. However, 'lung' pruning was not done on Needwood and the removal of all the branches at once did not seem to produce any noticeable adverse effects. By the time I left the field I felt I knew how pruning should be done and had tried my hand on a couple of small bushes, using the kangany's knife. The requirements were quite simple but it needed practice and some strength to produce the desired result. In fact, rather as most Frenchmen consider themselves experts on wine, most planters consider themselves expert pruners - although many probably don't prune a bush from one year to the next. I felt that my first efforts did not enhance my planting prestige and surreptitiously covered the ragged stems with prunings before making what I hoped was a dignified departure.

I spent the rest of the morning making my rounds of the various works and practising my Tamil on the people I met. It was quite tiring trudging up and down the steep hillsides along the roads, paths and steps and by the time I reached the top of the Division I felt I needed a few minutes rest. A path ran along the upper boundary of the estate, separating the montaine jungle above from the tea below. I sat on a rock in the shade and looked out over the tea-clad slopes towards the distant sea. It was peaceful up on this path below the jungle and the noisy chatter of the work gangs on the slopes below came only faintly on the breeze, mingled with the distant shouts of children and the occasional lowing of unseen cattle in sheds dotted here and there near the labour lines. Besides, I felt I could have a brief respite up here from being constantly on view, acting the part of the planter and being an object of intense interest to the labour force and their offspring. Bird calls echoed from the shady depths of the jungle and the wok-wok-wok of barbets came from trees across the sunny slopes while high above me a circling serpent eagle gave its intermittent plaintive mewing cry.

The montaine forest here was not tall, the largest trees reaching only about 30 ft or so, but it was very dense with thick undergrowth and the trees themselves were festooned with Spanish moss (actually the lichen *Usnea*) and various epiphytic plants. These comprised several kinds of ferns and orchids (one with dainty sprays of tiny white blossoms) and a mistletoe-like growth with red and yellow tubular flowers which I thought might be a kind of *Loranthus*. This was a parasitic plant like mistletoe which attacked many of the shade trees in the tea (especially the *Grevillea*), growing as bushy clumps on the branches and debilitating the trees. The red and golden flowers attracted birds to their nectar and, again like mistletoe, produced sticky berries which the birds relished and inadvertently spread from tree to tree. About once a year a gang would be sent round the estate to cut out the growths, but six months later they would be just as numerous. Nearby a tiny stream emerged from the forest and cascaded down the bank, across the path and on down the mountainside, eroding a stony bed and forming small pools of crystal clarity. Someone had placed a leaf to form a little *peeli* (spout) for drinking and, conscious that there was no contamination above, I sampled the water and found it delicious. Various water-loving plants grew amongst the stones and trailed their roots in the water. One (which I later discovered was the orchid balsam, *Impatiens acaulis*) made a bold show with its long-spurred pink flowers which would have enhanced any rock garden. The banks formed where the path had been cut into the hillside were covered with lichens, mosses, liverworts, ferns and various other small plants. The leaflets of one fern I recognised had snowy undersides where they were encrusted with a white mealy covering. These fronds I knew from childhood experience made a dainty pattern, often accompanied by satisfying exclamations of surprise and shock, when placed on some unsuspecting person's clothing and given a sharp smack. The rear of shorts or trousers were best for this effect.

The factory hooter sounded at noon, marking the start of an hour's break. Labourers working in fields too far from the lines to return for a midday meal brought something to eat with them or arranged for it to be delivered. Many children, often tiny tots, could be seen shortly before midday making their way from the lines to the fields carrying parcels of food for their parents or relatives. The food was always carefully wrapped, perhaps in banana leaves or in an earthenware chatty pot tied in a cloth. The older children often carried these on their heads, but more elaborate curries were transported in many-tiered tiffin carriers.

I made my way down to the bungalow for lunch with Mr Meikle, whom I found seated on the veranda reading *The Scotsman*. Lunch consisted of well-peppered soup, well-peppered steak and fruit salad (fortunately sans pepper). After lunch there was a short interlude during which we sat on the veranda, Mr Meikle returned to his *Scotsman* and I read some of the airmail *Telegraph*. At one thirty Mr Meikle rose and, with Haggis in close attendance, departed for the office in the Landrover, leaving me to repeat my morning round of the estate works.

At 4.00 p.m. the factory hooter again sounded for evening muster. This was also held at Needwood Factory, but the centre of activity shifted from the muster ground to the reception and weighing-in of the leaf under the shelter of the roof covering the rear entrance to the factory. As I made my way down the mountainside I could see gangs of labourers converging on the factory from the various parts of the Division where they had been working. The leaf plucked during the day was weighed and collected twice in the field, at mid morning and at noon, but for the evening weighing the pluckers brought their baskets to the factory. When I arrived the pluckers from the nearest field were standing in line awaiting their turn while the Assistant KP operated a large spring balance and called out the weights of leaf to the KP, who was standing behind a lectern or small desk raised to chest height on long legs. Each plucker emptied the contents of her bulging basket into a large, saucer-shaped weighing basket which was then lifted and hung by its three strings from the large hook on

*View north over the Uva Basin, showing Idulgashena Factory in the foreground, 1958. This is a typical, medium sized factory building, clad in silver-painted corrugated iron. The gap in the mountains on the horizon is framed by Narangala (5,011 ft., with Keenakelle Group on the other side) on the right and Gommaliya (5,511 ft., with Kirklees Estate, Uda Pussellawa, on its slopes.) on the left. The Uma Oya, a tributary of the Mahaweli Ganga, flows through the gap. Aislaby factory can be seen on one of the lower hills in front of Narangala.*

the spring balance. Steadying the balance dial with his hand, the Assistant KP called out the weight to the KP, who entered it in the check-roll against the plucker's name. After the weight had been called out, the two labourers on duty seized the basket and emptied it onto a sheet of hessian at the rear, returning the empty basket for the next weighing. Meanwhile the growing pile of leaf on the hessian was being rapidly stuffed by yet more labourers into open-mesh sacks made of coir string and these were carried away up to the withering lofts. All this was accompanied by much loud chatter, argument and shouted instructions above the hum of the factory machinery and the regular thump-thump-thump of the factory engine blowing out of the tall black exhaust pipe.

Tea factories were large, long buildings, usually with a brick- or stone-built ground floor and two to five floors above. These were the withering lofts and contained endless banks of hessian tats, or shelves, on which the tea leaves were spread to wither partially before being processed. These floors were constructed of wood, often with a steel framework, and clad in corrugated iron sheeting, usually painted silver with aluminium paint. Both Needwood and Idulgashena factories were typical of their kind.

Tea manufacture is quite a complicated business. Most Ceylon tea factories at that time made black tea of the kind that was sold in packets in Britain and most other countries. Tea bags had not yet made their appearance, and I believe that green tea for the Middle East market was only produced by a few estates.

*A tea factory rolling room, showing two rolling machines (background) and a roll-breaker (foreground) with the dhool heaped in front of it. The cloth end of the leaf chute is visible above the nearest roller.*

On arrival in the withering lofts the fresh leaf would be spread on the stretched hessian tats, which reached from floor to ceiling. Under the influence of a draft provided by the wind coming through the open windows or by the large fans at each end of the building, the leaf withered to a flaccid state. This was closely checked by the Assistant Teamaker, who would order the opening or closing of windows, operation of the fans, or the application of warm air to achieve just the right consistency. This was why many factories were built in elevated and exposed positions where they would receive wind for the withering process. When there was sufficient leaf, factories worked 24 hours a day, and the factory staff and labour were organised in shifts.

The withered leaf was then put down a chute into the rollers. These large machines consisted of open cylinders, with tops which could be screwed down to compress the leaf within them, which rotated in an eccentric fashion over ribbed circular tables. After 30 minutes or so of this treatment, the battered leaf became screwed up into little twists which were thickly coated with concentrated tea leaf sap. The resulting dhool, or batch of rolled leaf, was emptied from each roller onto 'roll-breakers' - vibrating sieves which broke up any lumps of leaf which had formed in the rollers and also sifted it into two or three size grades. The coarsest grade might be put back into the rollers, with or without more leaf, and the rest was then spread in thick layers on wide concrete shelves to ferment for a few hours at room temperature. This fermenting period was rather critical and was one of the key differences between black and green tea manufacture. The colour of the rolled leaf slowly changed from dull green to take on a reddish or coppery hue and at the appropriate time the fermentation was stopped by 'firing' the leaf in the dryer. This was a kind of large oven, rather like the ovens used commercially to bake biscuits. It had a wide, perforated moving surface onto which the leaf was loaded to a depth of an inch or two. This moved slowly through the machine against a stream of heated air from a furnace burning either locally grown timber or (as had become more usual) fuel oil. The leaf emerging at the lower end of the dryer was black and now recognisable as tea, with a wonderful aroma which permeated the whole factory and its surroundings. The various constituents of the tea were also now more easily seen, with stalks and fibres showing pale brown or straw colour and the much prized 'tips' - the very youngest leaves, which were slightly hairy – showing up with a silvery sheen. When cool, the tea would go through a final cleaning and sifting into numerous grades before being packed into chests.

The grades mostly had traditional names deriving from their Chinese or Indian origins. The main grade was Broken Orange Pekoe or BOP, which looked like ordinary packet tea and formed most of the production. Then there was Broken Orange Pekoe Fannings, which looked much like BOP but with smaller particles, Orange Pekoe, which had elongated, wiry particles, Dust, which looked like its name, and Broken Mixed, which was a low quality grade accepting tea which could not be put into better grades. There were numerous other grades and different estates produced various combinations of grades. Grades which had an unusually high content of tips were sometimes denoted as 'Flowery', so one could have Flowery BOP or Flowery BOPF, and these were considered highly desirable. Samples of the various grades were regularly sent off to the agents in Colombo to be reported on by the tea tasters. Great store was set on these reports, although they could vary considerably between tasters. It was considered very underhand and reprehensible to send down unmarked duplicate samples although, if tasted by different people, it was possible to receive very different reports on the same batch. Of course samples were also tasted at the factory, by the Head Teamaker and by the PD of the estate and the SD responsible for the factory. The Head Teamaker's office usually had a tiled bench on which a couple of dozen white porcelain cups with perforated lids and a similar number of small white bowls would be arranged in a row. Samples of each grade and batch to be tasted would be set out behind each cup and bowl by the Assistant Teamaker and his labourer assistant, and measured quantities would be placed into each cup for infusing with boiling water. When the liquor had brewed, the infused leaf was exposed for examination on the perforated lid while some of the liquor was tipped into the appropriate bowl so that its strength and colour could more easily be seen. The Head Teamaker, PD or SD would then arrive and with due ceremony would examine each sample and infusion. Tasting would be done with much sucking and slurping of air and spitting of the tasted sample into a handy spittoon. The terms used for describing teas are as many, various and outlandish as those for wine and, like wine aficionados, most PDs considered themselves proficient, if not expert, tasters. However, in reality, only a few could make a professional tasting assessment of quality. Mr Meikle never made any attempt to teach me anything about tasting or factory management, so I had to try and pick it up for myself.

Very few tea factories were then on the mains electricity and power for all the machinery, fans and local electricity generators was usually provided by a single huge diesel engine located at one end of the factory. By means of pulleys and a gigantic belt, fully a foot wide, which was kept tacky by the occasional application of some kind of proprietary goo, this drove shafting which ran the whole length of the factory. Power was taken from the shafting via more pulleys and belts to drive all the other machinery. Needwood factory was typical and I always enjoyed visiting the engine room, where the turbaned engine driver lovingly cosseted his charges with oil can and polishing cloth. The main engine was a large flatbed single cylinder diesel, with a gigantic flywheel ten feet in diameter for which a channel had been cut in the floor. The cylinder was the size of a battleship gun barrel and the engine seemed covered with rotating knobs and reciprocating rods, each shining with an oily gleam and dripping into strategically placed little trays. The paint work was forest green, which contrasted well with the polished brass casing edges and name plate, which read 'Ruston Hornsby, Lincoln, England', with the serial number stamped in the middle. There was also a slightly smaller, standby engine of similar design for use when the main engine was out of action, as not infrequently happened. The engine driver always wore a khaki jacket of military style, as befitted his elevated status, and would delight in explaining to me the latest breakdown or difficulty in obtaining a spare part.

*The engine room of a large tea factory. The nearest engine is a two cylinder model.*

All the many moving parts of the engine were quite unguarded, the only sop to safety being a rather flimsy wire grill over the power take-off, to which the huge drive belt came and went through holes in the wall. I am not sure what safety regulations might then have been in operation, but factory inspectors did sometimes appear. However, their visits did not seem to have any effect on the organisation of the factory or the introduction of any new safety precautions. One, I remember rather vividly, delighted in showing me a whole album of gruesome photographs portraying factory accidents of every kind imaginable, and many which would never have occurred to me. In one, the engine mechanic had somehow contrived to get his unravelled turban entangled round both an engine shaft and his neck, with spectacularly fatal results. Evidently the inspector had either been on hand with camera at the ready to record this event, or the body and machinery had been carefully kept unmoved until his arrival. I wondered if the Needwood incumbent realised the risk his headgear represented.

Tea manufacture has changed enormously over the past few decades and today uses very different methods to achieve much the same ends. Withering is done by blowing warm air through the leaf in long troughs, so the great withering lofts on the upper floors are not required, and the so-called CTC (cut, tear and curl) manufacture does not use rollers, but cuts and shreds the leaf in something the same way as tobacco is shredded for cigarette manufacture.

By the time I returned to Needwood bungalow the sun was already sinking behind the mountains. The garden was in shadow and the golden evening light on the plains below threw the foothills into sharp relief. Haggis came waggling towards me as I climbed the steps and for a brief half hour I wandered in the garden before darkness fell. The kitchen coolie meanwhile had been stoking the hot water boiler with wood from the felled *Albizzia* trees and I gratefully soaked my weary legs in a hot bath. The remainder of the evening never varied in procedure during the whole of my time at Needwood. Until dinner time Mr Meikle would read his magazines and papers while seated in his dressing gown on the pouffe, sipping a whisky and soda of which I was never invited to partake. Meanwhile I attempted to learn some more Tamil vocabulary or perused the products of the Gardener's Book Club. Dinner maintained its format, starting with the inevitable soup or baked eggs (a speciality of Paikiam's) and ending always with the delicious but doubtful junket.

Later in the evening, when Paikiam and the kitchen coolie had cleared away the meal, washed up the dishes and put the oats to soak for our breakfast porridge, they both appeared at the sitting room door to say 'good night' and signal that they were going off duty. This little ceremony was repeated in European planters' bungalows throughout rural Ceylon and often in town households as well. In large households with several house servants it became quite an elaborate and lengthy procedure and it was certainly a very traditional part of everyday life in my parents' household.

As with most estate procedures, strict priority of rank was observed. Firstly the appu would enter with appropriate dignity, bearing before him, as though carrying the mace before the Speaker of the House of Commons, a small circular tray on which reposed the large kitchen alarm clock. This he would present to my mother with great aplomb, as if delivering up the city keys to the sovereign. The appu (in common with many Ceylon house servants) had a heavy hand with clocks, believing in winding them up so thoroughly and vigorously that they usually survived only a few days before coming to an untimely stop with a disintegrated spring, and to stem the excessive turnover of kitchen timepieces my mother insisted on winding them herself. Taking a pace back, the appu would then say 'Good night, Lady' to my mother 'Good night, Master' to my father, and so on as appropriate for each member of the family and any visitors who happened to be present, my sister being 'Missy' and I (even when adult) 'Little master'. My grandmother (who lived with my parents) was always addressed as 'Big Lady', a literally translated title with which she was never entirely happy but which in fact denoted her senior status. The appu then withdrew and the houseboy stepped forward to bid each of us '*Salaam*' in turn, and was followed by the kitchen coolie. English was used only by the appu, who regarded this as another status symbol, and responses were always made as appropriate in English or Tamil by each of us in turn.

At Needwood the ceremony was rather abbreviated, as there were only Mr Meikle and myself, Paikiam and the kitchen coolie. Nevertheless, it was always duly observed and marked the end of each day.

# Supernumerary planter

The centre of social life for the planting community was the district club. In colonial days, when the European planting community was much larger, the up-country district clubs had been much more numerous. However, the increasing numbers of Ceylonese planters seemed to feel less inclined to associate with their brethren at the club than did their expatriate colleagues who were far from their native lands. Therefore, as the numbers of European planters dwindled in the years following independence in 1948, the local planting clubs began to close or amalgamate. By the time I arrived on the scene this process had come to a stage when the less viable and smaller clubs, often in the more remote areas, had closed but the remainder were still very much in functioning order. Up-country there were also larger, provincial or area clubs, which served several districts and boasted facilities such as rugby pitches and squash courts which the smaller district clubs could not match. Such clubs were the Uva Club in Badulla, the Kelani Valley Club at Avissawella, and the large clubs at Radella and Darrawella in the famous tea-planting districts of Dimbula and Dickoya. In the larger towns there were also other clubs which served as centres of expatriate social life, such as the Cricket, Yacht, and Swimming clubs in Colombo and the Golf Club in Nuwara Eliya. Although nominally existing to serve their chosen sport, such clubs certainly did not insist that members actually took part or even had any interest in these. A considerable proportion of the membership tended to be 'drinking members' only, whose main activity was to prop up the bar and take part in the social events. Some of the larger clubs, especially those in Colombo, also provided cheap but comfortable accommodation, which was much appreciated by outstation members. There was also a system of reciprocal membership, mainly between the larger clubs, which meant that members of one could claim members' privileges and sign chits at others.

A typical up-country district club would be a low, single storey building tucked into a fold in the tea-covered slopes and roofed with the inevitable corrugated iron. Outside there was usually an area for parking cars, some minimal bits of lawn and a few flower beds, and several tennis courts overlooked by the club veranda. Tennis was by far the most important outdoor sport for planters, as it did not require large teams or much space. Inside there would be a large room for dances and other functions, a card room, a library (often just a cupboard full of books), a billiard room (where snooker had long since ousted billiards) and, most importantly, a bar. This would be presided over by the club steward, who knew everyone and became a friend of many. He was responsible for the running and maintenance of the club and its premises, overseen by the club committee, and the success of the club largely depended on him and his assistants. Although he had no official perks except sometimes accommodation for himself and his family, most club stewards were adept at creative accounting and could substantially augment their meagre pay by creaming off a surplus from the bar. If done carefully, this could hardly be detected and was almost accepted as a normal part of the rewards of the job. However, sometimes the incumbent was too ambitious, over did it, and either decamped with as much of the bar proceeds as he could lay hands on, or else the bar (and often the rest of the club as well) would be gutted by a mysterious but convenient fire, just before an audit of the bar accounts was due.

Because of this, a central element of the club system was that no money changed hands on the premises. All drinks and other items were recorded on 'chits' and were signed for by members, who received a bill at the end of each month supported by all the chits signed, which often made a bulky package. Convenient as this system was, it was all too easy, especially in moments of inebriated largesse, to go on signing chits far beyond one's means. But non-payment of the club bill, or even a lengthy delay, was regarded as a serious matter. SDs could be hauled before their PD to explain themselves and might be barred from leaving the estate until the debt had been settled. Recalcitrant PDs had to be dealt with more circumspectly, perhaps with a quiet but firm word in the ear by the club president and, if all else failed, eventually by expulsion from membership and reciprocal exclusion from most other clubs as well. Breaches of protocol or the prevailing social code were also regarded as serious matters and, although in Britain the first faint signs of the swinging sixties might have been emerging, out here in the backwaters of ex-colonial society attitudes were still firmly stuck in the 1930s. Any senior planter would always expect to be addressed as 'Sir' by anyone more than 15 or 20 years his junior and wives of similar status were always 'Mrs So-and-so' to the young SDs of the district. Further deference in all things was expected by one's own PD. His wife, even though she might take a motherly interest in her husband's SDs to the extent of inviting them occasionally to tea, would have been quite scandalised if any of them had addressed her by her first name. At the club the younger elements of the community were welcome at the bar and on the tennis court, but tended to be admitted only on sufferance to the billiard room. The card room, unless one happened to be an expert bridge player, was virtually impregnable after dark when serious play began.

The district clubs operated on Sundays and the afternoon of one week day, on which it was universally accepted that one could (and in fact *should*) take a half day off to attend. Non-attendance at the club was definitely regarded as peculiar if not downright antisocial and pressures could be brought to bear on those SDs who failed in this duty.

Mr Meikle did not often attend the club during the week and, if he did, he did not suggest that I joined him. However, on my first Sunday at Needwood I gladly accepted his invitation to accompany him to the Haldummulla Club. This was the nearest club to Needwood and had been located in Haldummulla village at the foot of the estate. However, it had been one of the first to suffer the effects of the decline in the European planting population and some years previously it had been moved to Haputale Estate, near Haputale town, where it was able to draw on a much larger club-going planting population.

On Sunday morning at 11 a.m. sharp, Muliniandy had the black Vauxhall Cresta washed and polished and standing ready in the sunshine outside the garage at the foot of the bungalow steps. Attired in the pukka tennis whites which custom and the Club rules demanded, and clutching my school tennis racket, I joined Mr Meikle on the back seat. Muliniandy set off at a sedate pace down the tarred but tortuous cart road, negotiating each hairpin bend with care and leaving little room for the few pedestrians we met. These were mostly estate labourers in family groups returning from Sunday shopping at the caddies in Haldummulla village, the man always in front, umbrella or stick in hand, followed by his wife carrying the bundles of purchases perched on her head or manually in knotted cloths. The children brought up the rear in descending order of age, also carrying bundles of proportionate size. On our appearance all would step aside into the ditch or onto the grassy verge, the woman steadying the bundle on her head with one hand, and a chorus of '*Salaam Dorai*' echoed down the line as we passed by.

By the time we reached the junction of the cart road with the main Colombo road we had descended nearly 1,000 ft. from Needwood Bungalow and turned left to pass through Haldummulla village towards Haputale. The centre of the village consisted of numerous caddies facing onto the road, a public medical dispensary and cottage hospital, and a small post office. As usual, all the caddies seemed to sell the same things. Hessian sacks of lentils, green and black grams, and various kinds of rice were arranged on the floors, each with a measuring scoop ready in the top of the sack. They were accompanied by baskets of red onions and dried chillies, while on the counters at the front of the shops were arranged large blocks of sticky, dark-brown compressed tamarind fruit and doughnut-shaped piles of green betel leaves arranged with each leaf pointing outwards. All sold matches, and tobacco in various forms. Neither the Sinhalese villagers nor the Tamil estate labourers smoked pipes, but most were very fond of locally made cheroots and cigarettes, both the normal kind and the small, very thin, *beedies*, all of which could be bought singly for a few cents. Many different varieties of bananas and plantains, green, yellow, and pink, hung in bunches from the eaves. The long, starchy, green plantains were for cooking and were often served as chunks in curries or mashed, like potato. When tasted raw they would fur up one's mouth like a crab apple or sloe berry. The best kind of bananas for eating fresh were the short, fat, yellow and slightly acid *Kollukootthu* variety, for which the caddykeepers always charged a premium.

At the far end of the village Mr Meikle indicated a whitewashed bungalow standing back from the road down a short driveway.

'That's the old Haldummulla Club' he said, 'Used to be a lively place years ago when I was SD on Idulgashena, but gradually all the estates below the road got sold to the wogs and eventually membership dwindled so much it was decided to move it up to Haputale. It's a lot further for us, of course, but at least now we have a reasonable membership.'

I found it difficult to imagine that rather forlorn and dilapidated bungalow thronged with the young Europeans of the district in the 1920s and 30s. Had Mr Meikle sat on that grubby veranda behind the now broken trellis sipping his pink gins? We left the village behind and began the long and twisting climb up the Haputale Pass. To the right as we climbed higher the view opened out, mile upon mile over the foothills and plains to the blue horizon. From time to time we passed neatly painted signboards at the entrances to estates: Batgodde, Berragalla and Blackwood to the left, on the slopes above the road, with Kalupahane and Wiharegalla below, on the right. Subsidiary signs directed one to 'Factory and Office' or 'Superintendent's Bungalow'. Presently the road levelled out and turned sharp left into Haputale town. Here Sunday shopping was in full swing with labourers from the surrounding estates crowding the caddies and a market was in operation near the railway station. Haputale was quite an important place, giving its name to the planting district, but was no more than a village and not nearly as large as the town of Bandarawela which was several miles further on, near the boundary with Badulla District. Nestling strategically in the gap of the Haputale Pass, Haputale was the next station along the railway line from Idalgashinna and was also a crossroads where the Dambatenne and Glenanore roads joined the main Colombo - Bandarawela road. There was also a rest house and a main post office. Quite often it was enveloped in the mists which tended to form and drift through this gap in the mountains, but on a clear day the view down the main street continued straight out to the distant sea.

Continuing through the town, we soon turned off left down the hill through Haputale Estate. Crossing the railway line, we turned up a gravel road bordered by fir trees and arrived at the club house. The Haldummulla Club was one of the smallest of the district clubs, consisting of a main room, a library-cum-card room, bar and veranda. The latter overlooked a clay surfaced tennis court and there was a second court out of sight at a lower level below. This was overshadowed by trees and tended to be rather damp and slippery.

Mr Meikle made some perfunctory introductions and disappeared into the bar, leaving me with the tennis spectators on the veranda. A game of frighteningly high standard was already in progress on the top court and perhaps a dozen people were either at the bar or watching from the veranda. They were about evenly divided between young SDs (who nevertheless seemed considerably older than myself) and older planters and their wives. There were no European planters in the District who personally owned their estates or other land, so there was a complete absence of the 'settler' community found in many African countries. Unattached women of any age were conspicuously absent. A few late-comers arrived to swell the numbers and I soon fell into conversation with the group of spectators, for whom my evident youth was something of a curiosity. There are many accounts of planters having started as teenagers in pioneering days, but in my time very few planters started their careers before their early to mid twenties, often after trying several other occupations and, of course, national service, which was then still in operation and which I had avoided through having left Australia when I finished school. Inevitably, I was invited to make up a doubles at tennis, at which I fear I did not make a very good impression. My awkwardness was accentuated by trying to pay for a beer in the bar, which raised difficulties, eyebrows, and disparaging looks from the florid-faced clientele. This was eventually sorted out by arranging with the Club Steward that I could sign chits as a prospective member, and the time passed pleasantly enough. When most of the afternoon had also passed, I was beginning to get hungry and wondered how long it would be before we returned for lunch. Slowly, people began to depart, some joining others for lunch at one or other of their bungalows, but Mr Meikle showed no signs of preparing to leave. Together with two or three cronies, he was ordering and consuming numerous rounds of brandy and ginger ale or gin and tonic, progressively becoming more and more florid, more and more Scottish, and less and less coherent. Eventually, only two of us remained outside the bar.

'I hope you're not expecting lunch soon' said my companion, 'Because you'll be lucky to get it before dark. Your boss is usually just about the last to leave.'

'Well', I said, feeling increasingly pessimistic about the chances of getting lunch, 'at least I'm lucky he doesn't have to drive us back.'

'Oh yes, good old Muliniandy', he replied, 'How he puts up with the old bastard, I don't know. He nearly left him behind on one occasion; old Leslie came out of the Bow Club in Bandarawela one evening after a heavy session like today's, got into the back of the car, and Muliniandy set off for home. What he didn't realise was that the silly old bugger had opened the other door, gone straight through and fallen out the other side. Muliniandy was half way back to Haputale before he realised and came back in trepidation, only to find that Leslie was back in the bar. He was lucky the old geyser was too far gone to realise quite what had happened.'

Eventually, my companion also departed and after an hour of relatively sober solitude, the group in the bar emerged. Mr Meikle had now assumed an almost purple hue and had slight difficulty remaining upright.

'Ah, . . . David', he exclaimed, as if he had previously been unaware of my existence, 'Ah, . . . och . . . errrm, . . . ah . . . eh? . . . errrm.' He moved unsteadily towards the door, 'Och . . . nothing like a wee clack and dichter to see one on the way. . . . Muliandy! . . . ah . . . errrm *...bungalavuku.'*

In the car he slumped in the corner of the back seat and revived only as we arrived back at Needwood about three quarters of an hour later. It was now well after five o'clock but Paikiam, by some miraculous ingenuity known exclusively to all bungalow appus, had a curry lunch waiting.

I had known that lunch would be curry, not only because it was the custom - almost a ritual - on Sundays, but also because I had heard the sounds of its preparation in the kitchen from early morning. Besides the basic rice, which was usually coloured yellow by turmeric or saffron, a typical Ceylon curry consisted of a dish of curried beef or fish and four or five supplementary dishes of curried vegetables, including *dhal* (a sort of pease-pudding made from orange lentils) and whatever else the appu could lay hands on. Usually these would feature *brinjal* (aubergine), some kind of beans, and perhaps beetroot or pumpkin. Finally, there would be several *sambols*, including *sini-sambol* (of sugar and onions), *pol-sambol* (coconut and chilli) and a little dish of coconut milk with slices of tomato, onion and green chilli. In the centre of the pol-sambol there would usually be a small ball of ground spices, the bright vermillion colour of which derived from its high chilli content and it was the sambol of which one had to be the most wary. In fact it was the sambols which took much of the preparation work. The noises I had heard were those of the kitchen coolie grinding the numerous different ingredient spices, using a stone roller on a flat stone bed, which was a basic piece of equipment to be found in all Ceylon kitchens. He would develop a regular rhythm to the grinding, with a back and forward motion of the roller without letting it completely rotate, and every so often he would add some water, a little more cumin or coriander seed or pepper corns to get the blend right, scooping the ground mixture back into the centre of the stone with the crook of his little finger. Besides the sambols, there would often be other accompaniments, such as sliced bananas, chutney, and poppadums. In general, the heat of Indian curries increases the farther south one goes. Sri Lankan curries continue this trend and can be very powerful indeed. However, so long as it does not fry the taste buds, I rather enjoy a hot curry and so did not mind Paikiam's heavy hand with the pepper and chilli. On this occasion the curry was relatively simple, but nevertheless had all the salient features and Mr Meikle was recovered sufficiently to consume a hearty share. It was indeed almost dark by the time we had finished and Mr Meikle returned to his papers and magazines.

This proved to be the usual pattern of Sundays at Needwood. I enjoyed the visits to the club, as these gave me my only opportunity for any socialising, but the remainder of the day passed slowly and I chafed at the lack of my own books and contact with others of my own age. Because I had no transport of my own, it was not possible to accept invitations back to lunch on other estates, but on one occasion I was invited by 'Dickie' Dickinson to his bungalow to hear his new hi-fi apparatus. Long-playing records had only recently made their appearance in Ceylon and several planters had invested in new electronic sound systems. Dickie was another bachelor of about the same age as Mr Meikle but with a rather unassuming manner and was on Kahagalla, another of the Gibson Estates. He was generally considered slightly eccentric, as evidenced by having no desire for a modern car and not believing in taking out insurance. Through good luck he seemed to get away with this and would hold forth on the iniquities of rapacious insurance companies. As it was only a couple of miles from Haputale, Mr Meikle agreed to pick me up at Kahagalla on his way home from the Club and I found myself given a lift with several other people who had also been invited. In fact I gathered that these were fairly regular musical occasions when Dickie would put on a recital from his extensive collection of LPs.

Kahagalla Bungalow was set in an attractive terraced garden and we were ushered into the rather dark sitting room, the windows of which opened onto a closed-in veranda. A fireplace with mantelpiece occupied one corner; there were several chairs with thick cushions, a settee, and a large, double-doored cupboard of darkly-stained wood which housed the record collection stood against one wall. We settled ourselves in the chairs while Dickie busied himself with selecting the records and telling us about the merits of having the loudspeakers in a 'corner reflex cabinet'. In those days the records were all mono recordings and there was only one set of speakers. 'Corner reflex' apparently meant that the speaker cabinet was set to face into a corner of the room, which was considered to produce a better tone and ambience of sound. He then increased the gloom still further by half-drawing the curtains and the music commenced. Dickie had a taste for the more romantic classics, of which he seemed to have an inexhaustible supply. Although these were not entirely to my liking, this was such a pleasurable interlude from my Needwood routine that I would have enjoyed almost any kind of music. Apparently the dim light was intended to increase one's concentration on the music and its quality and was a feature of all Dickie's recitals. However, on this occasion it seemed to have a soporific effect on several members of his audience, including myself, who had great difficulty staying awake through the lulling strains of Delius, Debussy and Grieg. Nevertheless, I enjoyed the occasion and I was sorry when the Vauxhall Cresta arrived to collect me.

Mr Meikle did not often entertain, at least while I was with him, but occasionally he would have visitors for Sunday lunch. This was always bad news for me as it meant no visit to the club and I was also required to remain out of the way while they were in the bungalow. This always made me feel awkward, especially so when I actually knew the visitors. Ginger and Daphne Davidson from Nayabedde Estate near Bandarawela were two of Mr Meikle's closest cronies and on one occasion they visited accompanied by their daughter Judy, with whom I had been at school and who was out from the UK for a holiday. What could otherwise have been a rather enjoyable occasion for me was totally marred by having to be seen and heard as little as possible. Judy, whom I had not seen since the age of 13, enquired how I came to be living with 'Uncle Leslie' as she called him, but I was banished almost before I could explain and took refuge outdoors.

Mr Meikle was obviously a confirmed bachelor and showed very little interest in the opposite sex. However, this indifference was not complete. On Dambatenne Group, at the end of the road leading east out of Haputale town, there lived Monty and Nancy and, when she was out for a holiday, Nancy's daughter, Julia, by a previous marriage, reputedly to a Teutonic aristocrat. Nancy was a very vivacious and attractive person who was well known throughout the District (and beyond) for her various social exploits. She and Mr Meikle evidently got on very well, having common interests in the bar, and occasionally Muliniandy would be sent over to collect her from Dambatenne for a day out on the Horton Plains. On arrival at Needwood she would transfer to the Landrover and, with Mr Meikle at the wheel and a large crate of beer in the back, they would disappear for the rest of the day, returning late in the evening.

The Horton Plains were difficult of access, especially so from these southern slopes of the mountains. The only route up was through the Lower and Upper Ohiya estates in Haputale West District, which bordered Needwood to the west. This road was even more precipitous and with more hairpin bends than the Needwood road up to Idalgashinna. It was also considerably less well maintained. At the top a rough track branched left up to the Plains, another thousand feet higher, while the road continued on to cross the railway at Ohiya station. These expeditions did not endear Mr Meikle to Monty but, as far as I was aware, he put up with the situation, although under protest.

At Needwood on week days I was out somewhere on the estate from dawn to nearly dusk and had very little time to myself. Apart from a short period before and after dinner each evening, my only free time was the early part of Sunday morning, before going to the club. Mornings were almost always fine, as this area of the mountains did not get the south-west monsoon and during the north-east monsoon it usually rained only in the afternoon. I spent these morning hours in the garden or reading but, apart from Mr Meikle's supply of papers and magazines, reading material was limited. Of course there were always the dreaded volumes of the Gardeners' Book Club, and in fact through sheer lack of alternatives I did read quite a number of these. Inadvertently I thus gained some idea of such topics as how to grow and propagate fruit, how the duration of daylight affects the flowering of many plants, and how seeds of various different species of vegetables and flowers require different conditions for germination, all of which came in useful many years later. Naturally all the books were concerned with gardens and plants for conditions in Britain and northern Europe, but some of what they said could be applied in the Ceylon hills where, especially at the higher elevations, very many European garden plants could be grown most successfully.

One of the few volumes on Mr Meikle's shelves which was not a product of the Gardeners' Book Club was entitled *The Advance of the Fungi*, by an author named E. C. Large. Attracted by the unusual title, I dipped into it and was held entranced as the story of the investigation of plant diseases and their influence on history was unfolded. Until this point I don't think it had occurred to me to wonder whether plants had diseases or whether they were caused by agents similar to those causing diseases of humans. In fact I had come into contact with plant diseases but they had made so little impression on me that I had not registered their existence. When the plants in the vegetable plot I had had as a child had died I had simply accepted it as a fact of life, an act of fate, and I did not query what the cause might be. Nearer at hand, one of the work gangs on Needwood spent their time spraying the tea with a chemical against blister blight, but I had not really wondered at the nature of this disorder and Mr Meikle had not enlightened me. E. C. Large not only made the study of plant diseases interesting; he made it come alive. One felt one was looking down the microscope with Anton de Bary or sharing experiments with Louis Pasteur up on the Mer de Glace. The Irish famine of the 1840s was revealed as due to potato blight and, most pertinent of all, the tea industry of Ceylon was shown to derive from the destruction of the original coffee plantations by the coffee rust fungus. One felt the frustrations of Harry Marshall Ward as he grappled with the difficulties of his investigations, the pig-headed coffee planters, and the bureaucracy of the Ceylon colonial government. I read the book from cover to cover. It made a great impression on me at the time and gave me much food for thought as I made my endless rounds of the estate, but I did not realise at the time how great an influence on my life it would have.

*Needwood Bungalow and garden, 1956.*

Another pastime for Sunday mornings was bird watching. Many different kinds of bird visited the garden, most of which I knew well from childhood days. The red-vented bulbuls, brown birds with red under the tail and a dark head and crest, were always common and often nested in the shrubs. They had a friendly, rather throaty call, and stupidly built their nests in ridiculously exposed situations, with frequently disastrous consequences. Black and white magpie robins behaved very like European robins, feeding on insects and worms, and most gardens had a resident pair. Perhaps the daintiest birds in the garden were the purple-rumped sunbirds, which fed on small insects and nectar, for which they probed blossoms with their slender curved beaks. Their nests were quite delightful pear-shaped purses with an entrance hole at one side sheltered by a tiny porch, and were suspended from the tip of a slender branch or creeper. The whole construction was woven together with cobwebs and felted with soft feathers and thistle down to make it watertight and comfortable. The *totakaran* (gardener) did not share my interest in the garden birds and in fact, like most of the estate labourers, seemed almost totally unaware of them. Mostly, no doubt, they were much too concerned with the hardships of daily living to be bothered with such things. On one occasion a pair of sunbirds decided to start nest building in the creepers on the bungalow wall. Mr Meikle (who was quite a bird enthusiast in his way) and I watched the nest slowly take shape and looked forward to seeing the chicks being reared. However, one day we were dismayed to find the whole construction gone. On questioning, the *totakaran* explained that he had cleared away the mess of *nool* (woolly thread) which had been spoiling the creeper.

The *totakaran* was not the only destructive force with which the birds breeding in the garden had to contend. There were the handsome black coucals or jungle crows with rufous wings, the shiny green lizards, occasional snakes, and the chipmunk-like palm squirrels or tree rats as Mr Meikle called them, all of which enjoyed eggs or baby birds when they could find them. The squirrels proliferated enormously, building untidy dreys under the eaves and between the rafters, rather like sparrows. In the heat of mid day they would fill the garden with their shrill *pink-pink-pink* calls, uttered from a roof top or hanging head downwards on the trunk of a tree, their bodies and tails jerking at each *pink*. Eventually their numbers grew so large and the unfortunate birds seemed to be having such a difficult time rearing any young that Mr Meikle decided something would have to be done and one day he produced an air gun and a tin of pellets.

'Here you are, David', he said, 'We'll fix the buggers. Have a go with this.'

I did not relish the idea of shooting the squirrels, but it was difficult to refuse and there certainly was a problem with the birds. I also rather prided myself on being a crack shot (as I had discovered by my performance with the rifle team at school) and I suppose I did not feel averse to demonstrating this to Mr Meikle. Anyway, I took on the job, enthusiastically aided and abetted by Haggis. I found the air gun both powerful and accurate, so fortunately there were very few squirrels which needed finishing off, much to his disappointment. Eventually, after we had eliminated a couple of dozen, the birds seemed to be recovering and to my relief the campaign came naturally to an end.

One Sunday I decided to try my hand at writing an article about a visit I had made to the Yala national park for the journal of the Ceylon Wildlife Protection Society. This was called *Loris* and had an attractive picture of this tiny primate on the front cover. It was read quite widely among the planting community, as most planters had an interest in wild life one way or another. Frequently this was in duck and snipe shooting, which was sometimes combined with a more serious ornithological interest. Others went in for shooting larger animals such as wild boar, spotted deer and sambhur, while a few had a genuine interest in conservation and the preservation of areas in which the extraordinarily varied ecological systems of the Island and their constituent animals and birds could survive. To my surprise my article was accepted and I had some satisfaction in that it was noticed by several people in the District.

After a few months, I got to know Needwood Division quite well and no longer had to be told where the boundaries of the fields were or the names of the kanganies. My Tamil had also improved and I found I could hold a reasonable conversation about the work being done when I met labourers in the field. Sometimes I would take the place of the KP during the morning weighing-in of leaf. This was good practice for my Tamil numbers and I also got to know the names of the regular members of the plucking gangs. Holding the pocket check-roll book in which all the names were listed, I would station myself at the weighing point with the two labourers who operated the spring balance. Each plucker would empty her (or his) plucked leaf into the weighing basket and the labourers would then lift the pole from which the balance was suspended. I would then read the balance, mentally subtract the weight of the weighing basket, call out the net weight and enter it against the plucker's name in the check-roll. One had to be quick in order to get through the gang in a reasonable length of time and allow them to resume work. However, at first I had to ask each plucker his or her name, and these did not always seem to match what was listed.

'What's your name?'

'*Barbartee'nger*' would come the reply. I could see nothing like this.

'Say it slowly', I would say. This would produce embarrassed giggles and the woman would draw a corner of her headcloth over her mouth.

'*Par-par-tee*'

'Oh, *Papartee*' (butterfly), 'OK' And I would go on to the next.

Occasionally Mr Meikle would decide he should check on what I was doing. Either he would suddenly appear in the Landrover, or sometimes he would ask me to meet him at a particular place. He would then walk round with me for half an hour or so before being collected by Muliniandy at some predetermined point. These sessions were unpredictable in content. Sometimes Mr Meikle would quiz me about work being done (or not being done) as though it was I who was responsible for its organisation and not the conductor. Sometimes he would be in a mellow mood and full of anecdotes from former times. A favourite place for our meetings was at a bend of the cart road near a grove of *toona* trees. These trees (*Cedrela serrulata*) have graceful leaves like the European ash and make good timber with a reddish heartwood. The sprays of opened seed capsules look like bunches of little bells (and I well remembered as a child painting them to make attractive decorations for our Christmas tree). The flowers are tiny but emit a repellent smell, especially after rain, and I spent as little time as possible waiting for Mr Meikle at this spot during the flowering season.

One day when heavy rain had encouraged rapid growth, I found that the pluckers had been picking coarse leaves and stalks too far down the stems of the shoots. This would have resulted in much extra work at the factory and probably lower grade tea so, before allowing the weighing to proceed, I had insisted that the whole gang empty out their baskets onto their hessian waist cloths and pick out all the coarse material. This had been done and the first heap of green leaf was just being loaded into the weighing basket, when Mr Meikle appeared.

'Ah, David', he said, 'How are things today? Bit of coarse leaf, eh? You must keep a very close eye on them, you know.'

'It's not too bad, Sir,' I replied, 'I've had them pick it all over very thoroughly.'

I turned to gesture at the heap of weighed leaf now being stuffed into the mesh leaf sacks when, to my horror, I noticed the old stub of a cheroot on the surface of the pile. How it had managed to get mixed up with the leaf, I don't know - no one had been smoking - but almost at the same instant Mr Meikle also spotted it, just as the labourer gathered it up with the leaf to go into the sack. Well aware that it could severely contaminate a large batch of tea if it should go through the factory, I dived into the heap and managed to extract the offending item and dispose of it with the other debris, but Mr Meikle wouldn't let me forget it.

'D'ye realise what damage that thing could do in the factory?' he expostulated, 'Why, ye could contaminate a whole consignment with that thing reeking away. Ye just canna be so careless.' At the club the following Sunday he took pains to explain to all the incredulous members how I had been allowing cheroots to get into the tea.

All manner of accidents and damage could occur to the tea, both while on the bush and after plucking. However, I was surprised on one occasion when I came round a corner of the path to find a small black cow placidly grazing on the bushes. Tea is normally unpalatable to grazing animals because of its high tannin content. In any case, the cow had no business to be there, as the labourers were only permitted to keep livestock if they kept them under cover and did not allow them to wander about the estate. I therefore gave the cow a prod with my umbrella, expecting that she would make off whence she had come. But the cow was evidently not easily deterred and continued to consume the tea with every appearance of relish. I gave her another, firmer, prod. This distracted her from her meal, but instead of departing she lowered her head and advanced towards me in a slow but determined fashion. She was really quite a small cow, without horns but with a hump on her back denoting some Zebu ancestry. She continued to advance and I took a step back, at the same time whacking her over the head with the umbrella. This was a mistake, as the umbrella snapped off, leaving me looking foolish with just the handle in my hand. I felt at a disadvantage without my brolly and, as the cow advanced further, I took another step back. I had not realised that at this point there was a deep drainage ditch with a silt pit just behind me and into this I suddenly vanished, ineffectually waving the brolly handle at my assailant, and the bushes closed over my head. Seeming rather bewildered at the sudden disappearance of her adversary, the cow then wandered off, leaving me to emerge ignominiously from the silt pit (which fortunately was dry), hoping that none of the labourers had witnessed this undignified accident to the *sinna dorai*.

Although Mr Meikle was on quite informal and friendly terms with old Veloo, the Head Kangany, with whom apparently he used to go duck shooting in the days when he had been SD on Idulgashena Division, he had very little time for any labourers. In fact he seemed to have an almost pathological antipathy to them, often remarking that the Nazis had had some very good ideas about disposing of their ilk and ending up with excellent manure. This attitude was vividly demonstrated one day during one of our joint estate walks when a labourer leapt out onto the path in front of us and crouched in front of Mr Meikle, loudly salaaming and bowing to touch his forehead on the ground in a gesture of extreme deference. The colour almost instantly flooded into Mr Meikle's face as he shouted peremptorily to order him out of the way. He tried to walk around the prostrated figure, who then moved in front of us again, now explaining that his son had been unable to get any work, had a family to support, and beseeched Mr Meikle to take him onto the labour force. This had the worst effect on my boss, who turned positively puce and seemed in danger of apoplexy, the veins standing out dark against his florid cheeks. Shouting that he should know better than to ask such a thing and that he should go and ask the KP (who of course had no authority to make such a decision), Mr Meikle stepped over the crouched man and marched on down the hill. Turning to me, he remarked 'The Tamil coolie, David, is a bastard. Treat him as a bastard and he is OK, but never give him a chance or he'll take every advantage of you.' Coming from that most unusual social group, a planting family with liberal views, I always felt acutely embarrassed by such pearls of wisdom and most often took refuge in silence, lacking both the courage and confidence to demur and knowing that it would certainly do nobody any good if I did, especially me. Mr Meikle seemed happy to accept this as total acquiescence.

A conspicuous feature of Needwood Division was the aerial ropeway which connected the factory with the railway station up at Idalgashinna. Such ropeways were a common means of transport on estates which covered rugged terrain, where they were easier and cheaper to build and operate than a road. The system on Needwood must have been about two miles in length with a rise of 1,200 ft. and was supported on pylons at intervals up the mountainside. It had been built in the days before the cart road had been extended up to the railway and was then the principal means of transporting heavy goods and supplies between the factory and the station. Although transport by road was now possible, the ropeway was still used regularly for movement of such goods as fertilizer brought in by rail and firewood cut in the eucalyptus plantations above the railway, for which it was quicker and probably cheaper than using the estate lorry. Powered by a belt from the main drive shaft at Needwood Factory, the steel cable snaked up on one side of the pylons and down on the other over a series of little wheels. The cable had hooks at intervals to which sacks or bundles of goods could be attached. Sometimes the cable passed high overhead across the ravines but at other points it came low over ridges and hummocks. These points were well known as risky, not for danger to persons (although one always felt uneasy when heavy items passed overhead), but because a deft shove with a stick or pole could unhook sacks of fertilizer or rice, which could then be made to disappear without trace. The mists which often swirled over the slopes during the monsoon made such incidents all too easy and frequent. For this reason there was very careful monitoring of what was loaded on at one end and what came off at the other, which was made much easier when a telephone was installed at each end of the system. As far as possible, the ropeway was not operated after dark or on days when there was thick mist, but sometimes this could not be avoided. Since the construction of the road up to Idalgashinna the transport of finished tea to the station was always done by lorry, but in former times it had all gone by the ropeway and what had been loaded at the factory had often been disconcertingly different to what had come off at its destination.

One day Mr Meikle and I paused to watch the ropeway in operation carrying packages of plywood tea chests. These arrived packed flat in a knocked-down state as kits and were assembled into chests at the factory by forming the sides into shape and fitting a top and bottom.

'I reckon I could hitch a ride on that', I said, raising my walking stick to poke a package as it came by low over my head.

'Och, I'd be careful, if I were you,' said Mr Meikle. 'Old Bob Sarson had a nasty shock doing that when he was SD here years ago. He used to make quite a habit of hooking the carrier with his stick and hitching a ride up the hill. Then one day when it was fairly misty he got a bit too ambitious and decided he'd go right across that little valley to the ridge the other side. Anyway, he hooked on all right and held tight as he moved out over the dip there, where there happened to be a gang of pluckers. At that moment the mist came down, so he couldn't see much, but he knew it wasn't very far and he was a pretty strong lad, so the only problem was when to get off. In fact there wouldn't have been a problem if the system hadn't stopped at that moment for another load to be put on at the factory. There he was, hanging in the mist with his arms getting longer and longer wondering when the bally system would get going again. Well, there must have been some problem with the loading, because it stopped for quite a while and old Bob knew he'd have to let go. So he did. The pluckers were all jabbering away as usual, and the kangany was probably asleep, when suddenly there was old Bob's frightful roar and he plummeted out of the mist bang into the middle of the gang. Well, they all thought it was a *peria pasarsi* [arch devil] and scattered in all directions and the leaf went all over the place. It took quite a while to convince them that he was himself and get them all back into the field. Lucky he didn't have too far to fall so no great harm was done.'

However, I found Bob Sarson's idea of hitching a ride on the ropeway quite a good one and I sometimes tried it myself, although I never had the strength or courage to attempt the crossing of the ravine. It was also rather difficult to maintain one's dignity when suspended from the ropeway by one's walking stick, so I did it only when there seemed to be no one about, becoming a sort of closet ropeway hitcher.

The end of the north-east monsoon came and, after the usual bright and fine months of February and March, the skies more often became overcast as the south-west monsoon drew near. In Ceylon this usually broke in the middle of May, bringing heavy and prolonged rain to the south-west sector of the Island and dry but overcast weather to the eastern hills of Uva. By this time I had been on Needwood nearly six months and I was fully familiar with the Division and the various estate works. My Tamil was fluent enough for use in connection with the usual daily routines, although I soon got confused if the conversation took an unexpected turn. Six months was the period that a creeper normally served before being appointed to an SD post and six months training had been mentioned in my letter of appointment. In my case, as I had already had some months' experience with my father and elsewhere, I had expected that I might not spend so long.  However, I had heard nothing from the Agents, George Steuart & Co., and I began to feel impatient to be on my own and to test myself as manager of a Division.  But where could I be posted?  I did not know of any possible SD post which would soon become vacant.  In June, after I had been on Needwood nearly seven months I decided to tackle Mr Meikle.  He was impassive and uncommunicative in response to my questions.  Eventually, I asked what would be my position, if no post for me became vacant.

'You'll be supernumerary', he said.

# First billet 4

It was usual for young SDs to be appointed first to some fairly easily managed division where they could be closely supervised by their PD. After two or three years they would then be moved on to more responsible or difficult posts, often on different estates, in order to gain experience. If the company owned many estates or the agency firm was a large one, they might make several moves over eight or ten years before they got the chance of a PD posting. Usually this would be to act for the permanent PD while he was away on his six-month furlough ('home' leave) and, once started, one would normally continue to act in succession for various PDs on different estates, moving on every six months, until appointment to a permanent PD position was gained. This would be a very unsettled period in a planter's career, especially as by this time he was often married and with a family, so the relief on receiving a permanent posting would be considerable. After that, moves became less frequent and would be dependent on the retirements of more senior PDs and on the merit of the planter in the opinion of his Visiting Agent (VA) and the directors of the Agency firm in Colombo who in practice were his employers. VAs were very important and influential persons in the planting world and, for good or ill, featured largely in the life of estate PDs. Where the relationship was not a happy one, PDs could be driven into a state of apoplectic rage by the merest mention of the VA's name, whereas in other cases there was mutual respect and friendship. In Mr Meikle's case there was a distinctly convenient arrangement, as he and his great chum, Ginger Davidson, were VAs for each other. Their visits of inspection would usually develop into grand sessions during which the emphasis on discussion of estate management to the accompaniment of copious quantities of brandy and ginger ale would gradually become reversed, until they were reduced to beaming at each other in a state of mutual but incoherent bonhomie.

The origin of VAs could be traced back to the days of coffee, when they were responsible for estimating the size and value of the developing crop as a basis on which the agents, banks or other lenders could judge the size and security of any monetary advances needed to keep the estate going until harvest. Gradually their responsibilities had increased until they advised on every aspect of estate management. Normally they would visit each estate in their practice twice a year - and woe betide any PD who failed to carry out their recommendations, once these had been accepted by the agents.

If he was well thought of, had good friends in the Colombo Agents' office (or, even more advantageous, in the London Head Office) and had reasonable luck, a PD would gradually move up the seniority ladder in much the same way as eighteenth century naval captains used to move up the

Captains' List in the Royal Navy. In this case, however, he would be appointed to larger and more prestigious estates instead of larger men-of-war, but the effect was much the same. Eventually, if everything went well, he would attain the senior PD position on the flagship estate of the company: the largest or most profitable estate in the firm. By this time, like Mr Meikle, he would probably have been appointed as VA to other estates and might eventually become a full-time VA or go on to a senior position in the Agents' office in Colombo, or even in London Headquarters, the ultimate achievement being a seat on the Board after retirement. Planters have produced much doggerel over the years and there are numerous planters' songs (mostly unprintable). However, I rather like the following, which evidently comes from the planting community of north-east India sometime about the early twentieth century. It gives a rather nostalgic reflection on the planting hierarchy, which somehow rings true:

**The Assistant**
I wish I were a manager
With umpteen quid a year,
What a glorious life with a handsome wife
And never a boss to fear.

With unlimited powers and no fixed hours
And never a care about muster
(To go out at night and return when it's light
Is an old managerial *dastur*).

With a bungalow like an old chateau
And a most expensive car,
A blooming toff with all day off -
For that is what managers are.

**The Manager**
I wish they would say 'you can be the VA
And keep the whole gang up to scratch',
I've been so long in tea that they couldn't fool me,
And would find I was more than their match.

I'd make them obey and grow tea my way,
Especially old so-and-so;
He can't argue the toss if I am the boss,
Which is one thing I'd soon let him know.

To come out in October and talk about *goeber*
And compost and pruning and such,
And find out their dodgings (such as free board and lodgings)
Would suit this tired soul very much.

**The Visiting Agent**
If I could afford to get on the Board
And smoke my cigar at the table,
With a nice dividend at every year's end,
I'd get forty per cent, if I'm able.

I'm tired of Sylhet, but I'm not too old yet,
And I want a nice house by the sea,
But I must have the cash, for the wife cuts a dash
To make up for the years spent in tea.

If I'm made a director (a profits collector)
I'll see they're kept short in Assam,
I'll live in good style and I'll die worth a pile -
That's the kind of man that I am.

**The Director**
I wish I could be an Assistant in tea
And start my life over again,
You've only two-fifty but needn't be thrifty,
For that's not the way with young men.

The ladies adore you, your life is before you,
You've the nerve and the legs for a horse,
And dance till the dawn then set to with a yawn
And take life as a matter of course.

But I spend my life playing bridge with my wife
And discussing the past with my cronies;
I've got money and gout, - and I long to come out
And be young with my debts and my ponies.


All this was far from my thoughts, which were occupied in wondering when an SD post for me would materialise, and what would happen to me if it did not. At last, in July 1956, I heard from the Agents that I had been appointed as SD on the Lower Division of Meeriabedde Group as from 1st August. This was encouraging. At last I should be on my own and able to order my own life more completely than I had ever been able to do up to this point, through childhood, school, and my time on Needwood. My salary was to be 580 rupees per month (about £43). This was very average as a starting rate of pay for SDs and would cover living costs and the employment of an appu as cook and personal bungalow servant. One also had to consider some means of transport. Traditionally young planters got around by motor bike - the more powerful the better - and exuberant speeding on the tortuous up-country roads took a considerable toll in road accidents, which were quite often fatal. Despite the fact that my father had been typical in this respect yet had survived, my parents were anxious that I should not succumb to motor bike mania and very generously passed on to me their old Morris Minor, which certainly achieved their aim. In view of this, in recompense for occasionally using my own transport for estate purposes, my salary was to be augmented by a 'motor bike allowance' of Rs 50 per month (£3.70), for which there was provision in the company rules.

Another pleasing condition of my appointment was that my period as a creeper was to be counted towards the four years of my first tour of duty, after which I would be eligible for my first long leave or furlough, as it was known, of six months. This was considered by my employers to be extremely generous and indeed my father had had to do a first tour of five years excluding creeping. However, conditions had changed a lot for European planters in the intervening 30 years. At the time my father had started planting, in 1924, he had been given the choice of going either to Mauritius or to Ceylon. The Anglo Ceylon and General Estates Co. Ltd. (of which my grandfather was then a director) had estates in both islands, but my grandfather strongly advocated Ceylon on account of the excellent social life. By the 1950s expatriate social life upcountry had declined to a shadow of what it had been in the 1920s and the opportunities for finding a wife or even acquiring a girlfriend of one's own background within the immediate planting district had diminished to something near zero. The more progressive companies, such as the Scottish Tea and Lands, were beginning to accept this and had started to introduce shorter leaves of three months after 21 months' service, but not The Gibson Estates. Part of the trouble was that the shorter period of leave really necessitated travel to and from the UK by air, which at that time was considerably more expensive than the normal two-week passage by sea. All this did not worry me unduly at the time and in fact I did not think much about it. My long leave seemed so far off that the difference between four years and four and a half seemed almost academic. Meanwhile there was a lot to think about and plan.

One of the first essentials was to get myself an appu, without which any moderately civilised existence was almost impossible. Estate bungalows were not designed to be operated by the planter himself, as even the basic essentials of cooking food and operating the water heating system required much splitting of firewood and stoking of wood-burning grates, and keeping the place clean was often more than a full time job. Such things as oven-ready meals had not been invented and even semi-prepared food was not usually available. For chicken dishes the cook normally started by catching the chicken. Besides, one's reputation would have been severely dented if it had become known amongst the labour force that the *dorai* was actually cooking his own food and was too parsimonious to give anybody employment to look after him. Bungalow servants were very often drawn from the estate labour force when they first started in domestic work and so were usually Tamils on the up-country estates. Also expatriates, who often did not speak much Sinhala anyway, found them easier to deal with.

There was a well established system for acquiring domestic servants, which started with placing an advertisement in the appropriate columns of one of the national newspapers. This normally elicited voluminous replies which one then sifted and invited a few applicants to attend for interview. There was a registration system for domestic servants which theoretically made it almost impossible for anyone dishonest or unsatisfactory to be re-employed. However, it did not always work out the way it was intended and sometimes either backfired on the employers or else unjustly penalised blameless servants who for one reason or another happened to have incurred the wrath of their employer. Professional domestic servants, when registered, were issued with a passbook, something like a passport, in which their appointments were recorded, with dates, and in which each employer could enter a reference comment when the employee left service. Such registration was not compulsory but, for those who were more than casually employed in domestic situations, registration and the passbook gave them some professional status and authenticated their history of employment. Where it started to fall down was when it came to employers' comments. In these days one could not be outright derogatory, even when commenting on the most unsatisfactory miscreants. These were not colonial times and there might be some faint risk of legal action, but another deterrent was the possibility of a visitation from a posse of the dismissed rogue's even more unpleasant friends, who might do something nasty to oneself or one's property. Then again it was seldom possible to prove theft or other wrongdoing with hard evidence or witnesses, so dismissal was often done on some other pretext and a bland comment made in the reference section. Also, even when dismissing someone unsatisfactory in one's own employment one did not necessarily wish to blight completely their chances of getting another job. Therefore, for one reason or another, a bland comment was made perhaps more often than one that was pertinent and helpful to a future employer. However, after perusing a number of references one became quite proficient at reading between the lines and deducing whether the applicant had left his last job because he had to return home to look after his sick mother (as he claimed) or whether he had been dismissed. After selecting a few possibles, the best course was to contact their former employers (who might quite often turn out to be one's acquaintances or friends) for a genuine opinion. In my case I did not know any of the former employers, but made a selection on the written references and interviews. In any case, such appointments were always something of a gamble, as an appu or houseboy might suit one employer very well but could be considered lazy or impudent by another, so even a favourable reference was no guarantee of satisfaction.

Gomez claimed to be an experienced cook who had held the position of appu in several large bungalows, but who was now getting rather elderly (he was in his fifties) and anxious for a position in a smaller household with less responsibility. He appeared at interview dressed in a spotless white sarong with an immaculately ironed khaki jacket and spoke good English. He also appeared to write English reasonably well, which I felt might come in useful. I decided to give him a trial. He was rather short in stature (perhaps reflecting the Portuguese ancestry his name implied), and looked rather frail with grey hair and a deeply lined face. I arranged with Gomez that he should be at the Small Bungalow on Meeriabedde Lower Division on the appointed day and that his pay would be, I think, Rs.85 per month plus an allowance of rice and tea.

I had not visited Meeriabedde Group and nobody seemed to think it necessary for me to do so before taking up my post - or billet, as it was called in planting parlance which, as usual, had a certain military flavour. In fact I had only a vague idea of where it was, just above the village of Koslanda, about five or six miles down the road branching off the foot of the Haputale Pass and leading eastwards to Wellawaya and the south and east coasts. The main part of the estate occupied the middle portion of a rather narrow valley with steep sides, the Lower Division occupying the lower slopes on either side of the valley, while the Upper Division covered the higher slopes on the western side, on the eastern shoulder of the Dambatenne massif and bordering the famous Lipton property of Dambatenne Group. There was also another division, named Mahakanda, which was not contiguous with the rest of the estate, but lay in the next valley to the east, surrounded by the neighbouring Poonagalla Group. These estates represented the last outposts of tea on the higher hills to the east of Haputale. Beyond them, to the east and south, the land rapidly fell away through undulating foothills to the lowland coastal plains. Meeriabedde could also be reached from the north via a road from Bandarawela which wound through various estates, such as Nayabedde, Ballagallaella, Leangawella, and Ampittiakanda for some 12 miles before reaching Poonagalla, through which an estate cart road descended for another couple of miles to Meeriabedde and eventually connected with the road from Koslanda. On the whole, Meeriabedde was not as good an estate as Needwood: the average elevation was lower, the quality of the tea was generally poorer and on the steep, eroded and stony slopes yields were considerably less.

The change around of staff in The Gibson Estates which created the SD vacancy I was to fill involved several moves. On Meeriabedde I was to replace Trevor LaBrooy, who in turn was to replace Wimal Wickremasinghe on the Haldumulla Division of Needwood. Wimal, as the company's senior SD, was to start a period of 'acting' in PD positions on other estates within the Agency of George Steuart & Co. but which might not always be on one of The Gibson Estates.

On the appointed day I loaded my suitcase and the few other chattels I had accumulated at Needwood into the green Morris Minor, said farewell (accompanied by suitable sums as *santosums*) to Paikiam and the other bungalow staff, and set off down the cart road. Turning towards Haputale on the main road, I forked right at the foot of the Haputale Pass and about 20 minutes later came to the Koslanda village sign.

At this time, public roads in up-country Ceylon, although twisty and narrow, were generally reasonably well maintained, with tarmac surfaces and furnished with signposts. This was to the credit of the Ceylon Public Works Department (known universally as the PWD) which, to be sure, had more than 100 years of experience in road construction and maintenance. In the early days of British rule the military undertook all public works in Ceylon, but they became a civilian responsibility in 1833. Very few roads suitable for wheeled traffic had been inherited from the former Dutch administration (which in any case had largely been confined to the coastal areas), so that even the main roads had to be routed and built more or less from scratch. The present extensive network of main roads is largely due to the efforts of Lieutenant (later Major) Thomas Skinner, who came under the patronage of the then Governor, Sir Edward Barnes. Skinner (who, although coming from a long line of military ancestors, seems to have been no relation of the better known James Skinner of Skinner's Horse in the Indian Army) was appointed to organise road construction in 1820 at the tender age of 16, having received his commission a year earlier. He was concerned at first (and in fact throughout his career) with the Colombo-Kandy road, but was also involved with many others, numerous surveys, and particularly the mapping of the higher hills in the Adam's Peak area. From time to time he was appointed to other positions, but always returned to road construction and eventually became Commissioner of Public Works, a position which he held for many years until his retirement in 1867.

Upcountry, in the planting districts, the pioneer planters often acted as contractors for road construction. As apparently they were paid by the mile, there was little incentive to take short cuts or to choose direct routes, and gradients had to be negotiable by ox carts, all of which explained why the roads wound round every contour and circumvented every minor obstacle. Nevertheless, kerb and culvert stones were regularly whitewashed (a great help on dark and misty nights) and each culvert was individually marked with the mile number from the main town and the serial number of the culvert within the mile. One could therefore easily describe a location on the Colombo road by saying, for example, that it was 'just past culvert 58/17', this being the 17th culvert in mile 58 from Colombo. Village and town signboards were clearly lettered in the three official languages and the PWD was gradually rewriting them with Sinhala at the top and English at the bottom, in contrast to the practice in colonial days.

At Koslanda I turned up to the left, where the Meeriabedde road diverged and climbed steadily through Koslanda Estate. At this point the road was lined with flowering trees of various kinds commonly planted in tropical countries: the feathery-leaved blue jacaranda, the orange-flowered South African tulip tree (*Spathodea campanulata*), and the scarlet-flowered flamboyant tree. Unusually also here was the curious 'cannon ball' tree from South America which sprouted its waxy pink flowers and cannon ball fruits on stalks directly from the main trunk and branches. This tree was endeared to the Buddhist population because the central part of the flower (the pistil) was thought to resemble a Buddhist *dagoba*. Passing various labour lines and the Koslanda factory, I entered Meeriabedde estate and continued up past Meeriabedde factory, more labour lines, and round several hairpin bends until eventually I turned up a short driveway marked 'Meeriabedde Small Bungalow'.

The drive opened into a large yard, wide enough to turn a car, with a large open garage on the left facing the side of the bungalow to the right. The bungalow itself was sturdily built of dressed granite blocks, with large casement windows and roofed with the inevitable red-painted corrugated iron. At the rear, and connected to the main bungalow by a covered walk-way, was a separate block containing the kitchen, a storeroom and a servant's room and toilet, all opening onto a small back veranda.

Trevor was large, genial and welcoming. He came from a well-known burgher family and had several planting relatives. Several years older than myself, he had been on Meeriabedde for two or three years and now seemed to be looking forward to moving to Needwood, which he felt was less remote. My few possessions were soon unloaded by the kitchen coolie and Gomez, who had appeared and enthusiastically took charge of my interests.

After a cup of tea, Trevor announced that he had been instructed to take me up to the estate office, near the Meeriabedde 'Big' Bungalow to meet my new boss, Bill Horne. Trevor wheeled out his motor bike and, with me as pillion passenger, set off down the hill, over the stream at the bottom

*The author at Meeriabedde Small Bungalow, 1988. The protective boulder can be seen on the hillside above the bungalow.*

of the valley, and up round a hairpin bend the other side to the main office and bungalow. Bill Horne was one of the old stalwarts of The Gibson Estates, a contemporary of Mr Meikle. Tall and dapper, he would have looked well in military uniform. Like Mr Meikle, he had been a bachelor all his life and seemed likely to continue as such until he had visited Australia on his last long leave. There, to the astonishment of his entire acquaintance, he had met and wed his new wife, Maxime, who had introduced quite a new dimension to district social life. Small, not too slim but bubbling with unsuppressed energy, she bounced about like a rubber hand grenade, exploding social taboos and what she regarded as stuffy British colonial decorum at every turn. This I believe she did from natural exuberance and not from any sense of wanting to shock or to prick expatriate snobbery, but she caused the dignified Bill Horne much acute embarrassment. Tales of a sword dance on the table at a club dinner were circulating and one did not need to be very close to hear her loudly telling inappropriate or scurrilous anecdotes in Australian tones strong enough to mangle every vowel in the language. She was also very kind hearted and never stood on ceremony when entertaining us SDs to tea or lunch.

After a short talk in the office about the estate and ongoing works, I was introduced to the Head Clerk, an important personage on any estate. Trevor and I were then entertained to tea by Maxime before returning down the hill on Trevor's motor bike to the Small Bungalow, where I was taken on a tour of the premises. Situated on the western slopes of the valley, the bungalow nestled below a gigantic boulder almost as large as the house. This, apparently, was no accident, as further up the hillside was a small cliff from which large rocks occasionally became detached in the rains and came crashing down the hillside. The boulder provided good protection against this hazard, for which I was to be thankful during the next monsoon.

The front of the bungalow faced onto a small garden, beyond which the tea-covered hillside fell away down the slopes of the valley. A path, bordered on either side by flower beds, led from the veranda and joined an inspection path which wound down through the tea towards the muster ground some distance below. From the garden the view southwards over the lowland plains was framed in the V of the valley sides, so that the extent of the low country visible was rather curtailed, especially as this elevation was considerably lower than at Needwood Bungalow. However, on clear days the sea was still visible, and on clear nights the flashes of the lighthouse ten miles out to sea on the Great Basses could easily be seen. We walked down to the muster ground and then on a short way to a dam, stemming the flow of a small stream. The dam was quite small, scarcely half an acre in extent, but was surrounded by trees and grass which made it a pleasant focus for an evening walk. A white-breasted waterhen was busy at the margin of the water and scuttled into the long grass on our approach. Trevor was mourning the loss of his dog, which had died a short time previously and had much enjoyed this walk. Apparently he had had quite a number of dogs, sometimes several simultaneously, which he had used for hunting, and had always been much distressed when they died. Several of their graves were sited in the vegetable garden, although I did not notice any great benefit to the adjacent vegetables. August being the middle of the dry weather in Uva, the stream was scarcely running and the dam was only half full. Its main purpose was to feed a small turbine-powered generator at the factory, which provided lighting for the bungalow and some of the estate staff houses. Standing on the dam wall, one could see the pipe going down the hill and in at the end of the factory wall. The current produced was erratic, weak and fitful, especially when the water was low, but in the monsoon rains it was usually not too bad. At the end of the dry weather, when the stream had more or less ceased to flow, a small diesel engine had to be used to power the generator. In either case, the generator was only operated from about 6 to 11 p.m. each day unless prolonged by special request.

Returning to the bungalow, we repaired to the veranda for a beer while Trevor told me the basic facts about the Division, the labour, and the junior estate staff. He was convinced that the Head Teamaker was fiddling the books and smuggling out tea, but in spite of midnight patrols and surprise visits to the factory by Trevor in the small hours of the morning, he had so far been unable to catch the culprits or accumulate enough evidence to take action. Nevertheless, there was no love lost between him and the Teamaker and he advised me to be on my guard. These night activities were much enjoyed by Trevor, who would have been an excellent companion to have around if one was engaged upon a dangerous patrol behind enemy lines. Besides being large and genial, he was also immensely strong being, apparently, in the Ceylon national weight-lifting team. This was useful on several occasions, but especially in the Case of the Dead Ducks.

Trevor had been returning in his car from the club late one night when, passing the labour lines at a fair speed, some ducks had waddled out into the road just as he came by, and he got three of them. The next day the irate owner of the said ducks appeared at the bungalow office carrying their mangled remains and demanding suitable compensation. Although visibly ordinary in appearance, these particular ducks were apparently most valuable, so the owner said, owing to them being an especially superior breed and only recently purchased at vast expense. Furthermore, they were just about to breed, so compensation was needed to cover not only the ducks themselves, but also the many valuable offspring they were sure to have had almost immediately. Trevor was unimpressed by this tale and told the complainant in no uncertain terms that he should take more care of his valuable ducks, that in fact they looked extremely ordinary to him and, further, if he didn't get out of his sight very quickly indeed, he would bring his dogs to finish off the remaining ducks. This had the desired effect of removing the complainant from the bungalow premises, but rumours reached Trevor that the duck owner was planning revenge. Some days later Trevor was again returning up the cart road late at night when, coming round a sharp bend, he found a large boulder placed in the middle of the road. Getting out of his car, he investigated the rock and decided he might just be able to move it. Crouching with his back to the stone, he gripped it behind him and, giving an almighty heave, managed to move it over the edge of the road and send it rolling thunderously down into the ravine. He then got back into the car and continued his journey home. However, it soon became apparent that his rock-rolling prowess was widely known. Eventually, he heard that the boulder had been placed there by the outraged duck owner and three friends, who had struggled between them to shift it into the middle of the road and had then waited, concealed, in ambush. However, when they saw Trevor shift the boulder single-handed with such apparent ease, they had decided not to push their luck any further, remaining hidden, and nothing more was heard from them.

Trevor was not a naturalist but was interested in wild life (even if this interest was usually gastronomic). He was also something of a herpetologist and had apparently kept a variety of snakes and other reptiles in cages on the bungalow veranda. This had the added advantage, he said, of keeping off any potential burglars, as everybody on the estate knew about the snakes and had no wish to make their closer acquaintance. Mid-country tea estates harboured quite a number of snakes, but one did not see them very often, although their cast skins were common enough in the garden and amongst the tea, often draped over a rock or stump. Sometimes these skins would be so perfect that they gave the impression of a ghost snake on which one could count every scale. Probably the commonest snake on most estates was the rat snake, a charcoal-grey, non-venomous snake, which could grow to six feet or so and was often common around bungalows and buildings, sometimes getting into the lofts to catch rats, mice, bats and lizards. Then there was the Indian cobra, known in Tamil as *nulla parmbu* (the good snake) because of its role in sheltering the Lord Buddha from the sun by means of its spread hood, on which the characteristic whitish 'spectacles' mark provided easy identification. Although quite numerous, it was not an aggressive snake and was treated with respect by the labourers, in spite of the fact that most were Hindus. Much more feared, and with reason, was the Russell's viper or *tik-polonga*. This viper had beautiful markings, a large triangular head, and virulent venom. It would also attack with relatively little (often inadvertent) provocation and the bare feet and ankles of the pluckers were very vulnerable. The estate hospital kept a supply of antivenene, which was put to use fairly regularly. However, many of the locals, so Trevor said, did not have much faith in western antivenene but put their trust in traditional remedies, such as snake stones. These were small, pumice-stone-like objects, possibly consisting of some kind of bone, which the practitioner of traditional medicine applied to the fang punctures on the patient. The snake stone would apparently adhere tightly to the spot and could not be easily removed. The stone was supposed to absorb the venom from the bite and, when this was done, it would drop off of its own accord. I never saw this method used, but it was reputed to achieve considerable success (although, of course, only a few of those bitten by even the really deadly snakes would die anyway, as many would have received only a fraction of the full lethal dose).

Apparently the jewel of Trevor's collection had been a python of some nine or ten feet in length. This he had fed on small chickens for its infrequent meals and it had become quite tame. However, evidently it had not been entirely docile as he declared he had had to release it back into the wild because it bit him 'too much'. Pythons were relatively rare on the estates, but a few lived in pockets of jungle in the ravines or on land too rocky or steep to cultivate. They were much more common in the low country jungles, especially near rivers and tanks, where they reached a length of about 15 or 16 feet. There were also various grass and tree snakes which were either back-fanged or non-venomous. Although interested in the snakes, I could not help feeling rather relieved that he had disposed of the collection before my arrival, and I also wondered whether any of them might retain an attachment to the area of their former home.

The bungalow had two bedrooms, but Trevor explained that the second bedroom was more or less unfurnished and that he had arranged for me to share his room for the couple of nights we were to overlap before his departure. When we retired to bed, I noticed with some apprehension that there were no mosquito nets. Moreover, the large windows were open to the warm night and nobody had attempted to use any anti-mosquito spray. Trevor was good-naturedly dismissive of my doubts and assured me that there were hardly any mosquitoes around, especially in the dry season, and that he was never bothered with them. So saying, he turned out the light and was soon asleep. Now, normally I would stand a good chance of winning any getting-to-sleep-first race, but the unfamiliar surroundings must have handicapped me just enough to allow the mozzies to mount a pre-emptive strike. Almost immediately I became aware of the high-pitched whine of a million tiny wings and a few seconds later the first of the dive-bombers zoomed past my ear, to be followed by successive waves of its brethren. Slapping and smacking to no avail, I retired under the sheets, through which I presently felt the tiny pricks of the sheet-piercing squadrons as they got to work. Then Trevor started to snore. Not a mild, soothing, regular snore, but rich and vibrant yet so irregular one was constantly kept in a state of nervous anticipation waiting for the next blast. . . . .The two nights were very long ones for me and I felt far from refreshed when daylight came.

The next day we were up at dawn to attend muster. The muster ground was only five minutes walk from the bungalow down the path through the tea, with the dim grey of dawn developing into glowing colours in the strengthening light and wisps of wood smoke rising gently from the labour lines. At muster I was obviously the centre of much interest, and here I met the KP, whose name was Ramasamy, the Assistant KP and the various kanganys. As usual, muster acquired the aura of a military parade and one almost expected to hear the commands 'Shoulder, mamoties!' or 'Present . . . alavangoes!' as each gang was issued with the tools for the day. Old Ramasamy was an experienced and responsible KP who had seen many a young SD come and go. I got to know him well during my time on Meeriabedde and I always valued and respected his good sense and his ability to manage the labourers without overtly exercising his authority.

In the afternoon a small crowd gathered in the bungalow yard. This consisted of the KP, Assistant KP, all the kanganys and various other members of the junior estate staff together with a few hangers-on. It turned out that this was to be a farewell ceremony for Trevor and we therefore retired for a moment to don jackets and ties in order to mark the occasion with proper respect. Chairs were brought for Trevor and myself and we were garlanded with the traditional *poomalay*s. These were made of dense strings of white jasmine, golden marigold and purple bouganvillea, their sweet and heavy scent filling the bungalow yard. When we were seated, Ramasamy made a lengthy speech, saying how well-liked Trevor was, what a lot he had done for the Division, and much else which I could not follow properly. The kanganys and other staff stood round us in an admiring semi-circle to hear this oration, at the end of which, amidst a round of applause, a box was produced and placed on a little table in front of Trevor. This was a farewell gift, and when the lid was opened a very handsome set of table cutlery was revealed, to loud noises of appreciation from the assembled throng. This was the cue for Trevor and he rose to his feet with appropriately gracious demeanour. Having had lifelong experience of both Tamil and Sinhala, and having attended school in Ceylon at which both languages were taught throughout the school, Trevor then made a well-turned speech of thanks, saying how much he had enjoyed his time at Meeriabedde and how sorry he was to leave. As he sat down to more applause, all eyes swivelled to me and I suddenly realised that I was now expected to make my contribution. Panic suddenly assailed me. Now, although my Tamil had come on a lot in recent months, it was still very imperfect, even for general conversation. For off-the-cuff speeches it was totally inadequate.

Nevertheless, it was obvious that I had to say *something* and it would have been much too ignominious to ask Trevor to translate for me. Rising to my feet in what I hoped was an authoritative way, I greeted them all and searched frantically for something simple yet appropriate to say. I cannot now remember what I eventually came up with, but it was something to the effect that I would say very little, that I thanked them for the food and drink (which I could see were about to be produced) and that I would see them all around the Division. I then collapsed back onto my chair and we were offered little cakes of lurid colours and the currently available fizzy drinks (Lanka Lime being a deep and vivid green and Orange Barley equally brilliant in its own hue). Meanwhile a photographer from Koslanda village had appeared, equipped with a large full-plate camera complete with black hood and massive tripod. The assembled multitude then arranged themselves behind us and with much good humoured jostling and instructions to the photographer to be sure to include the centrally-displayed cutlery, the picture was eventually taken.

These farewell ceremonies were (and probably still are) quite a traditional feature on Ceylon estates where managers change every few years. They were not held invariably at each change-over, but were usual when managers had been in post for several years, or when they were particularly liked by the estate staff. They also varied greatly in complexity from simple and straightforward, like the one for Trevor, to really elaborate affairs complete with traditional dancing and firewalking, such as I remembered attending as a small child for one of my father's moves. The cost of the gift and other expenses were covered by contributions from the estate staff and I always felt that somehow expensive gifts should be discouraged, as junior staff salaries were so low that almost any contribution would seem excessive. Yet the staff always felt that only a substantial gift would be appreciated and that one which was only a token would not properly represent the esteem which they wished to convey.

Trevor duly departed for Needwood, leaving me to take stock of my new home. The main part of the bungalow consisted of a central dining room with a sitting room on one side and the main bedroom and bathroom on the other. The dining room windows gave onto a small veranda facing the view down the valley. Behind the sitting room was a second bedroom, with a rather more rudimentary bathroom, while behind the main bedroom was a small office. Outside, the front garden consisted of a slightly sloping lawn of coarse 'buffalo' grass, unequally bisected by the path and flower beds, which contained some rather scrawny gerberas and African marigolds. A low, dry stone wall formed the boundary on the lower side and the garden was partly shaded by large mango and African tulip trees. At the rear of the bungalow a flight of steps led up to the rather shady vegetable garden. This was divided into beds which contained little except a few beetroot, kohlrabi and one or two pappoy or papaya trees. Known elsewhere as pawpaw, these were a great standby as they provided both fruit and vegetable fare. Papaya trees could live for many years but became progressively less productive, so they needed replacing every few years. They grew very quickly and normally had a single trunk carrying a topknot of large, many-lobed leaves on long, hollow stalks. These could be joined together to form temporary pipes for distributing water in gardens or at roadside springs. The fruits were borne close to the stem, interspersed with the leaves at the top of the plant. They were melon-sized and when ripe good ones had delicious, aromatic golden-yellow flesh with masses of globular, black seeds in the hollow centre. The unripe fruits could be cooked and tasted like a rather insipid marrow - a godsend to appus short of vegetables to provide for the dorai's meal but dreary if served up too often, and many an appu must have received irate instructions never to serve cooked papaya again. The garden also had a few other fruit trees, of which the grapefruit trees bordering the drive and the mandarin tree outside the bedroom window provided excellent fruit, but the mangoes were small, stringy, and tasted like turpentine. In Ceylon the best mangoes grew in the dry lowlands of the north and east, and good fruits were seldom obtainable up-country.

Gomez immediately took charge of my domestic arrangements. Besides the rent-free bungalow, my allowances also included a young kitchen coolie cum houseboy named Arumugam and a venerable *totakaran* named Palaniandy, both of whom were paid by the estate. In addition I received 3 lb. of tea and 1.5 'yards' of firewood per month. Firewood was always measured in 'yards', these actually being cubic yards, since for measurement the wood was cut into three-foot lengths and piled into rows 3 ft. high.

*Taking over the Lower Division on Meeriabedde, 2 August 1956. Trevor LaBrooy (on left) and the author (on right) together with the junior staff of the Division, the kanganies, and others. Ramasamy KP (standing on left) and the Assistant KP (on right) are garlanded, with dark jackets. Arumugam is seated on the ground near me and Trevor's appu near him. The small axe-headed pole is carried by the turbaned bungalow watchman.*

The first thing to do was to get myself some supplies, so I asked Gomez to make a list of everything basic which he thought he would need for the next month. I then took him in the car down to Koslanda village, where I arranged to open an account at the main general store, Karamaraj Bros. Here we got everything on Gomez's list, - if Karamaraj didn't have an item then they would obtain it from a neighbouring establishment. All was supplied on credit and I paid the bill at the end of the month. This seemed an admirable arrangement as everything was itemised, and the monthly shopping trips to Koslanda became a regular feature of my life.

Koslanda was a relatively large village and not only was there a large range of caddies and a main post office, but also a hospital with a resident District Medical Officer, Dr Gunasena, whom I met on one of my early foraging trips. Dr Gunasena was genial and pipe-smoking and invited me to come along to the hospital on Tuesday evenings to join their social group for a game of tennis. This I did and met a small number of tennis players who were mostly minor officials and staff from neighbouring estates. The hospital tennis court had obviously seen better days, the net being much mended and the balls worn, but it still provided an enjoyable game and at a standard with which I felt I could cope. As yet I had not had the opportunity to make many friends, so a little socialising was also very congenial. I was gratified to find that I was made welcome (I was the only European who attended) and I got the feeling that it was appreciated that I did not disdain their company. Over the next few months I got to know several of the group quite well, especially Dharamadasa, a clerk from the Post Office, who was not much older than myself. However, as time went on and my horizons and acquaintance widened, I found my attendance becoming increasingly irregular. I often had other invitations for Tuesday evenings. Then one day Bill Horne took me aside and said he had heard I was playing tennis at the hospital and he had nothing against that, but he felt I should beware of becoming too socially involved with a crowd which might include some of my own junior estate staff. At this point I was not sufficiently involved to feel I should make a protest on this as a matter of principle, and in any case I was spinelessly but logically anxious not to upset my boss at the very start of my planting career. So my tennis evenings in Koslanda gradually came to an end.

Estate bungalows were usually provided with 'hard' furnishings; basic furniture and mattresses, while the 'soft' furnishings such as curtains, mats, and more special items of furniture were supplied by the occupant. In my own case I was lucky in that I was able to receive surplus items from my parents, and an early visit from my mother ensured that I had curtains and cushion covers made to her satisfaction. However, many young SDs had no such family support and, if they were not very domesticated, their bungalows permanently gave the impression of a temporary camp.

The large casement windows in every room of my bungalow were quite without any kind of bars or mesh to keep out unwanted intruders, either with two legs or with six. Security was not then even thought of as a problem and, except on very wet nights, I always slept with my bedroom windows wide open. To be sure, all PD and SD bungalows had a night watchman, or *karvalkaran*, who would come on duty each evening carrying a staff tipped with a kind of small axe head, which seemed to be a badge of office. However, the watchmen usually spent most of the night soundly asleep on the back veranda. Burglaries and theft, other than by bungalow staff themselves, were rare on estates and violent incidents extremely so. These were usually the culmination of some grudge held against a harsh manager or where he had got involved with local women on his own estate, thereby breaking the most cardinal of all planting rules. At night, if I left the light on for any length of time, especially during the monsoon months, the curtains would become covered with moths of every size, shape and colour. Their diversity was truly amazing and they clung to the curtains like thousands of enamelled brooches on the folds of a gown. Interspersed with the moths were numerous other creatures of the night, mostly small to medium-sized beetles, some with fearsome horns, and various delicate lacewings and colourful plant bugs. At this elevation the noise of the crickets was deafening after dark, hundreds of species and millions of individuals stridulating with all their might in frantic competition.

After my experiences when sharing the bedroom with Trevor, one of the first furnishing adjustments I made was the installation of an ample mosquito net. Mosquito nets vary considerably in shape and structure, a different design seeming to have evolved in each tropical country. In Ceylon the normal design incorporated a stout cane hoop about two feet in diameter, from which hung the ample folds of the net. The hoop was suspended near the ceiling by a distinctive type of cord (known universally as 'mosquito net cord') which passed through a pulley screwed into the ceiling. The net, which came in a wide range of colours, was long enough to be tucked in under the mattress. With this in place, and in the absence of Trevor's snores, I slept soundly. On the floor in a corner of the bedroom I discovered a length of two-inch steel shafting, as used in tea factories for transmission of power to the various machines. This was evidently a remnant of Trevor's weight-lifting equipment and no doubt he did overhead lifts with it. It was heavy: very heavy. In fact I found it was quite a struggle to get it off the ground at all. No wonder the Duck Man had been impressed. Calling Gomez, I asked him to remove the unwanted object and suggested he enlisted the help of Arumugam and probably, I said, he would need Palaniandy as well. Gomez eyed the shafting: 'Sir', he said, 'I do not think that will be necessary', whereupon he seized the bar and carried it away, leaving me to cope with my chagrin in utter astonishment.

As part of the anti-mosquito campaign, Gomez also instituted a ritual at dusk every day in which he must have been drilled by previous employers, as it was practised in most estate bungalows. Armed with a bamboo cane, he would come into the sitting room in the gathering gloom, switch on the lights, and with the cane he drew the curtains over each window. When all the bungalow curtains had been drawn, he then reappeared with a Flit can. This was bright yellow and decorated with graphic pictures of slaughtered mosquitoes and flies, all in positions of abject surrender with their legs in the air. The can was a manually operated pump action sprayer which, when vigorously operated, dispersed the famous pyrethrin-based insecticide Flit as a fine spray, which Gomez proceeded to direct over all and sundry, but especially into dark corners and under the desk, where mosquitoes liked to lurk. This gave fairly good mosquito control, but in fact in those days they were of nuisance value only. Malaria had been virtually wiped out in Ceylon with the advent of DDT in the years just after the second world war and Ceylon was often quoted as a textbook example of successful malaria control. Unless one was to spend a long time in the remotest jungles, nobody took any antimalaria precautions and the disease was almost unknown upcountry. It was very different before the war in the days of Leonard Woolf and John Still, when malaria could decimate a village population. It is now again a major hazard.

There were many other co-habitants of my bungalow with which I sometimes had to contend. Ants, especially the small black kinds, were always numerous and would home in within minutes on most kinds of food, particularly anything sweet. Meat safes and food cupboards were always stood with their legs in *shundus* of kerosene, which was very effective in keeping them at bay. Besides a meat safe, the estate provided three main items of kitchen equipment. There was a wood-burning cooking range (often a 'Dover' stove), a large water filter on a stand, and a refrigerator which operated on kerosene. This was a great convenience in bungalows without a continuous supply of electricity and, once one got the hang of them, they worked very well. White ants (termites) were also much in evidence and would quickly honeycomb and devour any untreated softwood which came within reach. This included books and cardboard boxes and, indeed, door and window frames, their reach being extended by the construction of hemispherical mud tunnels across inedible surfaces. Books needed a weekly dusting and beating, not only to discourage the genuine book worm (a beetle grub) but also the masonry or potting wasps. These were handsome yellow and black wasps with pin-thin waists, which delighted in constructing their pot-like mud nests on the rear surfaces of books, invisible within the bookcase, which they would then provision with a few choice paralysed caterpillars before laying their eggs and sealing the nest.

All this cleaning provided ample work for Gomez and Arumugam when they were not occupied in cooking, chopping firewood, or other domestic tasks. My mother, I knew, had a bungalow cleaning schedule which governed the work of my parents' bungalow staff. On each weekday one of the rooms of the bungalow was thoroughly cleaned and the whole bungalow would thus be cleaned every fortnight or so. The cleaning was by no means superficial. The furniture would be carried out of the room (into the garden, if necessary) and the carpet or matting would be lifted and hung on a line. Here it would be rhythmically beaten by two of the houseboys, using special paddle-shaped rattan carpet-beaters, to the accompaniment of loud grunts and clouds of dust, which would drift about the garden in the sunshine. The floor would then be polished, using wax if it was wooden, or the ubiquitous red polish if it was concrete. Fitted carpets would have been quite impractical as they would have provided a wonderful haven for all kinds of insects and *poochies*. Most carpets and mats were of local or Indian origin. Woven coconut matting was cheap and was produced locally in various colours and patterns. For more comfortable bungalow furnishing, Indian 'Bangalore' carpets and felt 'Numdah' rugs with colourful embroidery were commonly used. I did not institute a cleaning schedule for my small bungalow and Gomez seemed to be well versed in cleaning matters without any instruction from the inexperienced me, so all I had to do was to keep an eye open for any areas which had been missed.

Washing of clothes and linen was not a job done by the appu nor any of the bungalow houseboys. Washing machines were unheard of and all washing was entrusted to the local dhobi, of which there were several on every estate. The dhobi was usually paid a flat rate on a monthly basis, the amount depending on the size of the household. In my case this was, I think, Rs 15, and I left dealing with the dhobi in Gomez's capable hands. In larger households, however, dealing with the dhobi could occupy a considerable amount of time and effort. Many less reliable appus and dhobis would try devious ploys to increase their profit or pay so, after long experience, my mother always dealt with the dhobi herself.

The simplest ruse was to make items which might find a ready sale in the local market unobtrusively disappear. This, of course, was easy to prevent if one did the business oneself, and my mother kept a little 'Dhobi Book' in which all the items sent were recorded each Dhobi Day. Another ploy was to substitute a worn or poor quality item for a new or high quality one. This was more difficult to spot in large piles of clothes and linen, and each item had to be examined if dress shirts and silk blouses were not mysteriously to evaporate.

The dhobi's technical expertise might also leave something to be desired. After soaping, using large yellow bars of Sunlight soap, the traditional method of washing was to work the soap into the material by beating the clothes and linen into a lather on a flat rock in a stream. This was followed by rinsing in the stream and vigorous manual wringing-out, finally leaving them to dry spread out in the sun on some grassy area. Some items, such as handkerchiefs, might be boiled in an empty 4-gallon kerosene tin or 'debbie'. However, clothes could suddenly shrink if washed in water which was too hot. Also, curious stains could inexplicably appear in the most awkward places, while the more delicate fabrics did not take kindly to being beaten on rocks and would sullenly develop frayed edges or even dissolve into holes. On Dhobi Day my mother could often be heard complaining in her mild way:

'But, Dhobi, this stain is *new*, and look at this, it's still quite dirty.'

'No, Lady,' would come the reply, 'this stain there *before* washing. But coming clean, Lady.' And back it would go for re-washing.

A good dhobi was a treasure indeed, and some seemed to possess almost magical powers for removing stains or restoring shrunken garments to something like their original size. Ironing was done with large hollow flat-irons filled with glowing charcoal and sometimes operated with the feet. An expert could produce perfect results with this equipment. The less expert sometimes produced scorch marks or even burns, but these could be concealed from casual view by clever folding and stacking.

Clothes and linen were also under constant attack by pests and *poochies*. Clothes moths abounded and anything woollen which was not accompanied in the drawer by a liberal quantity of mothballs would come out as if it had been machine-gunned. For storage of blankets and linen, my mother and many other estate wives relied on their 'zinc-lined chests'. These were wooden chests, usually made by the local carpenter, of about the size of a large trunk. They had locks, and handles for ease of transport, although their weight always made them difficult to manoeuvre. The inside was lined with galvanised metal sheet, the joints being soldered to give an effective protection, not only against all manner of *poochies*, but also against damp and mould.

All tropical buildings have their resident geckos (kinds of small lizard) and in the comparative warmth of the mid-country elevation at Meeriabedde two species shared the bungalow walls. One was larger, dark coloured with some white patterning while the other, more ubiquitous, kind was only two to three inches long and transparent to the extent that one could discern its heart and innards in action when illuminated from below (as when resting on a lamp shade). I got quite fond of these small creatures, which broke the silence of my evenings with their 'chick-chick' calls. Their great delight was when the termites swarmed, usually at the beginning of the north-east monsoon. Great columns of winged termites would issue from termite nest entrances like smoke from some volcanic fumarole and rise high into the still and humid evening air. Bats and birds, frogs and toads, all had a gastronomic orgy on these occasions and so did the geckos, but I never saw termites used as human food as they are in Africa. As soon as the bungalow lights came on a swirling mass of flapping termites would assail the windows and doors and some would inevitably find their way in. Strategically placed bowls of water trapped some and others were easy game for the geckos, who were well capable of catching much more wary prey. They would devour the whole termite, wings and all, with a gulping motion and would then pause for a few minutes to let their digestions get to work. However, I noticed that each successive termite took rather longer to go down until at last, after about five or six had been consumed, the gecko could take no more and would rest, often with the wings of the last termite still protruding from its mouth. This made it look fairly ridiculous and one felt like reprimanding it for biting off more than it could chew. But usually, after a short rest, the wings would be eased in millimetre by millimetre, sometimes with help from a 'finger' or 'thumb', until they finally disappeared and the gecko retired to the picture rail or corner of the ceiling with a smug and self-satisfied expression.

The local populace were superstitious about geckos and considered it especially bad luck if (as not uncommonly happened) one fell on you. Although geckos had no difficulty in running up vertical walls or across ceilings, occasionally one would lose its footing or would be dislodged during competition with a rival. Another disconcerting habit was that, like most lizards, they would drop their tails if these were gripped by a predator. The disconnected tail would writhe vigorously with muscular spasms, which was usually enough to distract the predator while the gecko made its escape, and it would eventually grow a new tail. I was decidedly off-put on one occasion when opening the dressing table drawer to find a large dark gecko tail hopping about amongst my handkerchiefs. Evidently I had pinched a gecko's tail when opening the drawer, which had caused it to take this drastic evasive action.

I quickly settled into my new and delightfully independent life style. I had a wonderfully euphoric feeling that I could, for the first time in my life, do more or less as I pleased and did not have to consider whether my actions would be acceptable to my family or school authorities. I suppose everyone who moves into a home of their own for the first time experiences this feeling, but with me it was very strong (perhaps in reaction to my eight months on Needwood) and it never really left me during the two years I was on Meeriabedde.

# Estate life                                                           5

---

I do not remember receiving any formal notification of what my duties and responsibilities as SD on Meeriabedde would be. It was generally accepted that SDs could be required by their PD to do more or less anything, but an SDs routine duties were so well established in planting circles that it was probably considered superfluous to set them out. In fact they did not seem to differ very much from those I had had as a creeper, except that I was now expected to assume responsibility for the various field operations, to ensure that they were done in a timely and proper manner, and it was I who received the muster list each day from the KP. I was also responsible for making various small payments and for these I had to keep a cash account which had to be balanced and submitted monthly to the estate office. Nobody actually instructed me as to how the cash book should be balanced, but it was a simple matter to follow what had been done previously. It also seemed clear that I was *not* responsible for tea manufacture at Meeriabedde Factory, although it was on my Division. The technical aspects of this were the responsibility of the Head Teamaker, under the direct supervision of Bill Horne, and I dealt only with such things as the allocation of labourers to the factory, repairs to the surroundings, and any problems with the delivery of leaf from the field.

A new responsibility, which I found much more demanding, was sorting out any minor disputes which might occur amongst the labour force or junior staff. Again, I had received no training or advice on this and all I could do was to apply common sense. The main thing, clearly, was to be very fluent in Tamil and I made some effort to continue improvement in this direction. At muster one morning soon after I had taken over on Meeriabedde, old Ramasamy asked me for a note (a *tundu*) to get *savukaram* from the estate stores for the labourers who were to work on repairs to the cart road. *Savukaram* was not then in my vocabulary and I presumed he was asking for a *sauku murram* (grevillea tree). This was quite a common request on the occasion of funerals or weddings, the tree being used as firewood for cooking the large amount of food necessary on these occasions. However, Ramasamy made it clear that this was not what he wanted and I could not think of anything else which sounded similar which could possibly be needed. We had almost reached stalemate when, with a prodigious feat of memory, Ramasamy murmured 'so-aap'. Of course! They would need soap to clean up after using the emulsified Colas tar. Another word was indelibly added to my memory. Later on, when I had become quite fluent and was much more confident, I had a genuine request for a *sauku murram* but forgot to give the supplicant the desired *tundu*. When he reminded me some time later, I thought I would be clever and try a pun: 'Oh, *murramtiten*', I said with a smile (*murrantiten* being 'I have forgotten'). He looked at me completely blankly, obviously thinking the young *dorai*'s Tamil was worse than he had feared. I did not feel up to trying to explain the joke and avoided puns thereafter.

In my father's day, young SDs were introduced to Tamil by a book imperiously titled *Inge Va* ('Come Here'). My father's copy of this had disappeared in the mists of time (perhaps fortuitously, in view of its evidently colonialist tone). By the time I came along it was long out of print and the only book available for those trying to learn the kind of Tamil spoken by estate labourers was a slim volume entitled *Cooly Tamil* by W. G. B. Wells, published by the Ceylon Planters' Society. It was used by generations of European planters in Ceylon and south India, but changed its title in later editions to *Colloquial Tamil* in deference to the modern view that 'coolie' was a derogatory term. Easy to use and employing the Roman alphabet, it was the mainstay of my linguistic efforts.

Of course, in pioneering days (and for some considerable time thereafter) many, if not most, planters learned their Tamil or Sinhala with the aid of live-in local mistresses universally known as 'sleeping dictionaries'. Although this was often encouraged by the girl's family, who derived financial and other benefits from the arrangement, and was a much pleasanter way of learning the local language than battling with a dry textbook, the pressures of colonial society gradually made this method socially unacceptable. Thereafter, although sleeping dictionaries did not entirely vanish from young planters' households, they were not overtly paraded and certainly had to be concealed from one's PD.

A few months' after my arrival on Meeriabedde, Bill Horne told me that he thought I should enter for the Junior Tamil examination of the Ceylon Planters' Society (or CPS, as it was known). The CPS was in fact the planters' representative organisation; a sort of trade union, in fact, although most of its members (and their employers) would have been horrified at the use of such a term. In 1854 the early pioneer and proprietary planters had formed the Planters' Association to look after their interests, especially in dealings with the government of the day, and this it had done very effectively. However, by the 1920s and 1930s, when most estates were no longer managed personally by their owners but by salaried superintendents, the interests of the PDs and SDs had diverged from those of the owners (their employers). After abortive attempts to re-organise the Planters' Association into two sections catering respectively for employers and employees, the CPS was eventually formed as a separate organisation in 1936. In addition to the dissatisfaction with the Planters' Association, the formation of the CPS was given strong impetus by the Depression of the 1930s and the associated deterioration in conditions of service, including salary cuts and poor or non-existent arrangements for pensionable retirement. Many well-known planters had served as its chairmen, including Bill Horne in 1950. The CPS took its duties seriously and besides endeavouring to improve conditions of employment, tried also to improve professional standards by organising examinations in the Tamil and Sinhala languages and in tea manufacture.

Even before I had become an SD I had been encouraged to become a member of the CPS and I had done so soon after my appointment, so I was already eligible to take the examination. The Junior Tamil exam was entirely oral - only the Advanced Tamil required a written paper. However, before I could enter, I had to undergo a preliminary test by more senior members of the CPS to check that I was ready and would not waste the Society's resources by being likely to fail. This was done one evening at the club, after tennis and before repairing to the bar. Colin Mulrenan from Gonamotava Estate and Jim McLachlan, then on Glenanore, were to be my examiners.

'What', said Colin, 'is the Tamil for "hair"?'

'No, no', he went on after I had replied, 'I mean "hair", not "hare" '.

'Now for something a little more complicated', said Jim. 'How would you say "Take my umbrella, go to the plucking field and bring back a basket"?'

This was all fairly easy stuff and after ten minutes they decided I could go on to take the exam in far-off Kandy (where the CPS had its headquarters) and we repaired to the bar.

ᐯ

The Queen's Hotel was the focus of colonial Kandy, and even in these post-imperial days it still retained an aura of faded grandeur. Apparently it was originally established in the nineteenth century by a Mrs Perichaud, who obtained fresh produce for her customers from a farm several miles away near Kadugannawa (later Farm Group). As I entered, I recalled my first memories of it as a small child waiting at the front entrance for my father after we had stayed the night for some social function. I always used to be fascinated by two glass cases in the foyer, now long since disappeared. One of these contained a colony of green 'leaf insects', which were related to stick insects and were scarcely distinguishable from the leaves on which they lived. The other enclosed one of those coin-operated crane-like grabber machines. This case was full of the most desirable goodies, any of which theoretically could be mine if only I could get the grab on the crane to pick it up and deposit it in the opening at the back of the case. However, no matter how carefully one manipulated the grab, the desired object always seemed to slip out of its jaws just before it could be manoeuvred over the chute which would deliver it into my eager hands.

*The Queens Hotel, on the corner of Ward Street and Trincomalee Street (now renamed), Kandy, 1991.*

The Queen's Hotel was also the best vantage point for watching the great *perahera* procession. This was (and still is) held each year during the ten days leading up to the *poya* (full moon) during *Esala* (a period mainly in August), increasing in complexity and length until its culmination on the final night. Famous since the days when Robert Knox was held prisoner in Kandy in the seventeenth century, this honours the sacred tooth of the Lord Buddha, which is taken from its resting place nearby in the *Dalada Maligawa*, or Temple of the Tooth, and paraded within its bejeweled casket on a magnificent and lavishly caparisoned tusker. The temple containers of holy water are also replenished with due ceremony from the waters of the Mahaweli Ganga, the greatest river in Sri Lanka, where it passes near Kandy. The perahera procession takes a good hour to pass. In the vanguard come troops of male Kandyan dancers in their bells and silver filigree finery, followed by squadrons of tom-

tommers, drummers, and whip-crackers. In the centre are the stately Kandyan Chiefs, each wrapped in yards of silks and brocade, either walking with their retinue or carried aloft on elephants with decorated howdahs. Finally come more dancers, jugglers, pot-throwers and acrobats, all illuminated by flaming torches carried by lines of bearers on either side of the procession. Electric lighting is limited to embellishments on the elephants' caparisons and howdahs, powered by 12-volt batteries carried unobtrusively on their necks. In all, a sight not to be forgotten, and I always thought of this whenever I visited the Queen's Hotel.

The CPS language examinations were held in one of the first floor bedrooms, so I ascended the wide stairs down which I had often seen my mother descend in her evening dress, ready for some dance, dinner, or other function dimly remembered from colonial childhood days. The dark wood panelling and ornate banisters seemed to reflect more stable and stolid times. I entered the room in some trepidation as I knew my examiner would be the professor of Tamil at the University of Ceylon and I expected difficulties in understanding what would doubtless be his faultless grammar. However, he was kind and made an effort to keep his conversation simple and akin to that spoken on the estates. After half an hour I emerged not only with some relief, but also feeling there was some hope, and when the results came through a few weeks later I found that I had done quite well with 79% - thus missing a Distinction by one mark.

*The Perehera, Kandy, viewed from the Queens Hotel.*

Very few books were available which dealt with the practice and business of tea planting. Considering that many, perhaps most, planters came into the job without any formal training, this was quite a disadvantage for those who wanted some works of reference, and it put much emphasis on what they learnt during creeping (which, as I had discovered, varied a great deal). One book which could be found on the shelves of many planters' bungalows (sometimes almost the only book) was *The tea planter's vade-mecum*. This purported to tell the young planter all he needed to know about the business he had entered and covered everything from propagation of the tea plant to marketing of the finished product. However, it had not been revised very recently and I found it old fashioned and of little help. In fact SDs on large estates were usually fully occupied in carrying out instructions received from their PDs and did not often have to take agronomic or manufacturing decisions independently. In contrast, a book which was a veritable mine of information (and which I had received as a parting gift from my father) was H. F. Macmillan's *Tropical planting and gardening*. H. F. Macmillan had been the Superintendent of the famous and prestigious Royal Botanic Gardens at Peradeniya, near Kandy, from 1895 to 1925 and, by a curious coincidence, I had known his granddaughter when we had both been aged about 13 or 14. The book was a sort of botanical counterpart to Mrs Beeton's cookery volume and gave information on a huge range of crops and ornamental plants. It was written with special reference to Ceylon and it advised on everything from plant breeding to laying out a garden and what plants were suitable for growing at different elevations. There were tables showing the weights of various seeds and for converting bushels of rice to pounds and ounces. It was written in true colonial style and in dealing with the problem of water supply to upcountry gardens it assumed that 'a diverted stream can generally be made to meet requirements'. It has never been superseded by a single volume and I still refer to my copy, although a new edition appeared in 1991.

After muster and then breakfast, my daily routine on Meeriabedde was to make a round of the estate field works until lunch time and a second round in the afternoon until evening muster and the final weighing-in of leaf at 4 p.m. Weighing usually continued until 5.30 or 6 p.m., after which I could go back to the bungalow for a cup of tea. The rounds of the field works meant that I quickly got to know the Division and were usually enjoyable. Each day I walked about 10 or 12 miles along the paths or tracks through the tea and up and down the hillsides. The view was magnificent (except when the monsoon brought thick mists) and, besides the estate works, there was always something interesting to see.

During the dry season, when the flush of young shoots diminished, fewer labourers were needed for plucking and more were put on to other works. At one point the cart road was being extended to give better access to the upper areas of the Division and the dry season was always the time when roads were repaired and the drains cleaned, so during my first few weeks on Meeriabedde I spent quite a lot of my time on roads and drains. In fact 'Roads and Drains' was a well-known financial vote on all estates and was the classic account to which unscrupulous planters traditionally charged the labourers which they dishonestly employed on their own bungalows or businesses including, occasionally, their mistresses as well. Because of this, it was always scrutinised by the auditors and the VA but, unless the vote was grossly overspent or there was little accomplished to show for it, it was really only the SD of the division who could say whether there had been any misappropriation.

Cutting a new stretch of cart road was always interesting. There was considerable satisfaction in determining the best route and then the cutting into the hillside always revealed something of the geological structure. The underlying rock of the Ceylon hills is granite and granite boulders and outcrops were a common feature of the steep and stony Meeriabedde terrain. The general direction of the new road was already decided, but the actual route had to be determined and was largely up to me. As far as possible, it was necessary to avoid very steep gradients and major obstacles, such as large granite outcrops. The gradient was measured with a road-tracer and the course of the road was marked out with stout wooden pegs positioned on the line of the outer edge of the new road. A road-tracer was a simple instrument, a sort of idiot's theodolite, which had not changed very much since Roman times. It consisted of a small, low powered optical viewfinder set in a brass mount suspended from a swivel on a pole. By adjusting a small screw, the angle at which the viewfinder hung could be altered and this was indicated by a pointer on a scale calibrated in gradients from zero through 1 in 100 up to 50 in 100, or 1 in 2. I was told to avoid gradients steeper than about 1 in 12 and tried to keep slopes moderate, but this was not always possible, especially on the hairpin bend. To use the road-tracer one positioned the base of the pole at the foot of the last peg and got an assistant to take the sight pole (which had a cross on it at the same height as the viewfinder) and hold it upright about 10 or 12 yards further on. Setting the desired gradient, one then squinted through the viewfinder and had the assistant move the sight pole about until the cross was aligned with the corresponding mark in the viewfinder. A peg was hammered in at the base of the sight pole and so one moved on. The actual cutting of the roadway was done entirely by hand, the width being measured simply with a 12-foot pole and the camber by eye. A drain was always made at the inner margin of the roadway and the bank cutting was sloped slightly away from the vertical to minimise risk of collapse. The labourers used mamoties and alavangoes for the actual cutting and the loose earth was carried away in round cane baskets.

Rock outcrops and large boulders sometimes could not be avoided and had to be cut back or removed. As far as possible this was done piecemeal, using steel wedges to split the rock, if possible where there was already a visible crack or where one could be made with a sledgehammer. Otherwise one had to resort to blasting. Formerly, it had been usual to employ elephants for removal of large rocks and boulders, and they had done much of the work for which a JCB would now be used. I well remembered, as a child, seeing elephants working on local road works, manoeuvring huge boulders with great intelligence and delicacy. However, by this time working elephants had become scarce and expensive, while JCBs were unavailable.

The making of a new road always involved some work in smoothing the carriageway and crushing gravel or broken road metal into the surface by means of a roller. Good gravel was difficult to obtain, but small sized road metal was produced by hand. This was a job often given to the more elderly women, who would sit all day taking lumps of granite from one heap and breaking them into small pieces with long-handled hammers to produce another heap of broken metal. A piece of hoop iron was used to retain the lump on a larger stone, which was used as an anvil, and each stone breaker had another loop of hoop iron as a gauge of size. Although stone breaking is regarded elsewhere as almost synonymous with punishment work, it was quite popular with the elderly on estates as it did not involve walking far, was not physically demanding, and there was plenty of opportunity for chit-chat. Provided the kangany in charge was not too officious or conscientious, it was far from arduous and usually the day's norm of broken stone was not very great or rigidly enforced.

All estates had large rollers for road construction and maintenance and these also used to be pulled by elephants. When elephants could not be hired, oxen sometimes did the job, but otherwise there was nothing for it but manpower. It took quite a large number of the most muscular labourers to manoeuvre a large and very heavy roller on narrow estate roads, which also were usually anything but flat, so when a new, motorised, and much lighter roller was advertised as being equally effective, this attracted considerable interest. It was arranged that the agents would bring one of the new rollers along to the estate for a demonstration on the new stretch of road and a small crowd of KPs, kanganys, and the inevitable hangers-on gathered in anticipation.

In due course a Landrover appeared with a trailer containing the famous roller. This (although we did not know it at the time) was an early example of the now common or garden vibrating roller. The salesman proceeded to tell us of the revolutionary and elegant design of this machine while its minder clambered onto the trailer and filled it up with fuel from a can (this action alone diverting attention from the salesman's eulogy and drawing muttered wonder from the crowd, who had never before seen a roller with an engine which was not a full-sized steam roller). With a flourish the roller driver started the engine and coaxed the machine down the ramp from the trailer. It was indeed relatively small and did a very good job of flattening the new layer of stone metal put down for it. While the salesman was explaining its finer points to Bill Horne and the senior estate staff, the driver was busy giving his own version to the rest of the crowd and obviously enjoying his status as pilot of this new wonder of technology. At this point, having gone back and forth several times over the trial section, we were interested to observe that the roller was moving ahead onto uncharted territory. Moreover, the driver had broken off his patter and seemed to be frantically fighting with the controls. This had no effect whatever and the roller continued its inexorable course up the road, puffing out its merry exhaust and towing along the hapless driver, clutching the handle and still fiddling with the controls. Roller and driver disappeared round the bend just as the salesman became aware that something was amiss and set off in pursuit. Now, this part of the road was only just finished and I knew that not very far round the corner there were still large rocks waiting to be removed or broken. Sure enough, there came a muffled thud, the noise of the engine abruptly ceased and was immediately replaced by a sudden babble of raised voices. On rounding the bend we discovered the rather dented roller surrounded by a gesticulating throng in the centre of which the salesman and the driver revolved in antagonistic circles. This was obviously going to take some time, so we quietly retired and left them with the problem of getting the dead roller back onto the trailer. We never did buy one for the estate.

On most estates there were usually several skilled stonemasons, of whom one or two would specialise in the business of blasting. Holes in the rock were drilled using steel 'jumpers' like large cold chisels. Carefully choosing the best spot on the rock, the mason would position the jumper and smite the end with a club hammer, giving it a quarter twist after each blow. Settling into a rhythm which he would keep up for most of the day, the regular hammer blows could be heard far across the valley. The jumper would be changed every half hour or so, and at the end of the day all the used jumpers would be taken to the estate blacksmith for resharpening by heating, hammering, and tempering the cutting tips in water. Very slowly the hole would deepen and the rock powder was removed at intervals by adding water and sponging it out with cloth on the end of a stick. Usually two or three usable holes could be finished in a day. The mason would ensure the holes were dry and then would measure a suitable charge of black gunpowder into each, inserting lengths of white fuse and plugging the holes with hammered-down bungs of frayed hessian. Next came the exciting part of the process. Usually the actual blasting was done after work on the road was finished for the day and all the labourers had departed. Making sure that nobody was nearby, the mason would give two or three shouted warnings. Then he would light the fuses and he and anyone else in the vicinity would hastily take cover behind a convenient rock. After the explosions we would all emerge and gather round to examine the results. On one occasion I happened to be on the opposite side of the valley when I heard the mason's familiar shout but, as I was so far away, I did not think it necessary to take cover. I had a fine view of the blast, but my interest departed almost instantly as some large lumps of rock whistled by and crashed into the tea uncomfortably near. Since then I have found it much easier to appreciate the remarkably long range of cannon shot.

The estate's stonemasons were always in demand, not only for road repairs but also for terracing works to guard against or repair the effects of erosion, and for building walls and other structures, either with or without mortar. After heavy rain there would always be repairs needed where overflowing field drains had started an erosion gully or where a terrace retaining wall had collapsed. On the steepest slopes terracing was used around even individual tea bushes and on all estates there were well-known erosion black spots. Where large gullies had formed, the masons would construct low dry stone walls across the channel to partially stem the flow of water and allow the silt to deposit. When the silt had accumulated to the level of the top of the wall, the wall would then be raised and the process would be continued until the gully had become a series of low steps down which the storm water could cascade without causing further damage. The job was then finished by planting paspalum grass along the sides to bind the soil. All these retaining walls and terracing were built dry, without mortar. Rock was plentiful everywhere and was trimmed with club hammers, the large stones being fitted so that they held together and the interstices filled with small stones or earth.

Besides granite, the rocks were sometimes composed of other constituents. Sedimentary rocks were rare up-country (and the water was notoriously deficient in lime), but some other igneous and metamorphic rocks occurred, accompanied by various minerals. Quartz and quartzite of various kinds were very common. The quartz was usually cracked, milky in colour and crystals were never evident, but one could sometimes find pebbles or larger pieces of attractive clear or rose-coloured quartz. In some places flat lumps of mica (muscovite) were common and these could be split into wafer-thin transparent sheets. Plumbago (graphite) also occurred in pockets in the clay or laterite, in soft silver-grey flakes, and in some areas of the Island plumbago mines were operated. There was usually little topsoil, as the early planters had aligned the rows of coffee or tea up and down the slopes and erosion had taken its course. The subsoils were often reddish, yellow, or purplish lateritic clays, merging lower down the profile into soft, gritty rock known as *kabook,* which was used to surface the estate roads.

One of the first tasks given to me by Bill Horne was to investigate the possibility of obtaining some timber from the neighbouring Dambatenne Group. Dambatenne was something of a showpiece in the estate world and had been so since the days when Sir Thomas Lipton used to take guests up to a spot at the top of the mountain (now known as Lipton's Seat) and, with an expansive wave of the hand, demonstrate his estate acres rolling away over the hills as far as the eye could see. This was actually something of an exaggeration, but was more or less correct if one was facing in just the right direction. The border between Dambatenne and Meeriabedde ran high along the shoulder of the mountain between the Meeriabedde Upper Division and the Mousakellie Division of Dambatenne. Rather unusually, the gravel cart roads of the two divisions did in fact connect, although both were narrow, steep and tortuous in the extreme. Old *Grevillea* shade trees were being felled on Mousakellie and Bill Horne thought that we could use some of the timber for construction of an extension to the blacksmith's workshop at Meeriabedde factory.

It took quite some time to ascend to the Upper Division by the road which climbed up the face of a near vertical slice of the mountain, too steep even for tea cultivation, by means of numerous hairpin bends and fearsome gradients. Above this, the land flattened out as a high shelf before rising steeply again to Mousakellie. This shelf accommodated the Meeriabedde Upper Division, which was run by a Conductor almost as an isolated mountain fiefdom. The Conductor was a short but stout gentleman named Inch, who travelled about on an ancient motorbike, dressed in a voluminous wind-cheater. This ballooned out in the wind to become even more spherical than its owner, with the smaller sphere of his head protruding from the collar. Viewed from behind, little of the motorbike was visible, and the ensemble had somehow the appearance of an enormous cottage loaf precariously balanced on two wheels. I had arranged to meet him at the Upper Division muster ground and he came forward to greet me as I toiled up the slope.

'Good morning, Sir, welcome to Upper Division', he smiled, introducing himself, 'I am one Inch'.

Well, he *was* rather short, but this was excessive and in a moment his meaning became clear.

'Hello, Mr Inch, good morning,' I replied, 'thank you for coming to meet me. I shall rely on you to guide me to Mousakellie.'

Mr Inch was as jovial as he was rotund and talked almost incessantly throughout my visit.

'Certainly, certainly' he beamed. 'Let us go to Mousakellie and come, uh? I have been wanting very much to meet you since you arrived. Are you now settled in? Now they are felling some big trees on Mousakellie and we should be getting some good timber.'

We chatted as we crossed the culvert marking the boundary between the two estates and passed through the lockable barrier. Soon we could hear the crashing of branches, shouts and the thud of axes. The trees were in an area of tea which was evidently due to be pruned and, as with the albizzias on Needwood, the opportunity was being taken to fell them before pruning. Any damage to the tea bushes could then be tidied up during pruning and damage to tea in bearing would be avoided. Where the trees had already been felled, the pruning gang was advancing, leaving a sea of cut branches behind, while before them a small team of axemen were tackling the trees still standing. These were big old *Grevillea* trees (the Australian 'silky oak') which yielded a strong and fairly hard, pale-coloured timber with an attractive grain, but which tended to distort rather strongly during seasoning. Reggie, the SD on Mousakellie, was in attendance and I discussed with him the possibilities of obtaining the various types and quantities of timber we required.

The felled trees were being converted into timber on the spot, as was not uncommon on estates, which were always in need of planks and laths (known as *pallagies* and *reapers*) for repairs and minor building works. As usual, the sawing was being done entirely by hand by a group of Sinhalese sawyers, recruited on contract from a village in the lowlands. A sawing platform had been made by setting the ends of two roughly trimmed logs into the steep hillside and supporting their free ends on vertical trunks so that they were level and parallel. The log to be sawn was supported over the gap between the trunks by means of cross-pieces at each end and secured by wedges. The operation was done, as no doubt it has been done all over the world before mechanisation, by a team of two men with a gigantic ripsaw some 6 ft long. This tapered slightly from the upper to the lower end and had teeth of which any shark would have been proud. The lower handle was attached directly to the lower end of the saw, while the upper handle was at the end of a curved stalk extending from the wider end. Having taken slices off opposite sides of the log, it was turned over and the flat surfaces scored with guidelines. The sawyers then set to work with a regular rhythm, the bottom sawyer working in a pit hollowed out from the hillside and gradually filling with fragrant sawdust. The top sawyer had the responsibility of guiding the cut and keeping it on course, the ferocious saw teeth biting into the wood at each stroke with a loud rasping noise, barely an inch from his bare toes.

I watched the timber cutting process for some time, fascinated by the skill of the sawyers in producing even planks with few blemishes. Nearby sat a third member of their team, sharpening and setting the teeth of blunted saws. He sharpened each tooth with deft strokes of a well-used file and after sharpening he set the teeth by eye with a small punch and hammer against a wooden block. Judging by the rate and ease of cutting, this was evidently very effective.

Timber sawing in this way was a common sight by the roadside all over Ceylon, which produced many beautiful and strong hardwoods. One of the foremost of these was the satinwood, which took a high polish and produced a blonde and beautifully figured surface. This species was not uncommon upcountry, while the halmilla (*Berrya cordifolia*), which grew in the low country jungles, produced an excellent dark brown timber. Teak was not native to the Island but was widely cultivated in plantations in suitable areas at low elevations. There were many others, including less exalted woods such as jak, which was used for many local purposes and of which much of the furniture in upcountry bungalows was constructed. Jak was a spectacular wood when fresh, as the sapwood was a bright golden yellow and the heartwood dark brown. However, the yellow colour did not persist and when seasoned and finished it was a warm brown, with the heartwood much darker. A relative of the breadfruit, the jak was also notable for its gigantic fruits, each up to the size and weight of a sack of potatoes and carried on stout stalks directly on the main trunk of the tree. The outer rind was tough and covered with conical points, something like a large warty pineapple without its leafy topknot. In fact the flesh was not unlike the consistency of pineapple, but without the sweet juice. The large seeds, about the size and shape of a Brazil nut, could be boiled and tasted rather like potato.

I took my leave of Reggie and returned to Meeriabedde accompanied by Mr Inch regaling me with Interesting Facts about the Upper Division.

'Oh, yes, Sir,' he exclaimed earnestly as we passed the labour lines, 'we are getting some simply tremendous storms up here in monsoon times. On one occasion we had the lightening bolt. It was coming in through the window that you see there, turned the corner and passed through two rooms before it went out again at the back. My God! It was really frightening, and when I was coming to see what had happened the labourers were in a state of shock, Sir. But no one was hurt. It was simply amazing.'

From the edge of the slopes of the Upper Division, as I started to retrace my steps down the cart road, I could see over the ridge to Poonagalla, Mahakanda and, in the far distance, the jungles of the low country stretching away to the east and south. Back at my bungalow I wrote a short report for Bill Horne, which I delivered to him at the estate office later in the afternoon. He seemed pleased, and was even quite complimentary, so I felt it was a propitious time to broach the subject of the redecoration of the Small Bungalow. Sometime earlier he had told me that the bungalow was due to be repainted inside with the usual 'distemper', a sort of oil-based emulsion paint. I enquired whether I could choose the colours and he had told me to get the colour chart from the clerk. This had kept me entertained for a considerable time as I had mulled over the merits of eau-de-neil or aquamarine for the dining room, or whether I should have something more adventurous, such as orchid pink in the bedroom. Perhaps I should be ultramodern and have one wall of the sitting room a completely different colour? . . . 'Jungle Green', I thought, might look quite effective. Eventually I had assembled quite a list, with a different colour for each room and I was looking forward to seeing the results of my first efforts at interior design.

'By the way, Sir,' I said, 'I've been thinking about the distemper for my bungalow and this is a list of the colours.'

He took the list and gazed at it at arm's length with an expression of increasing incredulity.

'Good God, David, what's all this rubbish?' he exclaimed, at length.

'Well, Sir, you said I could choose the colours, . . . and, er, those are the ones I'd like.'

'Nonsense,' he said, 'I didn't say "go mad". . . . This isn't a massage parlour, you know. . . . What's this? "Eau-de-neil" - what the hell's that?'

'It's a sort of blue colour' I ventured, feeling considerably crestfallen, 'Er, rather pale, . . . quite nice really.'

'Never saw such a load of bullshit in all my days' said Bill Horne, 'I'm not having estate funds wasted on some bloody weird poofter colour scheme. Do the whole place in Magnolia.' So done it was.

Bill Horne was quite right, really, and after a few months of Magnolia Throughout I felt quite relieved that I was spared having to live with the elaborate colour scheme I had so enthusiastically designed.

One day Bill Horne informed me that we were to go to a neighbouring estate to see a demonstration of a new construction system. Apparently someone, I think in Australia, had developed a method of building walls of compacted earth. Tea companies were always on the lookout for cheaper methods of building construction, especially for labour lines, and what could be cheaper than making them out of earth? The shareholders (and, with any luck, the VA) would be delighted. An excursion off the estate on business was a rare event, so I was very ready to acquiesce.

The demonstration was on Golconda Estate, a few miles back along the road towards Needwood. Arriving at a building site, we joined a small group of rather sceptical planters standing around a half-built house or store and listening to a confident speaker who was evidently the salesman for the company marketing the various bits of equipment needed for 'rammed earth' construction, as it was called. We heard that in fact this had not been invented by the Aussies but, on the contrary, had been in use in biblical times and that ancient dwellings made in this way could still be seen. What had been done was merely to adapt an ancient method to modern materials. We then saw that the system was indeed quite simple. A mould the width of the wall, with wooden sides and removable ends, was positioned and a layer of damp earth mixed with a little cement was put in. This was tamped down with a heavy weight on a pole, another layer was added, and so on until the mould was full. The rods holding the sides of the mould in place were then removed and it was moved along, ready for the next filling. The finished section of wall certainly seemed extremely solid and hard and when I kicked it (the customary test for a newly built wall) I merely hurt my toe. Everyone came away murmuring that they intended to try it out. However, I never saw anything which had been built in this way, and certainly not any labour lines.

Labour lines were almost always depressing places. The oldest type were squalid in the extreme while the very newest were reasonably habitable, but usually only because they had not yet had time to become overcrowded. When village peasants had first been brought from India as indentured labour, the pioneer planters had housed them in free accommodation which had much the same sort of facilities as a village hut and, indeed, probably lived in not much better housing themselves. After the pioneering days were over, labour lines were built of brick or stone and roofed with corrugated iron or tiles, but little attempt was made to improve the facilities. However, in the early days the peasant-labourers probably found them, if anything, an improvement on what they had been used to back home in their south Indian villages. The accommodation usually consisted of one large room per family, with a covered veranda at the front and sometimes a lean-to shelter for a cooking stove at the back. Each 'line' consisted of six or eight rooms in a row. Water was supplied from a stand pipe outside and latrines were built a few yards away from each line. Where there were no cooking facilities, cooking had to be done either outdoors or in a corner of the room or veranda. Such accommodation was probably not too bad when it was first built and occupied by small families. However, families inevitably increased and grew older, and the upkeep of the lines was often perfunctory. Old lines were therefore horrendous, with soot-encrusted rooms bursting with innumerable ragged children, cracked and crumbling drains, leaking stand pipes and stinking latrines.

When aged about 12, I had come to the conclusion that most of the world's troubles could ultimately be attributed to over-population and it seemed to me that the labour lines were a graphic demonstration of this. Perhaps my youthful thoughts had been prompted by early sights of estate lines. Anyway, although my notion was simplistic and did not take into account a multitude of other relevant factors, I saw that ultimately the lines (and the world, as increasing numbers of people are now beginning to realise) must have a finite accommodation capacity and that this was rapidly being reached. Even if the population of either had not reached maximum capacity, it was clear that by the time it did, the environment would already have been destroyed. Nearly all the line verandas had been covered in with makeshift walls of corrugated iron and plywood to make another room, while the capacity of the large rooms was increased by flimsy partitions, hanging possessions or hammocks from beams, and raising sleeping benches above the floor. As far as I was aware (and indeed I was extremely ignorant of such things) the estate made no attempt to provide any family planning advice or services, but then the contraceptive revolution of the sixties had not yet arrived and it was difficult enough in those days even for rich and educated Europeans to obtain such services, let alone poor estate labourers, even if their beliefs had not banished such options. I was only aware that the lines were full to bursting point, that it was practically impossible to find any accommodation for newly married couples, that we already had more labourers on the estate payroll than were needed, and that more and more children were arriving.

Matters were not helped by the government's refusal to accept Tamil estate labourers as Ceylon citizens. This harked back to colonial times when there was still considerable coming and going by estate Tamils to and from their home villages in south India. However, by this time this link had been virtually severed and many, perhaps most, estate Tamils were second or third generation born and bred in Ceylon and had never been near India in their lives. Nevertheless, there was a requirement for estate Tamils to prove that they, their parents and, I think, at least one grandfather, had been born in Ceylon before citizenship could be granted. This of course was very difficult to do, even for those who qualified, because in their grandparents' day births had not always been registered, even in estate hospital ledgers. Return to their (often impoverished) ancestral districts in India was not an option without Indian nationality, while lack of citizenship rights denied them the opportunity to seek regular employment elsewhere in Ceylon, exacerbating the unemployment problem on the estates and the troubles of the SDs who had to deal with it..

Apart from seeing that routine maintenance was carried out, there was little I could do to alleviate matters, as estate companies would never vote capital expenditure for accommodating more labourers than were needed and were reluctant to replace even the worst of the lines with more modern buildings. I always disliked my duty visits to the lines which, no matter how often they were swept or repaired, always seemed to be surrounded by filth and litter, with crowds of curious children, grandmothers peeing into the gutters, and numerous mangy pie dogs snapping at my heels. The paved areas around the lines were also disfigured by red stains where betel-chewing people had spat. The estate labourers, both men and women, were much addicted to betel chewing, and betel leaves, which were about the size and shape of a laurel leaf, were sold fresh in the caddies. A chew was prepared by cutting a small piece from an arecanut, smearing it with chunam (lime paste) and wrapping it in a betel leaf. The arecanuts came from the very tall palms with impossibly slim trunks which grew in almost every village and many people had special arecanut cutters for cutting the hard nuts. After chewing for a while, saliva became an unattractive bright red colour and, over years, it tended to rot the teeth.

Estate spending on labour welfare was usually parsimonious, but had improved somewhat since pre-war days. Every estate of reasonable size, and each division of larger groups, had a junior school, a hospital or dispensary, a crèche, and sometimes a volleyball court and clubhouse. However, these were very often of a rudimentary nature. On Meeriabedde Lower Division the school had just one classroom with a blackboard, teacher's desk and very little other furniture. The children sat on the floor and lessons were mostly learned by rote. As I passed by I could hear the children chanting their spellings and tables, and singing various songs. The crèche was also a single room and was supervised by an ancient crone with a slightly younger assistant. It took babies aged from a few weeks up to crawling age, but could not cope with those who could run about. Much of the space was occupied by sleeping babies in cradles consisting of cloths formed into open-ended slings, which were suspended from the ceiling like fruits on long stalks. Any cries were dealt with by giving the appropriate baby a push to set it gently swinging. This usually seemed to have the desired effect and whenever I visited, most of the cradles seemed to be swinging with one of the ladies intoning a suitable lullaby.

Another practice which could be classed as a kind of social welfare was the issue of rice. This was arranged by the estate at, I think, a subsidized price with the cost being deducted from earnings each month. The rice was issued from the rice store and was often collected for a whole family by a responsible child if the parents were both out at work in the field. The rice would be in a great heap on the floor while the Assistant KP would stand nearby with the rice ration book to call out the amount that each family should receive. Measurements were in bushels, down to quarter bushels, and below that in shundus. The bushel, half bushel and quarter bushel measures were beautifully made cubic boxes of dark polished wood with brass bands around the rims and brass corner pieces. Brass handles were fitted at each side and there was a smooth wooden rod which would be drawn across the top of the measure to ensure that it was filled flat and not heaped. Nevertheless, there were various ways in which slightly more or less rice could be got into the measures and one had to be careful that the measures for everyone were filled in the same way. They would be emptied into the cloth bags or simple cloths which the family representative had brought and these bulging receptacles would then be hoisted onto heads, sometimes with friendly assistance, before being carried away.

Another new duty was paying the labour force. Coolie pay day was at the beginning of each month and the pay system was a well-established ritual on all estates. The cash had to be collected from the bank in the local town, in our case Bandarawela, and transporting it to remote estates was a notoriously risky business. Hold-ups and robberies, with or without violence, occurred occasionally and some planters carried a shotgun (if they possessed one) on these journeys. Bill Horne, however, went unarmed but always insisted that I and 'Kunay' Kunanayagam (the senior SD, who was on

Mahakanda Division) accompanied him in the Landrover. We would meet him at the Big Bungalow at 8.30 a.m. and set off for Bandarawela with the three of us in the three front seats. It was nearly an hour's drive to Bandarawela and at the bank there was much counting of bundles of well-thumbed notes. All the cash, amounting to perhaps a couple of *lakhs* (two hundred thousand rupees), had to be checked, the bundles examined to make sure that they contained notes all the way through and the bags of coins opened to see that they did contain what they were supposed to. The three of us would divide up the bags and bundles between us for checking. When this had been done and the amounts and denominations of notes and coin checked against the order, it was bundled into a canvas *tappal* (mail) bag, the brass half-moon hasp secured with the padlock, and put in the back of the Landrover for the return journey.

Back on Meeriabedde the cash was handed over to the Head Clerk and his office staff, who then had to complete the long process of parcelling it out according to the wage bills of each division, make sure that there were enough notes and coins of appropriate denominations for each division, and re-bag the cash in time for paying to begin at the same time as afternoon muster. Usually, Bill Horne would offer us a beer before we returned to our own bungalows for lunch, and this was really the only regular social contact we had with him and Maxime.

Bill Horne had known old Mr Gibson (who had built up The Gibson Estates) quite well in his younger days and regaled us with various anecdotes. Gibson apparently had a well-deserved reputation as a skin-flint, but Bill Horne had not experienced this at first hand until he had occasion to stay with him at the Netherbyres Bungalow, his residence on Kahagalla Estate. At this time, apparently, the mains electricity had not yet come to the district and Gibson had refused to install a generator at Netherbyres. When it came to bedtime, Gibson took the oil lamp from the room and disappeared, saying 'I'll find you a candle'. A few moments later he reappeared with a candle holder containing the last remnants of a candle stump. Taking this, Bill Horne retired to his room and quickly completed washing and changing, with one eye on the flickering flame. This became rapidly dimmer and, just as he got into bed, went out altogether. This, he had thought had been merely his bad luck but, on comparing notes with others who had experienced a night at Netherbyres, it appeared that this was the norm and that old Gibson could judge to a nicety the minimum size of candle stump necessary to light a guest to bed.

On pay day afternoon I would return to the main estate office to collect the pay bag for the Lower Division and at four o'clock I would be at the factory, where a long line of labourers would already be waiting. To make it more difficult for a surprise raid to succeed, paying was always done on a wide landing on the first floor. A chair for me would be set at a table and the KP and Assistant KP would be standing to one side with the checkroll on a simple lectern made for the purpose. I would have made a check of the total amount when I collected the cash from the office, so it remained only to lay out suitable bundles of notes and trays of coins and pay could begin. Names in the checkroll were in Roman script and in alphabetical order. The labourers knew from long experience the order in which they would be called and lined up accordingly, coming forward one by one as old Ramasamy called out their names and the amounts. Men, women and children were all paid individually into their own hands what they had earned during the previous month, less any deductions for loans, foodstuffs, insurance, or other legitimate items and with additions for weeding contracts or other extra work. I would repeat the amount as I paid them and the Assistant KP would explain at intervals that if they thought there was any mistake, they should say so before they departed. They would then sign against their names to acknowledge receipt of their pay, and the illiterate ones would do the same with a thumbprint.

There were always various hangers-on present amongst the throng on pay day, some less desirable than others. The small traders, selling domestic items, cloth, or clothing we tolerated so long as they did not become a nuisance. However, there were also the money-lenders who made loans at exorbitant rates of interest, and these were escorted off the estate when detected. Nevertheless, many labourers got into their clutches and the money-lenders could not always be recognised so, after receiving their pay, the unfortunate borrowers sometimes had to run the gauntlet of those waiting to extract their pound of flesh.

It took about two hours of concentrated work to finish paying, by which time the light would be getting dim and I would be getting tired. It was accepted that any deficit in cash could only be caused by one's own carelessness and that therefore any shortfall had to be made up out of one's own pocket. Likewise, one could appropriate any unexpected surplus, with the possibility that it might be used to correct an underpayment, if this could be shown. Usually, the cash worked out correctly to within a few rupees and I can remember only one occasion when I was as much as 40 rupees short. However, I was always glad when pay had been successfully completed and I could return up the hill to relax at my bungalow with a cup of tea.

Having never before had a garden of my own, I had a burst of enthusiasm for gardening in my early days on Meeriabedde. The grapefruit trees looked a bit neglected and I decided they needed pruning. Perusal of Mr Meikle's collection of Gardeners' Book Club publications had given me the impression that this was a necessary part of the maintenance of all fruit trees, but I was doubtful where to start. However, I had a good new pruning knife (which was partly the reason for feeling that pruning would be a good idea), so I set to work. Luckily I did not do much damage and in removing some dead wood may even have done some good. The trees survived and continued to produce fruit, which Gomez used to make a delicious grapefruit drink and I always looked forward to this on returning from my estate rounds during the grapefruit season.

Up in the vegetable garden there were a few banana trees. These grow in clumps and when one stem has produced its crop of bananas, you cut it down and another takes its place. The elevation of Meeriabedde Small Bungalow was a little high for growing good bananas, and those produced in the vegetable garden seldom ripened properly if left to their own devices. However, old Palaniandy had a patent system for ripening them. Digging a hole in the ground large enough to take the bunch of unripe bananas, he would carefully line it with soft dead grass and moss and lay the bananas in this kind of nest. He then covered the bunch with a thick layer of more dry grass and moss, finally covering the lot with earth to make a grave-like mound. Sticking out of the top, like the funnel in a pie crust, he arranged a tube or spout consisting of a short length of bamboo stem or even a piece of metal pipe. The earth was moistened, patted down firmly, and then he would drop down the spout small pieces of glowing charcoal collected from the kitchen range. The idea was to get the dry grass and moss to smoulder very slowly for a week or so when, hey presto!, he would unearth the now ripe bunch of bananas. This always seemed like magic to me and it was not until many years later that I learned that ethylene was active in promoting the ripening of fruits. Presumably the smouldering material surrounding the bananas produced a certain amount of ethylene and this effected the magical ripening. Much later I also discovered that this system was not old Palaniandy's own invention but that a very similar procedure had been observed in the Badulla area by Edward Sullivan in the early 1850s and is recorded in his book *The bungalow and the tent, or a visit to Ceylon* (London, 1854).

The larger of the two small lawns at the front of the bungalow sloped gently towards the low wall at the edge of the garden. I determined that it should be levelled and to replace the coarse buffalo grass with the finer 'blue' grass (a variety of *Cynodon dactylon*) which was used at the higher elevations to produce lawns which would have graced any garden in Europe. Palaniandy seemed rather taken aback when I broached the subject to him and was firmly of the opinion that such a project would be absolutely impossible without the allocation of 'rend'-munu aal' (two or three people) for a couple of weeks. Hard heartedly I said this was quite unnecessary and that he could do the job himself little by little. I hammered in pegs to show the level and over a month or so Palaniandy made a very good job of digging away the higher ground and building up the lower to produce a flat and level area.

I got a bag of blue grass trimmings from someone on a neighbouring estate and these Palaniandy dibbled in at intervals of a few inches so that by the middle of the rains I had an excellent new lawn.

The north-east monsoon usually arrives in the Uva hills in October. For some weeks the clouds had been piling up in the north and distant rumbles of thunder could occasionally be heard with faint flickerings of sheet lightning in the night sky, but at Meeriabedde the drought continued, with dry stream beds and the brief evening electricity produced by the stand-by diesel generator. One afternoon I was on the eastern side of the valley when the clouds thickened over Bandara Eliya on the heights of Dambatenne, darkening and settling on the upper tea-covered slopes to dim their emerald foliage to the darkest green. Thunder rolled and crashed, reverberating up the narrow valley and, even as I watched, merged into an increasing roar as the heavy clouds started to release their rain. The upper part of the mountain gradually disappeared behind an advancing wall of dark grey water and the noise became louder, as when one approaches a waterfall. But on that afternoon the storm did not advance to embrace the whole mountain, remaining confined to the upper slopes and giving me a spectacular display of lightening. Then, as the grey veil of rain began to thin, I became aware of a new noise, again a rushing of water as a thousand small ditches, streams and hollows filled with muddy turbulence. One by one the streams coming down the mountainside could be seen to fill and come gushing over rocks. Small waterfalls formed as the frothing water rushed headlong into the valley, carrying before it small collections of twigs, leaves and other debris of the long dry season. By the time I reached the river in the valley bottom it was already a raging torrent, rendering the stepping stones at the upper end of the valley impassable and threatening to rise over the small bridge carrying the cart road.

One of the things I liked most about the garden was the abundance of large trees, mostly set in the tea or uncultivated areas just beyond the perimeter. They attracted a great variety of birds, and various species of barbets, bulbuls and babblers could be seen or heard calling from their branches at most times of the day. Many garden birds had no very well defined nesting season and a few nests could usually be found at most times of the year. However, nesting was commoner during latter part of the monsoon rains, which generated more insect and vegetable food and made the worms easier to find. The black robin was one of the commonest and tamest birds on the estate and frequently nested in hollows in roadside banks or drains. As its name implies, it is closely related to the European robin and about the same size, the cock bird being black with a white wing patch and the female brown. They are cheerful little birds and often sing from vantage points on rocks or stumps. I would frequently find their nests in banks as the birds flew out on my approach, leaving their two or three heavily speckled eggs or yellow-gaped youngsters often very exposed to view. Although the labourers and their children did not seem to be very observant of birds, inevitably these exposed nest sites resulted in considerable mortality from both human and other predators. I was therefore pleased when I found that a pair of black robins was nest building in the garden. Unfortunately the place they had chosen for a cosy nest was the horizontal spout of a rainwater down-pipe and at the next rain storm their careful construction was ignominiously shot out into the drain. Nothing daunted, they tried again, but the same thing happened. Mornings are usually fine during the north-east monsoon, with the clouds gradually piling up and a deluge arriving daily at about 2 p.m. The robins persisted with their nesting efforts until, after several disasters, I decided to see what could be done. Getting a Quaker Oats tin (they were always sold in tins in Ceylon), which was about the right diameter, I blackened the inside and lashed it alongside the drainpipe spout, temporarily blocking up the spout with the lid. This worked very well, the birds built a new nest in the tin and raised a family of three alongside the intermittent cataract of rainwater which the monsoon produced every afternoon.

The north-east monsoon coincided with the winter months of the northern hemisphere and the monsoon winds brought not only rain but also large numbers of migratory birds. These remained in Ceylon until about March the following year and characterised the season almost as

68

much as the change of climate in higher latitudes. Amongst the migratory garden birds were several species of flycatcher, particularly the robin flycatcher with blue-grey upper parts and orange breast, and the beautiful northern race of the paradise flycatcher in which the cock is pure white with an immensely long tail and a black head. In the resident Ceylon race of this flycatcher both sexes are rufous brown with black heads, although the male does sport his long tail. The robin flycatcher would take up residence in the garden and I could always be fairly sure to find him (or her) on favourite perches during the six months they were present. The migratory paradise flycatcher, however, was itinerant and would pass through the garden every week or two, never staying longer than a few hours.

Perhaps the bird which was the most characteristic herald of the north-east monsoon was the Indian pitta. After migrating from north and central India, it always seemed to make its first appearance on one of those dank, wet and misty evenings at the onset of the monsoon. There would have been heavy rain during the afternoon, with rumbling thunder and, as dusk began to fall, the deluge would have eased while thick white mist (for some reason it was never referred to as 'fog') rolled down the valley, reducing even the big trees round the garden to dim shadows and muffling the evening sounds, faint shouts and radio music drifting up from the lines. The roar of the rain on the corrugated iron roof would have dwindled to a faint patter, accompanied by heavy drips from the sodden garden foliage and the evening chorus of frogs and crickets, when a low whistle would announce the pitta's arrival. Looking out, I would often see the bird come into the light cast by the bungalow windows and sometimes it would come to take refuge on the wet veranda. If very tired, they would just crouch in a dark corner, but otherwise they would hop around in search of insects attracted to the bungalow lights. Sometimes, especially if the mist was very thick, there would be a dull thud at the window pane and I would find a dazed pitta crouching in the wet flower bed, recovering from its sudden impact with the bright glass. They were dumpy little birds, like a very stout and solid thrush with a short, perky, tail, but there the resemblance ceased. Their plumage was a riot of colours with brilliant carmine under the tail, salmon underparts, greenish back and blue rump, all set off by a blinding white eyestripe and white patch in the wing. One would take up residence in the garden for the duration of the monsoon, skulking unobtrusively beneath bushes and undergrowth, and departing in March or April for the Indian breeding grounds.

There was another bird which made its presence known in the evenings. I never saw it, although on several occasions I searched the nearby trees with a torch. Sitting alone in the bungalow after Gomez had served the evening meal and retired for the night, I would be reading or writing (for the radio was too full of atmospheric interference) when an eerie, almost imperceptibly low sound would drift in through the window. 'Hummmm, . . mmmmmm', and then a pause, 'Ummmmmm, . . . mmmmmmmm'. At first I was curious and slightly alarmed. However, when I discovered this was the characteristic call of the Ceylon fish owl, the calls ceased to be sinister and became almost friendly; a part of the normal night sounds around the bungalow. I did not feel particularly lonely during these silent evenings, as I seemed to have plenty of activities to keep me busy and I had not had any experience of living with anyone other than my parents and family. Photography was a great interest but, although many people took colour slides, these were expensive and had to be sent out of the country for processing. I preferred to do my own developing and printing. It was not really practicable to undertake colour printing in the bathroom where I did my processing, so I confined myself to black and white materials. However, I did want to record some of the wild plants which grew on the estate and so tried my hand at painting them in water colour. I became reasonably competent at this, although very slow, but it gave me much satisfaction and made me much more conscious of botanical structure than I would have been had I simply photographed the plants as colour slides.

After a few months, I had acquired a small circle of acquaintances, mostly young SDs from other estates in the district, and a few who had graduated to their first PD positions. All were interested in wild life to some extent, but they differed in the aspects which appealed to them. Some liked exploring in remote areas, some were interested in natural history, some in shooting, and some in all three.  In the club one evening someone had the idea of spending the forthcoming holiday covering the Hindu festival of Deepavali (or 'Dee'vali', as it was called) camping in the jungles down in the south-east lowlands near the pilgrim town of Kataragama.  Although very much a newcomer, I was invited to join the group and eagerly agreed to do so, if I could get the necessary couple of days leave.  This would be my first real camping trip to the jungle and I very much hoped that Bill Horne would not be difficult about the leave and prevent my participation.

# The jungle and the sea                                        6

Ceylon was always a heavily forested country. Even in the days of the ancient irrigation-based civilisations centred on Anuradhapura and Polonnaruwa, which endured for more than 1,500 years up to the fourteenth century, the amount of land cleared for cultivation must have been relatively small in relation to the vast forests covering most of the island. As the civilisations declined, the cultivated land was reclaimed by the tall jungle which, when the Portuguese arrived in 1505, must have covered a greater area than at any time during the previous thousand years, especially in the northern plains. Samuel Baker, who later gained fame and a knighthood for his African explorations, spent eight years in Ceylon as a young man during the 1840s and 50s. He wrote of hills and plains thickly covered with forest, in which he enjoyed much time on his numerous hunting exploits. However, he lamented that the untouched forests indicated a lack of development and enterprise by both the local population and the colonial government of the day. Describing a crossing of the Mahawelli Ganga (river) near Monampitiya he says 'I was struck at the time with the magnificent timber in the forests on its banks, and no less surprised that with the natural facilities of transport it should be neglected.' The land remained heavily forested well into the twentieth century and even in the 1950s the lowland forests could be seen from Haputale extending to the horizon with little apparent interruption to the south and east.

The nature of the forests varied with their situation. The lowlands to the north, east and south of the central mountains were covered with dry, deciduous forest, while the mountains, especially on the western side, supported thick, evergreen montane forest but with a canopy much lower than on the plains. The really awesome forests were those in the lowlands of the south-west, where the two monsoons per year created true rain forest unsurpassed in magnificence by anything other continents could produce. Unfortunately, this area of the island is also the most populous and the rain forest area, never very large, has shrunk to a residue now officially protected as the Sinharaj Forest near Ratnapura. The only area which has never carried thick forest is the extreme north and north-east of the Island and the Jaffna peninsular, which are very dry and in places verge on semi-desert.

The coast and the jungle of the lowland plains to the south and east were fairly easily accessible from estates in the Haputale district and those around Koslanda were the nearest. The main road continued on eastwards from Koslanda, gradually descending until it reached the village of Wellawaya, which was at the foot of the mountains. A couple of miles beyond Koslanda the road passed below the Diyaluma Falls. These are said to be the second highest falls in Ceylon, although I always felt that they do not look as high as the 628 ft stated on the roadside sign. The volume of water is not great, especially in the dry season, but the massive and sheer granite cliffs are imposing and they always look picturesque. The brown toque monkeys which frequent the patch of jungle below the falls can usually be seen as one passes by. Wellawaya was about half an hour's drive from Koslanda and here one could either turn south to Wirawila and Hambantota or continue east to Monaragala and Arugam Bay. To the south one could reach the coast in little more than an hours' drive while Arugam Bay was about half an hour further. The two areas differed considerably in topography and population, especially near the coast. The east coast near Arugam Bay consisted of long beaches of golden sand, backed by low scrub jungle and interrupted at intervals by the estuaries of small rivers, while the south coast near Hambantota was much more populated and the beaches there were often backed by dunes and large, shallow lagoons or *lewayas*, some of which had been converted into salt pans. However, the greatest difference between the two areas was in the people. Arugam Bay is in the Tamil area, a part of the Tamil-populated provinces of the north and east, whereas Hambantota is in the main Sinhalese area covering the rest of the Island. On the southern coast the boundary between the two lies somewhere in the sparsely populated area to the east of what is now the Ruhunu National Park. The heart of the Park was originally the Yala Game Sanctuary (one of the first protected areas to be designated for the conservation of wild life) and the Park is still popularly referred to as 'Yala'.

The areas around Hambantota and Arugam Bay each had their own attractions for me. On the east coast there was superb swimming, birds on the estuaries and shallow *villus*, and of course the advantage that I could communicate fairly easily with the local Tamil population. On the south coast the *lewayas* were Meccas for wading birds, especially for the migratory species during the north-east monsoon, and wild animal life was rather more easily seen in the areas on the outskirts of the National Park.

Hambantota itself was a busy little town and probably had not changed very much since the days when the young Leonard Woolf was based there as Assistant Government Agent (AGA) between 1908 and 1911. As described in his autobiography, the salt industry has long been important in the area and part of his duties was to 'arrange for the collecting, transport, storing, and selling of the salt - a large-scale complicated industry'. Salt has always been a government monopoly in Ceylon and although by the 1950s it was no longer administered by the AGA, the industry was operated by a publicly owned company, the National Salt Corporation. I enjoyed visiting the salt pans on the northern and eastern outskirts of Hambantota when they reached a certain stage in the concentration of salt which promoted the growth of red algae, giving them a rosy pink hue. This was reflected in the rosy tints of the large flocks of flamingoes often found there and, indeed, their colour was largely due to the algae in their diet. Evidently they had inhabited these lagoons before they had been modified into salt pans, as Leonard Woolf describes how a small flock of about 30 flamingoes regularly passed along this part of the coast from west to east at the same time each day. At the point on the headland where stood the Residency, they turned inland over the house to reach a large lagoon just north of the town.

If bound for Hambantota, one turned right at Wellawaya. The road ran straight and almost due south for about 40 miles to Wirawila before curving round to reach the coast at Hambantota about ten miles further on. The surface was tarmac, but it was narrow and much patched, with crumbling edges sometimes resembling minor cliffs. This did not matter very much because the amount of traffic was slight. However, the width of the tarmac did not permit two vehicles to pass without at least one of them setting the nearside wheels on the verge. If one was unlucky and met a bus or lorry, it was unlikely to move from the centre of the road and prudent car drivers did not attempt to argue, either moving completely off the road or keeping the offside wheels only just on the tarmac. With other cars one could be somewhat bolder (depending how confident one was at playing 'chicken'), while for motorcycles or bicycles one kept all wheels on the tarmac, merely making a gesture of moving over. Dealing with vehicles going the same way as oneself was much more difficult. Overtaking was virtually impossible with lorries and buses (behind which a smoke screen of diesel fumes obscured the road ahead, even where passing might otherwise have been possible). However, with buses one could sometimes squeeze by when they stopped to pick up or set down passengers. Occasionally, cars could be induced to move over if one came up close behind and gave loud and prolonged hoots, but this was always somewhat hazardous as one would have to drop the offside wheels onto the verge whilest accelerating and there was always the chance of hitting a stray rock or branch, or cutting the tyres to shreds on the jagged edges of the tarmac. There was also a good chance that the driver of the car in front would be completely oblivious of what was behind him. The numerous hire cars (and often private ones too) were usually bursting with passengers, some of whom often had to extend portions of their anatomy out of the windows to avoid asphyxiating their fellow travellers or rendering the driving controls inoperable. As a rule of thumb, local drivers seemed to reckon on one passenger per unit horsepower so, what with the din of shouted conversation, the rattles of the car, and the complete obstruction of the rear window, it was not surprising that the hoots of cars wishing to overtake often went unheeded.

The Wellawaya - Hambantota road had been built about 1840 to provide a more direct and economic route to the coast for the export of coffee from the estates which by then had been opened in the Badulla District. In those days and for very many years afterwards it must have cut through undamaged mature forest for much of the way. By 1956, however, the road was bordered for many miles on either hand by shifting cultivations or *chenas*. Here the forest would have been cleared and burned, leaving only the remains of the largest trees lying charred where they fell. Between the debris crops of maize, cassava, beans and ash pumpkins would be planted for a couple of years by the *chena* cultivator, who would usually build himself an oblong hut on the site, with thatched roof and walls of wattle and daub. Two or three successive crops would exhaust the soil of the nutrients accumulated over the centuries under forest and from the burned timber. The cultivator and his family would then move on to clear a new patch, leaving the first clearing to develop a choking tangle of *Lantana* scrub and thorn bushes. These would often be so dense as to prevent the regeneration of the original forest by shading out any forest tree seedlings which managed to struggle through the ground, resulting in a permanently degraded form of vegetation.

The *chenas* tended to cluster near the few villages through which the road passed and away from these the forest still pressed close to the roadside for many miles. Here one might see troops of the black-faced grey langurs or 'wanderoos' foraging by the roadside, a spotted deer might leap across the road or a *talagoya* (the land monitor lizard) might rush up a tree or rock as one passed by. At Wirawila the road ran along a causeway which bisected Wirawila Tank. This 'tank' was a large example of the ancient irrigation reservoirs to be found throughout the drier lowlands, even in the remotest jungles. Many were disused and silted up, a paradise for birds and animals, but many others, like Wirawila, were in current use and were managed by the Irrigation Department. Wirawila tank was quite an extensive stretch of water a couple of miles in width, and was surrounded by jungle except for the area at the southern end of the causeway where the small village of Wirawila was situated. Unless the water was very high, there was a strip of grass, perhaps 50 or 100 yards wide, between the water and the edge of the jungle. This was usual for most of the tanks and lagoons in this area and provided grazing for the local herds of water buffalo (both wild and domestic, between which there was little visible difference), cattle, spotted deer, and many other herbivores which were not usually visible during daylight hours. It also provided foraging and nesting grounds for the many species of wading birds, such as the red- and yellow-wattled lapwings, and other less common plovers, stone-plovers and pratincoles. The shallows would be occupied by black-winged stilts, sandpipers, redshanks and stints, while herons, egrets and storks would forage where the water was slightly deeper. Out on the open water there would be dark rafts of little cormorants with various species of ducks in attendance, and the many dead trees protruding from the water offered perching facilities for the Indian darters, where they would half spread their wings to dry, and for the many other birds which frequented the area such as whistling teal, rollers, bee-eaters, and pied kingfishers.

A few miles off the main Hambantota road to the east of Wirawila lies the small town of Tissamaharama. Tissa, as it was invariably called, was the capital of the ancient kingdom of Ruhunu, dating from around the third century BC when King Kavantissa constructed several large tanks in the neighbourhood, including the beautiful tank now known as Tissa Wewa just north of the town. Legend has it that the beautiful Viharamahadevi, daughter of a neighbouring king, was sacrificed by her father as a penance for killing a monk. Being no doubt reluctant to use a more positive method and wishing to let the gods take the final decision as to her fate, the option he employed was to send her out to sea in a frail boat. By a happy chance (or the benevolence of the gods) she was washed ashore again on the coast not far from Tissamaharama. She eventually married King Kavantissa and their son was responsible for the liberation of Anuradhapura from one of its many occupations by invaders from India. The legend is a popular one and the large public park in Colombo, originally named Victoria Park, has now been renamed in honour of Queen Viharamahadevi.

There are various ancient monuments in the vicinity of Tissa, including several dagobas, dating from the time of the ancient kingdom. These are Buddhist buildings, solid, almost hemispherical in shape with a pointed spire on the top, and contain relics of the Lord Buddha. They are very characteristic landmarks in Sri Lanka and those in good repair are painted a dazzling white. The Tissa dagobas were crumbling and sprouted wild figs and other vegetation from fissures in their brick structure. However, being remarkably ignorant of the local ancient history, I paid them scant attention beyond appreciation of their graceful form and the atmosphere they imparted to the landscape.

*Tissa Wewa at Tissamaharama is an ancient tank (irrigation reservoir) about 500 ha in extent, probably built in the third century BC. Nearby are many historic dagobas and archaeological remains. The road runs beneath huge rain trees along the retaining bund, from which this view to the north shows the Kataragama hills in the distance.*

What appealed to me was the beautiful countryside and its wonderful birds and other wild life. Tissa was the centre of an area of intensive rice cultivation, with acres of rice paddies stretching into the distance, some of them still irrigated from Tissa Wewa. The paddy fields were interspersed with outlying homesteads surrounded by trees. Amongst these were a sprinkling of feathery-leafed toddy palms and the tall, thin, arecanut palms, which added much to the attraction of the landscape. There is nothing quite so green as a paddyfield with young rice and the brilliant green of these, together with the sparkling irrigation streams and channels, combined to complement the beauty of Tissa Wewa and the other tanks of the area. The Wewa was about a mile across and had a small island situated a few hundred yards from the eastern shore. On the shore just opposite the island was the Tissamaharama Rest House. This was a government rest house built, like dozens in towns and villages up and down the country, principally to accommodate government officials on their administrative travels. Although they were still occasionally used for this purpose, the ease of modern travel made this much less necessary and they were mainly used as small hotels where casual travellers could rest in pleasant surroundings, obtain something to eat or drink, and sometimes stay the night. The design of rest houses varied with their situation, those up-country often resembling English suburban houses while those in warmer areas were more open and airy. The one at Tissa, like many in the lowlands of Ceylon, had open plan lounge and dining areas surrounded by a colonnaded veranda beneath a tiled roof. There were a few bedrooms for overnight accommodation and one could have simple meals cooked by the rest house keeper and his assistant. Unlike many others, the Tissa Rest House Keeper at this time was a reasonable cook and on my visits I often sampled the results of his expertise. He spoke good English but, like many of his brethren, tended to confuse his 'f's and 'p's with disconcerting effect: 'Sir, we have no frawns today as the man is not yet coming from Hambantota, but we have curried pish'.

The road to the rest house ran along the bund of Tissa Wewa and was bordered for part of the way by majestic rain trees (*Pithecolobium saman*). These were huge, umbrella-shaped trees with feathery leaves and massive trunks and branches. In season, pinkish flowers like small powder-puffs covered the canopies. As one passed along the road they formed a magnificent frame for the view across the wewa to the Kataragama hills, a low range with characteristic outline beyond which lay the small town of Kataragama, about ten miles to the north. The trees were also home to a resident troop of wanderoo monkeys which I never tired of watching. Mothers would settle on fallen logs while their babies played and the older males sat in the branches grooming each other or searching the trunks for edible insects and vegetation. When they walked their very long tails would arch in a graceful question mark over their backs and their black faces, framed by pale grey fur and surmounted by a topknot, would often carry a puzzled or worried expression. This was often well founded, as the locals did not share my liking for them and often aimed stones and rocks at the troop to try to prevent their depredations on the papayas and other fruits in the village gardens.

Tissa Rest House was a convenient place to stop and enjoy its beautiful setting on the shores of the tank, surrounded by huge and magnificent wild fig trees. These attracted a large variety of birds and animals (including regular visits from the wanderoo troop), especially when they carried ripe fruit. The Rest House also served as a focus for everyone who happened to be visiting the area, so one frequently met friends or acquaintances there and, indeed, often also made new ones.

It was probably at Tissa Rest House that I met Bill Butler, a tall and slightly elderly character who lived in a modest bungalow on the outskirts of Hambantota. Rumour had it that he was a remittance man and the black sheep of the Butler family, the most famous member of which was then the British Home Secretary and Deputy Prime Minister. I never presumed to enquire if he was a sibling or, indeed, any kind of relation of R. A. Butler, although he would have been about the right age. As 'RAB' Butler's father was a distinguished member of the Indian Civil Service, whose children were born in India, it was plausible that one of them might have ended up in Ceylon. It was not until many years later that I learned from 'RAB' Butler's autobiography that his only brother had been killed in the Second World War. Bill Butler (who's initials were actually A. E.) was a mild and kindly person who always seemed pleased to see me and to enjoy my company, in spite of the difference in our ages. His bungalow was long and low, with a netted-in veranda running the length of the building. Onto this opened the living room and Bill's bedroom, both simply furnished and the former containing a large, glass-fronted bookcase in which reposed a complete set of the then published volumes of the Collins 'New Naturalist' series. He was in fact a good naturalist and we would sit and discuss the arrival of the latest migrants or the fluctuations in the local crocodile population over a beer or a cup of tea. He was obviously not well-off and I do not remember that he had a car (perhaps he had a motorbike). Usually he was dressed in just shorts and locally made sandals and would greet me or say farewell with a cheery wave from the gate of his compound.

If one did not turn south at Wellawaya, but continued eastwards, one came next to the little town of Monaragala. Situated some 35 miles from Wellawaya, it was at the foot of Monaragala mountain, an isolated and rocky massif rising from the plain to about 3,500 ft. This massif formed the isolated planting district of Monaragala in which there were only six or seven estates altogether. The lower slopes were covered here and there with rubber plantations and a few small areas of cacao and cardamoms, while higher up there was a little tea. The road skirted the mountain to the north and then continued eastwards, past the junction with the road north to the huge new irrigation scheme and reservoir on the Gal Oya river until, about 80 miles from Wellawaya, one arrived at Lahugala. To the east of the Monaragala hills most of the way was through intact jungle, dry for much of the year, and with many trees of the Ceylon laburnum (*Cassia fistula*). These hung out their chandeliers of yellow flowers in April and cast their leaves, like many other species of trees in these dry jungles, during the drought months from June to September.

Lahugalla was another ancient irrigation tank of considerable size, a little way off the road on the northern side. It was probably nearly two miles across at its widest extent and, standing on the low and overgrown bund one could see the blue outline of the Uva hills in the far distance. Slightly nearer, the immense monolithic block of Govinda Hela (also known as 'Westminster Abbey') could also be seen, rising in the distance from the Bintenne jungles. Although Lahugala tank was large, it had silted up considerably and much of its area was scarcely more than marsh. The water was also thick with rushes and water grasses and covered with floating plants so that rather little open water remained, even where it was of some depth. Dense jungle surrounded it on all sides and there were few people nearby except for a couple of irrigation workers and their families, housed in a small block of living quarters. The birds and animals therefore had the place very much to themselves and consequently it was well known to those of the Uva planting community who were interested in wildlife as one of the most rewarding places to visit on a day's outing.

Ten miles further on one reached the coast at Pottuvil, where one could turn either north, towards Akkaraipattu or, as I usually did, to Arugam Bay, a couple of miles to the south. Arugam Bay was in fact not really a coastal bay at all, but a large, shallow lagoon (known by the Tamils hereabouts as a *kalapuwa*) formed by the combined estuaries of a couple of small rivers. Except on rare occasions when flood waters breached it, the mouth of the kalapuwa was closed by a wide sand bar, from which local fishermen often cast their hand lines and throwing nets. Not only fish, but very fine prawns of several kinds were plentiful in the shallow waters and fishing was an important occupation for the local population of Pottuvil village and the small fishing hamlets on the shores of Arugam Bay. If one was lucky and happened to arrive when a fishing canoe had just returned with its catch, one could sometimes buy excellent large, black-banded prawns the size of small crayfish. Three of these would make a substantial meal. The road, gently deteriorating as it went, continued south for about 30 miles from the southern shore of Arugam Bay to the small settlements of Panama, Okanda and Kumina where, as a rough track, it reached the banks of the Kumbukkan Oya. This was one of the largest rivers in south-east Ceylon, rising in the Monaragala hills and forming a major barrier to travel along the coast when the few fords were too deep to be passable. It supported luxuriant forest along its banks, where thrived the many stately kumbuk trees (*Terminalia arjuna*) from which, presumably, the river derived its name. With their massive pale trunks and flaky bark, they always reminded me of the London plane when it is allowed to develop its full potential as a specimen tree and not hemmed in and cut about as it is in London streets.

The road did not cross the Arugam Bay lagoon but, as in many similar situations up and down the east coast of Ceylon, a ferry operated to provide access to the southern shore, a distance here of about half a mile. This ferry was of simple construction, consisting of two pontoons with a deck large enough for a bus or two cars, and propulsion was effected (very slowly) by the ferryman and the inevitable assistant hauling on a fixed rope. Nevertheless, it worked well, was cheap, and provided employment. I often used it, as the southern shore was wilder, less populated, and therefore better for swimming from the beach on the seaward side. There was also rather more vegetation and the trees, stunted as they were in this dry area, had been damaged less by the local firewood cutters. On one of my early visits to Arugam Bay I found one tree that contained a large orchid, perched in a crotch about ten feet up. It was magnificently in flower, a blue haze appearing at a distance to temper the dark green of the leaves and the silver stems. Drawing closer, I could see that each flower was the most wonderful sky-blue colour, with veins of darker hue. Although I did not know it at the time, there is little else this species could have been but the famous blue vanda, *Vanda caerulea*, now a rare item indeed in this its native habitat. When I looked for it again on a subsequent visit, both it and the tree had gone.

In later years I found the east coast around Pottuvil and Arugam Bay wilder and more attractive than the more populated southern areas between Tissamaharama and Hambantota, but as a 'new boy' I was only too pleased to accept the invitation to join my friends on their camping trip over the Dee'vali holiday, no matter exactly where we might go or what we might do. In fact the plan was to camp in an area just to the north-west of the town of Kataragama, outside the national park and where there should be some game for the hunters of the party. It was not to be a shooting trip as such, but the intention was to shoot for the pot and accordingly Paul would bring a shotgun. Hans declared that he had a rifle which he would bring. On later examination this proved to be a rather ancient army rifle and I wondered whether it was in fact the weapon issued to Hans during his Swiss national service and which, like all Swiss citizens, he was required to retain in a state of readiness, although I had doubts as to whether this extended to its transport to Ceylon.

It was decided that we would hire a bullock cart in Kataragama to take us father on and each of us contributed to the equipment and stores needed for the four day trip. Of the five of us in the party, Hans and Paul were Swiss, and the remaining (English) members were John, Mervyn and myself. Both Hans and Paul worked for the Swiss agency of Bowers & Co., Hans on Kinellan Estate near Ella, not far from Bandarawela, and Paul over in the Dimbula District. John was the senior SD on Pita Ratmalie, not far from Haputale, while Mervyn was on Dyraaba, the other side of Bandarawela.

I hoped that Bill Horne would be agreeable about allowing me the necessary two or three days off. Although it was over a weekend and there would be no work on the estate on the Saturday or Monday because of the Dee'vali festival holiday, I needed to ask for leave on these days together with the preceding Friday. I had been in my post for only three months, so it was with some trepidation that I broached the subject of leave. My terms of employment, such as they were, stipulated only the amount of 'home' leave and said nothing about any local leave during the qualifying four years of my tour of duty. Local leave was left entirely to the discretion of the PD in charge of the estate and so varied considerably. In fact I need not have worried. Bill Horne told me in a kindly way that although everyone knew planters were on duty 24 hours a day, he did not expect me to seek permission every time I wanted to leave the estate (as did some PDs) but that he did expect me to ask if I wished to be away overnight. As he himself would not be away over Dee'vali, he would have no objection if I took leave.

I arranged to meet the rest of the party at Kataragama and motored down on the appointed day in early November. The north-east monsoon was at its height and a lot of rain had fallen. However, although the sky was grey with low cloud, the day was dry and the track to Kataragama not too difficult to negotiate in the Morris Minor. Kataragama's claim to fame lies in the Hindu Temple situated nearby, which is a major shrine of pilgrimage at the time of the festival in January, when thousands of pilgrims swell the population to many times its normal size. Out of the pilgrim season, the population at that time was probably only a few hundred and the little town consisted of no more than a couple of streets of caddies built of wattle and daub with cadjan roofs. A few administrative buildings and more substantial houses of brick and tile were scattered here and there. *Cadjans* were the local equivalent of thatch, but were in fact one of the many products of the coconut palm, consisting of one side of a leaf frond with the leaflets woven together to produce a flat basket-like surface and trimmed to a length of about five or six feet. These cadjans were used for many purposes including partitions, screens and roofing, for which they were laid overlapping, as with tiles or slates, to give an excellent waterproof roof. In fact cadjan production was quite an important cottage industry in the coconut-growing areas and it was common to see loads of them being transported around the country.

I met up with the others of the party without difficulty and we then transferred our gear into a covered bullock cart which someone had arranged to meet us. The bullock cart owner had a 'cousin-brother' (i.e. a relative of some sort, perhaps a distant one) who was the proud owner of the Weerasiri Hotel. This establishment or, rather, emporium, since it served neither meals nor provided accommodation, occupied a central position in a row of caddies. Leaving the cars in the charge of the cousin-brother at the rear of the Weerasiri Hotel, we started off at a slow but steady pace set by the two hump-backed bullocks which were yoked on either side of the single shaft of the cart. Hans carried his trusty rifle slung over his shoulders, Paul his shotgun, and the rest of us our cameras or walking staves. The bullock cart driver was a rather taciturn individual who did not say much except a few words to Hans's houseboy, Shanmugam, who accompanied us and rode in the cart with the driver.

These bullock carts were not unlike a small version of a voortrekker's wagon, but with only two wheels and a cover consisting of large cane hoops covered with cadjans. They were the main means of long distance transport in the villages and are still commonly used where motor vehicles cannot be afforded. Village transport contractors often owned several bullock carts and, together with those of others, these frequently formed into lengthy caravans for long distance transport of village products or necessities such as rice and foodstuffs, kerosene, earthenware chatty pots or firewood. The bullocks could keep going at their slow and steady pace of about two miles per hour for a long time and the caravans often travelled overnight, providing a considerable hazard for motorists on the long and straight but narrow low country roads, as they frequently carried no lights. As the bullocks automatically followed the cart in front, only the leading cart needed any active direction and then only seldom, as road junctions were few and far between. The carters often slept soundly en route and allowed their beasts to plod on without hindrance. As the leading carter also often appeared to be asleep, I wondered how often the caravans missed their way or took a wrong turning, and whether the carters sometimes found themselves at unexpected destinations. Stories commonly circulated at planters' gatherings as to how the leading cart could be quietly turned around and the whole caravan, complete with its slumbering crew, sent plodding back whence they had come. This invariably elicited much merriment in imagining the bewilderment and horror of the drivers when they awoke in the morning to find themselves back at their point of departure. However, this exploit always seemed to

*Crossing the Menik Ganga at Kataragama. Note the cow tethered to the rear of the bullock cart as a walking dairy to provide us with fresh milk.*

have been performed by someone other than the raconteur and no doubt in most cases it was simply a good story or wishful thinking.

Another and more serious hazard on the lonely low country roads at night were the herds of wild or semi-domesticated water buffalo. These seemed to enjoy the residual warmth of the tarmac surface and would settle themselves comfortably in groups, calmly chewing the cud and completely blocking the road. No amount of hooting would induce them to move until the car or vehicle actually threatened to touch them, when they would very slowly rise and lumber a few yards before collapsing again. As one might be doing a fair speed at night on a straight road, one needed to keep a sharp lookout for large dark lumps on the road ahead and especially as one rounded bends, when one could be upon them with little warning, with potentially disastrous consequences for both car and buffalo.

Crossing the Menik Ganga ('river of gems') by a ford just outside Kataragama town, we continued along a rough track on the eastern side of the river through scrub and grassy areas grazed near the town by cattle and goats and further away more often by buffalo and spotted deer, although we did not see any of the latter. A few rice paddies and patches of cultivation could be seen at first, but these soon disappeared and the vegetation became thicker with occasional glades. After a couple of hours the track had largely disappeared and we came to taller gallery forest on the river bank. Great kumbuck and fig trees rose from the water's edge and we made camp on a grassy patch a few feet above the clear water, which here flowed fast over a shallow gravel bed. We had two tents, one smaller one which Hans and Paul shared (thus becoming the 'Swiss tent') and a larger one shared by the other three of us. Shanmugam and the bullock cart driver erected their own shelter a short distance away.

The camp was rather primitive in that we had no tables or chairs and we sat around the camp fire on logs or stones. Shanmugam served up a very reasonable stew, which we ate by the light of a hurricane lamp, listening to the lapping of the water flowing over the shallows and the sounds of the jungle night. These were mostly of insect origin and composed of a cacophony of various crickets, grasshoppers, katydids and cicadas. Moths and other winged insects of every description converged on the lamp from all directions and soon it was the centre of a ring of singed corpses and dazed creepy-crawlies, while the light was dimmed by a frantic swirl of innumerable gyrating winged creatures.

Occasionally there were other noises: the bark of a spotted deer, the yap of a jackal, the screech of an owl and, once, the distant 'sawing' of a leopard. This is the sound leopards make when on the prowl and is half growl and half purr, uncannily like someone sawing timber. It carries a great distance and is full of threat and menace, a real sound of the Ceylon wilds.

At that time hurricane lamps were the universal source of light in camp and, indeed, in all rural settlements without access to electricity. Only very well-equipped campers, village shop and bar keepers, and well-to-do village householders had Tilly pressure lamps. These were expensive, but gave an excellent and brilliant light. They were fuelled by kerosene and worked in much the same way as a Primus stove, with a delicate mantle as for a gas light. This was inevitably broken during transport each time camp was moved and a good supply of spares had to be carried. The butane gas cookers, lamps and other gadgets which are now such a commonplace part of camping equipment were not then available, at least in Ceylon, where much camp equipment dated from pre-war days. One basic item, which was available in most of the larger hardware stores, was the wide-mouthed thermos. These came in an enormous range of sizes, from moderate to gigantic, and were most useful for carrying butter and cold foods. However, they were somewhat temperamental and had to be cosseted and coddled against the knocks of jungle travel as they tended to explode (or, rather, implode) with a tremendous bang and shower of glass if they received too hard a knock or if one inserted a spoon which was too warm. By the 1950s a few innovations in camping equipment had made their appearance, and one of the most useful of these was the Volcano kettle, which would boil a couple of pints of water with only a newspaper as fuel. It consisted of a metal base with air vents, on which rested a conical aluminium water jacket, tapering around a central space to a circular hole at the top. Through this one dropped strips of newspaper which were ignited from the base and flames then appeared from the top, from which effect the kettle got its appropriate name. One continued to feed in newspaper until the water in the jacket boiled. This was amazingly quick - a matter of four or five minutes, and it was always maintained that the more inflammatory papers hastened the process. One essential prerequisite was that one first removed the cork from the filler hole in the water jacket, and forgetful campers who omitted to do this were startled by a loud report, closely followed by a cork projectile and a column of steam.

About half way through our first night the distant rumbles of thunder we had heard earlier in the evening drew nearer until they crashed and reverberated over the camp, interspersed with sizzling flashes of lightning which lit up the interior of the tent through the canvas with a strange greenish light. Soon the gurgling of the river in the shallows and rapids was drowned by the roar of torrential rain on the canvas and on the trees above. By dawn the rain had eased off to a drizzle and the roar of water then came from the river, which had risen 3 or 4 feet and was in spate, lapping its banks not very far from the tents, which we anxiously considered moving. We eventually decided against this, partly because in fact there wasn't really any higher ground to which we could move, and partly because by mid morning the river seemed for the moment to have stopped rising. Nevertheless, during the next two days the skies remained grey and threatening with occasional bouts of drizzle, although it was warm - as it always is in the Ceylon low country. So warm was it, in fact, that we began to feel a dip in the now subsiding river might be a good idea. Soon we were all in the refreshingly cool waters, splashing about and swimming where it was deep enough to do so. The inflated Lilo mattresses on which we slept were soon brought into play and we had great fun zooming down the rapids on them. Suddenly, there was a yell from Mervyn. I looked round, knowing there were crocodiles about and expecting at the very least to see him in mortal hand-to-snout combat with some giant reptile.

'Bloody hell!'

'What's the matter?'

'I'm being molested by some bloody fish!'

Then I felt it too. A sudden tug and twisting of the hairs on my leg. Then another. Keeping quite still, I managed to see what was happening. A smallish fish about six inches long with a black spot near its tail, was hovering nearby. Suddenly, it darted in and grabbed a mouthful of my leg hairs, worried them with a tug, spat them out and retired. Then another took a turn. I could not make out the reason for this behaviour and can only assume that the fish mistook our leg hairs for the weed or algae on which they normally fed. These blackspot fish were very common in the tanks and rivers and if one left a leg in the water for more than a few minutes, it usually attracted their attention and tugs at one's hairs soon followed. It wasn't painful (as these fish had no teeth to speak of) and I eventually got to feel quite friendly towards them and sometimes dabbled a leg in the water to renew their acquaintance and feel the familiar tugs.

As it had been planned that we would shoot for the pot on this trip, we had not brought more than enough meat for a day or two, so on the afternoon of the second day Paul went off with his shotgun, promising to provide a tasty peafowl or jackrabbit for dinner. When it began to get late and he had not reappeared, we started to get anxious about the possibilities for supper. Meals always assume great importance on jungle trips, which sharpen the appetite wonderfully, and the thought of a supperless night was worrying. Hans got out his rifle and said he would go and see what he could find. At this point there was a loud crashing in the undergrowth accompanied by what we assumed were muffled German expletives, and Paul reappeared. He had been unsuccessful, he reported, owing to the extraordinarily shy nature of all the local fauna. Despite every cunning trick known to the hunter and the silence of his shadow-like movement through the forest, he had seen nothing. We replied that if he hadn't crashed about like an inebriated rhinoceros he would have had more luck. 'All right', said Paul, proffering me the gun, 'You have a go'.

Now, I had never actually fired a shotgun before, although I had watched clay pigeon shooting. Being put on the spot and in any case not being averse to demonstrating my prowess with the weapon, I accepted and set off. Hans meanwhile departed with his rifle in the opposite direction, accompanied by John and Mervyn.

I walked away from the camp up a faint game trail which took me through dripping bush interspersed with open, grassy glades and occasional tall fig trees. One of these had some ripe fruit and I could see there were pigeons in the canopy. Ceylon has many beautiful pigeons, including several species of green pigeon, which I knew were said to be very good eating and were also apparently very fond of ripe wild figs. As I drew near, two or three pigeons burst out of the tree and flew across my path at a distance of about 30 yards. Raising the gun (and somehow remembering to slip the safety catch as I did so), I fired, and to my amazement the leading bird plummeted to earth. But it proved not to be a fine, fat green pigeon; only a poor little bronze-wing, scarcely more than a mouthful. I picked up the body, eyes closed in death, and the grey-capped head hung limp, at an angle to the glowing bronze-green back and wings. Why hadn't I looked more carefully before firing? I felt ashamed of myself and started back towards camp. Suddenly I heard the characteristic shout of the cock jungle fowl: 'Jock, joy-joyce! Jock, joy-joyce!' Now, a jungle fowl really would make a tasty supper. I replaced the spent cartridge and crept slowly forward through the scrubby low trees and thickets. The call came again, quite near now, just the other side of a dense tangle of creepers growing over a fallen tree. I could see a fowl-like movement through the leaves, pecking and scratching in the darkness beneath the creepers. The light was going now, even in the open glades, and I moved slightly to get a clearer sight. There! I fired through the gap in the foliage. I was fairly sure I had hit the bird and I hurried round the thicket expecting to collect a fine cock jungle fowl, which are about the size of a large bantam and look quite similar to some breeds, with flowing golden brown feathers on the neck and back, an arched tail in iridescent green, and a flame-like comb in scarlet with a yellow centre. To my horror, I was confronted by an obviously wounded female bird in her dark hen-brown plumage, flapping frantically by the base of the bush. The cock bird, which had doubtless been displaying for the hen, was nowhere to be seen. I finished off the hen with the second barrel (I couldn't bring myself, inexpertly, to wring its neck) and feeling chastened and deflated I set off back to camp. I never fired a gun again.

I reached the river bank some distance upstream of the camp and as I turned left to follow the bank there suddenly came a tremendous bang from somewhere quite nearby. Then another and another. Compared with the shotgun the explosions of the rifle shots sounded huge. What could Hans have found? A sambhur? Or perhaps he had wounded a leopard! I fervently hoped not. Quite apart from my disapproval of killing a leopard (although they were then relatively numerous in many parts of the Island), a wounded leopard was one of the most dangerous situations which one could have in the jungle. It was now quite dark and I made my way back along the bank as quickly as I could, occasionally banging into branches or getting entangled in creepers. As I drew near camp I saw dim movements ahead and heard the sound of excited voices over the noise of the river. Shanmugam suddenly appeared swinging the hurricane lantern just as I came upon the rest of the party, their attention focussed on the opposite bank. Apparently a porcupine had come down to the river and Hans had hit it with his first shot, but it had required two more shots to finish it off. Shanmugam and the bullock cart driver waded over to collect it and returned with the disembowelled carcass. I had not seen a porcupine close up before and was impressed by the strong legs, the tail with short, stout, black and white quills, and the longer, more slender quills on the back, which were orange where the others were white. In due course Shanmugam produced an excellent porcupine stew, with jungle fowl as an entrée. I don't remember what happened to the bronze-wing pigeon. No doubt we ate it, but it was so small as to be unmemorable.

We sat around the camp fire to eat our rice and stew, which tasted rather like pork. This was the time of the Suez crisis and the last news we had heard had been grim. Israel had attacked Egypt and the British and French airforces had bombed Egyptian airfields, destroying large numbers of planes on the ground to widespread condemnation by most of the Commonwealth. We had no radio with us in camp (transistor radios had not yet reached us) and the conversation was of what might be happening and whether this could herald World War Three. I had not been following the news closely before coming away; my old radio emitted so many atmospherics that even listening to the BBC World Service news was a major effort. But somehow I could not believe that the world would really be thrown into another war when, after all, the last one had been finished for only a little more than ten years and the Korean war had been over for barely three. To my naive mind, things in Ceylon seemed so permanent and so remote from the goings-on in the Middle East and Europe that I could not envisage these events seriously impinging on our pattern of life.

'What will you do if there's a war, John?' asked Mervyn, while nibbling the meat from a porcupine bone in one hand.

'Join up, of course', replied John, with unhesitating confidence, as he spooned up rice and gravy from his tilted bowl.

I wondered what I would do, what I might have to do, and whether my life would really be disrupted as my parents' lives had been by the last war. We finished off with bananas and mugs of tea before turning in.

The remaining two days of our trip passed quickly and the weather gradually improved, but we did not do any more shooting. Somehow everyone had lost enthusiasm for hunting, although we subsisted on porcupine curry for the remainder of our stay. On the last day, John, Mervyn and I decided to try to walk back along the river bank, while Hans and Paul accompanied the bullock cart. We set off in bright morning sunshine with the river back to its normal level and its waters, the colour of weak tea, running clear over the sand. The journey was not difficult, necessitating wading in only a few places, and was uneventful. At one point we came upon the intact skeleton of an eight foot crocodile, perfect in every bone and tooth, drawn up facing the water as though about to slide down the bank. There was nothing to indicate what had been the cause of its death. Three hours later we were back at the Weerasiri Hotel, where the bullock cart party had arrived somewhat earlier, and by dark I was back at Meeriabedde, looking forward to a hot bath and a good supper of something other than porcupine. Unpacking, back in the cool air of the estate after a visit to the low country, it was always curious to feel the warmth of the clothes, which retained the heat of the lowlands as though straight out of a tumble dryer. The news on the BBC World Service reported that British and French troops had ceased their advance down the Suez Canal 23 miles south of Port Said, a cease fire had been arranged, and the threat of World War Three seemed to have receded beyond sight.

*Mervyn and John walking back to Kataragama along the bank of the Menik Ganga.*

After this I made visits to the jungle about once or twice a month at weekends. As Saturday was a full working day, these usually had to be on a Sunday unless there was a public holiday or estate work was stopped for the day, as happened when the growth of the tea slowed during the dry season and the plucking rounds lengthened. Sometimes I stayed the Saturday night at a rest house, but more usually it was a day trip, leaving at first light and getting back well after dark. However, there was a social price to pay. Much as I enjoyed jungle visits, on most of them I was alone. If Club Day had been wet and few people had turned up, I would have had no tennis and little social contact for a week or more, so I had to balance the attraction of the wilds against the social possibilities of the club on Sunday morning. During my time on Meeriabedde the novelty of being my own master and the relatively short travelling times often tilted the balance in favour of the jungle. In later years I grew to value social life more and the estates I was on were less convenient for day trips. However, although gradually I found it harder to forego my Sunday injection of conviviality, I managed occasionally to find a companion for a jungle excursion.

# See you at the club! 7

Tea planting was a very male-oriented profession and it also ranked high amongst the greatest bastions of male chauvinism. In my day it would have been unthinkable for a woman to be employed as a superintendent or assistant superintendent on any estate. All the PDs and SDs whom I knew (or knew of) were exclusively male and, as far as I know, this virtually complete male domination of tea planting (or any other planting, for that matter) still persists today. Of course, there were a few women estate owners who had usually inherited their properties and partly or wholly managed them, but I am referring to planters as employees, as were all the European planters of my acquaintance and experience.

It would certainly have made life a great deal pleasanter if some of my fellow SDs had been female. The sudden transition from single sex school to the male world of tea planting had done nothing to bolster my confidence with the opposite sex and I had developed something of an inferiority complex when girls came into my social orbit. Admittedly, not many did so but, I felt, why ever should they bother with me when there were so many other young men around, seemingly bursting with self confidence and experience? My remote situation on Meeriabedde also did nothing to help.

There were two planters' clubs in the district. Besides the Haldummulla Club there was the Bow Club at Bandarawela. To reach either took me an hour's drive along narrow and tortuous roads. For the Haldummulla Club I had to descend the estate cart road through Koslanda Estate to the main Colombo road, proceed seven or eight miles west towards Needwood, and then twist up the Haputale Pass for more than 1,500 ft. to Haputale. The journey to the Bow Club was scarcely less exhausting. First there was the estate cart road down to the river, the zig-zag up through Meeriabedde and neighbouring Poonagalla to reach the Poonagalla road, and then a 12-mile twisting drive down to Bandarawela, crossing the railway just before reaching the town. Heavy rain or mist could nearly double the journey time in either direction. So I greatly envied those lucky SDs who were within a few minutes drive of the clubs and social centres.

From its title, the Bow Club sounded as though it had been founded to promote archery. However, neither bow nor arrow were to be seen and, if archery was the reason for its foundation, I cannot remember anybody ever referring to this phase of its existence. The Bow Club was for Europeans only and contained within its rules something to the effect that membership was 'open to persons of predominantly European descent'. In this it was unique amongst upcountry clubs, all the others having long since opened their doors to all races. The only other clubs in the Island still retaining their Europeans-only membership rules from colonial times were one or two in Colombo, illustrating the remarkable tolerance shown by the post-colonial Ceylon governments up to that time. In the case of the

Bow Club, it had probably been able to avoid pressure to become multiracial because the non-European community had a much bigger and better establishment right next door, namely the Bandarawela Club.

As with all the planting district clubs, the main outdoor activity at the Bow Club was tennis and in the Bandarawela-Haputale area one alternated between tennis at the Bow Club on Wednesday afternoons and tennis at the Haldummulla Club on Sunday mornings. Although it was situated in the little town of Bandarawela, the Bow Club itself did not really have much more to offer than the Haldummulla Club. It had one more tennis court (making three), a cupboard full of library books, a card room, a billiards room, and a table tennis table. The town, however, offered considerably more than Haputale. For a start there was a cinema which showed a regular programme of English films. Then there was the hotel, a low building of colonial style with considerable atmosphere and set in gardens on the top of the small hill just above the main street. But Bandarawela's principal attraction was that it had a real department store. This was a minuscule branch of Millers Ltd., a large and well-known department store in Colombo which had several branches upcountry. The Bandarawela branch must have been the smallest of these but had a well-stocked drinks department, a cold stores department where one could get butter, cheese and bacon, and it was the only place in the district where one could buy ready-to-wear European clothing such as knitwear, underwear and socks. Other items of clothing were also stocked, but normally one had these, including shoes, made to measure by one of the excellent tailors or bootmakers which were to be found plying their trades in front of almost every shop in town.

The procedure for ordering a new pair of shoes was simple. First you explained what type of shoe was required. Usually one had an old pair to show as an example. Otherwise you could choose a style from a catalogue with pictures, or even an illustrated magazine advertisement. Next the shoemaker would produce various samples of leather and invite you to select a suitable colour and quality. Finally, he would sit you down and place two large sheets of paper under your feet. He then drew around your feet with a pencil to produce outlines of each foot. An appointment for a fitting would be made, usually for about a week later, at which you tried on the unfinished shoes and at which, with any luck, you could detect whether and where they pinched or rubbed. No matter how doubtful one felt about the fit, the shoemaker would always make light of any problem and give the most categorical assurances that the final fit and finish would be perfect. If there remained any tightness or if perhaps a squeak was apparent in the new shoes when you collected the finished article a few days later, the problem was always confidently dismissed with assurance that whatever it was would be sure to disappear after a few days wear. In fact this was often the case, as the hand-sewn shoes were elastic enough to mould themselves to your feet, but it was often more painful and took rather longer than one had been assured.

The procedure for having clothes made by one of the tailors was very similar and some of them showed a remarkable flair for making clothes the like of which they had seen only in some catalogue or magazine sent out from England. However, others could be less skilful and some were downright ham-fisted. Usually the tailor would calculate the amount of material needed and one could either choose and purchase this from the tailor's 'home' shop or from another of the numerous textile shops in town. Planting clothes for men, being simple, straightforward, and not varying much in style, usually gave the tailor little trouble. Women's clothes, however, were a different matter and sometimes the making of a fashion garment developed into a nightmare for both client and tailor. Sometimes this could occur even with less fashionable items. My grandmother in particular had great trouble in getting dresses made that she liked and which fitted comfortably. 'Now, tailor,' she would say, 'be sure to leave plenty of room *here* and *here*' (indicating beneath the arms). 'Yes, Lady' would come the reply, 'Lady not to worry, all will be just as Lady wishes'. Then on fitting day there would be cries of exasperation. 'Tailor, I *told* you to leave room under the arms, and now look - I can't lift my arm without raising the dress. And look at this, the neckline is too sloppy and out of shape. This won't do at all.' 'No, no, Lady,' would come the patient reply through a mouthful of pins, 'Coming right, Lady. I loosening seam here . . . and taking little tuck here, . . . and here. Lady come back tomorrow and all will be right.' Needless to say, it usually was not all right at the next fitting, and successive fittings would drag on for weeks before satisfaction was at last reached, by which time both the tailor and my grandmother would be in the last stages of nervous exhaustion.

On Wednesdays I changed before leaving the estate and I would arrive in Bandarawela dressed for tennis in my regulation whites. In these I felt faintly conspicuous (but not uncomfortably so) while walking through the throngs of sarong and sari-clad people in the town and doing my week's shopping before going to the club. Having then filled up the car with petrol at the local filling station, I would arrive at the club about four o'clock, which was the accepted time that most people turned up. Usually I would then start playing a singles with whoever was there or arrived next. Later the courts would gradually fill up and mixed or men's doubles were then the order of the day.

At about 5 p.m. the club tea would be served. This was quite an elaborate affair and was provided (with reimbursement from the club) by each married member in turn. Bachelors were spared this duty, it being considered that neither they nor their appus would be sufficiently well versed in domestic skills to be up to the challenge. Besides, it would never do to have a man preside over the teapot. However, bachelors were expected to help out in other ways, such as organising various events. The lady member doing the tea acted as hostess for the occasion and always had her appu (and sometimes also her houseboy) in attendance. Plates of bread and butter with fish paste, Gentlemen's Relish, or guava jam would be arranged alongside home-made cakes and scones of various kinds, sandwiches and biscuits. Icing sugar was often difficult to obtain, so iced cakes were uncommon. However, really determined appus would manufacture a sort of icing sugar by crushing ordinary white granulated sugar to a fine powder with a bottle or grindstone. The frequent appearance of oatmeal flapjack, shortbread and girdle cakes (known to Sassenachs as 'drop' scones) reflected the large Scottish planting population. In some districts keen competition could develop between the lady members as to who could provide the most sumptuous club tea. This could get out of hand, with more and more elaborate teas and increasingly exotic iced cakes being produced, so often (as was the case at the Bow Club) there were some general guidelines as to what sort of a tea should be provided.

Later on, tennis would be resumed by those feeling active enough to do so, watched from basket chairs lined along the open veranda by the remaining members digesting their tea. Between 6.30 and 7 p.m. it became too dark for tennis and the tea drinkers in the basket chairs would have transferred their attention to whiskies and pink gins at the bar or to bridge in the card room. The tennis players would then shower and change into trousers and shirts (usually with tie or cravat) and the remainder of the evening would be devoted to drinking, with occasional interruption for a game of snooker. By 10.30 most people would be thinking of leaving, except for the die-hards and those living very near. In my case I would also be thinking of having to get up for muster the following morning.

The drive back to Meeriabedde always seemed much longer than the outward journey; this effect usually being produced by a combination of tiredness and the consumption of several beers. As the lights of the car swung to and fro round the endless bends of the twisty road, they often illuminated nocturnal animals on the grassy roadside verges. Black-naped hares, looking remarkably like ordinary rabbits, were quite common, as were various mongooses and civet cats, the latter always conspicuous with their bushy black and white ringed tails. When reported to my friends they always attributed these sightings to over indulgence at the bar, and to be sure there were many times when I felt it wiser to draw onto the roadside for a short nap rather than attempt to continue. However, they enlivened the journey.

The constant weaving round innumerable bends played havoc with car tyres, which lasted only a few thousand miles. A retreading service had been started in Colombo and one could send worn tyres down by rail or by road carrier to be retreaded. However, the quality of rubber used for the retreads in these early days was often very poor and the retreads themselves lasted for even fewer miles than the originals (four thousand was considered quite average for front tyres). But this was no problem as one could simply send the tyre for retreading again. There was no sort of regulation preventing the use of defective tyres and people who were short of funds thought nothing of having the same tyre retreaded several times until the side walls were so weak it could not be used. Nor was one deterred by the fact that the tyre was so worn that several layers of canvas were showing. The retread came back looking as good as new (or nearly) and kept the car going for another few months. In fact speeds on upcountry roads were so slow that a blow-out usually did not spell complete disaster. Also, most journeys were relatively short and few people accumulated a large annual mileage.

As different firms started to compete in tyre retreading, all sorts of tread variants were offered. One memorable (and expensive) version was the wire-soled retread, in which short lengths of wire were incorporated end-on into the tread. This, as advertised, greatly improved road holding and minimised skidding but lasted only a little longer than the ordinary ones. Their effects were most spectacular at night when it could be seen that cars fitted with them left behind a shower of sparks as though fireworks had been lashed to the wheels. Strangely, I never heard of any consequential explosions. Gradually, the increasing competition caused the retread companies to diversify and eventually they would retread almost anything. Tennis shoes were obvious candidates (especially as these were one of the few sorts of shoe which the local shoemaker could not produce) and over the years I had several pairs done with reasonable results.

On Sundays the pattern of social activity was repeated at the Haldummulla Club on Haputale Estate, except that here a few Ceylonese members would be present. One simply *never* went to the Bow Club on Sundays, although it was not closed. I suppose that with the same few people forming most of the membership of both clubs, there were just not enough to keep both going on the same day and once the custom had been established, it was pointless going to a club where it was extremely doubtful that anybody else would turn up. Sunday morning tennis began about 11 a.m. and continued until about 2 p.m., by which time it would be either too hot or the contestants too inebriated, or both. Attendance at the bar and on the court alternated and games became considerably more jovial and sometimes even unconventional later in the day. My game gradually improved, but with relatively little practice this was slow.

Besides the fact that I enjoyed the game, tennis was obviously an important social pastime and I determined to try to improve my play. There was no question of getting any coaching (professional coaches for any sport were quite unknown upcountry) except from a few rather pedantic books. One which I found in the club library started the chapter on The Serve by stating 'The service is the only time when the player has complete control of the ball'. As at that time I felt my state of play showed a tendency for the reverse to operate, this was rather unhelpful. What I felt I needed was a practice wall, and I wondered whether I could arrange one at Meeriabedde. Summoning Ramasamy KP one day, I explained to him that I wanted the terrace retaining wall by the steps up to the vegetable garden made vertical and plastered with a smooth cement facing. The following day one of the stonemasons appeared, accompanied of course by an assistant, and within a couple of days the rather rough and sloping stone retaining wall had been dismantled and rebuilt. When covered with cement plaster it was transformed into a smooth-faced vertical wall about 7 ft in height and 15 ft. wide. With the addition of a white line at net height it made an excellent practice wall and the area in front of the garage was just about the size of half a tennis court. It only needed a few stones and bumps to be removed and my practice area was ready. I never enquired as to which account Ramasamy had charged the labour and no questions were ever asked, but I suspect it was to the good old heading of Roads and Drains.

With regular practice against my new wall every evening, my ground strokes improved immensely and I found I could hold my own against most of the other players at the clubs. At these elevations normal balls bounced much higher than at sea level and it was usual to play with special high-altitude balls. However, even these had a tendency to bounce higher than normal and I found it very hard to apply top spin. Instead, to keep the balls from going over the wire and into the tea, I developed an unorthodox but accurate chip shot which was effective on balls received at head height, but which was severely punished by good players. I am sorry to say that I have never been able to replace it with something better.

The high spot in the social calendar of most district clubs was the annual tennis tournament. Upcountry, these were always two-day affairs, arranged at a weekend. For some reason they were always called tennis 'meets', presumably reflecting the habits of the huntin' and shootin' fraternity to which many of the older planters belonged. Naturally they were usually arranged when good weather might be expected which, in Uva, meant the dry season of May to September. This had the added advantage that estates often stopped work for a day or two each week when the dry weather reduced the growth of the tea, and it was easier for planters to get away. There were tennis meets at one or other of the district clubs in Uva almost every weekend during July and August and, as this also coincided with the UK summer holidays, the social scene at this time was enhanced by an influx of planters' sons and (especially) daughters out for their vacations from college or university.

In some ways this was reminiscent of the 'fishing fleet' which was such a major feature of Indian (and, indeed, Ceylon) social life in colonial times during the months of the northern winter. However, although in rare cases it still happened that some young planters did meet their wives in this way, there were significant differences. In colonial times when it was less common for women to have independent careers, a 'good' marriage was of very much greater importance. By the 1950s the boot or, perhaps, the stocking, was definitely on the other foot. The girls were seldom consciously looking for husbands and regarded their visits merely as enjoyable but transient holidays before moving on to the main business of life at home in Britain. Now it was the young planters who were the ones anxious to establish relationships and make matches. In addition there was also increasingly a feeling amongst the parents of eligible daughters that perhaps a planter son-in-law was much less to be desired than it had been in the days of the Raj, when everything seemed so much more certain. In these days, instead of being wealthy entrepreneurs or the sons of well-to-do estate proprietors, young planters were almost invariably impecunious employees of planting companies who's jobs depended on regular renewal of the detested Temporary Residence Permits. The numbers of female visitors had also dwindled enormously and now, instead of a fleet, they could have been comfortably accommodated in a couple of dinghies. Whereas previously a large influx of young women had joined a sizeable resident colonial population of sisters and daughters related to numerous members of the European expatriate commercial, military and civil community, these few arrivals became the objects of desire for whole planting districts and every girl, no matter how plain, could count on being the centre of attention for numerous rival suitors.

Usually I managed to attend four or five tennis meets each year: those of my local clubs as a matter of course, and two or three further afield in other districts. The Uva Gymkhana Club, the big provincial club at Badulla, was within a day's travelling distance but others, such as the Passara Club at Namanukula or the Maturatta Club in the Upper Hewahetta District, usually necessitated staying overnight, and this was certainly the case for attending events on the other side of the hills at the big clubs of Radella and Darrawella in the Dimbula and Dickoya districts. Various planter friends were always very hospitable in offering a bed for the night when one attended the meet at their local club and often the club operated a put-you-up scheme amongst its members for those who had no contacts in the district. The proceedings started with postal entry to the various tennis events and those who had no partners for the doubles could draw for them. On the appointed weekend I would pack my case and, with a grant of weekend leave from Bill Horne, I would set off on the Friday evening. My host would usually be some fellow SD acquaintance and it was always interesting to visit other bungalows.

In spite of instructions received, bungalows were sometimes difficult to find, especially at night, up long, narrow and bifurcating gravel-surfaced cart roads which wound through the tea, over and around the hillsides. Most estates had neat signposts indicating the way to the 'big' and 'small' bungalows, but sometimes they were missing at vital road junctions. Should one take the upper fork, ascending into the blackness above, or the lower fork which seemed more in the direction of a few dim and distant lights? Sometimes it would be raining, but usually there would be someone passing by from whom one could ask the way. Winding down the wet and misted window, I would stick my head out into the cold night air and accost a dim shape covered from head to knee with a dark *cumbley* blanket. *'Entha rotu sinna bungalavaku poerathah?'* (Which road goes to the small bungalow?) I would ask and usually the reply would be *'Intha rotiley po'nga'* (Go on this road, Sir), or something similar. Often the bungalow road was the darkest one, leading away from the visible lights, because (in contrast to pioneering days) most bungalows were not sited near the labour lines and their lights were hidden amongst the trees with which most of them were surrounded. Eventually, and sometimes considerably late, I would arrive to a warm welcome, and once I had visited a bungalow I prided myself on always remembering the way thereafter.

There was a very characteristic and evocative aroma associated with upcountry bungalows, compounded from the individual scents of polished wooden floors, wood fires, and the fir trees which often surrounded the bungalows. This was absent in bungalows at lower elevations where suspended wooden flooring was replaced by solid concrete and cement, usually scored into square or diamond patterns and invariably covered with a red polish which imparted its own tang to the atmosphere. Furnishings in SD bungalows were often Spartan and sometimes I had to take my bedding with me. Occasionally there would be other people staying and with a few beers in front of a cheerful fire a pleasant evening would be had by all.

The following morning we would arrive at the club at the appointed hour and the first job was to check the draw for the tennis events, see who one had drawn as partners in the men's and mixed doubles and who was one's opponent in the first round of the singles. A mixture of local planters and people from further away would be arriving, some from other planting districts and, at the bigger meets, a sprinkling from the agency houses in Colombo. Then one could indulge in unaccustomed socialising, meeting friends and acquaintances and making new ones, and even meeting one or two unattached young women. Apart from daughters out for the summer vacation, there were two main sources of these: nurses from the Colombo or upcountry private hospitals (always referred to in those days as 'nursing homes'), and teachers from the Hill School, the European prep school in Nuwara Eliya. I felt disadvantaged by my youth and inexperience, however, as usually they would be some years older than I was, having spent several years at college or university and having perhaps worked in one or two other posts already.

The club premises would have been tarted up for the occasion with great vases of flowers, the veranda floor polished to a ruby shine, and the tennis courts and lawns carefully swept and manicured. Coming out to the court-side chairs, drink in hand, one could see the ball boys and their supervisor already out on court. Ball boys would be recruited from children on the local estate, and while the supervisor frantically tried, with limited success, to keep order, his charges would be chattering like sparrows and proudly displaying to their less fortunate brethren beyond the wire the smart khaki shirts which some clubs supplied. Tennis then commenced and was followed keenly by most of those present. The standard of play was quite high, with a sprinkling of players of about English inter-County standard. Usually I did not survive more than the first couple of rounds unless I had been lucky enough to draw an unusually good partner in the doubles. However, this was a mixed blessing as I then felt a heavy responsibility not to let her or him down. Often this was counter-productive in making me feel increasingly nervous, and the harder I tried, the more my game disintegrated. My serve in particular was very vulnerable to my nerves and on the worst occasions I could lose control completely, serving four double faults in a row or even (on one memorable occasion) hitting my very senior planter partner on the head as he crouched at the net. More usually in these circumstances I managed to put on an adequate game and we would lose only when we came up against strong opposition. Later on, as I became more experienced (and replaced my schooldays racket), I managed to support my partner sufficiently for us to be runners-up and even to win on a few occasions when the opposition was not too strong. Prizes were varied and could be items of household equipment or trophy cups, and the larger clubs sometimes also recorded the winning names on boards in the clubhouse. It was all very correct and ordered, although usually only the finals of each event would be umpired.

There would always be a raffle for prizes and one would be pressed (sometimes several times) to buy tickets for this during the course of the weekend. It was the custom in many clubs to put all the tickets into a bucket or other container so that each one was picked individually at random and to price the tickets in cents according to their number. Ticket number 22 would thus cost only 22 cents, while ticket number 513 would cost Rs 5.13 (a substantial price). I therefore evolved an economically satisfactory system which did not damage my bank balance yet often produced one or more prizes at the draw on the Sunday evening. This was simple. I would buy tickets until I had accumulated three which cost more than one rupee each. If I drew one costing less than a rupee, I would draw another and perhaps another until I had the requisite three 'expensive' ones. Sometimes I was able to accumulate 10 or 12 tickets in this way and often went home with a bottle of gin or several beers whilst simultaneously basking in general approbation at my generosity in buying so many tickets.

Sometimes there were subsidiary activities at club meets, such as a clay pigeon shoot or a snooker tournament. For clay pigeon shooting the machine throwing the clay discs would be set up in some suitable position in a bunker or small dell behind sand bags, often arranged so that the clays would fly out over a steep hillside. Even the worst shots then could blaze away without danger of accidentally damaging onlookers or some industrious soul busily weeding their contract in the tea. Each participant would take up their stance at the appointed place and would shout 'Pull!' each time they were ready to fire. The clay pigeons would be thrown up in pairs, spinning in arcs like miniature flying saucers (which, of course, they were). The object was then to score hits with both left and right barrels, sending showers of earthenware fragments into the tea below. In their excitement, inexperienced people often frustrated their efforts by forgetting to slip off the safety catch as they raised the shotgun, and much strong language could be heard by the onlookers on these occasions as the clays sped away intact to a chorus of ribald comments. Clay pigeon shoots were always very popular with the local population of small boys (*podians*) who delighted in scrambling for the spent cartridges after each competitor had completed the requisite five or ten 'pulls'.

Excellent lunches and teas were always served at tennis meets and if you were on court in the afternoon, you had to be somewhat restrained at the trough if you were to give of your best in a three-set match, especially if it was a hot day. On the Saturday evening there was always a dance, often to a live band. If one's host lived on an estate within about half an hour's drive from the club, one usually returned there to wash and change, and probably to have a light supper, before returning to the club. Otherwise one merely stayed on at the club and at dusk changed into evening attire. Then, after much preliminary moving of furniture and shaking of 'French chalk' (talc) onto the dance floor, the band would strike up and the evening would gradually get going as people returned from nearby estates in their evening clothes.

Although more modern styles of dancing and dance music, such as the Tiger Rag, had already made their appearance in Australia and Britain, in Ceylon dances were still stuck in the fox-trot and waltz era. An occasional Paul Jones or Scottish country dance would be thrown in for variety and to mix people up. In fact, of course, the young SDs did not really want to be mixed up and risk the nightmare of landing up with the elderly wife of the Club President or (worse still) their own PD's wife. On such occasions the brain went numb with the effort of trying vainly to avoid damaging their toes (which seemed to get everywhere one needed to tread) with clod-hoppers more appropriate to tramping round the tea *totum*, while simultaneously trying to keep time, get the steps right and make polite conversation. What the SDs *really* wanted was to dance with the few young unattached females available (and, if possible, get them outside for a spot of snogging). But there were often insuperable obstacles frustrating such plans and desires. Sometimes one of these would be a boyfriend in attendance. This did not always spell disaster, however, as sometimes the girl seemed quite ready to dump him for the evening and sample the wealth of local talent. Even if she did not, he could often be got sufficiently tight as to be immobilised at the bar for the duration without too much difficulty or expense. However, although there might be no boyfriend, there was always fierce competition. It was, of course, probably also a difficult situation for the girls, who suddenly found themselves the focus of fascination for half a dozen or more presentable young men. Although previous experience in most cases may not have taught them how to handle such a situation, many seemed to adapt to it with remarkable rapidity, ease, and even enjoyment. So much so, indeed, that some girls got quite spoiled with attention and could be very off-hand with those unfortunate males who were below the top rank in the pecking order. Those who, like myself, felt slow in wit and lacking in charisma, usually did not try to compete but withdrew to the bar to observe the goings-on with an assumed air of confident detachment, but with an eye open to take advantage of any opportunity which might present itself. This might occur when a girl's partner went to get drinks from the bar or disappeared into the 'gent's', and one could then nip in and exercise what fascination one could muster.

It was really very difficult to start anything in the nature of romance unless one was unusually favoured in appearance or by circumstances. At the end of the club dance it was generally impractical to offer to take a girl 'home' unless she happened to be staying on a nearby estate or (this was real luck) happened to be the daughter or guest of one's PD. Parents and hosts were always reluctant to entrust their beloved offspring or cherished charges to the clutches of local SDs whose intentions were automatically (and usually justifiably) suspect and whose transport was often two-wheeled. So for the majority of poor SDs the most they could hope for after the last dance was a chaste peck on the cheek, and many opted for consolation at the bar long before the end of the evening.

Being excessively young and inexperienced caused me difficulties even when events conspired to favour me. Gail was slightly younger even than myself and out for a few months after leaving school. Her parents, who had known me as a child, lived on Kumarawatte Group, a particularly remote estate growing rubber on the slopes of Moneragala mountain, down beyond Welawaya on the road towards the east coast. They had arranged a party for Gail the day after the end of a tennis meet at the Maturatta Club, a good two and a half hours' drive from their estate. As both she and I were attending the meet, would I be so kind as to give her a lift home and be at her party? You bet I would! I would have been 'so kind' even had it been five hours' drive! Gail had long blonde hair and a lively personality, attracting all the most dashing young men like bees to a honey pot. I was nowhere in the running and remained ignored on the edge of the throng until at the end of the evening the time came to depart for Moneragala.

'Are you ready to go?' I enquired, feeling particularly redundant as Gail disentangled herself from a vastly handsome male specimen from the fleshpots of Colombo.

'What? Oh, yes, in a mo'' she replied, turning back to her admirer and obviously having to explain (so I imagined) why on earth she was suddenly contemplating leaving with this gauche non-entity, 'I'll be with you in a minute'.

Half an hour later she joined me in the car park and we set off. The night was fine and an almost full moon bathed the hills and valleys in silver light as we wound our way first along the Uda Pussellawa road, the cart roads of Kirklees estate, and then on through a slumbering Bandarawela, and down the Haputale Pass. Gail was pleasant enough in a sisterly way, but it was not in a brotherly way that I wanted our relationship to develop. The more I searched for something witty and entertaining to say, the duller I felt and there seemed no way of transforming the situation and even less chance of getting it onto a more physical level. About midnight we had reached Wellawaya when I suddenly remembered that Gail was learning to drive. Would she like to have a go? She would, so we swapped seats. This gave me lots of opportunity for interesting instruction and guiding of hand on gear lever. I even draped one arm carelessly on the back of her seat, waiting for the moment to carelessly drape it around her shoulder. But it never seemed to come: Gail was much too competent a driver and did not seem to need any help from me. I began to feel redundant again and my right arm went to sleep. Even the narrow and contorted road up Moneragala mountain did not seem to trouble her and the headlights swung to and fro, illuminating the serried ranks of the rubber trees as we climbed higher and the gradient got steeper. Eventually we arrived at Kumarawatte Bungalow (which was one of the few with an upper floor) and, acknowledging the salaams of the *karvalkaran* (night watchman), we let ourselves in through the unlocked front door. We tiptoed up the stairs and Gail showed me my room. Would she give some sign that she might welcome any closer attention from me? Not a glimmer.

'Will you be OK in there?' she asked politely - too politely, I felt.

'Yes, just fine', said I, feeling desperately that I should do something now, but what? How could I make advances yet not appear to be forcing myself on her? A quick brush of her cheek and she was gone.

The party next day partially restored my spirits. Most of the younger planters in the area were invited and a few girls had been assembled from far and wide. Kumarawatte Bungalow was high on the shoulder of Moneragala (one of several mountains in the Island bearing the name 'Peacock Rock') and looked out over the lowland jungles to the south. There was a swimming pool in the garden but, although of a reasonable size, it was a very simple affair. There was no nonsense about disinfection or filtration. It was just filled with water from the hose and when the water got too green, it was changed. There were various bits of flotsam drifting about in it which were skimmed off from time to time by the *totakaran* when the pool was about to be used. There was also a considerable population of more animate objects. The small black squiggly mosquito larvae were numerous and were accompanied by other, less easily identifiable, denizens and several bobbing clusters of tree frog spawn. However, nobody took the least notice of all these except when they provided interesting diversions in becoming lodged in various parts of the girls' costumes.

Gail's stepfather and mother, Tony and Elaine, were most hospitable and put on endless supplies of food and drink. They were also enthusiastic and very knowledgeable about the local wild life. So the day passed very pleasantly, but I had to be back on Meeriabedde that evening and soon found myself alone once more, motoring back up the Wellawaya-Koslanda road, wondering how and when I was going to be able to find myself a girlfriend.

Not feeling able any longer to take advantage of the tennis group at the Koslanda Hospital, the social possibilities close at hand to Meeriabedde were meagre. Apart from Kunay, who did not socialise, the only young SDs I knew on the neighbouring estates were Reggie, high up in his fastness on Mousakellie, and John, who was the senior SD on Poonagalla. As I already knew, Reggie's establishment was accessible from Meeriabedde only with considerable effort, but John inhabited the Cabaragalla Division of Poonagalla, through which I passed whenever I visited Bandarawela. A long, thin and fair-haired individual with a nice sense of humour, he had spent his childhood on estates in the Nilgiri Hills of south India and had spoken Tamil as early as he had English. He could also reproduce perfectly the local 'chee-chee' English accent and phraseology and had a fund of entertaining anecdotes. Being rather older and more experienced than me, I found him both interesting and convivial, and I sometimes called on him in the evenings.

On Poonagalla there was an old canvas-topped Landrover which was a model fitted with a manual accelerator control on the dashboard. John sometimes used this vehicle, and a favourite trick of his was to set the speed with the manual control and drive along with the hood down reading a newspaper while a companion in the passenger seat unobtrusively steered. The expressions on the faces of passers-by, and especially of on-coming drivers, were apparently most entertaining.

A squash court had been built near the Poonagalla Big Bungalow which could be used by the senior estate staff. Although not an expert, John found a spare racket and introduced me to the game, which we subsequently played occasionally and badly. However, it was a pleasant social exercise and gave an excuse to retire to John's bungalow for a beer afterwards. On one occasion he seemed less lively than usual and said it was because he had had a bad night. There was a nearly full moon and apparently the pie dogs in the labour lines below John's bungalow had kept up a constant barrage of barking until he felt he could bear it no longer. Seizing his repeating shotgun, he rushed out onto the lawn in his pyjamas and loosed off the entire magazine into the night, after which he retired back to bed with some satisfaction. However, just as he was dozing off, there was a commotion outside and he could hear the night watchman trying to convince somebody that the *dorai* was in fact quite safe. Re-emerging from the bungalow, John had found the Conductor at the head of a motley fighting force which he had rapidly assembled under the impression that the bungalow was being attacked by *kalawanies* and had arrived to rescue John from their clutches. When they had been calmed, reassured and dispersed to the lines, taking their knives and sword sticks with them, the pie dogs had started up again. So John had not had much sleep.

Although I did not know him very well, Reggie kindly invited several people, including John and myself, to his bungalow for a curry supper. John and I decided to try to get through to Mousakellie directly from the Meeriabedde Upper Division, which would save us a good hour's drive. Leaving his Jowatt Javelin (a rather superior car) at my bungalow, we set off in my Morris Minor and slowly climbed the hairpin bends of the zig-zag road to the Upper Division. At one point the bend was so sharp that I had to reverse the car to get round it, with John keeping a lookout through the gloom to see that I did not back into a rock or over the edge. After passing through the Upper Division we came to the barrier at the border of the two estates. We had arranged with Reggie that this would be left unlocked and so I hopped out to open it. No sooner was it open than the car surged forward and accelerated up the hill, with me in hot pursuit. When I eventually caught up, I found John in fits of laughter, thinking it a huge joke, although I couldn't see that it was so frightfully funny. After that, I was careful to remove the key from the ignition whenever I got out. We then climbed about another 1,000 ft. on the loose gravel of the Mousakellie cart roads before we reached Reggie's bungalow, where an excellent (but all male) party was in full swing. Large quantities of beer were consumed, topped up with whisky, gin, curry, and whatever else Reggie had available, so that when the time came to leave, it was somehow quite difficult to locate the car. This was rendered more so by the night being very dark and the fact that for some reason it had been thought a good idea to remove most of the light bulbs from Reggie's bungalow and float them in the beer mugs. Nevertheless, eventually John and I were successful and, leaving one or two guests reclining in the flowerbeds, we carefully retraced our route down the mountain. On such occasions my head always seemed miraculously to clear as soon as I got into the car, perhaps because of the sobering realisation that one slight mistake could send me hurtling off the steep and serpentine roads into space and oblivion. We reached my bungalow again sometime in the early hours of the morning ready, like good SDs, for muster at 6 a.m.

Poonagalla Group was one of the few remaining estates still managed by members of the European family which owned most of the shares. The PD, Gorton Coombe, was an immensely tall man who had taken over management of the estate from his father. Poonagalla occupies the upper reaches of a steep-sided valley only slightly larger than that of Meeriabedde. Also like Meeriabedde, a small river runs down the valley and, after it leaves the tea-covered slopes behind, it leaps in cascades down several granite cliffs between steep valley sides covered with tall *maana* grass and dotted with small trees. Shooting over the final and highest cliff, the river transforms into the white floating ribbon of the Diyaluma Falls. Higher up, a channel in the rock forms a chute into a large and deep pool bordered with smooth granite rocks on one side and fringed by overhanging branches on the other. This could be reached by a path leading off the little road which wound down the valley from Poonagalla to Koslanda village. Known to everyone as the Poonagalla Pool, it made an excellent swimming place and picnic spot, where many a Sunday was pleasantly spent cooking sausages and bacon, swimming, and scrambling down the river to sit admiring the stupendous view over the low country jungles from the top of the Diyaluma Falls.

Being well away from human habitation and not on the way to anywhere, it was one of the few local places where one could picnic in relative privacy, free from the usual little throng of smiling children who would usually materialise in even the remotest spots and watch one's every movement with avid interest. It was therefore a good place to entertain any eligible females who visited the district. Owing to the intense competition, it was very difficult to make a date on one's own, but it was more practicable to make up a picnic and swimming party. Rosalind had appeared with her parents at the Haldummulla Club one Sunday while her father (who was a naval officer stationed at Trincomalee) was spending some local leave at the naval establishment not far away at Diyatalawa. Short dark hair framed her face and I noticed with approval that she had a good figure, which was well displayed by her bathing costume the following weekend when she attended a Poonagalla Pool picnic party. Being about my age, she did not seem to find me too young or too inexperienced, and we got on very well. Also present on this occasion was Julia, Nancy's daughter, who was out from England for her summer holiday. A few days later Monty and Nancy gave a party at Dambatenne for the benefit of Julia and Rosalind, inviting most of the young SDs of the district.

*The Diyaluma Falls viewed from the Koslanda-Wellawaya road.*

The Dambatenne Big Bungalow had been carefully built by Sir Thomas Lipton on a most spectacular site. Surrounded by a wide expanse of gardens, the bungalow occupied a gently sloping area just above a granite cliff, perhaps 100 ft. high, and the magnificent gardens swept down to end at the crest of the cliff. Beyond this, the view over the distant lowlands stretched away to the sea on the far horizon. Monty and Nancy dispensed good cheer and large quantities of drink and food were provided. At this point the grey-haired and dignified appu, who had evidently been superintending the production of the latter, appeared with a tray of small, crescent-shaped curry puffs and other canapés (always known as 'short-eats'). Unluckily for him, he happened to pass close to Monty who, on his fifth whisky, was holding forth on the topic of how one should keep the bungalow servants under control and not let them get notions above their station.

'Look', he exclaimed, shooting out a hand and seizing the appu by the hair, 'he respects me because I don't stand any nonsense, do I, Ramanathen?'

'No, Sir', replied the unfortunate Ramanathen from a semi-bowed position, deftly saving the tray of short-eats.

'And you like to know who's boss, don't you?'

'Yes, Sir'.

'There you are!' cried Monty, releasing the wretched Ramanathen, as though this was incontrovertible proof of the efficacy of his management style, 'Treat 'em tough and they'll love you for it'.

I was secretly horrified at this exchange, and particularly at the physical contact and humiliation of the appu for no good reason at so public a gathering. I had been brought up always to treat the bungalow servants with consideration and respect, and this confirmed my unfavourable opinion of Monty's ways. However, I did not dwell on this very long, being intent on chatting up Rosalind. A hi-fi set was playing dance music which Rosalind and Julia, being well up with the latest hits in England, found amazingly dated, but which I was quite unable to judge. Nevertheless, a space was cleared and we danced, on my part with unaccustomed delight. Julia and her partner then suggested a walk in the garden, which sounded like a good idea. Rosalind was willing, so we sauntered out hand in hand into the cool darkness of the lawns and shrubbery. In my state of excitement I must have gripped her hand too hard, for she exclaimed 'It's all right, - I'm not going to run away!' I cannot remember how long we spent in the darkness, but it was all too short as far as I was concerned. The strains of well-known tunes drifted distantly to us from the lighted windows as we held each other close. We said very little, but we exchanged a kiss or two before returning to the lights of the bungalow and the chattering throng. The party was coming to an end. Rosalind and her parents were due to return to Trincomalee the following day and she asked if I could visit them there for a few days. I said I would love to and would try to get leave, but I knew that in reality it was a forlorn hope. Trincomalee was a full day's journey away and I would need several days' leave, which I could not obtain. We exchanged a letter or two, but she soon returned to England and I never saw her again.

# Round the tea *totum* 8

It is said that if all Scots returned to their homeland, there would scarcely be enough room to accommodate them all. They certainly formed a disproportionately large part of the expatriate population in most British colonies and Ceylon was no exception. The Scots had been prominent among the early planting pioneers and this was reflected in many of the estate names, especially in the higher hills, where many a Scot christened his new enterprise after familiar places in his own native land. Names such as Stirling and Strathspey, Caledonia and Braemore, Logie and Tillicoultry, Balmoral and Glen Devon, tripped off the tongue and to me they now evoke the green highlands of Ceylon just as in former times they reminded lonely pioneers of the Scotland they had left behind.

Estates usually had two different names, one English (or Scottish) and one Tamil or Sinhala, depending on the language of the majority of the labour force. Occasionally there were three names, one in each language. Meeriabedde was known to Tamils as *Sinna Kanackie* ('Little Piece'), while Needwood was *Palia Totum* ('Old Estate'). Estate or division names were sometimes the same as the local village or area. In these cases, although the pronunciation might be virtually the same, it was common to differentiate between estate and place in the spelling of the transliteration. For example, the Haldumulla Division of Needwood was spelt differently to Haldummulla, the local village, and Berragalla was the neighbouring estate while Berragala was the mountain on which it was situated.

Perhaps because of the large number of planters who were Scottish or of Scottish descent, there was always a party organised for New Year's Eve - although it was never referred to as Hogmanay. Usually this was one of the largest (and often one of the best) parties in the District calendar. For the first New Year's Eve during my time on Meeriabedde, I was invited to a party by the Officer Commanding H.M.Cy.S. Diyatalawa. This sounds very naval and indeed it was. Diyatalawa was situated in the dry and undulating country in the centre of the Uva Basin and had a station on the railway line about mid way between Haputale and Bandarawela. The settlement had begun in the early years of the nineteenth century as a Wesleyan mission but was later developed as a military convalescent station for troops. During the period of the Boer War of 1899-1902 it had also acted as a prison camp, holding up to 5,000 Boer prisoners of war. Later still it became not only a convalescent station but also a recreation centre and a major base for all three of the armed services. I am not sure whether these operated independent units at Diyatalawa or whether there was unified command of the station. However, my invitation came from the naval commander, who at that time was still a British naval officer (no doubt on secondment to the Royal Ceylon Navy). I had not realised that it was the custom in British naval establishments ashore to name and run them as though they were ships;

hence H.M.Cy.S. Diyatalawa. The invitation was rather grand-looking with gilt edges and specified evening dress ('black tie'), so on New Year's Eve I attended at the officers' mess with expectations of a rather formal and stuffy evening.

Occasions requiring the wearing of dinner jackets were quite common and usual. A black evening dress suit was a very necessary part of a planter's wardrobe. It was also quite common to embellish this with coloured cummerbunds round the waist or, especially in warm locations, to substitute a white tuxedo jacket (often made of a shiny fabric known as 'sharkskin') for the black dinner jacket. I acquired all these items in due course. For special occasions it was not uncommon for both sexes to wear flowers of some kind and, as carnations and gardenias flourished in many upcountry gardens, these often featured as buttonholes.

On arrival, I found that most of the other local planters, European and Ceylonese, were also present, and numerous officers of the Royal Ceylon Navy in dress uniform. However, I was pleasantly surprised. Drinks of all kinds were supplied free and, as far as I could make out, on demand, so it was not very long before a lively party was in full swing. Although, as usual, there was a dearth of single women, the evening passed very pleasantly and the New Year seemed to arrive all too soon. The band played Auld Lang Sine and those who were capable of doing so joined in an eightsome reel. These were a minority of those present, partly because most of the Ceylonese and many of the Europeans did not know the dance, but also because a large proportion were by this time, in Wodehouseian terms, pickled to the gills. The proceedings eventually came to a rather chaotic end, and I departed on a slow journey home leaving various fellow guests propped against sundry solid objects in the hope that the cold night air would gradually restore them to normality before morning.

I had not been one of those joining in the eightsome reel as I knew the devastation which could be wrought by a well-meaning but choreographically ignorant (and slightly inebriated) dancer. Scottish country dances were often included in the dance repertoire at upcountry clubs, although it always seemed to me that the English were rather keener on them than the Scots. In any case, those who did not know the dances missed out on much of the fun and so, especially as I enjoyed the music and rather liked the unusual dance names, I made a point of learning the steps and sequences. I gradually became proficient at the commoner dances and soon was enthusiastically participating in the country dance waltz, Strip the Willow (or Widow, as the wags would have it), the Dashing White Sergeant, Hamilton House, strathspeys, and even, at last, the Eightsome Reel. However, many of the more esoteric dances, with names such as Broun's Reel and Mrs McLeod's Rant, remained beyond me and I left them to the experts.

By the time my twentieth birthday came round I felt quite well established, both on Meeriabedde and in the Haputale District. I knew the daily routine and how the various tasks on the estate should be done. I knew by name all the junior estate staff, the kanganies, and many of the labourers, and my Tamil was sufficiently fluent for me to feel at ease in dealing with the every day matters which were my responsibility. I was, by a year or two, probably the youngest European SD in the Province of Uva, if not in the whole of Ceylon, and I grew accustomed to feeling I was the baby of any social gathering. However, I now knew all the European planters in the Haputale and Bandarawela areas and many of the Ceylonese planters as well. I had also acquired a circle of planter friends to whose bungalows I was often invited for dinner, or for a curry lunch on Sundays. As my birthday fell during a period of slack work during the dry weather in August, I decided to combine a small celebration with repaying my friends' hospitality by giving a party.

The bungalow lawn which had been levelled and replanted with 'blue grass' so painstakingly by Palaniandy was now a fine and close sward, so I thought it would be a good idea to centre the activities on the veranda and garden, with lights in the trees. I bought a long length of lighting wire, bulb sockets, a three-pin plug, and connected them all up. However, on throwing the switch I was disappointed. Instead of bright fairy lights dangling from the branches, all I got was a dim glow which did not look at all festive. I took down the wire and checked all the connections, but the result was the same: what to do? I summoned Mr Rajaratnam, the estate electrician, from the factory and explained the problem. In ten minutes he had put matters right and explained to me that I had connected the bulbs in series instead of in parallel, which I should have realised from the elementary physics I had done at school. The next thing was the food and drink. Drink was easy; I simply obtained crates of beer and soft drinks from Karamaraj Bros. on a drink or return basis. Then there was the food. I explained what I wanted to Gomez, who made me out a list of necessary supplies. He seemed not at all put out or intimidated by the task or the extra work and, on the contrary, appeared to relish the challenge. I invited all the younger people in the District, including many young SDs and some of the younger PDs and their wives, but no unattached girls were available.

The event was a great success. Music from my new record player reached the garden through the wide open sitting room windows and even Scottish dances were done on the lawn under the lights hanging from the big tulip tree. Gomez excelled himself and produced an excellent spread of party food, the skills for cooking which he must have acquired during his long previous career (into which I never enquired too deeply) as appu in households much larger and more prestigious than mine. I rewarded him and, indeed, Arumugam also, with a suitable financial bonus.

Bill Horne had turned out to be a reasonable and fairly pleasant boss (although he had off days) and in general he seemed to be pleased with my performance. At least, he seldom offered criticism or praise but just let me get on with the work. Certain things never failed to amuse him, as with the ritual of Choking Off the Dogs.

The estate Landrover in which Bill Horne did his rounds of Meeriabedde and Mahakanda was a rather ancient canvas-topped short wheelbase model. Although the estate driver kept the bodywork polished and the interior in good repair, the engine was showing its age by its addiction to the consumption of large quantities of oil which, converted into clouds of dense black smoke, subsequently emerged from the exhaust. This happened especially after the Landrover had coasted down a hill, at the moment when Bill Horne accelerated to tackle the next rise. When he was visiting the Lower Division he often asked me to meet him at the Big Bungalow and we would set off down the cart road. The road first descended to a hairpin bend near the rocky seepage where in season a patch of ground orchids flourished in some profusion, and then continued down to the bridge over the river. Just across the bridge were some labour lines in which lived numerous assorted pie dogs. Seeing us descending on the other side of the valley, the dogs would emerge as a pack in full cry and high-pitched voice to assail the Landrover at the bridge, baring their teeth and snapping at the tyres. Having carefully conserved the oily mixture in the exhaust system all the way down the hill, this was the moment that Bill Horne had been waiting for and he firmly depressed the accelerator. We shot forward whilst simultaneously a black, oily cloud that would have done credit to a battleship smokescreen blossomed behind us. Looking back we could see the melee of dogs suddenly immobilised and almost obscured, coughing and spluttering in the inky fumes. The dogs never seemed to learn the consequences of chasing the Landrover and the result never failed to elicit chortles of mirth from Bill Horne.

The estate hospital was situated just a short distance above my bungalow and, as part of my 'patch', it was my responsibility to see that the place was kept clean and in proper order. Of course I was not expected to supervise any medical aspects, which were the prerogative of the estate Dispenser, who had some rudimentary medical training. The principal condition presented by the hospital patients seemed to be childbirth, but cuts and broken limbs, and the commonest infectious diseases could all be dealt with, while first aid could be given for more serious ailments before transferral to the hospital at Koslanda. One day Bill Horne decided he should inspect the hospital and asked me to meet him there at one thirty in the afternoon. I knew it would take me less than three minutes to get to the hospital, so at one twenty I was unconcerned that I had not finished the fruit salad I was having as a sweet for lunch. Suddenly there was a crunch of heavy wheels in the bungalow yard, revving of the Landrover engine, and the tall and irate figure of Bill Horne appeared in the doorway.

'David!', he bellowed, 'You're supposed to meet me at the hospital!'

'Yes, Sir', I said, rising from the table, 'At half-past one. It's now only just one twenty.'

'Don't argue, boy,' was the reply, 'I expect you to be there when I arrive. Get into the Landrover and come with me.'

I felt somewhat bewildered at this display of what seemed to me to be gross unreasonableness. However, I knew that further protest would only make matters worse and would do me no good, so I got in, leaving the remains of my lunch on the table, unconsumed, to be cleared by Gomez. We continued up to the hospital, found the Dispenser, and made a tour of inspection. Fortunately this did not turn up any major horrors and the worst discovery was a posse of cockroaches comfortably ensconced in cracks of the 'operating table'. Bill Horne seemed almost pleased to have discovered something amiss. Seizing a bottle of Jeyes Fluid (of which there were always copious supplies in the hospital), he applied liberal quantities to the areas sheltering the offending livestock which emerged, waving their feelers, in a state of consternation greater than my own at the interruption of my lunch. I knew how they felt.

'Look at the little buggers; running like hell!' he observed with approval as the cockroaches hurriedly vacated their quarters, dropped to the floor and disappeared.

The Dispenser and I got a doubtlessly well deserved ticking-off, but this event seemed to restore Bill Horne's good humour and by the end of the afternoon, after another successful exercise in choking off pursuing dogs, he was back to his usual self.

On upcountry estates one was a long way from normal standards of European medical care, which were certainly not to be found in the small district hospitals such as that at Koslanda. The big agency houses which employed many planters in Uva (such as my own employers, George Steuart & Co.) contributed to the Uva Medical Scheme. This Scheme employed a European doctor who was based in Badulla and was available to attend the planter employees of the contributing firms. The incumbent, Dr Ellis, had already retired from one medical career and seemed about ready to retire again. He always looked rather frail, but I do not think he was professionally very hard pressed, which perhaps he had anticipated when he took the post. However, he held a regular clinic at the Bow Club, particularly to give anti-typhoid and other inoculations. It was considered only prudent to keep up one's typhoid immunity, if nothing else, and I attended Dr Ellis's clinic annually to have my 'booster' immunisation. This was normally done after tennis at about 6 p.m. By the end of the evening my arm would have stiffened up so much that it made driving difficult and painful, besides which by this time I would have developed a headache and a mild temperature. However, in spite of the frequent need to turn the steering from lock to lock, it was possible to drive home single-handed, whilst changing gear as little as possible.

Dentists were a rare species and outside Colombo existed only in the largest towns such as Kandy and Nuwara Eliya, although sorely needed by the betel-chewing local population. Most planters took the opportunity to visit the dentist on their occasional trips to the capital, but it could be difficult if an emergency occurred between visits. Sometimes this could be dealt with by extraction, performed at the local hospital, but for more sophisticated treatment there was usually no alternative to making the slow journey to Colombo, nursing the aching tooth. One Friday an ache developed in one of my upper front teeth. I had never suffered with toothache before and wondered what I should do about it, as there did not seem to be any prospect of visiting Colombo for a week or more. I felt an almost academic interest as the ache gradually got worse and I wondered how bad it could become. As time went by the throbbing increased, a swelling appeared on the inside of my jaw, and I became fairly sure that I must be suffering from an abscess. However, just as I determined to consult my friend, Dr Gunasena, at the Koslanda hospital, I felt pus start to seep from around the affected tooth, the throbbing and ache subsided and the swelling diminished. The abscess had burst and I did nothing more about it, but when I eventually attended the dentist a month or so later, he declared that I had been lucky not to have had any complications. Apparently the tooth was now dead, and bits gradually broke off it in subsequent years.

Meeriabedde was certainly remote, but this did not really worry me as I was enjoying my independence and also I was not short of things to do. I started developing and printing my own films, for which I turned the spare bedroom into a temporary darkroom, and found this very creative and satisfying. I wrote more articles for the Wild Life Protection Society's magazine, and I started making botanical paintings of the local wild flora. However, it was a lonely situation and what I really felt I needed was a dog.

I have always liked dogs, but I have also felt that one should not purchase a dog any more than one should purchase a friend. So many dogs need homes that it seems particularly selfish and misguided to purchase a pedigree dog from a breeder who in effect is increasing the dog population for profit while depriving others of what could have been good homes. So I bided my time while keeping my ears open for anybody wanting to find a dog a home. When I had been on Meeriabedde about six months I heard that Chris and Anne were finding their dog tiresome and might not wish to keep him. Chris was the senior SD on Dambatenne and apparently had a lot of office work to do, so that often he could not exercise the dog in walking round the estate. At the first opportunity I sought out Chris and Anne at the club and made enquiries. Yes, they said, their Frodo was a beagle about one year old and needed lots of exercise which they could not always provide. He had taken to going off on his own, sometimes for several days at a time, and they felt he might be happier with someone who could tire him out every day. Would I have him?

I was delighted at the prospect and looked forward to the next club day when I should take charge of him. At that time I had not read Tolkein's famous trilogy *The Lord of the Rings*, then fairly recently published. 'Frodo' therefore meant nothing to me and I misheard his name as 'Fredo'. So Fredo he became and remained so all the time he was with me. Although later I read *The Lord of the Rings* and realised my mistake, it was by then much too late to make any correction - and anyway his character was nothing like his namesake. In fact his main interests in life were hunting and sex; most other things came well down his list of priorities.

Wednesday duly came round again and at the Bow Club I met Chris and Anne laden with Fredo's personal belongings: bowl, brush and lead. They opened the door of their car and out jumped a waggling and rather stocky hound in black, white and tan who, after a cursory sniff at my hand, immediately set about exploring the car park with his nose firmly to the ground and tail bolt upright with the tip curling forwards over his back.

On the way home later that evening, Fredo scrambled up onto the front passenger seat so that he could put his nose out of the window. This kept him fully occupied as he assessed and catalogued the numerous passing smells and he did not seem to be in the least concerned that he was going into the unknown with a strange new owner.

Fredo immediately took over the bungalow at Meeriabedde and became my constant companion. He also ingratiated himself with Gomez and Arumugam, who liked his open and friendly nature and were fascinated with one of his accomplishments, of which I slightly disapproved. Chris and Anne had evidently taught him to 'beg', which I find undignified in a dog, preferring that requests should be made in a normal doggy manner rather than in anthropomorphic style. However, Fredo was never loath to perform and if ever he wanted anything, up on his hind legs he would go, with a quizzical expression on his face, and usually he got what he wanted. He was a solidly-built dog with a deep chest, - perhaps rather too heavy for a pure-bred beagle. Nevertheless, his nose was superb and, except when sex got the upper hand, it ruled his life. He was in his element during my tours of the Division and must have covered three times the distance I did in his pursuit of squirrels, mongooses, hares and other small game. Whenever we flushed an animal from the tea or it crossed the path in front of us, he would be after it in a flash, giving tongue in authentic fashion. I could follow his progress from afar because the white tip of his tail was usually just high enough to show above the 'plucking table' level of the tea bushes and I would see it zig-zag this way and that like an animated periscope as his excited yelps disappeared into the distance. Unlike Haggis, he very seldom actually caught anything; the chase was all that mattered. Eventually, from afar, I would see him returning, panting somewhat and tongue lolling out, following his tracks with his nose still in charge if not always to the ground. If I called, he would look up, but often could not see me. Puzzled, he would then revert to navigation by nose, eventually arriving at his point of departure, from which he would then follow my scent until he caught up with me for a joyful reunion.

*Fredo.*

The estate lorry driver was another of Fredo's fans. I often hitched a ride in the lorry to another part of the Division when my route coincided with its rounds collecting and transporting leaf to the factory. There were no doors to the cab, and Fredo and I would scramble onto the bench seat where he would take up his position between me and the driver. As we slowly wound our way round the contours of the cart road, Fredo would sit with his eyes glued to the view ahead. Whenever, he fancied he saw something of interest, perhaps a squirrel, another dog, or even a moving branch, he would slowly rise to the begging position, much to the amusement and delight of the driver, who several times only narrowly avoided having a nasty accident through watching Fredo's antics instead of the road. Never taking his eyes off the subject of interest, Fredo would utter small yelps of excitement or quiet growls, as appropriate, and sometimes would have to be restrained. On one occasion a squirrel suddenly leaped across the road in front of us, only just avoiding the lorry's wheels, and disappeared down a deep culvert. This was too much for Fredo, who hurled himself out of the cab in pursuit and likewise disappeared down the culvert. Thinking he must surely have damaged himself severely, I stopped the lorry and hurried down to see what had happened. At first I could see nothing, but after a few moments Fredo emerged from the opposite end of the culvert, limping slightly but not much the worse for wear, and indeed he seldom seemed to come to much harm despite his occasionally reckless behaviour. The squirrel, needless to say, had disappeared.

Maxime Horne had a pair of miniature dachshunds, of which the female was particularly small and dainty. Fredo never seemed to have much time for his Teutonic brethren, but on our visits to the Big Bungalow he often had to suffer their barking barrages, which he studiously ignored. On one occasion we were in the garden with the Hornes when a group of largish pie dogs from the nearest labour lines hove into sight at the end of the drive. Fredo took no notice, but the two dachs rushed out, barking their heads off. The pie dogs, which normally would have avoided entering the bungalow precincts, could not believe their luck at these two dainty morsels actually rushing towards their jaws. Baring sets of large teeth and barking ferociously, they came rushing up the drive to meet them. About half way down the drive, and observing the pie dogs now rapidly closing on them to the sound of ferocious snarls, the dachs suddenly realised their mistake, turned about and rushed headlong for home, shrieking with fright. It was a near thing, but the male dachs just made it to Maxime's arms in time for her to frighten off the pie dogs with a large stick. The female, however, was nowhere to be seen and, fearing the worst, we set off down the drive in search of her. Drawing a blank, we were returning towards the bungalow when a slight scrabbling noise drew my attention to the orifice of a small drain pipe set in the roadside bank. From this, slowly and with extreme caution, the back end of a very small and very frightened dachshund was beginning to emerge. As she fitted the pipe like a shell in the barrel of a gun, her progress was somewhat slow. Eventually, however, she wriggled out and one felt there should have been an audible pop as she emerged. Chastened and rather muddy, she was nevertheless unscathed, and was scooped up by Maxime with cries of relief. After this incident, I noticed that the two dachs were much less liable to bark at visitors, much to Fredo's relief, and never again attempted to chase pie dogs.

I was now making fairly regular day trips to the low country jungles to the south or east. At Lahugalla Tank I had noticed that there appeared to be a heronry at the far end, about a mile distant. The white blobs of numerous egrets could be seen with the naked eye and with binoculars it was clear that several species of egret, heron and cormorant were nesting there in low bushes on the edge of taller forest. The water level was high in the first months of the year, at the end of the north-east monsoon, and the heron nesting season coincided with this. One Sunday I decided to try to visit the nesting colony and set off from Meeriabedde at first light as the resident pied robin was pouring out his fine song from the roof of the bungalow. On arrival at Lahugalla I left the car under some trees near the irrigation department lines and inspected the shore of the tank. The water was indeed as high as I had ever seen it, but almost the entire surface was covered with floating grass, water lilies, lotus, and other vegetation. It looked wonderful, in fact, as many of the aquatic plants were in bloom, with blue and white water lilies, pink lotus and the yellow flowers of another plant which had swollen floats at intervals along its stem. The shortest route to the heronry seemed to be round the eastern side of the tank, but an arm of water extended for some distance in this direction and would involve a considerable detour. This area was not always submerged and I knew that the depth was not great. Perhaps I could wade across?

Gathering my camera and binoculars into a bag which I slung round my shoulders, I found a stick which would do as a support and approached the water's edge. I had a good look round but, apart from a pheasant-tailed jacana, looking very dapper and tripping daintily over the lily pads with its long toes, no movement was visible. I knew there were crocs at Lahugalla, as at most of the wilder jungle tanks, but I had never seen any here and I guessed that even if one was in the area, it would be unlikely to attack, so I planted my stick in the shallows and stepped in. The bottom was muddy and shelved gently as I progressed, but the main impediment was the mass of floating vegetation. Slowly I pushed my way forwards and the depth gradually increased, first to my knees, then half way up my thighs and then I started to find my shorts dipping in at each step. Pushing through the water lily stalks and clumps of grass, I began to find that the depth was no longer increasing and slowly it became perceptibly shallower until soon I emerged dripping on the grassy farther shore. It had not been quite waist deep, but not far from it. I picked various bits of flotsam off my legs and inspected them carefully for leeches but, rather surprisingly, there were none that I could see, although I was somewhat anxious that one could have looped its way up into my pants. A quick inspection again revealed all clear, so I hitched up my bag and entered the forest along a game trail.

At this point the tall forest came nearly down to the water's edge. The sun, which had been hot while I had been wading across the inlet, now retreated behind clouds which had built up unnoticed, and the sky became overcast. In the deep shade under the trees the light was dim and gloomy. There was little undergrowth, but the ground was marshy in low-lying areas and I had to skirt round tongues of water encroaching into the forest from the brimming tank. My plan was to make a wide arc and rejoin the tank somewhere near its northern end, which I hoped would not be far from the heronry. I lost sight of the forest margin and squelched along in my wet shoes, feeling a little chilled. After about 20 minutes I became aware that I was no longer really sure in which direction I should be heading. Trying to suppress a feeling of alarm, I stopped and tried to get my bearings. The forest stretched into the gloomy distance in every direction. There were several marshy patches nearby, but none seemed actually connected with the tank. I listened. In the distance I could hear movements among the foliage, - probably a troop of monkeys, or could it be elephants? Lahugalla was renowned as an excellent place to see them. No, I could hear a wanderoo-like hoot. I decided to cast about in various directions from a recognisable large tree. On the second or third cast I came upon a flooded area which I felt must be connected with the tank and began to skirt the edge of the water. In a few minutes I saw more open country ahead and suddenly I emerged from the trees to find I was on the edge of the tank.

*Nest of median egret with three young, Lahugalla, January 1958.*

To my right I could now see the heronry, about 100 yards away, with much activity going on to an accompanying hubbub of squawks and cries. To my left I could look out across the full length of the tank and could just discern the irrigation buildings in the distance amongst the trees. The whole area of the heronry was flooded to a depth of about two feet, but many of the nests were at or only a little above water level, perched in scrubby bushes. Getting out my camera, I slowly waded over to the colony. Most of the nests belonged to egrets of various kinds, but there were a few cormorants, some night herons and one or two grey herons. The adults flapped off with raucous cries as I approached and I found that many nests contained partly fledged young, although a few still had eggs. This was the first time I had ever visited a heronry and I was fascinated and absorbed. I started taking pictures of the nestlings, which stared at me looking startled, some with tousled tufts of down still clinging to the tops of their heads, giving them a 'just permed' look. All were vibrating their throats in anxiety (or perhaps as a cooling measure). It certainly was hot and I could feel the sweat trickling down inside my shirt as I moved amongst the bushes. Some nestlings had come to grief, either by accidentally falling from the nest or perhaps in trying to escape from some predator, their bedraggled bodies floating in the water amongst feathers, droppings and other bits of debris. In fact it was not only hot but decidedly smelly. Eventually I ran out of film and decided I had caused enough disturbance for one day. I started back and this time kept nearer to the edge of the tank, making sure I knew my bearings. The return wade also passed without mishap and, after another leech inspection, I started my return journey.

On my way back through Moneragala I decided to call in at Kumarawatte to see whether Gail might be at home. She was not, but her mother and stepfather kindly pressed me to stay for dinner and seemed interested to hear about the heronry. The household at Kumarawatte was always full of animals, with several dogs and cats usually in residence. On this occasion there seemed to be more cats than usual. Dinner was a roast, and Gail's stepfather carved a large joint of meat for the houseboy to serve. He then sat down with his back to the joint. Sometime later, my attention was distracted by one of the cats leaping onto the sideboard and starting to lap the gravy. I wondered whether I should call attention to this activity, but Gail's mother could see quite well what was happening and did not seem to think it unusual, so I let the cat continue to enjoy its meal while I got on with mine. However, I did decline a second helping. This particular cat, a young ginger tom, was evidently a skilful operator in more ways than one. Gail's mother and stepfather apparently always slept with their bedroom windows wide open and the cat often came and made himself comfortable on the bed. This did not make for a restful night for the bed's slumbering owners, as bats frequently flitted in and out through the open windows. These the cat often caught with lightening leaps as they swooped low over the bed and the ensuing struggle and crunching repast were apparently considerably disturbing to the rightful occupants.

The day at Lahugalla had been wonderful, but I felt that to reach bird colonies such as the one I had visited I really needed some kind of boat. But what kind? Boats were not easily obtainable upcountry, they were expensive, and in any case I needed one I could transport with the Morris Minor, preferably without a trailer, which would have been very awkward on the steep and twisty roads upcountry and the rough roads of the low country. I decided that some sort of canoe would be the best design and that I would build it myself.

The garage at the Meeriabedde Small Bungalow was built out over the slope of the hill and was wide enough to hold two cars. Like the bungalow, it was solidly built of dressed granite blocks and roofed with corrugated iron sheets, but there were no doors as car theft was almost unknown and they were not necessary for protection against the weather. Some of the space enclosed by the retaining walls had been used for a small room beneath part of the garage floor. This was thus a kind of cellar, but most of it was not below ground and it had a window facing onto the tea below the garden boundary. It was reached by a short flight of stone stairs at the back of the garage. I decided that this would make a fine workroom and in it I assembled such carpentry tools as I had. I also got hold of some wood which I thought would do for the frame of the canoe. This was grevillea and may have come from the off-cuts of the timber sawn up on Mousakellie, which by this time was reasonably well seasoned. I worked away in my spare time and soon I had assembled a frame consisting of a main timber with curved sections at stem and stern, to which were attached ribs which I had laboriously cut from single pieces of wood. This looked quite like the pictures I remembered having seen of wooden boats being constructed in shipyards and I began to wonder what I should use to cover the sides. I felt quite proud of my handiwork and admired it from all angles. I imagined myself paddling away on the low country tanks and able to approach the water bird colonies for close observation. How stable would it be when afloat? I looked at it again and was suddenly assailed by an awful doubt: was I right to have designed the canoe to be semi-circular in cross-section?

The more I thought about it, the more certain I became that a semi-circular cross-section was not a good idea; indeed it seemed obvious that it would probably tip me out at the first wobble. Also, what should I use to cover the ribs? A clinker-built boat would be very heavy and I had no suitable timber for this. However, a few days earlier, I had happened to notice in the paper that Messrs Walker, Sons & Co. Ltd., the old-established Ceylon engineering firm, were advertising sheet aluminium at what seemed remarkably cheap prices. Why not use aluminium sheet for the sides of the boat? This would have the added advantage of being both light and easily worked. On the other hand, the tapering design of the canoe would make it difficult to cover neatly with the aluminium sheet and there would be long joins to waterproof. I therefore decided forthwith to abandon the canoe design in favour of a flat-bottomed punt-like craft. This was much easier to build and the sheet aluminium could easily be folded to cover the hull. I therefore ordered a couple of 8ft x 4ft sheets together with a large pair of tin snips for cutting it, some other tools which I felt I might need, and a gross of round-headed brass screws. Based on the size of the aluminium sheet, I therefore constructed a timber-framed punt, 2ft wide with sides 1ft deep and a total length of 9ft. I attached the aluminium skin to the frame with the brass screws and I sealed the joints and screw holes with bitumen. This craft would just fit through the gap between the boot and the interior of the Morris Minor when the rear seat had been removed and a couple of small notches made in the sides of the gap. Admittedly it did protrude rather a long way, but it was so light that the car remained quite stable. I painted the outside an environmentally friendly shade of green and brightened up the interior by painting the woodwork yellow.

To test the water-proofing of the joints, I took it down to a large pool in the river below the bungalow for its first launch. It came through this with flying colours and did not take in a drop of water, even when I scrambled in and crouched on the bottom boards, under the astonished gaze of a crowd of small children which had materialised on the bank. All good ships must have a name, but a suitable one for my brainchild eluded me for some time. Eventually, after practical navigational experience had revealed its tendency to move sideways, I settled on *Nandu* (the Tamil for crab). This I painted in Tamil characters either side of the bow (or at least, one end, since both ends were the same).

I now had the wherewithal to explore the low country tanks by water in more detail. One of my first trips, and one which remained a favourite, was to the small island in Tissa Wewa, which was about 400 yards off-shore opposite the Rest House. At this time there were no crowds of curious trippers and the island was undisturbed. A heronry had developed there on the bushes and low trees near the water's edge, and in the nesting season (during the early months of the year) the bushes were white with egrets, cormorants, night herons, and their droppings. This was a perennial source of interest to me and over the following years I made many visits to Tissa Island. I also explored the waters of many other tanks to which the *Nandu* gave me access.

After several trips with the *Nandu* I found that the design was by no means ideal. For a start it was very unstable when afloat and although I had constructed a couple of adequate thwarts, I had to sit or kneel on the bottom boards all the time in order to keep the centre of gravity as low as possible. Also it was awkward in sticking out of the car so far during transportation. It was not very long, therefore, before I embarked on a redesign and 'upgrade', as they say these days. First of all I cut the boat in half, fitted a bulkhead to each half, and hinged them together so that it could be shut up like a box for transportation, while metal ties secured with brass bolts and wing nuts ensured that this did not happen while afloat. In addition, I constructed an outrigger of the same design but half the size, which could be joined to the main hull with two lengths of Dexion slotted angle steel. When fitted, this made such an improvement in stability that I could even stand up in the boat, and for transportation the folded outrigger could be stowed inside the main hull together with the paddles, outrigger arms, bottom boards and removable thwarts. Although not very beautiful (and some of my uncouth friends rudely christened it the *Floating Coffin*), it was very practical for my circumstances.

*The Nandu at Lahugalla. This is after the modification and shows the two halves of the boat, but I am evidently using it without the outrigger.*

In my second year on Meeriabedde, the north-east monsoon continued late, with heavy deluges most afternoons. These often caught me far from shelter in some distant corner of the Division. With only my battered black umbrella for protection, I was frequently soaked to the skin and could acutely appreciate the discomfort of the field labourers as the paths became rivulets and the field drains, filling their silt pits, gushed forth into the streams. The small river in the valley bottom would suddenly swell to a terracotta-coloured raging torrent, no longer crossable by leaping from boulder to boulder.

One afternoon I was returning to my bungalow after heavy rain when a group of labourers came to me in a state of agitation. A child, they said, had fallen into the water and drowned, 'down there' they said, indicating the swollen river. I followed their direction and searched the river banks, where I soon came upon the body of a girl aged about ten, lying in shallow water. She was wearing a brown dress with full skirt, very usual attire for girls of her age, and she seemed to bear no marks or bruises. Her skin was pale in death with the palms of her hands white and crinkled from soaking in the cold water. At this point the river was nowhere more than a couple of feet deep and I wondered how the child could have drowned in such shallow water. Perhaps she had drowned higher up in one of the larger pools, or perhaps she had slipped and knocked herself unconscious on a rock. Was it really an accident? Wading in, I called to the labourers to come and help me lift the body from the water, but none would do so. I could not understand the reasons they gave, but only that they had some taboo on touching the dead girl, which I suspected had to do with differences in caste (although

106

they did not say so). Feeling impatient with them, and upset myself, I hurried to the muster ground nearby where I found one of the night watchmen (a Muslim of the Ceylon Moor community) and enlisted his help, at the same time sending for the estate lorry. With the watchman's assistance, I got the girl's body to the roadside, where a small knot of onlookers had gathered. We covered the body with somebody's spare cumbly, but nobody seemed to know who she was and there was no sign of any relatives. Eventually the lorry arrived and removed the body to the hospital, where I thankfully handed over responsibility to the dispenser and returned to my bungalow. I never did discover which family she came from or how the accident (if it was an accident) occurred.

Not long after this incident, I learned that Bill and Maxime Horne were soon to go to the UK on their long leave (or furlough) of six months. As the time for this approached, I also heard that apparently Bill Horne had accepted a new job to oversee the development of new tea estates in Mauritius and so would not be returning to Ceylon after his leave. He never mentioned this to me, even when I went to say goodbye to him and Maxime before they left, perhaps because he felt it inappropriate to discuss his movements with a lowly junior SD. Our employers, George Steuarts, also thought it quite unnecessary to inform me or 'Kunay' Kunanayagam, the senior SD who, like me, became aware of the situation only through his own grapevine. Naturally, I felt a keen interest in these developments, not least because I wondered who my new PD would be, but felt I could not ask Bill Horne. I was not left in doubt for long, however, as there was no shortage of ready informants at the Club, from whom I learned that Bill Horne was to be replaced on Meeriabedde by Bob Fleming, whom I did not know.

'What's he like?' I asked, being more than anxious to know.

'Oh, not a bad sort of chap', my informant replied, swilling his gin and tonic around his glass, 'Before he took up planting he used to play the trumpet in Sasha's Band at the Galle Face, just after the war, - he came in very useful for carol singing.'

I imagined my new PD somehow tootling his way around the estate, trumpet in hand, and wondered how much his musical past now featured in his planting life. When he arrived, however, Bob Fleming turned out to be a very normal looking planter, without any signs of musical genius. Of about middle age and height, his hair had thinned to give him a bald patch on top of his head and this was compensated for by a thick moustache. I found him pleasant to deal with as he was much less formal in his manner than Bill Horne and quite jovial, but I never did hear him play his trumpet. Neither my informants nor Bob Fleming himself told me whether he was only 'acting' as PD on Meeriabedde or whether it was a permanent appointment. In the absence of any indication to the contrary, I therefore assumed it was the latter. However, I was subsequently proved wrong, as Bob Fleming soon moved on and the permanent position was given to J. J. D. Scott.

*The author at Meeriabedde Small Bungalow, 1957. Photo: Norah Ebbels.*

# 1958

9

Although the birds of Ceylon had been studied quite intensively and several books on them had been published, they and their habits were very much less well-known than most European birds. Therefore there was always the exciting feeling that observations had not been made a thousand times before and there was the intriguing possibility that one might even turn up something new. I spent a lot of time bird watching in the garden and one of the commonest birds was the tailor bird. This was a cocky, lively little bird which behaved somewhat like a wren but was rather bigger and had a longer, cocked-up tail. It was a dull, olive-green,

For an island, Sri Lanka is blessed with an extraordinarily rich bird fauna. This is mainly due to the great diversity of habitats in the island, ranging from wet and cold to dry and hot, and from semi-desert to tropical rain forest. It is also the terminus of the migration flyways down the Indian sub-continent and receives multitudes of migrants from the Himalayas and northern Asia during the north-east monsoon (the months of the northern winter). Its long isolation from the Asian continent has also resulted in the evolution of 21 species and many sub-species of birds (and also many sub-species of animals) which are not found anywhere else in the world (technically being described as *endemic* to the island). These occur mainly in the central hills and the remaining tropical rain forest in the south-west lowlands, which have greater and longer isolation from similar habitats in India and elsewhere than the dry coastal plains in the north and east.

The ancient irrigation tanks and their surrounding wetlands form one of the richest habitats, both in terms of numbers of birds and in the number of species present, especially water birds. With luck and a little effort, it was possible to reach a tally of 100 species seen in one day. Great colonies of egrets, storks, ibises, spoonbills and herons nested at many of the large tanks, either in the dead trees which remained from times before renovation had increased the water level, or in the living trees around their periphery which, when the water was high, often stood in the water and were thus protected from many terrestrial predators. These ornithological spectacles were often spoken of by the older planters interested in wildlife, who described the wonders of the nesting colonies to be seen at Giant's Tank, up near Mannar, at Ridiyagama, down near Ambalantota, and at other more remote tanks of the eastern low country jungles. But all agreed that the most spectacular was at the bird sanctuary of Kumina, near a small village of this name on the south-east coast at the mouth of the Kumbukkan Oya.

I was very glad, therefore, that I had already completed the redesign of the *Nandu* when, in March 1958, I was invited to join my sister Valerie and two friends, Roy and Mary, on a trip to

Kumina over a long weekend. I lost no time in coaxing a couple of days leave out of Bob Fleming to enable me to join them. Although the weather is normally good at this time of year, there had been a lot of rain in the preceding month. Valerie arrived from Colombo in the old jeep which she had acquired for such expeditions. It was laden with camping equipment, jerry cans of fuel, and driven by a driver recruited for the weekend, named Mr Gunewardena and known as 'Gooney' for short. We set off from my bungalow at first light with both the jeep (containing Gooney and a camp assistant I had engaged for the trip, named Arunasalam) and my Morris Minor and made a rendezvous with the rest of the party at the Arugam Bay Rest House. We then set off southwards and took the ferry across the Arugam Bay lagoon.

As the ferry could accommodate only two vehicles, it needed to make a second trip to bring over the jeep, and we then proceeded a few miles along the little coast road to the village of Panama (pronounced 'Parnama'), where we had arranged to leave the cars at the office of the Wild Life Department. We had arranged for two bullock carts to meet us at this point, as from here onwards we expected the road to deteriorate rapidly. I transferred all the equipment from my car to the carts, but Roy and Mary elected to try and get further in their larger car (a Standard Vanguard). However, as expected, we presently found the track flooded for a considerable distance and after some deliberation they had to transfer to the carts before reaching the next village. This was Okanda, where we spent the night at the Forest Department circuit bungalow.

*Crossing Bagura Plain on our return journey, showing a fine palu tree and the small hill.*

The carts set off at 2 a.m. the next morning, taking the hapless Arunasalam with them, while we followed in the jeep at a more leisurely 6.15, accompanied by the local Game Warden. Our road, which had by now dwindled to barely more than two wheel tracks, lay across the Bagura Plain, a flat savannah-like area sparsely dotted with handsome palu trees (*Mimusops hexandra*). In the distance a rocky hill could be seen. This was probably the one on which Frederick Lewis and his little scouting party spent such an uncomfortably wet night after observing a suspicious ship anchored off-shore on 22 March 1917. Several ships, including the SS *Persia* and the Bibby Line ship SS *Worcestershire*, had been sunk by mines just outside Colombo. Lewis, who knew the area well from his years with the Forest and Land Settlement Departments, was convinced that it was a German vessel which had been mining the shipping lanes and was lying low while probing the defences of this remote coast. With considerable effort he carefully telegraphed this to the British military authorities who had asked him to make the reconnaissance, but he found his information pooh-poohed and belittled, for which he never forgave them.

After a couple of hours of the muddy and partly flooded track, we reached Kumina to find that the carts had already arrived. The Kumbakkan Oya was very full, with the water lapping the top of the banks, and we made camp on the highest ground possible, not very far from the river bank. However, although full, the river was not in spate and the water was clear. The huge kumbuk trees with their pale trunks grew close to the water's edge, the tracery of branches arching high above the surface in wonderful profusion. Bird calls echoed from the canopy, while the occasional hoots and sceeches of langurs and monkeys came filtering through the forest.

Later in the day the Game Warden and I made our way back to the seaward side of our track and prepared to launch the boat on the lagoon or *villu* which formed the heart of the bird sanctuary. Having put the *Nandu* together, we had some difficulty in pushing our way through the floating grass and warm mud before reaching open water, where an amazing sight spread before us. The Kumina Villu must have been about 100 acres in extent, having an oval area of shallow but clear water about 500 yards long in the centre. This was only a few feet deep, but overlay several feet of soft and squashy mud. The open water was surrounded by a partly submerged forest of 'water apple' trees (probably a relative of the 'rose apple', *Eugenia jambos*) which were in turn surrounded by a wide area of floating vegetation and marsh grasses in shallow water and muddy pools. One or two low islands rose from the surface and the perimeter of the open water was choked with a brown scum in which the occasional body of a luckless nestling could be seen. The water apple trees were festooned with the nests of all kinds of water birds: pelicans, painted and open-bill storks, ibis, egrets and herons of several species, cormorants and darters. The air was thick with birds coming and going to and from their nests, while the clamour of thousands of calls, croaks and clapping of bills was almost deafening. On the water flotillas of cormorants and pelicans paraded back and forth while darters swam with their bodies submerged and only their long necks protruding from the water like periscopes. I had never seen such richness of bird life and was almost bewildered, not knowing where to look or which species to examine first. The humid heat and the powerful stench of guano and decaying debris gradually made themselves felt more keenly and after an hour we made our way back to camp, leaving the boat by the water's edge.

The following day we returned to Kumina Villu and, as well as the *Nandu*, we had the use of a local dug-out canoe with outrigger. I was anxious to film the bird colony and arranged for my companions to leave me in a large tree while they explored further in the boats. However, filming was not as easy as I had anticipated. The tree was an awkward one to climb and, encumbered with a large and heavy Paillard-Bolex 8mm movie camera, it was very difficult moving about. I was also conscious that the slightest slip could send me or the camera (or both) into the water and the apparently bottomless mud beneath. The sun beat down with unrelenting intensity and it began to get extremely hot. Perched uncomfortably on a rather narrow branch like one of the awkward stork fledglings I was trying to film, I could feel the sweat pouring down inside my shirt and soaking my underpants and the waist of my shorts. Furthermore, I found that the lenses were not really powerful enough to film any but a few of the nearest nests. However, the others had disappeared, and when I sighted the dug-out the other side of the lagoon, they took no notice of my increasingly desperate signals. Eventually I was retrieved in a rather dishevelled and dehydrated condition and they seemed quite surprised that I had not had a wonderful time. It was quite a relief to be in the boat again and in fact I got some good film sequences from the bow of the dug-out.

*On Kumina Villu with the Game Warden in the dugout canoe.*

I returned to Kumina Villu later that day and again the following morning, but our time was running out and we had to start the long trail back. There had been heavy rain in the night, but we reached the Okanda circuit bungalow without difficulty at dusk and continued on our way the next morning. About mid morning we reached Roy and Mary's car, which nobody had considered might not have remained safe and sound by the side of the track. We then transferred their now rather muddy gear, discovering at the same time that the jeep seemed to have lost most of its oil, which was dangerously low. Administering what little oil we had with us, we continued as far as Panama. Here we paused on the bund of Panama Wewa, a delightful little tank covered with blue water lilies, while we sent Gooney ahead in the Vanguard to obtain more oil at Pottuvil. He returned unexpectedly early, looking somewhat agitated.

'Hello, Gooney, Did you get some oil?'

'No, Sir, there is a problem.'

'A problem, Gooney? What's the matter? Didn't the garage have any oil?'

'No, no, Sir, I did not reach the garage; there is a problem with the ferry. . . . It has sunk.'

We received this news with considerable consternation as all of us were expected back at our posts by that evening. Besides, we had no supplies for a longer stay. We quickly decided to see the situation for ourselves and soon arrived at the southern shore of the lagoon at Arugam Bay, where we found our informant had been absolutely correct. It *had* sunk. At least, if not totally sunk, it was more or less submerged with just the superstructure showing and definitely not likely to go anywhere in the near future. Apparently an inexperienced crew had steered it over one of the very few rocks in the vicinity and had holed it below the waterline.

This presented quite a 'problem', as Gooney had said. In the dry season it might have been possible to make a circuit around the western end of the lagoon to strike the main Moneragala road, but at this season the inland margins of the lagoon were marshy and quite impassable to ordinary cars. On the seaward side the mouth of the lagoon was blocked by a large sand bar which was breached only in times of flood, and I walked over the sandy area behind the beach to have a look. The bar was intact and in fact the recent tracks of tractor wheels showed that it was used by the local tractor-owning farmers passing from Pottuvil village to their paddy fields south of Arugam Bay. I followed the tracks and found that they wound through the bushes behind the sand dunes and eventually connected with the road. This would be passable for the Jeep (provided its engine had not already seized from lack of oil) but not for the cars, and the Jeep was not powerful enough to tow them through the deep sand. But perhaps we could get some co-operative tractor driver to tow us? Roy and I walked over the sand bar into Pottuvil village where we located a tractor and driver, but he was not at all keen, although we offered him what we thought were generous terms. It wasn't just a question of money, he explained, but the tractor wasn't his and perhaps the owner would not approve. Then what if something should go wrong? He would be blamed for any mishap and, besides, it was time for his dinner. No, no, we said, nobody would blame him and we would be very grateful if he would try. Eventually, after the agreed price had been considerably increased (to compensate for this delay to his dinner), our nervous tractor operator agreed and we rode back across the sand bar in style.

It was decided that my Morris Minor should be the first to be towed across. The tractor driver produced a long chain, one end of which I attached to the front of the chassis, giving the other end to the tractor man, who still seemed somewhat reluctant and nervous. In addition, although we were initially unaware of this, apparently he was unfamiliar with towing things behind the tractor. No sooner had he attached the chain to the tractor, than he climbed into the driving seat, let in the clutch with a jerk, and set off at a fair pace with never a backward glance. I was taken by surprise and nearly got left behind as the wretched Morris was yanked forward through the sand. Desperately, I tried to steer the car to follow the winding wheel tracks. However, the wheels could get no purchase in the deep sand and where the tractor followed a bend, the car took a dramatic short cut, squashing bushes and breaking through thickets. It was quite difficult even to determine whether the wheels were straight or on full lock. Suddenly a large stump loomed ahead which must surely rip the radiator, if not a wheel, right off the car. I hooted, shouted, banged on the car door, but to no avail: like a horse homeward bound at the end of the day, the tractor driver proceeded ahead, deaf to all commands, with his gaze firmly fixed on the other side of the sand bar (where, presumably, his dinner awaited). At the last second the front wheels of the Morris managed to get a grip on some more solid ground and with a deft twist I steered around the stump, which made only a nasty scratch on the paintwork. As we came out onto the sand bar, I discovered that the best thing to do was to hold the wheels straight, without attempting to steer to left or right and, much to my relief, somehow we reached the track on the northern side of the lagoon without major accident. After this experience, I was able to warn both Roy and the tractor driver of the hazards involved, and the Vanguard was towed over in a relatively sedate fashion. With the expedition safely on the northern shores of the lagoon, we gratefully paid off the driver. He disappeared as fast as his tractor would carry him in search of his dinner, considerably richer for his pains, while we made for the Rest House in search of similar refreshment before starting our long journeys home.

Perhaps because Bob Fleming was of a younger generation than Bill Horne, he also seemed to have more progressive ideas on estate management. One of these was the need for organic matter to improve the soil. In this he was probably quite right, as the steep sides of the Meeriabedde valley had long ago lost what topsoil they had had when first the estate had been opened from the jungle, and in many areas the gnarled roots of the tea bushes protruded straight out of the rocky subsoil. What was required, he said, was large amounts of animal manure, regularly applied. As the only animal manure available came from the few cows which some labourers managed to keep in sheds dotted about the estate and fed from the waste grassy places, there was no possibility of obtaining anything like the quantities needed. The solution, said Bob, was pigs. Pigs were apparently easy to keep, produced large amounts of manure, and in addition could be slaughtered to provide a profitable supply of pork.

Mr Meikle, as the Meeriabedde VA, approved of this idea and, accordingly, a piggery was established on some patana grassland up on the south-western shoulder of the Lower Division slopes. A Sinhalese Pig Man was appointed to look after the piggery and I was told that I had to manage the whole unit. However, I was far from enthusiastic about this enterprise, not because I disagreed with the need for organic manure on the estate, but because I felt that it had been set up without enough thought as to how it would operate and how we would market the pork produced. I also did not relish having to supervise the slaughter of the pigs, which I was aware might be a most unpleasant business. My misgivings were reinforced when I interrogated the Pig Man, Piyadasa, and found that apparently he had no knowledge of keeping pigs, at least not on a commercial scale. Nevertheless, the enterprise was pushed ahead, sties built, and some weaned piglets were obtained from the Danish bacon and ham producing farm at Nuwara Eliya.

I decided that Piyadasa and I needed some hard information on pig keeping, so on my next visit to Colombo I visited H. W. Cave & Co., which at that time was about the only bookshop of note in the whole Island. Amongst the few books on the shelf devoted to agriculture, I found a small volume on pig-keeping. Although written for British conditions, this contained some useful basic information which we were able to put into practice. The piglets, which appeared to be of the Large White breed (or something very similar), settled in well and were a lively lot. They would rush out to greet me when I arrived, jostling each other, squealing and grunting enthusiastically. I discovered that vigorously tickling their ribs would cause them to lie down immediately, almost as though their legs had been suddenly incapacitated. For some reason, Fredo took no notice of them at all and would busy himself hunting in the long *maana* grass of the surrounding patana while I was at the piggery. Except for one, which sickened and died from a mysterious disorder not described in my pig-keeping book, the piglets put on weight quite rapidly and I became quite attached to them. I also became nervous that they might soon be reaching slaughterable size. I questioned Piyadasa closely as to whether he had slaughtered a pig before and became even more nervous when he declared that he had not and moreover, as a good Buddhist, he had no intention of doing so in the future. What would we do? Would Bob Fleming expect me to do the job if the pig man would not? The prospect horrified me and I spent a considerable time wondering what I should do.

Although I was doubtful at the time, I am sure that in fact Bob Fleming had no intention of ordering me to stand in as chief pig slaughterer. However, my worries were overtaken by events and before the uneconomical longevity of the Meeriabedde pigs became widely apparent, I had left Meeriabedde for good. I have never fancied pig keeping ever since.

About this time in 1958, violent events occurred in Ceylon which, although we did not know it at the time, were to have serious repercussions throughout the next half century. The Sinhalese people, who now comprise a large majority of the population, originated in the Bengal area of northern India and migrated to Ceylon some time about the sixth century BC, gradually displacing the aboriginal population of Veddahs and settling mainly in the northern lowlands of the Island. The early history of the Sinhalese is told in the Mahawansa or Great Dynasty, an epic poem, the translation and elucidation of which was achieved in the first part of the nineteenth century, mainly by George Turnour together with a Buddhist priest named Gallé. Born in Ceylon in 1799, Turnour was a gifted linguistic scholar and colonial administrator. When he started this huge task in 1826, he was still aged only 27 yet was already the Government Agent (the senior administrator and government representative) of the

Saffragam District, stationed at the provincial town of Ratnapura. His translation, and subsequent work by later scholars, has shown that the Mahawansa generally agrees in substance with the archaeological record.

The early Sinhalese immigrants established a sophisticated civilization which was based largely on the culture of irrigated rice. Many of their great irrigation reservoirs survive as the beautiful tanks we appreciate so much today, often surrounded by jungle and supporting large and varied populations of birds and animals. Others exist as jungle-covered dry depressions with broken bunds. So successful and intensive was their agriculture that the ancient Sinhalese kings could boast that 'not one drop of rain water would reach the sea without having grown one grain of rice'. However, from about the sixth century AD onwards the Sinhalese kingdoms came into increasing conflict with the Tamil people, who mounted successive invasions from their kingdoms in southern India. This continued for the next 800 years or so and eventually the main centres of Sinhalese population moved to the south and west and into the central mountains, leaving the northern and eastern areas to the Tamils. The great Sinhalese cities of Anuradhapura and Polonnaruwa on the north-central plains were successively abandoned in the 11th and 14th centuries AD and became overgrown by the sparsely inhabited jungle, which thus divided the two races.

This division of the Ceylon population still largely survived in 1958, the peasant populations of the two races having very little contact with each other. The middle classes, however, mixed freely and worked amicably together in the civil service and in commerce, and they continued to do so after independence as they had done during colonial times. But there tended to be a disproportionately greater number of Tamils in such posts than might have been expected from the relative sizes of the two populations.

The indigenous Tamils of the north and east formed a quite separate population from the Tamils employed on the plantations who, as explained earlier, were originally imported from southern India by the British as indentured labourers. There was very little contact between these two Tamil populations, although in 1958 each accounted for about 10 or 11 per cent of the national population. After independence in 1948, the various ethnic populations in the Island began to exercise their political muscle, the Sinhalese to enhance the status which they felt rightly belonged to their majority, and the indigenous Tamils to safeguard their northern and eastern homelands and their status in occupying many prominent public positions.

The first governments after independence tended to continue with many policies which were not so very different from those which had been pursued by the British administration during the last years of colonial rule. However, the government soon passed the Ceylon Citizenship Act, which limited citizenship to those who had several generations of ancestors born in the Island. This not only disenfranchised most of the plantation Tamils but, as I knew from my own situation, restricted the eligibility of foreigners to reside and work in the Island to those in possession of a Temporary Residence Permit.

Nevertheless, the official administration of the Island, including the legal system, continued to operate in English, which was not understood by the vast majority of the population. For many reasons it was in fact very difficult rapidly to replace English with either vernacular as the language of national administration. For a start, many senior Ceylonese civil servants and politicians had been educated in English, spoke English at home, and felt uneasy about using Sinhala or Tamil for complicated official business. Although most would have studied both languages at school and used them in everyday communication with local people, many had not taken the languages to a high level of proficiency and sometimes could not read or write them fluently. Then there was the difficulty of using them in situations which would require a completely new format (such as for maps and telegrams) and for technical purposes for which they did not possess appropriate words. The roadside name-boards for towns and villages continued to give the Anglicized name centrally in large Roman letters, while the Sinhala and Tamil names were denoted in their respective but smaller characters at the top and bottom. However, the more radical of the Sinhalese politicians were determined that Sinhala should eventually be the national language, preferably to the exclusion of all others.

In 1955 legislation was enacted to replace English by the 'mother tongue' for official purposes. For the 1956 election the party which had been in power since independence, the United National Party (UNP), campaigned on the equal use of Sinhala and Tamil. However, the Sri Lanka Freedom Party (SLFP) led by Mr S. W. R. D. Bandaranaike, campaigned on making Sinhala the only national language (although apparently the English version of its manifesto provided for the 'reasonable use of Tamil'). The UNP, seeing the popular support for this policy amongst the Sinhalese majority, then changed its stance to 'Sinhala Only'. However, it was too late, and the SLFP won a landslide victory as leader of the MEP (Mahajana Eksath Peramuna or People's United Front) coalition.

The accession of the MEP to power with a large parliamentary majority consisting of many newly-elected, inexperienced politicians apparently engendered a feeling of giving power to the people. The government tended readily to accede to the demands of organised labour (many of the unions being led by politicians) and the police were discouraged from controlling MEP- or SLFP-supporting crowds or demonstrations too firmly. Indeed, in many places pressure on the police by local politicians resulted in the police being afraid to act too decisively for fear of being over-ruled or even penalised by commissions of inquiry. Incidents occurred where no action was taken against individuals creating violent disturbances and in some cases, apparently, arrested miscreants were released by order of the local MP. Police morale and efficiency consequently declined.

In early 1958 the registration plates of new motor vehicles appeared bearing the Sinhala character *Sri* in place of Roman letters. This was very unpopular in the Tamil areas, where the offending *Sri* was obliterated and replaced with the equivalent Tamil character. In turn this provoked reaction in the Sinhalese areas, including Colombo, where Tamil lettering was indiscriminately obliterated, and this was soon extended to road signs and even to attacks on Tamil people. In May, a plan to settle Tamil labourers from the closing British naval base at Trincomalee in Sinhalese areas was prevented by pre-emptive occupation of the land by Sinhalese. The accompanying unrest culminated in attacks in the Polonnaruwa area on trains thought to be carrying Tamil people from the Eastern provincial capital, Batticaloa. In the absence of firm direction or reinforcements from headquarters, the police and army units available were unable to maintain order and the situation in the Polonnaruwa District deteriorated into serious rioting in which a substantial number of Tamils lost their lives. The inter-racial strife and accompanying looting spread to other areas, around Dambulla, to many of the larger low country towns, and to Colombo itself. Many people, mainly Tamils, were killed or had their homes and property destroyed, and refugees of both races converged on Colombo. Eventually, a State of Emergency was declared by the Governor General, the police and army were required to take firm action, and within about three weeks the disturbances had been brought under control.

On estates in the Haputale District we saw practically no sign of these disturbances, which we heard reported on the radio from Colombo and even from our own provincial capital, Badulla. The estate Tamils, fearful of their situation as largely stateless persons, were reluctant to become involved in the language dispute or to engender antagonism among the Sinhalese in the local towns, and relations with the small number of Sinhalese on the estates continued to be amicable. No curfew was operated in rural areas or in the local villages and small towns and almost the only visible sign of the troubles was the painting out of Tamil lettering on roadside signs. This was soon followed by the tarring of the Sinhala lettering and subsequently often also, just for good measure, by the obliteration of the Roman lettering. However, the Declaration of Emergency and the firmer action by the police under this edict ended visible civil strife and within a few weeks life in the troubled areas seemed to have returned to normal. As I did not have occasion to leave the District during this time and, indeed, seldom even left the estate more than two or three times in a week, I was scarcely conscious that an

Emergency had been in force and life continued in its usual routine  Little did we realise in 1958 that these disturbing events were the precursors of a racial conflict which would escalate some 25 years later into a full scale civil war.

At the start of the dry season in 1958 I had been on Meeriabedde Lower Division for nearly two years.  This seemed quite a long time to me, and indeed it was then about ten percent of my lifetime.  I felt I could cope quite well with the job and I had settled comfortably into the expatriate social life of the District, with a number of friends amongst the SDs on various estates.  I was regularly invited to dinner by several of the married PDs, but seldom reciprocated, as young bachelor SDs were not really expected to host dinner parties in the absence of a woman's civilising influence and, in any case, Meeriabedde was too remote for easy visiting.

I did not think very much about the future or of my prospects in planting, and certainly Bob Fleming never discussed such things with me.  So I was surprised one day to receive an official letter from one of the Directors of Messrs George Steuart & Co. Ltd. in Colombo, informing me that I was to be transferred to the Idulgashena Division of Needwood Group as from the 1st August.  In fact I was to change places with 'Dinky' de Fonseka, who had been on Idulgashena since my days of creeping on Needwood.  While I had been on Meeriabedde, my predecessor, Trevor, had been on the Haldumulla Division of Needwood, where I suspected Mr Meikle felt he could keep a close eye on him.  So now we were both to be SDs under Mr Meikle.  I felt rather sorry to be leaving the small bungalow on Meeriabedde Lower Division, which had been my first independent home and which was so well-placed, on the south-eastern edge of the hills, for visiting the low country jungles and the south and east coasts.  However, Idulgashena was considered to be the plum SD billet in the Gibson Estates, being up at a cool elevation of about 5,000 ft and producing heavy yields of high quality teas from its well-covered slopes; very different from the scraggy tea and poor yields of rocky Meeriabedde.  Although I felt I had done a reasonable job, I doubted that I had done well enough to merit such an elevation.  So I was pleased that I was evidently considered to have done well enough to be given the responsibility of Idulgashena.  The move was not really a promotion, as it would carry no increase in salary beyond the normal increment of Rs.50 per month which I received on each anniversary of my appointment as an SD.  However, I could not understand why Dinky was being posted to Meeriabedde Lower Division (which was considered a junior post) as he was a lot senior to me and, as far as I knew, well respected for his ability.

I felt I could not question Bob Fleming on this point and he did not volunteer any information, so I remained somewhat puzzled for the rest of the week, until I happened to see Mr Meikle at the club the following Wednesday evening and had a few words with him about the move.

'Eh . . ., Ah . . ., Err . . ., Um . . ., Yes, David,' he said, taking another sip of his fourth brandy and ginger ale, 'I think ye'll enjoy Idulgashena. . . . Eh . . ., Ah . . ., I was there myself in my early days, too, y'know.'

'Really, Sir?' I replied, remembering very well his anecdote about the piano.

'Yes, . . . Ah . . ., Ehhh . . ., Yes,' he continued, 'and it'll mean y'won't have a black PD' he added, as though this was the real reason for my transfer. ' but, it'll come in time ye know, David, and I don't know what'll happen then.'

'Oh, I expect I shall survive, Sir,' I said, as he turned back to the bar, but I got no further information and it was not very long before I could hear his conversation with his buddy Ginger descend into almost total incoherence.

I felt rather crestfallen at this revelation: was this really the reason for the transfer and was it not on account of the merit of my performance?  But then, as far as I knew, the next PD on Meeriabedde was still likely to be a European and Bob Fleming showed no signs of turning black, in spite of his trumpet-playing ability.  So the mystery remained and I merely accepted the situation as fairly good fortune, although I certainly did not view the prospect of having Mr Meikle as my boss once again with unmitigated delight.

Packing up the bungalow for the move took several days, as I seemed to have acquired quite a lot of bits and pieces over the past two years. However, with the help of Gomez and Arumugam, we were ready when the estate lorry arrived to load my *sarmen* on the appointed day. I had had no intimation from the estate staff that any farewell ceremony was planned for me. I felt somewhat relieved about this, as I still did not feel up to making a farewell speech in Tamil, and I also did not want the labour force to spend their scarce cash on any gift. It was a pity that they evidently did not wish to say any formal farewell, but I could not really be surprised. Two years was a relatively short stint and, although I had looked after their interests as far as my responsibility went, I had never sought to become closely involved with labour welfare. They probably felt that I was rather cold and impersonal in my dealings with them and no doubt would not be sorry to see the back of me. However, as the last of my things were being loaded, old Ramasamy K.P. and a small group of the kanganys arrived to pay their respects and wish me farewell so I was able to thank them for their help and good work and to wish them well. When my things were all loaded and Gomez had added his few cases and bundles, we bid farewell to Arumugam and to old Paliniandy (both of whom I had suitably rewarded). The lorry trundled down the drive and Gomez and I followed in the Morris Minor.

# Idulgashena 10

The journey to Idulgashena took about an hour, half of which was taken up in negotiating the Needwood estate cart road and its 22 hairpin bends. The watchman salaamed loudly in recognition as he lifted the barrier near Needwood Bungalow and I received salaams and smiles from many others as we passed by on our way up to the Idalgashinna Gap and crossed the railway line near the station where Mr Meikle had originally met me. Idulgashena Bungalow, which was to be my new home, was in fact the cosy-looking bungalow with the red roof which I had noticed from the train just before my first arrival. To reach it, the road first passed over the level crossing, leaving on the right the Idalgashinna post office and the half dozen houses which formed the hamlet of Idalgashinna, and then descended the northern slope of the mountain to reach the Idulgashena factory a few hundred yards below the railway. From the factory it was about another half mile to the bungalow and the cart road then continued on via labour lines to climb back to the railway again at the westernmost point of the Division.

Presumably, Idulgashena Division had been opened originally as a separate estate from Needwood as the bungalow, having been built for the proprietor, was much larger and better appointed than bungalows built for lowly SDs. In fact it had a rather suburban air, which was accentuated by the tidy garden and the wonderful display of petunias which greeted me when I arrived. The bungalow was basically L-shaped and the outside walls were covered with rendering, contributing to the suburban effect. The front door was sheltered by a little porch, supported by two brick pillars on either side, leading directly into a large sitting room, the length of which covered the width of the building and in one corner of which was a brick fireplace. At this elevation the nights (and, indeed, the days, during bad weather) could be cold, although never frosty, and a warm log fire was a regular feature almost every evening. A central passageway led from the sitting room to the dining room, having two bedrooms with a bathroom between them, on either side. There was also a small office, and the smaller wing of the L was occupied by the kitchen and servants' quarters. Outside, there was separate accommodation for bungalow staff and a small shed housed a Lister diesel engine and generator for the bungalow electricity supply. A good-sized, flat lawn with a jam tree (*Muntingia calabura*) in the middle occupied the angle of the L. These trees grew amazingly fast and although this one was fully 15 ft high with a good spread, it was probably no more than 18 months old. In front of the bungalow, terraced flower beds descended to the garage. A tiny rill, bordered by arum lilies, tinkled down a depression to run into a pipe under the road and on the far side of this little valley a steeply sloping lawn rose up to a row of camellia bushes. Camellias are closely related to tea and grow very well in upcountry gardens. These were in almost constant bloom with red and pink blossoms, and formed the boundary of the garden with the tea.

At the rear of the bungalow was a back yard of beaten earth, which was shaded by several peach trees. Peaches and pears were quite commonly grown at elevations of about 5,000 ft and above, but they were far removed from the modern 'low chill' varieties grown in Spain and other moderately warm climates, and even further removed from any resemblance to the luscious fruits which appear in European greengrocers' shops. Being of an obstinate nature and bullet-like hardness, these fruits displayed an extreme reluctance to ripen or in any way ameliorate their wooden flesh into something softer. However, having allowed them as long as possible on the tree, they could be stewed into submission and, with liberal quantities of sugar, were then just about acceptable. Gomez tackled them with skill and determination and produced quite tasty stewed peaches or peach pie.

*Idulgashena bungalow, 1958.*

There was also a large vegetable garden, and at this altitude almost any European and most tropical vegetables could be grown to perfection with the fertile soil and in the cool but frost-free environment. It was the custom to allow the *totakaran* to sell the surplus produce from the vegetable garden for his own benefit (although some planters went in for vegetable production in a big way and gave the *totakaran* only a small percentage of the revenue). Personally, I was happy for him to get what he could out of it, so long as there were plenty of vegetables for the bungalow and that in his commercial enthusiasm he did not devote himself to vegetables to the exclusion of all else. This seemed to work pretty well, except that there were occasions when the produce seemed to consist of little other than kohlrabi and vast quantities of beetroot. The vegetables not only grew rapidly, but seemed to be giants of their kind and in complimenting the *totakaran* on his skill, I asked how he produced such prize specimens. The answer was simple: in the centre of the garden was a 44-gallon drum scrounged from the factory and in this was placed a goodly basket of cow manure obtained from a friend down the road. The drum was filled with water and allowed to mature for several days, with occasional stirring. The resulting powerful brew was decanted into a watering can through a basket filter and each day a little was used for watering the crops. They never looked back.

Cauliflowers were one of the few vegetables which often could not be grown well in upcountry Ceylon and around about this time it had been discovered that the reason for this was a lack of the element boron in the soil. Boron was apparently needed by the cauliflower plant before it would produce the cauliflower 'curd' (actually the young flowering shoot). Adding a trace of boron to the soil could rectify this deficiency and wonderful crops of cauliflowers could then result. This news quickly spread amongst planters and gardeners, who lost no time in purchasing a supply of borax from the chemist and adding it to their watering cans. The Idulgashena *totakaran* was fully up-to-date with the borax technology, but in his enthusiasm he overdid the dose. Wandering into the vegetable garden one evening, I was at first puzzled as to what vegetable he might be growing. On drawing nearer, this changed to astonishment as I realised they were cauliflowers, - but *what* cauliflowers! They had indeed all produced magnificent heads of creamy white curd but, not content with this, many had produced a second head from the centre of the first, and some even a third, giving the impression of a miniature, but particularly severe, atomic explosion. In congratulating the *totakaran* on his fine crop, I also suggested that he should go easy on the borax next time around.

Gomez settled in at Idulgashena with enthusiasm, taking charge of the separate residential quarters, the house boy, the *totakaran*, and relishing a larger and more prestigious domain on which to exercise his considerable domestic skills. His cooking also seemed to blossom in the new environment and, discovering a much better supply of eggs than was to be had at Meeriabedde, he went egg-mad. Hardly a dish appeared but contained eggs of some sort. Multi-egged omelettes, beaten to a golden froth and inflated like duvets, almost floated off the plate, while even rice puddings were forced to accept an egg delicately blended into their creamy bosoms.

Meat was available in Haputale (the next station along the railway line) and came by the 'beef-box' (the *errichi-petti*) on the train in the charge of the Beef-box Man who, at Idulgashena, doubled as the garden *totakaran*. The beef-box was a veritable institution in upcountry Ceylon and most planters depended on the system to obtain fresh meat, and sometimes poultry, fish, butter, and other supplies. In essence, it was what it was called: a box (often with a zinc lining) for transporting meat. Mine was about the size of a tuck-box such as used to be essential for boys attending British public schools. It had a hinged lid, a lining of zinc sheet, and there were perforations in the sides to provide aeration. It was closed by a hasp and staple with a padlock, one key of which was kept by the butcher in Haputale and the other by Gomez. Once a week on 'beef-box day', which meant the slaughtering day at the butchers, Gomez would put a list of meat and dairy produce needs into the box, which would then be carried away by the *totakaran* on his head. I paid his return fare to Haputale on the train and later in the day he would reappear with the beef-box containing, with any luck and amidst quantities of gory newspaper, sawdust and semi-melted ice, the meat and other items which Gomez had listed, for which I paid a monthly account. The beef-box run was much valued by the *totakaran*, who not only enjoyed the social aspects of a free trip to the fleshpots of Haputale, but who also was able to earn some extra cash by carrying out small commissions in the town for other estate people. Although the train journey was only about 20 minutes, the exercise usually occupied him for the whole day and, indeed, sometimes the social activities at the toddy and arrack tavern got the better of him and impeded his return until late in the evening, or even (a heinous crime) until the next morning. Even the best possible cuts of meat were invariably tough, and on one occasion an SD on Haputale Estate with closer access than I had, dispatched his appu direct from the dining table to the butcher with forceful complaint, bearing his plate with the offending roast and two veg in hand.

However, there were various things one could do to reduce wear and tear on one's teeth and jaws, and Gomez knew them all. The most basic treatment was to hang the meat like game for two or three days and then bludgeon it to relative tenderness with a blunt instrument. The sound of muffled thuds coming from the kitchen usually signified the preparation of dinner and not a domestic dispute. A more subtle method was to smear the meat with papaya seeds, wrap it in papaya leaves and leave it for several hours. The round, black, papaya seeds, each with a spherical gelatinous coat and rather like caviar in appearance and consistency, had a high content of the enzyme papain, which acted to degrade the meat fibres. The result was usually edible, although perhaps not for the weak-jawed.

Once the meat had arrived, the next problem was to keep it fresh. The estates almost always provided a refrigerator as part of the bungalow equipment, but where there was no mains electricity, as on Meeriabedde and Idulgashena, these operated on kerosene (paraffin oil). Kerosene fridges could work very well, but when old or badly maintained they could be a nightmare. The kerosene was contained at the base of the fridge in a shoe-box-sized tank which was fitted at the rear end with a wick and burner with a glass shade. The wick had to be trimmed and adjusted to perfection if the thing was to work properly and a little mirror was thoughtfully provided at the front of the apparatus so that one could check on the condition of the flame without crouching down. If for any reason these works were neglected, clouds of oily black smoke would arise, volcano-like, from the chimney at the top of the fridge and blacken walls and ceiling for yards around while the interior remained near room temperature. The workings of kerosene fridges were a mystery to most bungalow staff and, indeed, to most planters, so a facility to keep them working well was a much-prized asset in an appu or house-boy, and Gomez was an excellent example.

Kerosene came in oblong, four-gallon tins which had multitudinous uses. Tin smiths in every village used them as raw material to make all manner of household items and, beaten out flat, they were used like slates for roofs or were nailed to timber frames for the walls of houses. However, they were not easy to pour from and any attempt to fill the tank of the fridge directly from the tin, even with the aid of a funnel, usually resulted in pools of kerosene all over the floor. My parents' appu, named Muthu, who was most resourceful and intelligent, therefore hit on the excellent idea of distributing the kerosene into empty lime juice cordial bottles, which were easy to pour from and of which my parents had a plentiful supply. This worked very well until one day, after the usual weekly topping up exercise, the refrigerator flame gradually became smaller and smaller until eventually it disappeared altogether. No amount of coaxing would rekindle it, and my mother firmly kept the fridge door closed while anxiously quizzing the appu as to what might have gone wrong. The mystery seemed inexplicable until it was discovered that the new and old cordial bottles had somehow become mixed and the fridge had been topped up with neat lime juice cordial. This the fridge found particularly indigestible and it stubbornly refused to function until its innards had received a total overhaul. Still, as my mother remarked, it might have been even more unpleasant if the topping up had been the other way round.

As my bedroom I selected the one at the inner angle of the bungalow L, facing onto the lawn. The room was almost square and was simply furnished with a bed, chest of drawers, and *almira* (wardrobe). On the small table by the bed I placed the electric lamp I had won at tennis. Also on the table, at the end of a wire flex, was a bell-push with a white button. This was the cut-out for the generator and it felt most luxurious not to have to get out of bed to stop the engine. When one felt drowsy, one simply reached out and pressed the button. All being well, the light would then fade as the distant throb of the diesel engine slowed and died away. Unfortunately, this arrangement was not infallible and there were many nights when I pressed the button and then realised with sleepy wrath that the noise of the engine was *not* dying away and the blasted light was *not* dimming, but continued irritatingly bright and constant. Further and increasingly savage jabs at the button usually had no effect and I would then have to heave myself out of bed again, don my dressing gown, and go in search of the night watchman to get him to stop the generator with the manual cut-out on the engine.

The bathrooms were each equipped with a basin, a flush toilet (which discharged into a septic tank beneath the lawn), and a cast iron bath with giant taps and supported on stout legs with feet of the 'ball and claw' design. The bath in the bathroom adjoining my bedroom was badly stained and in places the enamel had been chipped down to the metal, so I decided to paint it. It was quite usual to do this and one could buy special 'bath enamel' paint for the purpose. I gave it two coats overall and more on the spots where the enamel was chipped, which rejuvenated it miraculously. I was rather taken by the 'ball and claw' feet, and I painted the claws white while picking out the 'ball' in black, which I thought looked very smart.

The bungalow office was just opposite my bedroom, across the central passage. Here there was an iron safe built into the wall, which contained the cash box. There was also a table and chair, and some shelves for the cashbook and a few reference books. I held a 'surgery' each day from about 7.30 to 8 a.m. for anybody who might wish to come and speak to me about any matter, and there were usually two or three people waiting outside the office window each morning when I entered the office. It was part of my job to make payments from the petty cash for small items and to enter up and balance the cash book at the end of each month. This was then sent down to the estate office at Needwood for the clerk to incorporate the figures in the estate monthly accounts. Also in the office were two telephones. One of these was for the estate internal telephone system, like the one I had had at the Meeriabedde Small Bungalow, but the other was connected to an external line on the Haputale exchange and this was a great perk of the Idulgashena post. The Company presumably permitted the external line because of the extreme remoteness of Idulgashena and the relative seniority of the post, otherwise I am sure it would never have been allowed. Perhaps there was also an element of compensation for the lack of a direct road connection to Haputale. This was quite deliberate and was primarily intended to make it more difficult for any thefts of tea from the Idulgashena factory to be smuggled off the estate. However, I could not help feeling that Mr Meikle was also not averse to the control it gave him over the movements of the incumbent SD on Idulgashena. There was a road from Haputale which ran along the northern side of the Berragalla mountain range, just below the railway, and connected the estates situated on its northern slopes: Glenanore and Beauvais. At their closest point, the Beauvais and Idulgashena estate roads were no more than three or four hundred yards apart, but this doubled the time needed to reach Haputale by road, the journey from Beauvais being only half an hour. It was frustrating, but there was nothing to be done about it.

I much appreciated being able to contact friends and family by telephone and in fact I sometimes acted as an unofficial telephone exchange for Trevor Labrooy on Haldumulla Division. Trevor found the lack of an external phone very inconvenient, especially in conducting his various romantic liaisons, and he would frequently ring me with an urgent request to contact some young lady on the external phone and connect him by placing the two handsets together on my office table, with further strict instructions not to listen in! Of course it seemed logical for both telephones to be installed in the same room, as in my office, but this was not always done. On Poonagalla, apparently, the phones in one of the SD bungalows were in different rooms. John, who's bungalow did not suffer from this defect, delighted in phoning the occupant on the internal phone and, while holding an animated conversation, he would then dial him on the external line.

'Just a minute', the Unfortunate One would say, 'I can hear the other phone ringing; hold on a sec, - don't go away' and the sound of him legging it down the corridor would float down the internal phone. A panting respondent would then answer the external phone in a polite manner which quickly dissolved into shouts of rage and abuse as the reply came back 'Hello, Old Boy, I haven't gone away!' This exercise seldom failed, as he was loath to leave the external phone unanswered and possibly miss a pleasant or important call.

For the first week or two on Idulgashena I made a point of attending muster each morning, as I had done at Meeriabedde. This gave me the opportunity to meet all the labourers, kanganies, KP, and other staff, and to become familiar with the works in progress. Muster was held on a flat area near the factory and seemed to be routinely conducted by the KP, who was very much in charge. I therefore decided to let him carry on, and thereafter I attended only occasionally, to keep in touch with what was going on and to show that I had not abandoned supervision of the KP. When muster was finished he would come and deliver the muster list to me at the bungalow. Very soon I had a summons from Mr Meikle, who wanted to come up and tour the Division with me.

At the appointed hour I was waiting for him by the railway level crossing where we had first met on my arrival. The bright morning sunshine felt pleasantly warm and a light breeze shimmered over the Idalgashinna Gap. Musical calls echoed across the tea-covered slopes from barbets perched in the tall shade trees and from other birds in the tea or in the small patches of jungle in ravines near the railway. It was not long before I heard the sound of the Landrover approaching and it felt rather pleasant to be able to greet Mr Meikle as the established Idulgashena SD on the spot where I had arrived as an ignorant and juvenile creeper.

Mr Meikle told Muliniandy to take the Landrover to meet us at the factory and we set off for the western end of the Division by walking along the railway. The upcountry line was all single track, standard gauge, with passing places only at stations. The narrow ridge at Idalgashinna station in fact accommodated three lines of track, including a passing line and a small siding. As was the case everywhere in Ceylon (and, indeed, throughout Asia) the railway was used as a thoroughfare by all the locals and we passed numerous people coming and going on the track as we went along. The sleepers were at a convenient distance apart for my stride and were universally of wood. Judging by their weathered, pitted and decrepit appearance, many could have dated from 1893, when this section of the line was opened. The building of the railway from Nanuoya to Badulla took 32 years but, although the engineering was difficult, the slow rate of progress was due principally to the political impediments put in the way of extending the line. There was endless correspondence between the Governor, Sir Arthur Gordon, and the Secretary of State for the Colonies in London, on the economics of the new line; whether the colony could afford the cost and whether it would be profitable. The indefatigable John Ferguson of *The Ceylon Observer*, as usual, got involved and was probably instrumental in convincing the Governor that, whereas the other extensions to Matale and Nanuoya only served the same traffic as was already using the Peradeniya-Colombo section, the proposed extension to Uva would capture new traffic, which at that time all went down the Ratnapura road. Eventually, the turning point came when Sir H. T. Holland succeeded Lord Stanhope as Secretary of State and agreed that he would not veto a proposal which had such strong support from such a rapidly developing industry. The Uva extension was started from Nanuoya in 1892 and the line was opened in sections as it was completed: to Haputale on 19th June 1893, Bandarawela in 1894, and eventually to Badulla on 5th February 1924. The economics, however, had changed over the past 60 years and Mr Meikle frequently complained about the cost of transporting Needwood tea to Colombo by rail.

'Well, Sir,' I said on one occasion, 'why not send it down by road? It would be much cheaper.'

'No, David,' came the reply, 'when the railway was put through here, all the estates agreed to support it, and I intend to continue to do so while I am here.' I later discovered that this was in fact the George Steuart official policy.

Although the mail trains were now hauled by diesel locomotives, most of the others, particularly the goods trains, were still dependent on steam locomotives. These occasionally dropped burning coals onto the sleepers, which merrily smouldered away until the next shower of rain or the track maintenance gang put them out. Each section of the line was inspected daily by the local overseer and his retinue, who travelled up and down the track on a sort of small trolley. At the front this had a wooden seat, rather like a park bench, on which the supervisor sat under a small canopy. Behind this was a flat platform with a manual device for propelling the trolley. This consisted of a post supporting a pivoted bar connected to a kind of treadle which in turn powered the wheels. With a man on each end of the bar, pumping it up and down, the trolley could be driven along at a considerable speed. Going up the gradient, they often hitched a lift by looping a rope over the coupling on the last wagon of a train. However, going downhill I often saw the trolley flying by with the two men pulling at the bar handles like galley slaves and the rest of the gang hanging on for dear life. On this particular morning at one point we had to move off the track to let the trolley go by and Mr Meikle was reminded of an incident which he claimed had happened on this stretch of the track during his time on Idulgashena.

'Och, yes, David', he said, 'In those days there used to be a Scottish engineer stationed at Ohiya' (the next station up the line) 'and he used to come down the line here on the trolley at a huge speed. This fella was immensely strong, - probably did tossing the caber, or something, d'y'know. Anyhow, one day he and his gang were coming down the line like greased lightening when he spied an old woman ahead, walking down the track with a large chatty of water balanced on her head. Well, he started ringing his little bell and shouting, but the old woman took no notice and continued walking along as if next week'd do, just steadying the chatty from time to time with her hand. So old Jock began to get a bit excited and he stood up and shouted and hollered and the gang shouted and hollered, but the old woman took not a blind bit of notice. What they didn't realise y'see was that in fact she was deaf. Anyway, they slammed on the brakes, but it was too late and the trolley was bearing down on the old woman at a great rate, so old Jock shouted to the overseer sitting next to him to hang onto him round the waist. Then, just as the trolley reached the woman, Jock leans forward, grabs her round the legs and tosses her clean over the back of the trolley! Well, that's how it was told to me, anyway, and apparently the woman was more surprised than hurt, but I doubt if it did the chatty much good!'

Mr Meikle seemed to be in a good mood and our tour of the Division seemed to go well. Fredo didn't take much notice of Haggis, but Mr Meikle liked dogs and Fredo made a favourable impression. At the end of the morning, as we approached the factory, Mr Meikle asked whether I had met all the estate kanganies and what was my opinion of the KP. Just as he got back into the Landrover, he seemed to have a sudden thought:

'By the way, David', he said, 'I want you to do the check-roll and have it ready for me to see on the days when I come up.'

Now I had not done the check-roll since I had left Needwood. It was universally accepted to be an integral part of a KP's job and Ramasamy KP had always done it on Meeriabedde. Here on Idulgashena I knew the KP would feel considerably slighted if I took this responsibility away from him. It was also an exceedingly tedious job which (depending on how many arithmetical mistakes one made, - and these were the days long before electronic calculators were available) occupied anything from one to two hours each day before the figures agreed, and I certainly had no wish to spend my evenings on this task.

'But Sir', I said, 'The KP normally does the check-roll here, I really don't think I should take it over from him. Besides, it would be difficult for me to do it on Club day. Why do you want me to do it?'

'Because it's your job, David,' he replied. 'I did it when I was on Idulgashena. I don't mind if you let the KP do it on Club days, but the rest of the time it's your responsibility. I shall be coming up again on Friday and I shall want to see it then. Muliandy, *bungalavuku.*'

Muliniandy let in the clutch and the Landrover disappeared up the road, leaving me feeling both irritated and deflated. I could not have objected if he had asked me to verify the check-roll arithmetic occasionally, as this was only prudent. But I felt that doing the check-roll calculations every day was a waste of my time, as well as being unreasonable. Times had changed a lot since Mr Meikle had been an SD. The job today was much less simple; the SD's authority now was not unquestioned, and much more management was involved, including dealing with the labour unions, which had scarcely existed in his day. I had felt I had achieved some merit by being posted to Idulgashena, and now here I was having to do the blasted check-roll as though I was a creeper again. I had to go and find the KP and explain to him that the *Peria Dorai* had taken this strange notion into his head that I should do the check-roll (except on Wednesdays) and that I would start as from tomorrow. From then on I did the check-roll every evening for about six months, when Mr Meikle finally relented. It was especially irksome on evenings when I had been invited out, as it delayed my departure and sometimes meant that it was impractical to go out in the evening at all, but it did have the effect of getting me to know the estate labourers by name quickly and thoroughly, which is probably what was intended.

Another irritating feature of life with Mr Meikle as my boss came to light at the end of my first month on Idulgashena. At Meeriabedde, Bill Horne and later Bob Fleming had been punctilious about paying salaries on the first day of each month (or the next day, if the first was a Sunday). However, it did not seem to occur to Mr Meikle that his junior staff might be anxious or, indeed, even desperate, to receive their pay promptly. My pay cheque seldom arrived in the first week of the month and frequently it did not appear until the end of the second week, or even later, which meant that it did not get into my bank account until the third week. Fortunately, this was not usually a problem for me, as I tried to arrange my finances so I did not live hand-to-mouth, but it was a serious matter for some of the junior estate staff with families, who complained bitterly to me about the unnecessary delay. Although I mentioned it to Mr Meikle on several occasions, he was unresponsive and the situation did not improve while I was on Idulgashena.

From the level crossing near Idalgashinna Station a path led off up the hill above the railway. This zig-zagged its way up the slopes of Tungoda, which was the peak on the western side of the Idalgashinna Gap. It was not a particularly spectacular peak, being just over 6,000 ft in height and covered with patana grassland at the top. The path did not go all the way up but, after passing through a patch of red gums (which probably dated from the days when the factory dryers were fired with wood), it flattened out and ran west along the northern slopes of the mountain, more or less parallel to the railway. I liked this path and often used it when I had to visit the tea fields above the railway. One got stupendous views all the way up, firstly looking down on Idalgashinna Station on its knife-edge ridge and through the Gap to the blue lowlands beyond, and then to the north over the Uva Basin, with the gentle rounded hills folded around Diyatalawa shimmering away to the distant ridge of Uda Pussellawa and the peaks of keel-shaped Narangala to the north and triangular Namunukula to the east. Sometimes I followed the path beyond the boundary of the tea and into the dense forest which covered these mountainsides to Ohiya and beyond, up to the Horton Plains. Here it was more of a bridleway than a footpath and Mr Meikle had told me that in the days before the building of the railway, this had been the main route from Haputale right through to Nuwara Eliya and the planting districts of Dimbula and Dickoya. I imagined the local planters mounted on their horses setting off to visit neighbours a day's ride away, or returning, perhaps somewhat the worse for wear, after a day at the Nuwara Eliya races. In those days the beef box came from Nuwara Eliya or Nanuoya and the beef box coolie would cover the 25 miles or so on foot in a day, with another day to carry back the full box.

I never seemed to have the time to follow the path more than a mile or two into the forest, but I never met anyone and enjoyed the solitude, with only the bronze-wing pigeons and olive thrushes for company. Sometimes sprays of tiny white flowers would hang from orchids perched on the moss-covered trees, and dark forest butterflies would alight where patches of sunlight evaded the dense shade. It was always cool in the forest and sometimes during the north-east monsoon it could be downright cold, with drizzle and damp mist swirling between the trees. On these occasions the labour gangs employed on field tasks, such as lopping of shade trees, would often light fires to warm their hands and keep out the numbing cold. Fredo always enjoyed visiting the forest and would disappear into the undergrowth on the tracks of porcupines or 'mouse deer', the tiny, foot-high deer-like chevrotain which tripped so daintily through the thickets that one heard only a slight rustle as they disappeared.

In wet weather leeches could be a nuisance in the forest, if one strayed into the undergrowth, and I kept a sharp watch for them on my shoes and legs in hopes of forestalling a bite. However, if they were numerous it was almost impossible to prevent one or two getting into one's shoes (often through the lace-holes) and working their loathsome way down between the toes, where they would painlessly suck away unnoticed until one removed the shoe and discovered a blood-soaked sock and bloated leech. The anti-coagulant injected during feeding usually prevented the blood from clotting

*View east over the Uva Basin from the Idulgashena gum plantation to Mt Namunukula, 6,679 ft.*

for some time after the leech had been dispatched and a cotton wool swab would be necessary between the toes attacked. Fredo did not suffer from leeches between his toes, although he spent most of his time in the undergrowth, but he did get them up his nose. This perturbed me for some time, as there seemed no way of getting them out, although he did not seem discomforted and would merely snort down his nose when they wriggled. They did not protrude from his nose except momentarily when he licked it or when he had a drink, and then the leech's tail would extend, wiggle, and quickly withdraw again. I then hit on a brilliant plan. When we set off on a walk I would conceal a pair of pliers in my pocket. After some distance, when Fredo stopped to have a drink at a stream or puddle, I would cover his eyes with one hand (as he hated to see the pliers) and, operating the pliers with the other, I would grip the tail of the leech when it protruded and whip it out. This seemed to work entirely satisfactorily. Fredo seemed to suffer no ill after-effects and merely gave a sniff as he trotted away. Estate life was ideal for a Beagle and Fredo enjoyed himself hugely as each day consisted mainly of two long walks. However, there were hidden hazards which neither of us appreciated.

Blister blight is a fungus disease which attacks young tea leaves. Closely related to the common leaf gall disease of azaleas in Europe, it causes a thickening and blister-like deformation of the leaf. This blister becomes white on the underside as the fungus produces spores and severe attacks render the leaf useless for tea manufacture. Originally Ceylon had been free from the disease, which was prevalent in Assam (whence the Indian type of tea plant originated) and also in the Darjeeling area. However, in 1946 the air currents of the north-east monsoon must have been exceptionally strong and, indeed, conditions were exceptionally wet, with much thick mist. In any case, somehow, in a few days, air-borne spores of the blister blight fungus travelled some 2,500 miles south-west from the tea areas of Assam and Darjeeling to infect tea on estates in the Mundakayam, Anamallai and Nilgiri Hills in South India, where it was first discovered in August of that year. On 25th October 1946 it was found in Ceylon on an estate in the Dolosbage District and within a very few weeks it was present in most of the districts on the wetter, south-western side of the hills. By the end of 1946, 68 estates were affected and it was apparent that at least several of the early outbreaks must have originated independently. My father, who was then in the Dickoya District, described returning to the estate in the New Year of 1947, after our Christmas holiday fortnight at the coast, to find the tea fields white with blisters.

In Ceylon at that time blister blight was the most feared of all the diseases and pests of the tea bush and was considered to present the greatest threat to tea cultivation. In an effort to keep it out, stringent laws forbidding the import of tea seed from India had been enacted. However, shortly before its arrival these had been relaxed as unjustified, as it was argued (correctly) that it was not spread with seed. Indeed, it was because the early tea plantations in Ceylon had been started with Indian tea seed and not with cuttings that Ceylon had remained free of the disease up to then. Nevertheless, its sudden appearance caused great consternation and recrimination amongst the tea planting community. Many feared that it would destroy the tea industry, just as the Ceylon coffee industry had been destroyed in the 1870s and1880s by the arrival of coffee rust disease. But this time, although the disease at first did much damage, satisfactory fungicides were available to control it and the tea industry survived, albeit with an added financial burden.

By the time I arrived on the scene in the 1950s, spraying against the disease was an established routine of tea estate management. Large, cylindrical brass sprayers were used, carried on the back in the rucksack position with webbing straps. They were pressurised by working a long handle which operated a pump at the base of the cylinder. The fungicides used were based on copper, either the coppery-red cuprous oxide, or the greenish-white copper oxychloride. These could not cure infection which had already taken place, but were prophylactic and had to be applied so that there was a protective deposit of copper fungicide on the leaves before infectious spores arrived. This meant that all the tea in bearing had to be sprayed regularly about every 10 to 14 days, and usually it was arranged that the spraying gang moved in just after the field had been plucked, so as to avoid contaminating the new growth which would be harvested on the next plucking round. The fungicides came as a powder which had to be mixed to the correct strength with water before application. Spraying used a lot of water, and in some areas of the Division there was no convenient stream to provide it. In these areas a few of the silt pits in the roadside drains were enlarged to a volume of about a cubic yard and these held enough water to supply the sprayers.

On one occasion Fredo had gone ahead, as usual, nose to ground, but when he did not return for some time I thought nothing of it and assumed that he was off on the trail of some mongoose or hare. However, as I plodded up the road I became aware of a sploshing sound and rounding a bend I discovered Fredo swimming round and round in one of the enlarged silt pits. This was not quite full, the water level being about a foot below the top, so he was unable to reach the rim or to get a purchase on the vertical sides and by the time I found him he was obviously getting very tired. There was no indication of how he had fallen in, but it was the work of a moment to haul him out by the scruff of his neck. If I had taken a different route, this incident might have had a tragic ending.

Soon after I moved to Idulgashena, my birthday came round again and this time it was my twenty-first. However, Idulgashena was much too remote to think of having a party: who would be bothered to come all that way and tackle all those 22 hairpin bends? So I made no attempt to celebrate but did the check-roll in the evening and went to bed early.

Other events soon gave me more serious things to think about. Gomez had come to me one day and informed me that he was thinking of getting married again. Perhaps he had been encouraged in this by the more spacious quarters he was now occupying and by the increase in pay which I had given him. I did not feel very enthusiastic about this news, although I congratulated him and wished him well. I felt even less enthusiastic when I discovered that his newly betrothed was a young girl in her twenties and not the comfortable, motherly figure of around his own age that I had at first envisaged he might select. An age gap of 30 years seemed to me, even inexperienced as I was, to spell nothing but trouble. Gomez, as befitted his ancestry, was a Catholic, and I had visions of numerous babies arriving to distract his attention from my household. Or, worse, perhaps the girl's affections would wander and I should have to deal with domestic strife. However, I felt it was not for me to try to dissuade him and, as I was probably younger than his intended bride, any adverse advice from me might not have gone down too well. So the ceremony took place at the Catholic church in Haputale and the young lady moved into the appu's quarters with the proud Gomez.

All was sweetness and light for a few weeks and Gomez went about his work like the proverbial dog with two tails. Then one night I was woken in the early hours of the morning by the *karvalkaran* (watchman) tapping on my window. Please would I come quickly as the appu had been taken ill. I knew the watchman would not have disturbed me unless there was a serious problem, so I dressed quickly, grabbed my torch, and hurried to the appu's house. Here I found the watchman, young Mrs Gomez, and several unknown hangers-on grouped around a bed on which Gomez was slumped. In the dim light of a hurricane lantern he looked to me to be in a fairly bad way, being scarcely conscious and breathing very shallowly. Someone helpfully suggested it could be heart trouble. I was woefully ignorant of first-aid and I had no idea what to do so I felt the best thing was to get him to hospital, the nearest being the little hospital at Haldummulla. With some difficulty, we carried Gomez down to the garage and got him into the front seat of the car. Thinking I might need some help, I told the watchman to get in the back and we set off up the hill, over the railway, and down the long and tortuous Needwood cart road in the thick night. At Haldummulla the hospital was in pitch darkness. Leaving the lights of the car to illuminate the front of the building, I entered the veranda and hammered on the door. Nothing happened. I walked around the building, but could see no other obvious point of entry, so I continued banging on the door and shouting. After what seemed an age, I heard a scuffling sound within. Soon the door opened an inch and a dim and rather bleary face appeared. I explained what the trouble was and asked for the Dispenser, my explanation in Tamil being helpfully amplified in Sinhala by the watchman (who was a Sinhalese). This personage was apparently not present, but the dim face apparently belonged to a medical orderly of sorts and he eventually prepared a bed on which we were able to get Gomez comfortable before leaving him.

When I visited the hospital next day, I was able to see the Dispenser who told me that Gomez did indeed have heart trouble and would need a considerable period of rest. I could not help wondering whether his unaccustomed exertions with young Mrs Gomez might have had something to do with this, although I did not say so to the Dispenser. For the next few days, while Gomez was in hospital, the houseboy bravely attempted to do the cooking. However, although he could do eggs in various ways, more complicated cuisine appeared to be beyond him. Gomez was discharged from the hospital with a recommendation for at least two months' rest, and it certainly did not appear that he would be able to resume his normal duties very soon. I felt in a serious dilemma. The houseboy, although willing and pleasant, could not run the bungalow and could not cook. There also seemed no guarantee that Gomez would return to normal, even after two months, and indeed there seemed every prospect of the problem occurring again, especially if young Mrs Gomez was still around. It might have been possible to get someone who could cook to stand in temporarily, but I could not afford to go on paying Gomez as well as another cook for any length of time. Very reluctantly, I came to the conclusion that the only course was to pay Gomez off and recruit a new appu.

Although Gomez had been more or less retired when he came to me, it did seem very hard that he should lose his job through illness. Never-the-less, this was not unusual and was an accepted hazard of life on estates (and most other situations at the time), where the extended family normally provided the essentials of social security. I arranged that his notice would correspond to his two months 'rest', during which time I went through the process of advertising for and interviewing applicant appus; a process which I certainly did not relish. Eventually I settled on Carupiah, who came from Attampettia Estate, not far on the other side of Bandarawela. Carupiah was young by Gomez's standards being, I guessed, in his early thirties, but he was pleasant and had very good references, so all I could do was hope for the best. Gomez and his entourage departed with dignity, and the gratuity which I gave him, and Carupiah moved into the appu's quarters.

Carupiah had a wife and family, but did not at first bring them to Idulgashena, which seemed to me indicative of a sensible outlook. His children were of school age and there was no suitable school for them at Idalgashinna, so they remained at Attampettia, although his wife appeared from time to time. We got on well and he turned out to be almost as good a cook as Gomez had been, so my domestic life gradually returned to normal although my bank balance took longer to recover.

I knew Attampettia and its neighbouring estate, Aislaby, quite well as it was possible to take a shortcut through these estates from Bandarawela to Uda Pussellawa, if one knew the cart roads. I was also sometimes a visitor to the SD bungalow on Aislaby, which had only recently been built. Very few new bungalows for senior staff were being built on estates at this time, so the SD bungalow on Aislaby was of special interest and fascinated visitors from other estates by having all the latest electrical and bathroom fittings. Its first occupants were Bill and his wife, Theresa, who had come to Ceylon from Rhodesia, where Bill had been in the air force. They were quite a young couple, although Bill was several years older than me. As the youngest SD in the District, it was quite a novelty to meet someone who had not been planting for as long as myself. Theresa was about my age, but already had three small children. However, they were very sociable. Theresa was an especially lively personality, and the children (with the help of an ayah) did not inhibit them entertaining. Not long after they moved in, and to celebrate the completion of the bungalow, they gave a housewarming party to which I was invited.

Now parties were few and far between, so the invitation was very welcome anyway. But this was especially attractive because they had apparently invited a couple of new teachers who had recently arrived from the UK to teach at the Hill School (the European prep school) in Nuwara Eliya, only about an hour's drive from Aislaby. As it was on a Saturday evening I decided I could do the check-roll on the Sunday morning, and I made sure that nothing else prevented my attendance. The hour-and-a-quarter's drive from Idulgashena would be a minor price to pay for a party with two real unattached young women present.

In the event, I felt the party hardly lived up to my (perhaps over-optimistic) expectations in spite of the fact that not two but three unattached young women were present. Most of the other young SDs in the district were also present and Bill and Theresa laid on excellent food and drink. All three girls were teachers from the Hill School. Anne and Shirley both had blonde shoulder-length hair and were rather quiet, while Pat was a lively brunette. Shirley had only recently arrived in Ceylon and no doubt was wondering what to make of this crowd of glib young planters, all anxious to make her acquaintance. Pat, like Anne, had been teaching at the school for a year or two, so was well versed in dealing with the advances she received. The three of them were the centre of attention and I didn't get much of a look in, especially when plans were being made for meeting up in Nuwara Eliya the next day. Quite apart from the check-roll obligation, it was really too far from Idulgashena for me to participate easily and, as often happened, I felt rather discouraged on my long drive home. However, I saw quite a lot of Bill and Theresa over the next few months. Theresa and I got on very well. I found her very lively and amusing and at least she provided some female company of my own age.

Wherever Scots are numerous, there is usually a Caledonian Society and the Ceylon Caledonian Society was a very active and prestigious organisation. It organised various activities, both in Colombo and up-country, and the height of its social calendar was the Caledonian Ball. This was held at the Galle Face Hotel in Colombo, which at that time was the best and most imposing hotel in the capital. The Caledonian Ball was always over-subscribed and tickets were difficult to get. I therefore felt delighted and complimented when friends told me that they had two spare tickets for the Ball and invited me and a partner to join them. There was just one snag: I had no partner. In fact, as far as I knew at that moment, there was no unmarried young female of any kind in my limited social circle. I was very loath to refuse the invitation, especially as I enjoyed Scottish dancing and ceremony and felt a certain kinship with the Scots through my Scottish great grandfather. I cast around in my mind for a solution and eventually decided to ask Theresa if she would accompany me. This she agreed to do, and I arranged for us to stay in Colombo with my sister and brother-in-law (or 'bil' as the Ceylonese would have it).

Being a staunch Scot himself, Mr Meikle was sympathetic to my request for a day's leave for such a Scottish occasion. My English friends, however, were ribald and on hearing that I was taking Theresa commented that the Ball was likely to be more like that of Kirrie Muir than Caledonia. Little did they know how naive I was. Nevertheless, on the appointed Saturday I called for Theresa at Aislaby and we had a pleasant drive to Colombo, arriving in good time to prepare ourselves for the evening's event.

For such a formal event as this, there was no doubt as to what one should wear. I donned my (woollen) dress trousers, my white 'sharkskin' jacket, maroon cummerbund and black tie, while Theresa produced an off-the-shoulder evening gown in pale blue, which complemented her dark hair very well and in the heat of Colombo was doubtless a lot cooler for her than my trousers and jacket were for me. In fact the heat seemed to be affecting me quite a lot and I did not feel too bright as we set off to meet our friends at the hotel.

The Galle Face Hotel is on the sea shore about a mile south of the Fort, the commercial centre of the city. Built in solid colonial style in 1864, it was unchallenged as the premier hotel of Colombo for more than 100 years. Set with the sea to one side, it faces north over the mile-long expanse of the Galle Face Green, an open grassy space with a promenade on the seaward side which stretches almost all the way from the Hotel to the city centre. It was originally laid out as the 'Galle Face Walk' between 1856 and 1859 at the instigation of Sir Henry Ward, the governor at the time. Half way along the promenade, set with its back to the sea, there is a granite commemorative stone. The inscription reads:

GALLE FACE
WALK
Commenced by
SIR HENRY WARD
1856
Completed 1859
and recommended
to his Successors
in the interest of the
Ladies and Children
of Colombo

These days the Galle Face Green is much used by the locals for romantic promenades, for political meetings and other public gatherings. Doubtless it was not actually the local ladies, children, and other citizens who now use it so much that Sir Henry had in mind when he started the project. However, the preservation of such a large area of public open space by the sea shore so near to the heart of the city warrants the memorial. Sir Henry left Ceylon soon afterwards to become governor of Madras, but died of cholera almost immediately he assumed his new post.

In the 1950s, and for as far back as I can remember, the Galle Face Hotel was painted a most distinctive brick red colour and each window had a canvas canopy in alternate black and white stripes, making it quite unmistakable. The entrance to the hotel was under a solid and extensive porch and on the evening of the Caledonian Ball it was a melee of cars and people. There were many men in kilts and some women in formal white evening gowns with tartan sashes. I had to park out on the Green, and Theresa and I then made our way through the throng, met our friends and found our table in the dining room. All the public rooms were huge, with high windows and many ornamental openings in the walls through which air could freely circulate. Rows of electric fans, suspended by long stems from the lofty ceilings, lazily stirred the thick and humid air, but this did little to combat the heavy heat of the tropical night.

By this time I was feeling quite unwell, but I attributed it to the heat and the activity of parking the car and getting us organised while clad in full evening dress rig. We had our dinner, during which the haggis was duly piped in with traditional ceremony. The hotel waiters were faultlessly trained and padded between the tables in their spotless white jackets and sarongs. Amongst them were several imposing personages with bristling moustaches and wearing the semicircular tortoiseshell combs denoting their senior social status. All went well until, with a sudden movement of my elbow, I managed to tip the contents of the gravy jug down Theresa's wonderful blue gown. How could I be so careless? Although I could see she was upset, she gallantly refrained from taking me to task as a clumsy oaf and cleaned herself up as much as the facilities of the ladies' room permitted. However, I am afraid that the dress could never have recovered from its sousing with good Scottish gravy.

After the meal, Scottish dancing began and we did many waltzes, strathspeys, reels, and jigs, until the band finished sometime after midnight. With the ceasing of the revels, I began to feel unwell again and felt I was developing a temperature. However, I was sure it was nothing that a couple of Asprin could not cure, my only regret being that I felt I could not be the lively companion that Theresa had been expecting. We returned to the house, said our goodnights rather quickly, and retired, with a dose of Asprin for me instead of the flirtation with Theresa which I had secretly been hoping for.

The next morning I did not feel much better; in fact I seemed to have developed a troublesome cough, and by the time we were ready to depart I was again running a temperature. Nevertheless, I felt I wanted to deliver Theresa back to Aislaby, as promised, and get back home to Idulgashena where I could deal with whatever infection I must have picked up. So we set off. It was still very hot and seemed to be getting hotter by the minute. By the time we reached Ratnapura I was finding it quite difficult to drive and the glare of the searing midday sun was hurting my eyes in spite of sun glasses. We decided to call at the Ratnapura Rest House for some lunch and a rest (although I did not feel like eating much). It happened that Henry, an acquaintance of mine from the Badulla area, had also stopped for lunch at the Rest House and we joined him for a chat. It gradually became clear that I would have considerable difficulty in completing the remaining two hours or more of the journey. Theresa did not drive, so Henry very kindly offered to take us on in his car, while I left mine at the Rest House to be collected later. Although rather reluctant, I was persuaded to accept and so Henry delivered me back to Idulgashena feeling very crestfallen and also very unwell, and took Theresa on to Aislaby.

Dosing myself with Paracetamol, I retired coughing to bed, nursing a headache which seemed to have the proportions of an earthquake. I awoke several times during the night to find myself soaked with sweat and, after several changes of garments, I wrapped myself in a towel in an attempt to keep the sheets reasonably dry. The next morning I was no better and felt worse. I informed Mr Meikle that I was out of action, and gathered from his tone that he seemed to find my feeling 'a bit peely-wally' rather a nuisance. Eventually I decided to make use of the Uva Medical Scheme. It was at times like this that the external phone at Idulgashena came into its own. I telephoned Dr Ellis Jones. On hearing my symptoms and the circumstances of their appearance, he diagnosed a severe hangover and prescribed Alkaseltsa. This irritated me considerably and in the evening, feeling depressed and

132

sweating again from the effects of the Paracetamol, I phoned my parents. Although I tried to conceal how unwell I felt, I was evidently unsuccessful. My mother decided I was in need of her care and, together with my grandmother, who lived with my parents and from whom she was inseparable, she set off for Idulgashena almost immediately.

They must have arrived sometime in the early hours, as they were in the bungalow when I woke the following morning. My mother took charge of affairs and contacted Dr Ellis Jones somewhat more forcefully than I had. This eventually prompted a visit from him, whereupon he pronounced a revised diagnosis of double pneumonia. My temperature was now rising alarmingly so, in addition, he ordered my immediate evacuation to hospital in Colombo. This was rapidly arranged, and I presently found myself on my way back to Colombo in the Uva Medical Scheme 'ambulance' (in fact a converted estate car), my destination being the Joseph Fraser Memorial Nursing Home.

The Fraser Home, as it was universally known, would these days be called a private hospital and catered to the needs of the expatriate and professional communities. Almost all planting families had had some contact with it over the years and in our case this included the birth of my sister there some 25 years previously. I had also had a previous admission when I had developed incipient septicaemia from a wound in the leg from a pruned tea bush. As on that occasion, my initial treatment on admission was a massive injection of penicillin. Fortunately, this acts on me like magic, and the following day my temperature was near normal, although it was a week before I was discharged to recuperate for another fortnight at my parents' bungalow.

# Anticipation                                          **11**

---

I eventually arrived back at Idulgashena feeling weak and out of condition, although Mr Meikle seemed to feel that I had taken a rather too generous amount of time recuperating. On medical advice I spent the next month quietly with very little social contact, and I kept away from the club. This gave me even more time than usual on my own in the evenings and at weekends, so I turned my attention to interests which had first been kindled at school.

Processing my own black and white film and making enlargements was one of these interests, which I had resumed while I was on Meeriabedde. I had bought an enlarger from a planter neighbour, but darkroom equipment and chemicals were expensive and difficult to get outside Colombo. However, I made a few purchases when opportunity arose and transformed kitchen baking trays into dishes for developer and fixer by covering them with white enamel paint. Light-proofing a space for use as a darkroom was always a problem, and I was compelled to restrict my photo-processing activities to the late evening, after it was fully dark and when there was no appreciable moonlight. A dark red 'safelight' bulb fitted in an ordinary table light made an effective darkroom lamp. I found the creation of black and white prints most enjoyable and rewarding, but clearing up after a session was tedious and tiring, especially as I seldom finished before midnight and had to be up for muster next morning before dawn. After moving to Idulgashena things were a little easier, as I used the second bathroom as a darkroom and did not have to clear up so completely between sessions.

I got some good results with my little Voightländer 35mm camera and joined the Ceylon Camera Club, which subsequently established a branch at Bandarawela. My subjects, of course, were largely landscapes and natural history and, after a while, I began to find the Voightländer, with its unchangeable lens and parallax-prone viewfinder, very limiting. Accordingly, after I had been on Idulgashena a few months, I bought a new camera on one of my rare visits to Colombo and sold the excellent but inflexible Voightländer to Bill on Aislaby. My new purchase was an Edixa Reflex, a relatively cheap but effective 35mm single-lens reflex fitted with a 'macro' lens capable of focussing down to 4 inches. This was excellent for plants and, before I acquired a telephoto lens for bird and animal shots, I made several close-up studies of plants and insects in the garden. My medically-enforced confinement gave me time to make some good prints, and one or two of these won Camera Club competitions at the Bandarawela Branch.

Another interest was in wood turning. There was a small room near the kitchen, at the back of the Idulgashena bungalow, which obviously had originally been intended for use by an appu or houseboy. However, as Carupiah used the separate appu's quarters, the room was unoccupied and I determined to fit it up as a wood turning workshop. First I employed one of the estate stonemasons to build a broad plinth by the window. I then purchased a half horsepower electric motor, and found two old bearings, a faceplate, and a short piece of discarded shafting in the Idulgashena factory. I got the estate blacksmith to thread one end of the shafting to take the faceplate and the other for fitting a grinding wheel. I designed two reciprocal cone pulleys, each with four positions which could use a car fan belt to transfer the drive from the motor to the shaft, and these I had made in Bandarawela by a local engineering firm. One was beautifully machined from a block of brass, which today would be impossibly expensive but was then quite cheap. They evidently had difficulty with the other one, which they made out of cast aluminium alloy. This looked as if it had been made out of a metallic sponge, as it was full of air bubble holes, but these were small enough not to interfere with the working of the pulley, so did not really matter. The only remaining difficulty was to devise some kind of clutch. After trying out one or two abortive ideas, I eventually hit on the plan of mounting the motor on a piece of channel-iron, pivoted so that it would tip and remain on one side or the other under its own substantial weight. The tipping was accomplished by means of a handle attached to the channel-iron. This arrangement worked very well; the weight of the motor held the belt amply taut in the 'drive' position to give sufficient power, but it would jump back without damage if there was any serious jam with the wood or cutting tool. The whole contraption was mounted on the plinth by means of upturned bolts set in a layer of concrete. Finally, with the aid of the grindstone, I made several excellent turning tools out of worn-out files from the blacksmith's shop. The machine looked a bit dull, so I cheered it up by painting the ironwork in bright yellow and green with the paint I had used for the *Nandu*.

Rather to my surprise (as I had little idea at what speeds the wood should rotate and had had to make a guess) my brainchild worked very well and I started to produce bowls and platters out of such woods as I could obtain. It was difficult to find well-seasoned wood in baulks thick enough to produce reasonably deep bowls, but I was able to get some imported Burma teak, and on one occasion I saved some satin wood from 60-year-old railway sleepers which were being replaced. I made my own French polish out of shellac dissolved in methylated spirits and I was well pleased with the good finish of the polished products. The only drawback was that I started to get hay fever from the thick and voluminous dust which my vigorous sandpapering produced, which was probably also not too good for my recently infected pulmonary system. However, this was easily prevented by using a simple mask with gauze filters.

With Carupiah's good cooking and Fredo leading me on my daily tours of the Division, my strength gradually returned and life resumed its normal routine. During my period of convalescence at my parents' home on New Peacock Group in the Pussellawa District, I had received a telephone call from the Secretary of the Ceylon Bird Club, inviting me to become a member. I already knew of this organisation, which had been started originally by the planter and naturalist, W. W. A. Phillips, and the ornithologist, Cicily Lushington, in the 1940s, mainly to gather data for the books they were each preparing on Ceylon birds. In fact 'organisation' was perhaps too pretentious a description, as there were only about a dozen members altogether and it was operated very informally. However, membership was only by invitation and was restricted to those whom the existing members considered competent observers and ornithologists, so I felt quite complimented. Members were expected to submit monthly reports of their observations to the Secretary, who's job it was to type these up and circulate them to all members as a kind of newsletter. This was really the only activity of the Club, as members were widely dispersed throughout the Island and so meetings were impractical. A very small subscription covered the costs of stationery and postage. I gladly accepted and looked forward to receiving the monthly reports.

The Wild Life Protection Society of Ceylon was a much bigger and more formal association which had been established as long ago as 1894. It was also very active, pressing the government of the day for establishment of new reserves and improvements to the wildlife protection laws. The WLPS held meetings at fairly frequent intervals in Colombo and occasionally also in the upcountry centres. Sometimes these were held at the Badulla Club or in Bandarawela and meetings often concluded with a show of slides or a film by one of the local members. I became a member of the WLPS very soon after I started on Meeriabedde and attended the meetings whenever I could. I soon got to know the people in the District who were interested in wildlife and its conservation and in turn became known myself, both through the WLPS meetings and through my articles in the WLPS journal *Loris*, for which I continued to write.

It so happened that the Hon. Secretary of the WLPS at the time was one of the local planters, Ted Norris, who was on Pingarawa Estate in the Passara District, about half an hour's drive from Bandarawela. Ted, and his wife Patsy, were stalwarts of the Society, for which they did a tremendous amount of work, and never missed a function. Besides being an expert naturalist, Ted was also quite a talented artist and often illustrated his articles with his own sketches. This struck a chord with me, as I had started to make botanical drawings and paintings of the local wild plants and Ted and Patsy were most encouraging and appreciative. I became a fairly regular visitor to their bungalow where I met many of the local leading figures in natural history and wildlife conservation. One of these was Max, who was also a planter in the Passara District. Although substantially older than myself, he was younger than Ted and was considered a rather dashing figure in the District, at least by several of the younger wives. Max had made himself an expert on the frogs and other amphibians of Ceylon and sometimes gave lectures on this topic. Eventually, his interests in natural history got the better of him and not long after I got to know him, he managed to get a post with the Game Department of Tanganyika and became a Game Ranger there.

Several of the larger tea companies had estates both in Ceylon and in East Africa, where production was being expanded. Some experienced planters were being recruited from Ceylon to strengthen the management of estates there and, just as Bill Horne had been transferred to Mauritius, one or two of my planting acquaintances transferred to East Africa. Gail's stepfather, Tony, was one of these and I was sad to see him and Elaine depart from Kumarawatte to take up a post on Kibabet, one of the estates owned by the same company in the Nandi Hills District of Kenya.

East Africa was a Mecca for anyone interested in natural history, especially birds or mammals, and a visit (or transfer) there was the goal of everyone in the wildlife fraternity. Some planters managed to visit East Africa as part of their home leave. They returned with wonderful accounts of their safaris, the magnificent landscapes, and the countless herds of game, sometimes giving a slide or film show to illustrate a talk. Everything seemed to be bigger, fiercer, more colourful, better or more numerous than in Ceylon, and (perhaps mistakenly) one gained the impression that the colonial governments of the East African countries took a greater interest in preserving their wildlife inheritance than did that of Ceylon.

On one occasion I was invited to dinner by an older couple who were on an estate not far away and, presumably to keep me company, they invited along another young S.D. After dinner they gave a slide show on their travels in East Africa, which kept me riveted. Our hosts were good naturalists and their slides were excellent. However, unfortunately they had misjudged the interests of my fellow guest, who evidently was not nearly so keen on East Africa or its fauna. He instantly went conspicuously to sleep and failed to wake up when the lights came on for changing the magazine. Although I confidently expected him to wake at any moment, full of apologies, this did not happen. He remained firmly asleep at the end of the show, continued asleep (with penetrating snores) through the serving of coffee, and was still asleep when I left half an hour later. Apparently he was not at all embarrassed when eventually they had to rouse him and suggest that it was time he went home as they were going to bed themselves. I never discovered if he was ever again invited.

As my first contribution to the notes of the Ceylon Bird Club, I sent in my more interesting records for the previous six months. The format started with a brief description of the weather and then gave short observations of resident birds breeding, migrants seen, and anything else of note, not limited to birds only, but including observations of wildlife in general. The following gives the general flavour of the notes:

*Idulgashena, 4,600-5,900ft., Haputale District, Uva Hills.*

October 1958. Rainfall 11.18in., 21 wet days.

Lahugalla area visited 11th. Tank very low. Azure Flycatcher, Black-capped Bulbul, Forest Wagtail, female Shama. One elephant visible on the north side in mid afternoon.

Indian Paradise Flycatcher. A fine male in full white adult plumage visited the garden on 31st and stayed all the day. I suspect the Idalgashinna Gap is used by migrants passing to and from the Uva Basin to the south and southeast low country.

Wild pig. A large boar caused consternation among the shade tree lopping gang on 21st when it was flushed from beneath a tea bush. In April a plucker was killed by a boar in the same locality. Pig are common in the jungle nearby.

· · · ·

April 1959. Rainfall 12.94in., 19 wet days; a damp month. The wind is backing round to the south-west, whence it was blowing strongly on 22nd.

Grey Wagtail. Those which had been resident here during the north-east monsoon had all left by the 2nd; very early. Single birds on passage were seen on 18th, 22nd, and 28th.

Brown Shrike. Still present in numbers on 30th.

Kashmir Flycatcher. Last definite record on 12th, but probably stayed longer.

Pied Shrike. Two cocks competing for a hen on 8th; tea area, 5,000ft.

Shikra. Pair suspected breeding in pollarded grevillea at 5,000ft. Hen flushed on 11th from what appears to be a nest at a height of 30ft from the ground and both birds appear frequently in the area. Female seen with a large rat at 8.30a.m.

Dusky-blue Flycatcher. Two very well-concealed nests found on 18th in the bank on the Ohiya track in thick jungle. One at 5,800ft with newly hatched young and the other at 5,900ft. with well incubated c/2. This bird had also been brooding a stone of irregular shape, but with no sharp corners, about twice the size of an egg. The stone had probably fallen from the bank overhanging the nest, but I could not be sure. Both at heights of 3-5ft. were in very dark recesses and the cups of the nests were very deep, making it difficult to see inside.

Large Ceylon Flying Squirrel. One was shot by a member of the estate staff on the evening of 18th in jungle at about 5,800 ft. I inspected this and found it to be a large male in good condition.

I relished the feeling that in Ceylon, unlike England, such commonplace observations had not all been made dozens of times before and that, even if my observations were not altogether new, they might still contribute towards confirmation of some aspect of bird biology or behaviour. For example, I did indeed confirm that the Idalgashinna Gap (the pass in the Haputale range occupied by Idalgashinna railway station) was regularly used as a migration route by birds passing from the Uva Basin and surrounding highlands to the southern lowlands and coastal plain.

In fact birds were not the only migrants using the Idalgashinna Gap. In the early months of the year it was also used by butterflies migrating from the lowlands northwards. These butterflies were of several different species, but all belonged to the Pieridae family: the yellows and whites. One would see them coming up the hillside from Needwood Division, flying in mixed skeins of a few dozen together and about 5 to 10 ft. above the tea, all travelling in the same general direction although with a butterfly's irregular flight. The station platform was a good place to see them as they passed over and continued down the northern tea-covered slopes, still following the contours of the land. Butterfly migrations are a regular occurrence in many parts of upcountry Sri Lanka and a widespread legend has it that the insects are on a pilgrimage to die at Adam's Peak, the spectacular 7000-ft conical peak in the Maskeliya District. This mountain is revered by several religions, each of which claim that the large 'footprint' on the summit belongs to one of their holy personages. Many Sri Lankan Buddhists believe it to be the footprint of the Lord Buddha and so call it *Sri Pada*. Because of the butterfly legend, it is also known as *Samanalakande* (Butterfly Mountain). In fact the direction of many of these migrations was indeed more or less towards *Samanalakande*. As I never observed a return migration in the opposite direction, there seemed no logical explanation for the biology of this phenomenon.

The Idalgashinna Gap has historical as well as biological interest, for it was through this pass in 1630 that the Governor of the Portuguese possessions in Ceylon, Don Constantine de Saa y Noroña, led his army of about 10,000 men in an attempt to annex the Kandyan principality of Oovah (as Uva used to be spelt). At this time the Portuguese had already been present in Ceylon for 125 years and ruled the lowland areas in a harsh and religiously intolerant manner. They had already made several attempts to annex the Kandyan kingdom in the mountains, but had been unsuccessful. On this occasion their substantial force included about 1,500 European troops together with the same number of half-castes, the remainder being lowland Sinhalese, presumably from the rival kingdom of Kotte, which occupied the south-west of the Island. Looking down now from the hillside above Idalgashinna at the sleepy little station idling peacefully in the bright sunshine, it is difficult to imagine a marauding army of this size, with its attendant baggage, weapons and provisions, pouring up the hillside through what is now Needwood, through the Gap and down into the Uva Basin in just the same direction as the migrating butterflies. Apparently Don Constantine had been informed that the population of Oovah was dissatisfied with Kandyan rule and would support his invasion. He did in fact encounter no opposition at first and penetrated as far as the capital at Badulla, which was sacked in true Portuguese fashion, and he then attempted to retreat the way he had come. However, at a pre-arranged point, the lowland Sinhalese deserted to their brethren on the Kandyan side and the Portuguese were massacred to a man, including the misguided Don Constantine.

During my time on Needwood and Idulgashena I never heard of any artifacts from this campaign being found. The only visible signs of this great invasion are rudimentary remains of the Katugodella Fort, built by the Portuguese as a staging post halfway up the mountain on a knoll not far from where Needwood Factory now stands. The mountainside here flattens out somewhat before falling away again for another 1000 ft to Haldummulla village and on down to the low foothills. The knoll rises at the edge of this area and commands a wide area of country. Today it is patana grassland and used for grazing a few cattle. Much patana grassland is of ancient origin and although in Portuguese days most of Needwood must have been thick forest, the knoll and surrounding area could well have been patana then, providing an additional reason for the location of the fort.

Surprisingly, while I was on Needwood and Idulgashena, I also never heard mention of the mansion which is now the Benedictine Monastery of Adisham, but which was then in private hands. Adisham mansion stands on the northern slopes of Beragala, just above the railway line and below the forest of the Tangamalai wild life sanctuary, looking out north over the Uva Basin. The access road connects with the Beauvais-Glenanore-Haputale road at the point where a path leads up into the Tangamalai Santuary. It was built, I think about 1930, for his retirement by Sir Thomas Villiers, and no expense was spared. The name was taken from the parish of Adisham in Kent, of which his father, Henry Montagu Villiers, was prebendary vicar. Thomas Villiers was a leading figure in Ceylon planting and political circles of his time. Starting off as a planter, between 1887 and 1906, he then went into commerce in Colombo and spent much of his business career with George Steuarts. He was prominent in local politics and served on both the Legislative and State Councils of Ceylon, receiving his knighthood in 1933, just after his retirement. Through his mother, Lady Victoria Russell, he was a grandson of the nineteenth century British Prime Minister, Lord John Russell, and thus a cousin of Bertrand Russell, the philosopher. Through his other grandfather, who was Bishop of Carlisle and then (very briefly) Bishop of Durham, he was related to the Earls of Clarendon and thus was a very well-connected and influential person.

The mansion has two floors and a steep roof covered with wooden shingles. The structure is of carefully-dressed granite blocks, with windows and doors having rather unusual, slightly arched outlines. The frames and floors are of Burma teak and the rooms were evidently handsomely decorated and furnished. The garden has terraces at the front and a huge lawn at the side. Sir Thomas left numerous relatives in Ceylon planting and commerce, one of them being Monty of Dambatenne, who was the son of Sir Thomas's cousin, Reggie Villiers.

Estate life continued in a steady routine and at evening muster I usually took charge of weighing the leaf, calling out the weights and entering them in the checkroll against the plucker's name preparatory to totalling the figures when I did the checkroll in the evening. At about half past four on the afternoon of 25th September 1959 I was, as usual, standing at the desk in the factory side entrance, surrounded by deep piles of green leaf and concentrating on calculating the weight of each load before entering the figures in the checkroll. Suddenly there was a commotion within the factory and when I looked round, the Assistant Teamaker emerged.

'Sir', he said, 'it has just been announced on the radio that the Prime Minister, Mr Bandaranaike, has been assassinated.'

I was somewhat nonplussed by this announcement: what should be the appropriate reaction on being told the Prime Minister has been assassinated? Horror, presumably, combined with shock, and concern for his family. Solomon Bandaranaike, although in many ways an opportunist politician, was very popular with most of the poorer Sinhalese population. However, his sympathy for socialist policies and for nationalisation of private business did not endear him to the planting community. I did not follow the political situation very closely, receiving no newspapers and seldom listening to the local radio. I could not feel great shock nor, being a rather calm person and a bad actor, could I put on much of a show of horror. The Assistant Teamaker was therefore probably disappointed at my lack of histrionics when I replied 'Oh dear, I'm sorry to hear that. Do they know who did it?' Very fortunately, the assassin turned out not to be a Tamil, which would have precipitated immediate civil strife, but a Buddhist monk who, like many of the Buddhist *bikkus*, apparently thought that S. W. R. D. Bandaranaike was insufficiently supportive of the Sinhalese and Buddhist causes and was giving too much away to the Tamils, Hindus and Christians. He was succeeded by his wife, Mrs Sirimavo Bandaranaike, who until then had not taken a public role in Ceylon politics but became the world's first female prime minister.

When I started on Meeriabedde, the four years tour of service which I had to complete before my first furlough (long 'home' leave) had seemed an absolutely interminable period. An event so far distant in the future scarcely entered my thoughts. However, in late 1958 several of my friends went on home leave and by the middle of 1959, when they started returning, it dawned upon me that this event, so long and so eagerly anticipated, was now drawing near for myself. What did I really want to do with such precious time? Well, one thing which had become clear in my mind was that I needed some female company. Absorbing as natural history was, and much as I enjoyed my freedom to pursue my various interests, I had begun to feel that they could not compete with sex, which was so conspicuously lacking in my life. This was accentuated when one or two acquaintances returned from leave having acquired fiancées, and Hans had actually appeared with a beautiful Swedish wife in tow. I was now nearly 22 and if I had to do another four years before my next long leave, I would have reached the incredibly advanced age of 26. Something had to be done about this, and I decided to spend quite a lot of time in England to see what opportunities might turn up. However, I was also determined to visit East Africa, so I started to gather information on what one could do and I wrote to Max, who by then was established as the game ranger at Lake Manyara. People also often bought a new car on leave and brought it back with them when they returned to Ceylon. This too seemed a good idea; one would have the use of the car duty-free while on leave, and because it would then be classed as 'used' one would pay less import duty when it was eventually imported into Ceylon.

I became quite busy with all these preparations, contacting people about East Africa, travel schedules, and reviewing the merits of various cars. I also suddenly realised that my leave would fall due on 1ˢᵗ December and that I would therefore be in England almost entirely during the winter, with very little prospect of some good weather, so I wrote to the Managing Director of George Steuart & Co., asking if I could postpone my leave by one or two months so that it would finish at the end of June or July instead of May. At that time the normal mode of travel to and from Europe was by ship, the passage each way taking about a fortnight (indeed, this was partly why six months was needed to make home leave worth while). However, it would be difficult to visit East Africa unless I travelled by air, at least on my journey from Ceylon to the UK. As planters were considered to have a superior social status (only just below that of the old colonial administrators), it was usual for shipboard travel to be First Class. It would never do to have one's estate superintendents and assistants mixing with that frightful lot of Aussies and Kiwis with which the 'tourist' class was usually infested. Air fares were expensive, but the cost of a First Class P&O passage, to which my terms entitled me, would just about cover an economy round-trip ticket by air. I therefore added a request to be allowed to convert my sea passage into an air ticket.

Nothing happened for a long time. However, a visit to Colombo gave me the opportunity to put my request in person. Whenever one visited Colombo, it was incumbent to call at the Agents' offices and pay one's respects, even if one had no specific matters to discuss with them. In fact such calls were very useful for PDs, who could discuss estate problems and policy more easily than over the crackly and uncertain telephone, but were less so for SDs like myself who had no input to the more general management of the estate. Nevertheless, they might have allowed the Agents' directors to get to know the more junior members of the senior plantation staff if a more relaxed atmosphere had been generated. At George Steuarts these visits were always very formal and the atmosphere generated was reminiscent of a headmaster reluctantly entertaining a tiresome and rather uninteresting pupil. I found the visits very stressful, especially as they necessitated being dressed in the smartest office attire, which was quite unsuited to the heat of Colombo. To wear more casual clothes would have been considered disrespectful. Now, although the temperature did not often reach 90°F, Colombo could be seriously hot and was also extremely humid. Within minutes of having a cold shower one would be sweating again and on humid nights without air conditioning or a fan one would lie tossing and turning in a sweat-soaked depression on the bed until sleep eventually came. Cars did not have air conditioning but most people used woven cane backrests, which prevented one's shirt from becoming completely soaked. If parked in the sun, which sometimes could not be avoided, cars became man-sized ovens and had to be ventilated for several minutes before one could get in. After half an hour in the sun, an egg could easily be fried on the bonnet, while the plastic-like Rexine fabric with which the seats were usually covered could burn the backs of the thighs of anyone wearing shorts.

Smart office dress in Colombo in those days consisted of longish white drill shorts and a white short-sleeved shirt with a tie. If one could sport an old school or regimental tie, so much the better. However, a tie had to be worn, and a fairly sober one. The outfit was completed by a white or cream linen or cotton jacket, long white cotton stockings reaching to just below the knee, and polished shoes. It was impossible to feel at ease when got up in this attire and by the time I arrived at the George Steuart offices in Queen Street, not far from the old clock tower cum lighthouse in the Fort (downtown Colombo), I was sweating profusely and had damp patches under the arms of my jacket. The office *peon* took my name and I was invited to wait on one of the cane-seated chairs in the hallway under the fan. After some time, I was ushered into a large and rather dark office where the director I was to see was seated behind a large desk. The office was air conditioned to quite a low temperature, which doubtless allowed him to feel comfortable in his jacket and tie, but which started to make my damp clothing feel cold.

'Ah, Ebbels!', he exclaimed, rising briefly to shake my hand, 'Do sit down. . . . Good journey?' He rapidly seemed to run out of pleasantries: 'Well, now, how are things on . . . er, let me see, . . . Needwood, isn't it?'

'Yes, Sir, Idulgashena Division.' I replied, 'I like the Division and I think production has been quite good during the last few months. . . . In fact I'm due to go on furlough quite soon and I wondered whether I could have a word with you about arrangements.'

A faint shadow seemed to pass over his face at the news that I had something to discuss, followed by a quick glance at his watch, but he listened to my request without demur. As I expected, however, he replied that there were many factors to take into consideration, which was why an immediate answer to my letter had not been forthcoming. Saying he would discuss it with the other directors and let me know as soon as possible, he quickly brought our conversation to a close and got the *peon* to show me out. A blanket of heat enveloped me as I passed through the door and I lost no time in divesting myself of the hated superfluous clothing.

Back at Idulgashena, I eagerly scanned the *tappal* (post) each day for a letter with the George Steuart frank, and several weeks later one arrived. It had been decided that, far from postponing my leave, it would be brought forward to mid November, but travel by air was agreed. This would have the effect of denying me any of the summer in England, but did at least mean that I could visit East Africa. At last I could get on with making definite arrangements.

However, I soon had other things to think about, and the final weeks before my departure did not go smoothly. By mid September the dry season had prevailed for four months and the growth of the tea had slowed so much that plucking rounds had to be extended to nearly double their usual length. This meant that there was not enough work for the pluckers and there was a shortage of other work too, as many jobs such as spreading fertiliser or weeding could not be done or were less necessary in dry weather. The usual way of dealing with this situation was to cease work on the estate for all the labour force for a day each week until things got back to normal with the advent of the rains of the north-east monsoon. On such days the only labourers who worked were those performing essential tasks, such as factory maintenance and cleaning of the drains and latrines in the lines. Normally this shortage of work lasted only a few weeks and the stoppage was only for one day per week. However, this year the drought seemed more severe than usual and I occasionally had to stop estate work for two days in a week. As the labourers were paid by the day, this meant that they lost a substantial amount of pay, about which they were not at all happy, which I appreciated. After a couple of four-day working weeks, I found the union representative outside my office window when I held my morning 'surgery' and he complained bitterly of the hardships being suffered by his members. The union rep was a young man named Rajanathan, not very much older than myself, and I found him a rather truculent person to deal with. I explained (as he knew very well) that because of the dry weather there was not enough work on the estate for full employment every day and that although I was sorry that the labourers were finding things hard, there was little I could do about it. Nevertheless, after another four-day week, Rajanathan was back at my office with the same complaint, this time expressed even more forcefully. I went through the explanation again, but this did not satisfy him and he continued to argue in a rather disrespectful way that I should contrive to find some extra work for the labourers. I knew that I could not do this: even if I had been able to create some extra work, with no harvested leaf coming in, the average cost of production would have increased rapidly and I would have been in serious trouble. Feeling somewhat irritated, I therefore re-iterated my explanation, but he would not accept this and persisted with his demands.  Finally, in exasperation, I said 'You know there is no work except sweepers' work; you can do that if you want.'

The sweepers were the people who kept the labour lines clean and tidy and part of their duties was to keep the drains unblocked and the latrines clean.  The only people who would do this work were those of the lowest caste, as I knew very well.  I also knew that Rajanathan came from a high caste family.  However, the union was supposed to disregard caste in its dealings, being of a strongly left-wing stance.  I knew, too, that he would get a much harsher response if he took his complaint to Mr Meikle.  Rajanathan took my remark as a deep personal insult and, ostensibly to protest about this, he organised a 'go slow' of the pluckers.  By this time we had had some rain and the tea was starting to grow more rapidly again, so the plucking rounds got behind, the shoots were overgrown, and I had to be very careful to prevent coarse leaf being sent to the factory.  Apart from an apology to Rajanathan, which would have been a major blow to my authority and which in any case did not seem warranted, there seemed to be no way of resolving the dispute.  I therefore referred it to Mr Meikle, who backed me up, but the 'go slow' continued until I went on leave.  I suspect that, once Rajanathan had made his point and I was no longer present, Mr Meikle was able to get his old friend Veloo, the Head Kangany, to restore normal working without much difficulty.

I had arranged to spend a month in East Africa before going on to spend the rest of my leave in the UK.  Having spent weeks writing letters, making lists and advertising my car, the calendar eventually came round to November.  In spite of the 'go slow', a small knot of estate staff gathered to see me off, so I said a few words, hoping that they would do their best to make things run smoothly during my absence and telling them when I would be back.  I always got into difficulties with my Tamil when I had to deal with unaccustomed subjects, so I kept it very short.  Leaving the bungalow to a chorus of loud salaams from the KP, kanganies, Carupiah and other staff, and with Fredo on the front seat beside me, I set off up the hill, over the railway and down through Needwood to the main road.  Fredo was to spend the time with my parents and I dropped him off at their bungalow on my way down to Colombo.  There was a lot to do, collecting tickets, arranging money matters, and delivering my car to its new owner.  As there was no direct flight from Colombo to Nairobi, I had to travel via Bombay.  My flight from Colombo to Bombay was to be my first experience of air travel and I felt both excited and slightly apprehensive.  On 12th November my parents, who had come to Colombo to see me off, gave me a lift to Ratmalana Airport, passing down the only stretch of dual carriageway road in the Island, which had recently been completed.  However, the locals had not yet quite got the hang of the situation, as we met a bullock cart coming in the opposite direction along the fast lane of our carriageway.  Fortunately traffic was very light.  Arriving at the airport, I had a sudden panic when I discovered I had left my cameras behind at my sister and brother-in-law's house, but this was soon dispelled when Alan arrived with them, just as I was wondering if there was time to retrieve them.  Boarding the Vickers Viscount, a rather fat little plane with short wings, I savoured the unaccustomed sensation as we took off and the palm trees retreated into a ruffled green carpet below.

The ponderous Viscount took three and a half hours from Colombo and got me to Bombay well after dark.  It was a long ride into town on the bus, which passed through the most horrendous shanty towns I had ever seen.  They seem to be constructed mainly of what looked like cardboard and made even the poorest areas of Colombo seem prosperous.  Further into town the pavements were covered with cloth-draped bundles which, on closer inspection, were revealed to be sleeping bodies.  Although of course I had read of the population living on the streets of Indian cities, it was nevertheless shocking to me to see at first hand the numbers of families in this situation.  It was a sight one did not see in Ceylon, except perhaps for the odd person here and there in the largest towns.

The Ambassador Hotel in downtown Bombay, at which I had made an advance booking, turned out to be a concrete, multi-storey affair set in a street with innumerable small shops.  The following morning my first port of call was the Air India International office, to check my onward flight and arrange to be collected by the airport bus. The friendly girl behind the desk then announced that one needed a permit to stay in Kenya for longer than 14 days, adding, helpfully, that nobody in Bombay could issue such a permit and that my plan for a month's stay would therefore be at the discretion of the authorities in Nairobi. This upset me considerably: were all my careful plans to be nullified by red tape and rules which nobody had told me about? Soothingly, she replied that very likely there would be no problem, but I retained nagging doubts. Next I proceeded to the West India Automobile Association to make arrangements for clearing my new car through Customs on my return journey, preparatory to driving south to Ceylon. It appeared to be quite impossible to arrange clearance in advance of my arrival, my presence being, apparently, essential. However, the helpful Tours Manager felt sure that it could be cleared within two days of my arrival and I had to be satisfied with that. Perhaps it was fortunate that I did not then realise how optimistic he was being.

The plane from Bombay to Nairobi was a Super Constellation. It was a lot less than full and departed on time with me in a window seat in Cabin A. After about eight hours we touched down in Aden where local time was about 4 a.m. Many passengers left the flight there, some perhaps to take up domestic positions with Arab employers, as became even more common in later years. From Aden we droned through the night until the faint and pale light of dawn again attracted my interest to the window. As if floating on the clouds, I could see the sharp and jagged peak of a mountain which I realised with a sudden burst of excitement could be none other than Mt Kenya itself. As we started descending towards Nairobi the cone of Kilimanjaro came into distant view on the opposite side, the early sunlight just finding the white streaks of its snowy cap and glaciers. East Africa at last!

*Approaching Nairobi from the east. First view of Mt Kenya from the plane.*

# East African interlude 12

Nairobi Airport borders the Nairobi National Park and as the aircraft made the approach to land I was thrilled to see giraffe and zebras out on the flat, tan-coloured grassland. I couldn't wait to get out there to see the animals at close quarters. Kenya was still a Crown Colony and at immigration there was no mention of a 14-day limit to my stay. A European customs officer chalked my case without demur and I was soon out in the sunshine amongst purple bougainvilleas in front of the terminal building. Once in town, I booked in at the Norfolk Hotel, which was then not nearly so superior as it is now. It was definitely regarded as second-best to the New Stanley in the centre of town, but I liked it better as it had a more rural air and a garden with trees in which I had my first sight of many East African birds.

I had last been in Nairobi in 1942 at the age of four. I, together with my mother, grandmother and sister had then been fugitives from the threat of Japanese invasion of Ceylon. However, we had been fugitives with a certain amount of style as we had carried with us innumerable items of baggage, including a portable wind-up gramophone, which my grandmother had purchased in Bombay in order that we should not be deprived of musical culture. I had no memories surviving from those days and in any case they probably would have been of little service to me, as I had the impression that Nairobi had greatly changed under recent economic prosperity. Although the Mau Mau movement had ended only a few years previously, there was an upbeat feeling about the city. New buildings with some attractive modern architecture were evident in the city centre, shops were bursting with goods and (a great novelty to me) European sales girls, - and the jacarandas were in bloom. Delamere Avenue (now Kenyatta Avenue) and the other main streets of Nairobi were lined with jacaranda trees festooned with blossom of that distinctive mauvy-blue so hard to capture on film. Showering to the ground, the foxglove-shaped flowers covered the pavements with a carpet of blue under each tree. Colombo had nothing like this. Parked between the trees were modern cars, many of them four-wheel-drive safari wagons or large estates, all with a heavy coating of dust. Some in fact had dust boards mounted over the tailgate to deflect air down over the rear window and keep it dust free. And then there was the climate. Instead of the sticky, oppressive heat of Colombo, here, at 5,000 ft. elevation, the sunshine raised the temperature to little more than a warm European summer's day. It was no hardship to wear trousers, but there seemed to be a fashion for safari jackets with matching shorts. Why did nobody wear these in Ceylon?

Through my kind neighbours, Pat and Beryl, on Beauvais Estate, next door to Idulgashena, I had an introduction to a CID police officer in Nairobi. John Baker and his wife were most welcoming and hospitable and took me under their wing. As the day following my arrival was a Sunday, they invited me to lunch. In the afternoon they took me out to the Nairobi National Park, scarcely half an hour's drive from town, where I had my first taste of viewing East African game in its natural habitat. I was simply entranced and distracted by so many species of birds and animals I had never before seen.

My first task was to set about acquiring some transport. I had already discounted hiring a car, which was prohibitively expensive, and had optimistically decided to buy one second hand and re-sell it on departure. I had arranged some funds for this and on the Monday morning I toured the Nairobi second-hand car dealers in the company of a 'minder' from the CID. 'What you need,' he said, 'is something with a reasonably large engine, so that you don't have to row it along with the gears, and good sized wheels for the corrugations in the roads'. In those days there were several sites in the centre of Nairobi which had not yet been built up, and some of these made convenient second-hand car lots for various dealers, European and Indian, to display their wares. Mr Davis's second-hand car business was on one of these lots and there I found a Volkswagon 'beetle' which seemed to be in reasonable condition. It also seemed to satisfy the criteria enunciated by my 'minder'. After I had taken it for a test drive, my 'minder' called in the CID for help again and had it checked over in the workshops of the Chief Inspector of Motor Vehicles. Although to my consternation we discovered that the car had had no less than seven previous owners, the mechanic's verdict was favourable and I purchased it for £300.

The following day I took the car to have its shock absorbers replaced, as recommended by the mechanic at the CIMV and enquired of Mr Davis what had happened to the tools, which seemed to be missing. Mr Davis was somewhat evasive about these and their fate could not be discovered, but he agreed to let me have a replacement set for 21 shillings. Finally, I visited a bookshop for a guide to East African birds and a Kiswahili phrase book. There was not much choice. The two huge volumes of Mackworth-Praed and Grant's *Birds of Eastern and North-Eastern Africa* (which at that time was the only detailed work available on East African birds) were impractical to cart about and beyond my pocket, so I purchased the more manageably-sized single volume of Roberts's *Birds of South Africa*, which I thought would cover sufficient of the East African species to be useful. For the Kiswahili I found a small booklet by an aristocratic gentleman, a baronet, no less, published by the East African Standard. As the author was apparently on the official government committee which was somehow authenticating Kiswahili words and phrases for modern terms, I felt I could do no better, although I had doubts as to whether I should have need of the section on big game hunting. Armed with these purchases I packed the car, noting that the engine seemed to be in the boot, while luggage went under the bonnet. This space was too small to accommodate my large suitcase, which I placed on the back seat. There was no petrol gauge on this model, but the previous owner had thoughtfully left behind a stick which one could insert into the tank through the filler pipe as a dipstick. I filled the tank and set off down the Mombasa Road.

I was soon out of Nairobi, following the wide and straight tarmac road across the undulating plains covered with short, khaki-coloured grass with here and there a thornbush or a flat-topped acacia tree. After about 20 miles I came to a junction near the village of Athi River and turned right where a signpost indicated 'Arusha'. This road was also wide but was of *murram*, the sandy earth of which most East African roads were made. In fact the surface seemed to be more of sand than earth and stretched away over the Athi Plains as a white and dusty ribbon to the far horizon. The car seemed to be going quite well, but I was slightly anxious as I had not been able to check the water when I looked at the engine, which seemed to have no water-filling point. As the afternoon wore on I became increasingly anxious and eventually drew up and had another look in the engine with the same result: nowhere to put in water. I knew that some engines were air-cooled, so I had to assume that the V W Beetle was one of these. The sandy road surface was not unpleasant to drive on, except where strong corrugations had developed. I soon got used to it and discovered that the ride was quite smooth if I kept the speed above about 45 mph. There was almost no other traffic and I passed only two other vehicles during the whole afternoon. They materialised in the distance like tiny comets with long trails of pale dust lit up by the westering afternoon sun, appearing and disappearing in the undulations of the road, until eventually my visibility was suddenly obliterated by the dust storm as they passed by.

In those days the Athi Plains were virtually unaffected by development and there were no fences or other signs of human activity or habitation. Large numbers of animals in varying concentrations were scattered over the plains as far as the eye could see and I was enthralled to see large mixed herds of zebra, wildebeeste, and Thompson's gazelle grazing by the roadside on the short grass sward, with an ostrich or a giraffe occasionally visible amongst them. At about mid afternoon I came upon two figures seated by the side of the road with large rucksacks beside them. As there was no vehicle, road junction or building anywhere visible, they appeared to have materialised on the spot. However, Barry (from South Africa) and Darryl (an American) told me that they had been dropped off by a pick-up truck which had turned off the road and disappeared across country. I fitted them into the car with some difficulty and we proceeded to the Tanganyika border at the small village of Namanga beneath the steep and high slopes of Ol Doniyo Orok. Here there was a bar across the road, but formalities were minimal and we were soon on our way again after signing a book for travellers at the police checkpoint. From this point the road became tarmac again and the sun was getting low, throwing deep blue shadows in the folds of the hills which now covered the landscape.

The road ran due south, with sharp volcanic hills on either hand rising from the plain on which numerous giraffe could be seen ambling along with their loose gait. Some of the hills, in fact, were quite spectacular, particularly the peak of Longido whose craggy summit, rising to well over 8,000 ft., towered above us as the road skirted its base. The huge bulk of Kilimanjaro rose on the eastern horizon, with the dark clouds swirling about its higher slopes just occasionally allowing a gleam of icy white in the last of the evening light. Making good speed on the tarmac, we entered Arusha just after dark. Barry and Darryl were obviously intent on finding the cheapest accommodation, so I felt slightly embarrassed in booking in at the (not very) swanky-looking New Arusha Hotel in the centre of town. However, we met later in the evening for a drink and a chat.

The following day I spent the morning making my bookings at the Tanganyika National Parks office and buying essential stores. Like Nairobi, Arusha also appeared modern and westernised compared to provincial towns in Ceylon. At night the sodium street lamps, which had not then reached Ceylon, bathed the town in their yellow light, while during the day European sales girls again caught my eye in the shops. Early in the afternoon I headed out along the Kondoa road with the 14,000 ft. apex of Mt Meru hidden in clouds behind me. After about 50 miles of smooth tarmac, I turned right onto a wide murram road covered in layers of fine and pale volcanic dust which hung in the air at the slightest disturbance. Approaching vehicles could be seen in the far distance at the head of dust plumes which stretched for a mile or more behind them. Any overtaking of vehicles was prohibited by reaching zero visibility while still far behind the vehicle in front. Luckily, traffic was very light and the lorry in front of me soon stopped to take on more passengers while I passed by. The landscape was largely open grassland, on which grazing antelope and zebra could be seen dotted here and there in small groups, while on my right the slopes of a substantial mountain rose into the golden sunshine. In mid afternoon a line of blue cliffs appeared on the western horizon, stretching as far as the eye could see on either hand. This was the western wall or escarpment of the Great Rift Valley, of which this section is generally known as the Gregory Rift, after the Scottish geologist and explorer, John Walter Gregory, who investigated the Rift Valley in East Africa during expeditions in 1893. In fact Gregory did not come as far south as this, his travels mainly being in Kenya, further north. Nevertheless, his careful observations and geological arguments (which of course did not take into account modern plate tectonics) publicised the geological wonders of the area with which his name is now associated.

I was heading for the Lake Manyara Game Reserve, where Max had become the Ranger. He had written to say I would be welcome for a couple of days, although he had no spare room in his

146

bungalow as his father and his brother, St John, were staying with him.  His headquarters were at a small village called Mto-wa-Mbu ('Place of the Mosquitos') at the foot of the escarpment.  I arrived in late afternoon and found the village was a collection of huts with thatched roofs set in cultivated *shambas* on either side of the road.  At first there seemed to be no sign of Max's headquarters, but after some enquiries I was directed up a track on the outskirts of the village.  After a short distance I came to his bungalow, where I was welcomed by Max and his father and brother.  The bungalow was on the top of a small hill, facing out over the village to the road by which I had come and towards the northern end of Lake Manyara, glistening white in the afternoon sun.  It was a very modest bungalow by Ceylon planting standards and had no garden to speak of, except the natural bush which bordered the hard earth of the clearing in front of the door.  On one side stood a huge baobab tree, its bulbous trunk swollen as if it would burst, while a dusty and rather battered Landrover stood in the shade nearby.

*The road to Lake Manyara, showing the western escarpment of the Gregory Rift with the Ngorongoro Crater Highlands beyond and my VW beetle.  Note the dust trail of the approaching Vehicle.*

At this time the narrow strip of land between Lake Manyara and the escarpment wall had not become the famous national park it is now.  However, its wonderful diversity of habitat and its amazing wealth of wildlife had long been recognised by the creation of a Game Reserve.  Only a few miles wide, but about 25 miles in length, it stretched south to about half way along the Lake.  Its northern end was thickly forested with big trees, their roots bathed in the water which seeped down from above the escarpment and emerged in springs and streams on the valley floor.  For this reason it is known as the Ground-water Forest and abounds with Syke's blue monkeys as well as other forest-loving animals and birds.  After a few miles this peters out into savannah woodland, with flat-topped acacias (*Acacia tortillis*) and much open grassland towards the shores of the Lake. This continues all the way down to the southern boundary.

After a welcome cup of tea, we piled into Max's Landrover for an excursion into the Reserve. Elephants were numerous and, unlike those in Ceylon, all except the juveniles had tusks, which made them much more spectacular. At the northern end of the Lake was an extensive area of marsh, which was alive with water birds and waders, with many unfamiliar species to add to my growing list of the East African birds I had seen. Sacred and glossy ibis and squacco herons probed about in the shallow water between the grass tussocks, while smart black and white blacksmith plovers ran about picking up insects and small creatures from the mud. As dusk began to fall we returned to Max's bungalow and I then followed him up the road to the top of the escarpment, about 1000 ft. above the floor of the rift valley. There is now a large and modern hotel at this site, but at that time the top of the escarpment was totally wild and only a tented camp and some foundation trenches marked the spot where the hotel was to be. Max had booked me in here for two nights and left me in the charge of Don, who was the camp manager. The tents were large and old-fashioned, made of heavy grey canvas and supported on thick poles. Mine was furnished with a comfortable camp bed, a chair and table, and a canvas washbasin on a folding stand. A hurricane lamp provided a soft light. Meals were served by the cook in the mess tent and, as I was the only guest, Don and I ate together.

The tented hotel above the escarpment at Lake Manyara, November 1959.

Ostrich nest on the soda flats, Lake Manyara. From right: Max, Assistant Warden Umtai, Assistant game ranger.

The following morning I was awakened at 6.30 by shafts of sunlight. The whole camp faced due east, straight out over the cliff edge to the plains far below and the pink and yellow dawn beyond the blue mountains. As if from the air, I looked down onto the Game Reserve and could just make out a family of elephants, in single file, picking their way through the woodland, and a small herd of giraffe moving across the grassland. The calls of hornbills, barbets, and the musical ring of the brubru shrike came echoing up from the trees below. After a quick breakfast I returned to Max's headquarters, where I found him busy on his routine morning radio-telephone calls. A pet baby ostrich named Booni (the Kiswahili for ostrich) wandered around the compound, pecking at anything which might prove edible. He had apparently adopted the waste paper basket as his nest at nights. When Max had completed the morning calls, we fitted the Landrover gun racks with his rifle and shotgun, collected the Chief Assistant Ranger, an experienced and knowledgeable man named Umtai, and entered the Reserve for the morning patrol. I had gratefully accepted Max's offer of a few hours in the hessian bird hide which he had constructed on some planks overlooking a pool out on the marsh, and they deposited me and my sandwiches there in mid morning. This was a wonderful experience for me and I scarcely noticed the time passing until they collected me again, hotter, dirtier and happier, in mid afternoon. A huge variety of birds paraded in front of the hide, not all of which I felt confident in identifying, and I took a large quantity of film (later lost in the post).

The previous several seasons in East Africa had been very dry and the levels of all the lakes were very low. Lake Manyara, which is a soda lake and very shallow, had receded perhaps a mile or more from the grass bordering its high water shore, leaving huge flats which were quite devoid of any vegetation, but were covered with a thin white crust of soda over the baked grey mud. As with the other soda lakes in this part of the rift valley (lakes Magadi and Natron), the soda (sodium carbonate) derives from the leaching of the very alkaline larvas produced by the many adjacent volcanoes, particularly from Ol Doinyo Lengai, the majestic cone in the rift valley between Lake Manyara and Lake Natron, which is revered by the Maasai and which is still occasionally active. Significant eruptions have occurred in 1966 and 2003/04.

Reunited with Max and Umtai, we toured the soda flats in search of young two-banded coursers, of which Max was making a study. As with stilts and other waders, the young courser chicks run well soon after hatching, but crouch immobile when danger threatens, when they can easily be caught. We ringed two with coloured rings. Far out on the baking flats, shimmering in the heat haze, a dark lump could be seen. As we approached, this gradually resolved itself into a male ostrich, which heaved himself to his feet and moved away to reveal a shallow depression with a clutch of 18 enormous white eggs. Apparently several females sometimes lay in the same nest, leaving the male to do most of the incubation.

The following day, I again went out with Max, Umtai and St John on a visit to the southern end of the Reserve to inspect the game fence. We saw large numbers of animals, although none of the cats, and found no more ostrich nests. There appeared to be no other visitors to the Reserve on the days I was there. A pink haze out on the Lake where the water began showed where the flamingos had congregated, although they were too far out to see well. Near the southern end of the Reserve was a place known as Maji Moto ('hot water') owing to the presence of hot springs. Steaming water was seeping and bubbling out of the ground here and the rocks were covered with blue-green algae growing in the hot and mineral-rich water. Not very much further on we came to the game fence. This had been erected in an effort to prevent elephants from leaving the Reserve and entering cultivated land, where they were often shot at by farmers or poached for ivory. The fence was a massive affair of steel cable attached to large trees and with stout poles at intervals. It seemed to be intact, but ended with the trees, leaving wide open soda flats with no barrier. Needless to say, it was ineffective and is now no longer there. It may be that the farmers also have moved, as elephants now move freely between Manyara and the Tarangire National Park to the south-east, as they have presumably done since time immemorial. But the threat of poaching remains.

St John and I discovered a mutual ambition to climb Kilimanjaro and we arranged that we should make an attempt together in a few days' time, after I had visited Ngorongoro. That afternoon I left the warmth of Manyara for the cool uplands of the Crater Highlands and the Ngorongoro Crater. Driving up the escarpment, I continued on along the red murram road over rolling agricultural land. Much of this was grassland with grazing livestock, but there were also wide areas bearing crops of wheat and barley. After an hour or so, the road began to ascend more sharply and to twist around the steep slopes, which became covered in forest. Monkeys were occasionally visible in the roadside trees and on one occasion I rounded a bend just in time to see the hindquarters of an elephant disappearing up the bank. After this I proceeded with rather more caution. Suddenly, I was on the Crater rim and the land fell away into the depths of a vast cauldron of swirling cloud. Now and then, as it momentarily cleared, I could dimly see a distant view of grassy plains far below and of mountain summits rising in the distance. I had joined a dirt road which ran round the rim of the Crater, undulating over grassy slopes and through patches of forest. Turning left, I followed the road round the Crater rim and after a short distance I came upon a cairn, built of rough stones and mortar in the shape of a pyramid. A small plaque on the side facing the road read:

MICHAEL GRZIMEK
12.4.1934 - 10.1.1959
HE GAVE ALL HE POSSESSED
INCLUDING HIS LIFE
FOR THE WILD ANIMALS OF AFRICA

At that time the Ngorongoro Crater had not achieved the pinnacle of global fame as a haven for wild life that it has today and was visited by relatively few people. Since then, countless stunning documentary films and TV programmes, articles and pictures, have brought Ngorongoro to the attention of almost everyone interested in natural history and to many of those who are not. But in November 1959, scarcely 10 months after Michael Grzimek's death, even the Grzimeks' own documentary had only just been completed and I, like most other visitors, knew nothing of the work Michael Grzimek and his father had been doing to survey the animal populations of the Serengeti and Ngorongoro to provide a scientific basis for their future management and preservation. Michael Grzimek had been killed when his light aircraft had been rendered uncontrollable after colliding with a griffon vulture over the Salei plains to the north of the Crater Highlands. He and his father, Professor Bernhard Grzimek, between them probably did more for the preservation of the large wild mammals of East Africa than anyone else before or since, and their book *Serengeti shall not die* vividly publicised their work. In particular, it was largely through their efforts, and Michael Grzimek's untimely death, that research laboratories were established in the Serengeti National Park. These have become famous in their own right and in them many now famous scientists have produced much of the work needed to set the science of wild life conservation on a sound foundation.

Although the first phase of the Grzimeks' work had just ended, in 1959 many initiatives which were to have far-reaching results in understanding and conserving African animals were just beginning. In south-west Uganda, Jill Wordsworth was studying the mountain gorillas of the Virunga Volcanoes long before Dianne Fossey brought them to world attention, and to the south, on the shores of Lake Tanganyika, Jane Goodall was just starting her pioneering work on chimpanzee behaviour. This, in turn, was at the behest and with the encouragement of Louis Leakey who, together with his wife Mary, was making key discoveries on human evolution at the Olduvai Gorge, situated between the Ngorongoro Crater Highlands and the Serengeti Plains. Although I did not know this at the time, I did gain the feeling that wild life study and conservation in East Africa was exciting and starting to develop a momentum which I only wished could be kindled in Ceylon. However, there was also much uncertainty. The Serengeti was still the only national park in Tanganyika and a long-running controversy over whether human or animal interests should take precedence in certain areas had just culminated in the excision of the Ngorongoro Crater from the Park in order to allow the Maasai people to continue to graze their livestock there. It had been specifically stated by the colonial government that if any conflict of interest should arise, those of the human inhabitants must take precedence over those of the animal population. Nobody knew whether this would result in the destruction of the wild herds which gave Ngorongoro its unique value, and many were fearful that the worst would happen. So far, except for the virtual eradication of the black rhino, it is pleasing to note that these fears were largely unfounded. In spite of the poaching, financial difficulties and agricultural encroachment which have affected wild life reserves all over the world, the Ngorongoro Conservation Area still retains much of the wild life it had forty years ago, the Serengeti is not dead, and I like to think that Professor Grzimek would have felt that his son had not died for nothing. There is now a second memorial cairn, situated at the junction of the roads on the lip of the Crater. This was erected on the occasion of the Serengeti and Ngorongoro Diamond Jubilee in 1981, marking the 60 years since the Serengeti had first received protection as a game reserve. The inscription lists details of six people, including Michael Grzimek, who lost their lives in the cause of wild life conservation in the Serengeti or Ngorongoro between 1959 and 1981. Sadly, this list could today be further extended.

Continuing along the road, I soon arrived at the Crater Lodge, which at that time was the only accommodation available at Ngorongoro. The Lodge had been built in 1938 in the South African rondaavel style, except that the dozen or so bedrooms were square log cabins instead of round huts. A larger, central building, also constructed of logs, contained a lounge, a bar, and a most welcome log fire. At this elevation of around 8,000 ft. the nights were cold and I was glad to find several blankets on the bed. No food was provided; visitors were expected to bring their own provisions, which the cabin 'boy' prepared. A separate bathroom cabin provided an excellent hot bath and I was much impressed by the sight of a rhino out of the bathroom window, just the other side of a small ravine. Where else could one rhino-watch from one's bath tub? The hot water was generated behind the bathroom cabin in what was known as a Tanganyika boiler, a simple contraption consisting of a 44-gallon drum over a log fire, the drum being connected on one side to a cold water supply and on the other to the hot water system. To prevent inadvertent explosion, there was also a vertical pipe which acted as a safety valve.

The weather cleared in the evening and revealed the Lodge to be on the Crater rim with magnificent views over the Crater floor, 2,000 ft. below, and to the opposite rim, 12 miles distant, with higher mountains beyond. Only two other parties were staying at the Lodge and I soon arranged with one of them to share a Landrover for a tour of the Crater the following day. We made an early start but, although a new road was being constructed down the Crater wall on the southern side near the Lodge, this was not yet finished, and we had to make a journey of many miles around the rim in order to descend by the old road on the north-east side, where the wall was less abrupt. There are now two roads into the Crater on the southern side, allowing for one-way travel up and down, such is the volume of traffic.

Today, the Ngorongoro Crater is so well known that its needs no further description. There are now several palatial lodges around the rim where thousands of tourists are accommodated in conditions no different to good hotels anywhere; only the view is unique. And holidaymakers from Sydney or Seattle, Stockholm or Strasbourg, take in a visit to Ngorongoro just as they would a visit to the opera. It is simply another item in the holiday package. The proportion of visitors which appreciate the amazing wealth of species and intricate ecological relationships when viewing the spectacle of Ngorongoro is probably no greater than the proportion which would appreciate the intricacies of an operatic production. I am glad that I visited Ngorongoro at a time when visitors had to make an effort to do so, when the talk in the bar in the evening was of animals and birds seen and not the comparison of package tours or the merits of their reps. My first experience of Ngorongoro that day made a lasting impression, although I now know that for Ngorongoro it was nothing special, and I hoped that some day I would return to East Africa, not as a visitor but in some capacity which would benefit its animal and human life.

The following morning I left the Crater Lodge soon after breakfast and my diary records in faintly aggrieved tones that my lodging cost me 30 shillings (£1.50) per night without food, as compared to Sh.27.50 including food at the Manyara tented camp. November brings rain to Ngorongoro and the Serengeti plains and I had been warned that the road to Seronera would be impassable for an ordinary car. I therefore planned to make my attempt on Kilimanjaro before returning north to Kenya and on to Uganda. After some slight delay due to elephants on the road (in such circumstances, with a precipitous drop on one side and a high bank on the other, car manoeuvrability feels remarkably restricted), I arrived back at Max's bungalow in mid morning. He then kindly took me out again to the shores of Lake Manyara for a photographic session on the flamingos, which had arrived in force during my absence. A wide pink swath along the shore was composed of huge numbers of both greater and lesser flamingos, forming a truly wonderful spectacle against the backdrop of white soda and the

*The Crater Lodge, Ngorongoro, 1959.*  *View of Kibo from the saddle at about 15,000 ft.,*
*Kilimanjaro.*

honking of flocks arriving and departing. At length we had to return and, after an excellent lunch, St John and I set off for Kilimanjaro.

Although rumours of snowy mountains in equatorial Africa had circulated amongst travellers since the middle ages, the great East African mountains seem to have been brought to the attention of Europeans first by the Spanish geographer Fernandes de Encisco in 1519. However, he was not writing from personal experience, but from reports reaching the coast at Mombasa, as he says:

> 'West of this port is the Ethiopian Mount Olympus, which is very high, and further off are the Mountains of the Moon in which are the sources of the Nile.'

This was remarkably accurate for the state of knowledge at the time, although it is not clear whether he was referring to Kilimanjaro or Mt Kenya, but of course readers had no way of distinguishing accurate information from the spurious and fanciful, of which there was a large amount also circulating and which often had greater appeal to the minds of the day. After this there seems to have been no published report referring to Kilimanjaro until a German missionary, J. Rebmann, reported sighting the mountain in his 'Narrative of a journey to Jagga, the snow country of eastern Africa' in the first issue of the *Church Missionary Intelligencer* in 1849. Immediately this ignited a scientific controversy in Europe as to whether it was possible to have snowy mountains near the equator. This seems strange, as it was already well known that the higher in the atmosphere one went, the colder the temperature became. In Ceylon there was a long-accepted rule of thumb that the average temperature decreased by 3 °F per 1000 ft of elevation, which seemed to match experience quite well. There seems no good reason why the European scientific community of the day should have supposed that this principle would not hold in tropical Africa. It was already known that several of the East African mountains were very high indeed and a decrease of temperature at their higher elevations to below freezing seems entirely logical. Nevertheless, the controversy raged for 40 years and was finally resolved only with reports of snow on the summits of the Ruwenzori by Stanley in 1888 and the ascent of Kilimanjaro by the German explorers Hans Meyer and L. Purtscheller, who reached the highest point on 5th October 1889 and named it Kaiser Wilhelm Spitz.

After this very few climbers actually reached the highest point until after the 1939-45 war, and for a long time there continued to be considerable doubt as to the exact height of the mountain. This was because the few measurements which had been made had used inaccurate methods (uncorrected aeronoid altimeter or determination of water boiling point). An authoritative triangulation was eventually made only in 1952 (seven years before my visit) by K. T. Pugh of the Surveys Division in Dar es Salaam. This was no easy matter because the large ice cap prevented a direct line of sight from Kaiser Wilhelm Spitz to the triangulation base stations down on the plain. Pugh also suffered from mental confusion as a symptom of mountain sickness, but eventually successfully made a subsidiary triangulation to a point in the Western Breach, where there is a gap in the crater wall and from where the base stations could be seen. This resulted in the figure of 19,340 ft, which remained the accepted height for the next half century. However, in 1999 new and highly accurate surveys of many of the world's high mountains were made by the University of Technology in Karlsruhe, using satellite techniques. These measurements have given new figures for the altitude of many famous mountains, including Kilimanjaro, for which the height now given is 19,330 ft., or just under 5,892 m. Considering the difficulties with which Pugh had to contend, the accuracy he achieved is remarkable and commendable.

In fact Kilimanjaro has three peaks. Kibo is the highest and retains the typical volcanic conical shape, with a caldera and a central hollow named the Ash Pit. To the west is the low dome of Shira (13,140 ft.) and to the east is the jagged eroded volcanic plug of Mawenzi (16,896 ft.). Between Mawenzi and Kibo there is a broad and high saddle at about 14 - 15,000 ft. Only Kibo has glaciers, and these have been slowly retreating since they were first examined 100 years ago. In Hans Meyer's day, the northern and southern ice fields were apparently connected, but the ice around the crater rim has gradually diminished to leave notches in the ice cap where the volcanic rock is exposed. These notches have been named, but eventually, presumably, they will link up. One, not far from the summit point (which is on the south side of the crater rim), is named Leopard Notch because the frozen and desiccated body of a leopard was discovered nearby. If it still remains, the poor leopard must be getting rather dilapidated as the Rev. Dr R. Reusch, a missionary and keen mountaineer, attempted to decapitate it for a trophy in 1927, but eventually settled for cutting off an ear. The mystery as to why a leopard should have climbed so far up the mountain seems to have caught the imagination of many, not least Ernest Hemingway, who mentions it in a preface to his short story, *The snows of Kilimanjaro*.

Thanks to Hemingway and many other authors, Kilimanjaro has been invested with an aura of excitement and romance which it fully deserves. I certainly felt this as St John and I drew near and beheld the full splendour of the mountain above us, with the glaciers on Kibo shining in the evening sunlight. The clouds did not part for long, however, and later we only glimpsed the snows from time to time, seemingly impossibly high and easily confused with the drifting white veil of cloud. We continued on through Arusha and past the little town of Moshi, turning left up the lower slopes of the mountain on the road to Marangu. The southern slopes of Kilimanjaro are home to the Wachagga people, who grow coffee and bananas on their small farms. The clan or tribe is divided into several chiefdoms, of which Marangu is one, which also gives its name to the village, where we arrived at dusk. The Marangu Hotel, where we booked in, was old fashioned and in some ways reminiscent of an alpine *gasthof* with stout wooden floors and balconies. At that time there were still many people of German origin in Tanganyika, dating back to the days before the 1914-18 war when it was a German colony, and they much favoured the Kilimanjaro area. We were therefore not surprised to find the hotel presided over by a Mrs Braun, who informed us that a party of climbers was already on the mountain, so we could not make a start the next morning, but must wait until the following day. So we busied ourselves for a day in Moshi buying various requirements, including some boots for St John.

The next day Mrs Braun produced gloves, hats, ear muffs, thick long-sleeved pullovers, long underpants, blankets and rucksacks. She warned us of the cold and the dangers of sun on unprotected skin at high altitude and supplied us with Vaseline for our faces (this being long before UV-blocking suncreams were invented). She then marshalled us into the kitchen to witness our food and other equipment being packed. Our guide, Syara, and four tough-looking porters appeared and, after introductions and distribution of loads, we set off just before 10 a.m. My rucksack had weighed 13 kg with my lunch and sleeping equipment, but the cine and still cameras increased this to about 17 kg. This was hardly a heavy load, as backpacks go, and the rucksack was comfortable, so I set off with a light step.

For the first three miles we wound in and out among banana and coffee small-holdings and then struck a broad grassy road which soon took us to the gate at the boundary of the Kilimanjaro Reserved Area (as it then was). Beyond the barrier the road entered the forest and continued to ascend steadily. Each of us walking at our own pace, we separated out and at one point our porters disappeared into a hut. The tall rain forest pressed close on either side of the road and rang with bird calls and other noises, some of which I wondered might originate from elephants. However, we saw no tangible signs of anything larger than pigs of some kind and occasionally glimpsed birds darting between the tall trees. These were difficult to identify except for Hartlaub's turaco, a pigeon-sized but rather parrot-like bird of tall forest, flashing brilliant blue and green with a wide crest. After about three and a half hours, including a short stop to eat our sandwiches, we emerged into a clearing on the upper side of which, with its back against the forest, was a small building of stone and mortar with a roof of corrugated iron. Situated just below 9,000 ft. and about 11 miles from Marangu, this was Bismarck Hut (now rebuilt and renamed Mandara Hut) which, together with several other huts on the mountain, had been constructed in German days. We were slightly put out to find a VW Beetle parked outside the hut, the owners of which were nowhere to be seen and were evidently up on the mountain. We felt that we could have driven up in mine, saving both time and effort. However, although we did not realise it at the time, it was probably good for us to have had the acclimatising walk and we should also have missed the wonderful views of the forest. Within the hut, on the right of the entrance door, were the kitchen and quarters for the porters, while on the left was the accommodation for tourists. Sleeping shelves, about two feet wide and in two tiers, had been built against each wall and probably had space enough for about a dozen people. A central table and a few chairs were the only other furniture, but a wood-burning stove provided some welcome heat. The rest of the day we spent bird watching on the edge of the forest, where golden-winged sunbirds were visiting the orange flowers of *Leonotis* plants. The mist had come down and drifted through the trees of the forest, but the male sunbirds still flashed brilliant bronze and yellow, with graceful long tails.

After enjoying a substantial stew, which our guide Syara had prepared for us, we did not stay up much later than nightfall. Syara joined us for the night and seemed to have no difficulty making himself comfortable on the shelves. Built of odd planks and covered with graffiti of names and dates of previous climbers, the shelves were devoid of any mat or pillow which might have softened their unyielding surface. Even tired as we were, it took us quite a long while to get to sleep. In the middle of the night I awoke in the pitch darkness to find an arm on my patch of shelf. As I was on the top tier and the others were below, this seemed curious. It appeared quite lifeless and I gingerly felt up its length, coming eventually, and with some relief, to my own shoulder. It took me some time to get feeling back into the limb and return to sleep.

The following day we rose at dawn. The night had been wet, but the rain had stopped by the time we set off. However, the path was slippery and dripping leaves emptied water onto us from every angle. Very soon we emerged from the forest onto moorland, covered with grasses and scrubby, heath-like plants. The path continued upwards over the moorland, skirting large lumps of rock and being very rough underfoot. Our destination this day was Peters Hut named, presumably, after Karl Peters, the German empire-builder whose dubious treaties with local chiefs gave Bismarck the pretext for Germany's proclamation of a protectorate over the area of Tanganyika in 1885. Situated at 12,500 ft., it was only about 4,000 ft. higher than Bismarck Hut, and we took the walk fairly slowly, having short rests at frequent intervals. The weather remained dull and the landscape appeared rather bleak and grey, with occasional glimpses of the dark volcanic crags of Mawenzi when the clouds permitted.

There was little wild life visible, but heavy-billed white-necked ravens appeared occasionally and once we had a sight of a small antelope; probably a bush duiker. After about five hours' walking, including a stop to eat our lunch, we arrived at Peter's Hut early in the afternoon. Both St John and I had sustained a few blisters on our feet, but nothing worse, and in fact I felt less tired than I had the previous evening.

Peters Hut (now long since rebuilt and named Horombo Hut) was in fact two huts, both built of corrugated iron on wooden frames. One of these served as the kitchen and porters' accommodation and the other was intended to accommodate visiting climbers. I was somewhat relieved to find that the Spartan sleeping shelves had not been installed here. Instead, there were bunks covered with hay palliasses, which proved to be quite comfortable. Again, a table, a stove, and a few chairs completed the furniture. Here it was cold enough to wear gloves and our views were obscured by mist and rain. A smart pair of stonechats which frequented the vicinity kept up a constant chat, sounding identical to hard flints being knocked together. Later the cloud began to lift and we had views of the jagged rock summit of Mawenzi, which showed a dusting of snow in the gullies. At about 6.15 the cloud partially cleared from Kibo, allowing us views of the glaciers on the southern side, and eventually, just after sunset, the view below cleared to reveal the plains in deep violet shadow against the salmon glow on the western horizon. Again we ate by the dim light of the hurricane lantern and turned in soon after nightfall.

St John awoke with a headache, which worsened after breakfast, so we rearranged our belongings into one rucksack which we planned to carry alternately. Things seemed to take us longer on this morning and we did not get away until after 8.30, following a narrow and winding path upwards through the misty moorland. It is a curiosity of the high East African mountains that some species of plants belonging to genera which are represented in northern climates by low-growing herbs, here grow to the stature of trees. This particularly applies to the groundsels (*Senecio* species) and the genus *Lobelia*. Because they inhabit only upland areas, members of these two genera have diversified in isolation on individual mountains, just as they might have done on isolated islands. The result is that there are many species of giant groundsel and lobelia which are endemic to particular mountains, not being found anywhere else. The giant species of *Lobelia* usually have also evolved adaptations for pollination by various local species of sunbird. Depending on the geography and geological history of the mountains, there are also other species of these genera which are rather more widespread in their distribution. On Kilimanjaro there are two species of *Lobelia*, including one endemic, and at least seven species of *Senecio*, including three endemics. After leaving Peters Hut we began to be aware of these giant groundsels, standing alone like shaggy sentinels dotted over the landscape, but as we climbed higher they became less frequent and eventually disappeared.

After about an hour we reached scattered patches of snow, which gradually coalesced until soon we were treading through an inch or two of a fresh fall which covered the ground. It is said that the people living at the base of the mountain believed the snow to be a powerful *dawa* which could cure many ills and that some wily Wachagga chiefs made good use of its propensity to turn into water to demonstrate its magical properties. Until this point I had not noticed that one of the porters was barefoot, but he gave no indication of any difficulty, striding apparently easily through the snow along with the others who wore shoes of various descriptions. They were all dressed in thick clothing, much of which looked as if it could have been army surplus, and they seemed a cheerful lot, murmuring amongst themselves. St John's headache had persisted and he was not feeling very bright, so I continued with the rucksack, leaving him to carry the lantern. Presently the slope of the ground levelled off and we found ourselves on the broad saddle between Mawenzi and Kibo at about 15,000 ft. The overnight snow still covered the rocky ground here, with larger rocks looming dark through the mist. We turned to the left to follow the saddle west towards Kibo and, as it had done on previous days, the mist gradually lifted to allow brief views of Kibo against an unnaturally deep blue sky. Occasionally, brilliant shafts of sunlight penetrated the clouds, which instantly set us shielding our eyes with our goggles and sun glasses. We paused frequently for rests and at one point met a party of 10 on their way down. Most of them had apparently reached Gillman's Point (the first point on the crater rim reached on the route up) but had been unable to go further because of deep snow.

St John began to complain of acute tiredness and slowed his pace. The Kibo Hut was now visible as a speck of grey in the dark jumble of rock at the base of the final cone of Kibo peak. However, it took me another hour to reach it and a further half hour before we had all arrived, St John feeling very sick with a throbbing head and making straight for his bunk. This hut, at about 16,000 ft was smaller than the others, with very cramped living space. Built of a mixture of corrugated iron and larva blocks, it offered little more than shelter and a few makeshift bunks. A bitter wind swirled around and assaulted anyone stepping outside the door, so this was avoided as much as possible. However, occasionally it could not be avoided. The privy, which was also constructed of corrugated iron, but with large gaps at the joints, must hold the record as the coldest in Africa and guaranteed that the absolute minimum time was spent therein. One had little time or inclination to reflect upon the curious situation of occupying a privy higher in elevation than the top of Mont Blanc, with a drop into what was effectively a deep freeze. In fact this explained one reason for the fascination of Kilimanjaro for nineteenth century European geographers, mountaineers and physicians. Because the onset of mountain sickness usually occurs only near this elevation, it was not a phenomenon which could be studied in Europe, - or anywhere else more readily accessible than East Africa, and so its effects on East African climbers were of considerable interest. Mountain sickness (basically symptoms brought on by exertion in conditions of depleted oxygen, which sometimes prove fatal) is now regarded much more seriously than it was in 1959, when it was treated as little more than a nuisance and an unpredictable hazard for climbers.

After a rudimentary meal and some tea, we retired to rest in preparation for starting our final climb soon after midnight. By this time I had developed a severe headache myself and found it impossible to get to sleep. At the appointed hour we arose and dressed in all available clothes. For me these included three pairs of socks and stockings, short and long underpants, pyjamas, corduroy trousers, two shirts, two pullovers and a windproof jacket, gloves, mittens, and a balaclava. St John had been sick again and neither of us was feeling very well. However, eventually we set off about 2 a.m., following Syara, who carried the lantern. Our way lay directly up the steep and scree-covered rocky slope above the Hut. The snow gleamed pale in the starlight and later on a crescent moon rose and we could see the jagged crags of Mawenzi. We were both short of breath and we found the loose scree very tiring, slipping down half the height of every step we took. In silence we gradually gained height until we were on a level with the top of Mawenzi. We were now resting every 10 yards or so, and then every five, but slowly we plodded on. After about two hours, St John began increasingly to flag and our rests gradually got longer and longer. Eventually he vomited violently and came to a stop, saying he felt he could go no further. Syara stood by with the lantern, but otherwise gave no advice or encouragement, saying impassively that we were not yet half way to the Crater rim (I guessed we must be at somewhere just over 17,000 ft.). I now felt in a considerable dilemma. St John appeared to be in no fit state to go on (and said as much). The thin air and freezing wind struck icy cold right through our many layers of clothing as we stood considering our position. I myself also felt pretty sick and had a severe headache, although I did not feel as yet at the end of my tether. However, it was out of the question to leave St John alone in the dark on the inhospitable scree slopes for what might be a quite considerable length of time. Syara did not attempt to encourage or cajole us into continuing and I felt there was no other choice but to turn back.

*View from Kibo Hut across the saddle to Mawenzi (16,896 ft), Kilimanjaro.*

Once we had agreed on aborting our climb, we made good time back to Kibo Hut, taking only about 30 minutes to cover the distance we had so laboriously ascended. After about an hour's rest we left for Peters Hut in weather which was at first clear, but later deteriorated when a thick mist enveloped us as we traversed the Saddle. We found we made remarkably good speed downhill, feeling better with every step, and took only two and a half hours to reach Peters Hut. Here Syara made some porridge for us, which I found very welcome. St John could not eat anything but, sensibly, was anxious to descend as rapidly as possible and we soon set off again, reaching Bismarck Hut in another two and a half hours. Here we found that our appetites were starting to return. But, while our heads felt fully recovered, our legs started to suffer from fatigue. We had some food and debated what to do. Normally, climbers spend the final night at this hut, descending to base the following morning. However, in our semi-exhausted state, neither of us was anxious to spend another night on the dreaded sleeping benches and we decided to continue down to Marangu. This took us another three and a quarter hours, without our packs, and we felt mightily glad to see Frau Braun and her hotel, where we arrived at 5 p.m. After descending more than 12,000 ft. in about eight and a half hours, we were even more delighted to see hot baths, a meal and our beds, into which we thankfully collapsed.

The following day we started to suffer the after effects of our climb, both of us being very stiff indeed. I also found that, in spite of liberal application of the Vaseline, exposure to high altitude UV radiation had reduced the skin of my face to a hard, parchment-like surface which cracked and then gradually flaked away over the next few days, leaving it tender and pink. It took the remainder of my time in East Africa to regain its customary texture and hue. We felt rather chastened that such fit young fellows as ourselves had succumbed so readily to mountain sickness. St John had been living at sea level in Colombo, where he worked in one of the agency houses, but at Idulgashena I had been living at 5,000 ft. and I felt I could have been expected to cope better. Nevertheless, as Frau Braun pointed out, this only illustrated how unpredictable mountain sickness was, and how fitness was no guide to susceptibility.

Frau Braun charged us Shs.330 (about £16.50) each for the trip, inclusive of hire of clothing and equipment, which even then seemed very reasonable, but of course there were also gratuities to give to our guide and porters. Rather regretfully, we climbed into the VW Beetle and set off down the road to Arusha. Here we had lunch and St John arranged at the National Parks' office for a lift back to Lake Manyara the next morning. We then bade each other farewell and I set off for the return journey back to Nairobi. We never met again.

The journey north was not as straightforward as I had expected. There had been rain on the Athi Plains since I had been in Tanganyika and the dusty murram road on which I had come south turned into a quagmire after I crossed the Kenya border. However, it was in these conditions that the VW Beetle showed its suitability for East Africa. With its light body, and the weight of the engine directly over the large driving wheels, it ploughed through mud which might have defeated even a four-wheel-drive, and I continued without delay until I came within about three miles of the Mombasa-Nairobi road. Here there was a very muddy area with several lorries and buses stuck and slewed off the road. There seemed nothing to be done but to make an inspection, plot the best route and try my luck. This seemed to hold until I was nearly through, when the car came to rest with mud up to the doors. I got out and had a look at the situation. I had no implements and there seemed no easy way of getting out of the mess. While I was standing looking at the car and wondering what to do, a Landrover full of people came up and I was pleased to find that it was the American party I had met at Ngorongoro. They took a determined run at the mud, weaving back and forth, and eventually got through without much trouble. They then kindly came back for me. With several willing people pushing, the Beetle seemed to float over the mud and emerged on firm ground, looking more like a dung beetle than a VW. But I was through and, with thanks to my American friends, we each resumed our journeys. By nightfall I was back in Nairobi at the Norfolk Hotel.

# Uganda                                    13

For the second part of my East African journey I planned to go west into Uganda. However, on the way it seemed a good idea to visit various acquaintances in the Kenya tea-growing districts from whom I had had kind invitations. One of these was from Gail's parents, Tony and Elaine, whom I had last seen on Kumarawatte Estate down at Moneragala. They were now on Kibabet Estate in the Nandi Hills, to which Tony had been transferred by his employers, The Eastern Produce and Estates Co. Ltd., which was expanding in East Africa. Before leaving Nairobi I had a Sunday of enforced rest, which enabled me to get the car unearthed from its muddy coat and to make visits to the Coryndon Museum (now the National Museum of Kenya) and to the drive-in cinema on the Fort Hall road, which I found a great novelty. The Museum itself was impressive compared to its counterpart in Colombo, even though it then had none of the fossil hominid exhibits for which it is now famous. I was particularly struck by the gallery of beautiful botanical paintings by Joy Adamson, who at that time, in pre-*Born Free* days, was unknown outside East Africa. My diary records my impression of them as 'masterpieces of botanical illustration', which I still feel is not an overstatement.

Another task to be done in Nairobi was to obtain the car's registration book from the dealers, Davis & Co. My hurried departure after purchasing the car had allowed no time for the transfer of ownership to be made, but Mr Davis had assured me he would have it done in time for me to collect when I returned to Nairobi. I called at his office, only to discover that Mr Davis was away and his Indian second-in-command was out. After further calls during the morning, I eventually located this deputy, who then revealed that the transfer had not been made. This was a serious nuisance as, without the transfer, I could not legally sell the car. He charmingly assured me that it would definitely be done that day and that he would post it to me at Kibabet. I had doubts about this, and visions of the book chasing me around East Africa but never arriving were all too vivid. However, there seemed to be no alternative so, impressing on him the importance of posting the log book as quickly as possible, I departed on the Nakuru road.

The wide and smooth tarmac road led me west, up through Muguga to the crest of the escarpment, before plunging 2,000 ft to the floor of the rift valley. This was truly spectacular scenery and from the top of the escarpment one had a stupendous view out over the rift to Mt Suswa, Mt Longonot and far in the distance the blue humps of the Mau highlands, rising to over 10,000 ft. Down on the floor of the rift the land seemed to be occupied mainly by ranches, and a few rather rangy cattle were visible here and there. The land was still dry and brown, and the rains had apparently not yet arrived. However, as I approached Nakuru I ran into an electrical storm with torrential rain so heavy that I was forced to stop for a while until it passed. Soon I was climbing out of the rift valley again, up to Mau Summit, where the road narrowed, and presently I turned left onto a murram road signposted 'Kericho'.

Kericho was the centre of the older tea-growing area in Kenya while the Nandi Hills, over on the other side of the wide Kavirondo Valley, formed a relatively new tea district. However, the tea area was being rapidly expanded in both districts by several large companies and during my visits over the next few days my friends were able to show me newly-planted clearings covering hundreds of acres. It was obvious that major capital investments were being made by these firms and the differences from tea planting in Ceylon were dramatic. Even the topography was very different. Here tea was grown on flat land or gently rolling slopes which contrasted emphatically with the precipitous hillsides of Ceylon and some working practices were strangely the reverse of those to which I was accustomed. For example, in East Africa field cultivations are traditionally done by women, while the tea plucking is done mostly by men. Most of the labour force seemed to be only temporary, with workers coming for a few months and then going again, - so different to the established and static labour populations on the Ceylon estates. Then when we visited the factories, they were relatively new and full of new machinery, some of it quite different to that used in Ceylon, especially the automatic system of withering the leaf in troughs and the CTC machines which cut and tore the leaf instead of rolling it. I was impressed with the new thinking and new methods (although I thought the quality was well below that of good Ceylon tea) and I felt rather old-fashioned in the face of all this innovation and pioneering vigour. Blister blight was unknown and production costs were low, so it also seemed obvious that East Africa was going to be a strong competitor for Ceylon in the world tea market.

After a couple of days in Kericho, staying at the Brooke Bond 'Tea Hotel' I moved on to Nandi Hills where I was made very welcome by Tony and Elaine. Kibabet bungalow turned out to be very similar to many tea estate bungalows in Ceylon and there was even a local club which would not have been out of place in any Ceylon upcountry planting district. I found that Gail had recently married an assistant factory manager and was living quite near by. In East Africa at that time many of the junior estate staff were Europeans, which would have been quite unheard-of in Ceylon. We met at the club and when I left I gave her a lift into Eldoret (the local town), but I felt too diffident to reminisce very much about Ceylon days.

Eldoret, high on the Uasin Gishu plateau of western Kenya, had started as an Afrikaner settlement. After the Boer war, when the Afrikaners found that the British did not interfere too much in their local government, the anti-British antagonism generated during the war died down and in 1908 a large party of Afrikaners decided to settle in Kenya. With encouragement from the colonial government of the day (which was interested in opening up the area), they had made a pioneering trek from the railhead at Nakuru up onto the plateau grasslands, - a re-enactment on a miniature scale of the voortrekkers' migration from the Cape to the Transvaal in the1830s. The first party had been followed by a second wave a few years later and the settlement of huts built near the Sosiani River was known as 'Sixty Four', after the surveyor's number for the farm on which it was situated. The name Sixty Four was changed to Eldoret after a public meeting in 1911, but the town really started to develop only after the arrival of the railway in 1924. The town became the centre of a large area producing heavy crops of cereals and sheep and the countless herds of game animals for which the plateau had previously been famous were soon eliminated.

I found Eldoret was now a busy market town with wide main streets (designed, no doubt, as in other Boer towns, to permit the turning of a span of oxen) on the main road west to Uganda. There were numerous modern-looking shops and all the services necessary to maintain a prosperous farming community. European-run cafes and tea-rooms serving such luxuries as strawberries and cream gave it a very un-tropical air and we took advantage of their pleasant hospitality for lunch before I continued on my way. The state of the roads was of course of vital interest to me, especially with the rains now in progress and, as I knew there was a long stretch near the Uganda border which had not yet been sealed, I did not delay longer than necessary. Road works were actually in progress at various places on this stretch of murram road but, although somewhat churned up, it did not present any difficulty to the VW Beetle. Like the voortrekkers, I appreciated the benefit of large wheels when coping with rough terrain.

The tarmac began again soon after I crossed the Ugandan border. The name Uganda derives directly from the ancient Kingdom of Buganda bordering the northern shores of Lake Victoria. In colonial times Uganda had an enviable reputation as a model of development and prosperity and, with considerable justification, was once described by Winston Churchill as the 'pearl of Africa'. Being relatively small, with abundant water, adequate rainfall and fertile land, it did not have the problems which beset the larger and more arid territories. By the 1950s a network of good tarmac roads linked the main administrative centres, while the production of cotton textiles and the development of other manufacturing industries and copper mining, together with export crops such as cotton, sugar and coffee, had made the country generally prosperous. The Baganda people, like the Wachagga of Kilimanjaro and the Kikuyu of central Kenya, were also notably sophisticated and enterprising so that economically and socially the prospects for Uganda seemed bright. At the time of my visit no one could have conceived that the country would lie in ruins only ten short years after independence in 1962.

As with Kenya and Tanganyika, this was actually my second visit to Uganda. The epic journey that my family and I had made as refugees from Ceylon in 1942 had continued to Uganda after our stop in Nairobi. We had travelled on by train to Kampala and a kind family friend, who at that time was in the Ugandan government administration, gave us a refuge at his bungalow at Entebbe, near the shore of Lake Victoria. I remember little of the three months we spent there except a general impression of the bungalow being set amongst lush vegetation and that the veranda and windows were closed in by fine wire mesh against the lake flies (actually a kind of midge). These could often be seen rising from the water, out on the open lake, like columns of smoke and could roll inshore in countless billions as a dense fog. There were even tales of fishermen choking to death when caught up in a dense swarm. However, the local populace caught them in nets, compressed them into cakes, and ate them with relish.

Now, seventeen years later, my main objective in Uganda was to visit the famous national parks in the west and north-west of the country. The Queen Elizabeth Park was on the shores of Lake Edward, between the Ruwenzori mountains and the highlands of Kigezi, while the Murchison Falls Park was on either side of the Nile, just before it enters Lake Albert. I would have much liked also to visit the Ruwenzori, or Mountains of the Moon, which seemed so mysterious and inviting but, unlike Kilimanjaro, there was no simple way of doing this in a few days, and I had not allowed unlimited time.

The road ran through plantations of sugar cane and endless groves of what seemed to be bananas, but were actually *matoke*, the large green cooking plantains which are the staple food of the populace in these parts. Occasionally there were patches of thick forest and, passing through one of these, I suddenly felt the accelerator go slack and the car came to a halt with the engine just ticking over. This was bad news, as I had little or no knowledge of car engines and this part of the road seemed to be deserted, the dark and high forest pressing close on either side. I got out to investigate and discovered that the accelerator cable had snapped off near its connection to the throttle on the carburettor. This was quite a problem, but I thought that if I could find a piece of wire, I might be able to tie the end of the cable to the throttle lever. Although I was on the main highway from Nairobi to Kampala, I had seen very few other vehicles during the afternoon. However, I presently heard the noise of an approaching engine and soon a large truck appeared, laden with a heavy load of *matoke* and large sacks of indeterminate content. On top of this load were perched about 20 passengers, who craned forward with interest as the driver stopped at my request. The driver was a large and burly Sikh, but he seemed rather nervous and was reluctant to get out of his cab. With some persuasion, he agreed he might have a bit of wire and after some grubbing about he produced a piece of electrical flex. However, as I turned back to the car, he smartly let in the clutch and accelerated away down the road. The flex was not really suitable for my purpose as I found it almost impossible to connect it to the accelerator cable. The tool set which Mr Davis the Dealer had supplied was not very comprehensive but did contain some pliers and a screwdriver and, after much fiddling about, I eventually managed to pull the broken cable far enough through to reconnect it to the throttle. This worked, but the engine ran at frighteningly high revs and I had to use the clutch carefully to control my speed during the remaining hundred miles to Kampala.

At Jinja, about halfway to Kampala, the road crossed the Victoria Nile at the Owen Falls Dam. The dam is several miles downstream from the point where the Nile actually leaves Lake Victoria and has completely submerged the Owen Falls, although these were apparently more a series of rapids than actual falls. This is a hydroelectric scheme, supplying a large proportion of Uganda's power, which was opened about five years before my visit, in 1954. It still looked quite new and I stopped to view the waters of the Nile gushing out of the turbines' exhaust duct at the base of the dam in a gracefully curving arc to start their journey to the sea at Alexandria. It seemed ignominious for the Nile to issue from what was in fact just a glorified pipe, but the volume of water was certainly sufficient to fill the river bed below the dam.

The remainder of my journey to Kampala was uneventful, passing through more heavy forest with occasional areas of sugar cane. As far as I remember, there was little choice of places to stay and I booked into the main hotel, The Imperial, which, true to its name, was a solid building furnished in a rather dark and sombre style. The next day I hastened to Coopers, the VW agents in East Africa, to get the accelerator cable replaced, which they did within a couple of hours. While waiting, I walked into one of the city parks, which were well kept and free of litter. A group of school girls, dressed in pink, were keeping up a lively chatter while they pursued some active quarry in the hedge with paper bags. Every now and then one of them would make a grab at something and then stuff it into the bag with triumphant shouts. As I drew near, I saw that their quarry was a kind of large, green, grasshopper, of which there seemed to be a swarm in the park. These, they said, were excellent eating and they would have them for their supper. The Spanish geographer of 1519, Fernandes de Encisco, would have been proud of them. After his mention of the 'Ethiopian Mount Olympus', he goes on to say 'further off are the mountains of the moon in which are the sources of the Nile. In all this country are much gold and wild animals and here devour the people locusts.' How right he was!

Leaving Kampala about mid day, I followed a smooth-surfaced main road to Masaka. Half way there, a circular monument and a line across the road marked the equator and for the second time in as many weeks I crossed into the southern hemisphere. Masaka was a small district centre with some new buildings, but I paused only for a late lunch, continuing on to Mbarara and then turning north. A murram-surfaced road then led into hilly country, often thickly forested, where recent rain and the twisty road slowed my progress. Late in the afternoon I came over a sparsely populated range of hills to find myself in a volcanic area with neat, round craters about 500 to 800 ft. deep, each with a circular lake at the bottom and some with cultivated terraces up the sides. The road followed the rims of these craters, giving excellent views of the moon-like landscape and also, more distantly, to the Mountains of the Moon, the Ruwenzori, which, most unusually, were free of cloud and I could distinctly see the white gleam of the glaciers and snows on the highest peaks of Mount Stanley. Like Mount Kenya, Mount Stanley has twin peaks, Alexandra and Margherita (the latter being marginally the highest at 16,763 ft.), although at this distance the separate peaks were not distinguishable. It is partly due to his journalistic flair for self-promotion that Henry Stanley is usually credited as being the first European to see these mountains, on 24 May 1888 during his last central African expedition, when he apparently had a clear view of the snowy summits from the western shores of Lake Albert.

However, there is considerable controversy about this and it is probable that several officers in the early, pre-Mahdi rebellion, administration of the Anglo-Egyptian Sudan had seen the mountains from Lake Albert in the early 1870s without realising their significance. This was probably due to the almost permanent shroud of thick cloud which covers their highest peaks, although one officer, Romolo Gessi, privately recorded that he had had 'a strange vision in the sky, as of a mountain covered in snow'. Evidently he doubted his own eyes or sanity, or thought (probably correctly) that nobody would believe him. Even Stanley had probably had an earlier sight of them, from southern Uganda during his expedition in 1875, but they appeared only as 'a faint . . . enormous blue mass afar off' and he did not recognise them for what they were. The cloud cover evidently also hid them from Samuel Baker during his travels on and near Lake Albert in 1864 and 1872. In fact Stanley made no attempt to explore the mountains themselves and the higher regions remained virtually unknown, even to the local people, until the British Museum expedition of 1906. This was followed later the same year by an Italian expedition, led by Prince Luigi Amedeo, Duke of the Abruzzi, which named many of the main geographical features and made first ascents of the highest peaks on 18th and 20th June.

Even though sunset was later here in the extreme west of Uganda than in other areas of East Africa, dusk was rapidly falling as I arrived at the entrance to the Queen Elizabeth National Park (now renamed, rather inappropriately, Ruwenzori National Park), not far from the village of Katwe. Here I bought a guide book and some excellent maps of the Park (which would no longer be a possiblity in most East African national parks these days), and continued towards Mweya Lodge in the gathering darkness. The murram road followed the crest of a narrow peninsula extending into Lake Edward and the lights of the lodge were visible in the distance when I suddenly found the car surrounded by elephants.

Although not travelling fast, the road sloped steeply downwards and I had to brake carefully on the loose surface to keep the car on the road. Coming to a stop within a forest of pillar-like, gnarled grey legs, I turned off both lights and engine and sat in some trepidation to see what would happen. The herd comprised about 15 adults, but many were accompanied by very small calves, which increased my anxieties. However, I need not have worried. The herd took very little notice of the car and moved slowly around it across the road, their giant limbs moving smoothly like well-oiled machinery and their feet swinging forward silently and deliberately at each step. Once I found that they displayed no interest in the car, I was able to enjoy the privilege of being in their midst and did not move again until all had passed out of sight.

Mweya Lodge is situated at the end of a peninsular with Lake Edward on one side and the Kazinga Channel, which connects Lake George to Lake Edward, on the other. It was then a delightfully informal affair, built almost entirely of round timber, with *makuti* thatch (woven palm frond panels like Ceylon *cadjans*) both on the roof and walls. There was a central building with lounge and dining areas, a library and a laboratory, and three or four bedroom blocks. The library had a good collection of reference books for identification of birds, mammals and other creatures, while the laboratory had a small collection of bird skins and mounted bird specimens. Like most East African national park lodges at that time it was mainly intended to serve the resident local population, both indigenous and expatriate, and was relatively inexpensive. It made no pretensions towards the unnecessary and inappropriate five star luxury to which so many such lodges now aspire and perhaps consequently the clientele was equally congenial and appreciative of the natural wonders with which the area was blessed.

The few other guests included a team making a promotional film for East African Airways and three young prospective settlers en route to Kenya. Patrick, Barry and Richard had driven south from Europe, crossing the Sahara in their Landrover, and intended to start farming in Kenya. No Wind of Change had yet blown through the British Government and, now that the Mau Mau crisis was over, the Kenya government was again welcoming settlers. Many of my fellow guests at Mweya were knowledgeable naturalists, two were ethnological artists in the process of painting portraits of members of the local tribes, while the Welsh Lodge Manager and his Russian wife were keen ornithologists, kindly identifying the amazing variety of local birds for anyone who was interested. Magnificent brown and white fish eagles were common all along the shore of the Kazinga Channel and had nests at regular intervals in the large candelabra *Euphorbia* trees. Their haunting cries echoed along the shore, while the incessant coo-cooing of the ubiquitous ring-necked doves provided a soothing accompaniment. Another bird which nested along the Kazinga Channel was the hammerkop. This was a curious, dull brown bird, about the size of a bantam, with a stout horizontal crest at the back of its head which provided the reason for its name. It fed on frogs and other aquatic creatures at the water's edge, but its main claim to fame was its extraordinary nest. This was a huge affair, about the size of a car, which was built of sticks in a stout tree or on a rocky outcrop. Quite unlike any other nest, it had an entrance hole at one side, which was smoothed with mud. I was told that the birds took several months to build this structure, which seemed hardly surprising. They were also relatively tame, which may result from a widespread local belief that it is unlucky to interfere with them.

*View from the launch: elephant by the Kazinga Channel, Queen Elizabeth National Park.*

I spent three wonderful days at Mweya, watching elephants and hippos from a launch on the Kazinga Channel and making trips with Patrick and his friends to various parts of the Park. On my last day we drove down to the south-western area of the Park where it abuts the border with the Congo, and saw huge herds of topi, buffalo, and Uganda kob. I lingered as late as I dared and eventually left at dusk as I knew the route to Fort Portal was along a good tarmac road. The lights of the town were in sight when I was stopped at a police road block. In later years this would have been cause for serious alarm, but I received only politeness and an apologetic explanation that they just wanted to check my driving licence. I spent a comfortable night at the Mountains of the Moon Hotel and the following morning I followed the road north out of the town with the cloud-topped blue mass of the Ruwenzori on the western horizon. The tarmac soon ended and shortly after this I was overtaken by a large, fast Mercedes. There was a loud bang, as if from a pistol shot, and the windscreen frosted up in a crazed pattern, leaving only a small clear area through which I could still just see the road. When I had recovered from the shock, there seemed no alternative but to continue at a slower pace and this I did until, a few miles further on, the windscreen suddenly disintegrated. Luckily I was wearing sun glasses and I sustained only a few cuts and scratches, but my lap and the interior of the car were full of granular pieces of glass. I stopped again and spent some time knocking out the remainder of the glass from around the windscreen pillars and sweeping up the mess. I discovered that, if I kept all the windows shut, the blast through the open windscreen was not intolerable as the air within the car itself acted as a barrier. There were few other vehicles on the road, so dust was not severe and the main problem was the larger insects, of which there were a great many. It was no joke to be hit in the face at 40 mph by a large grasshopper or fat carpenter bee.

Early in the afternoon I arrived at the little town of Masindi. This had been the capital of the chiefdom of Bunyoro and it was here in 1872 on his second visit to these parts that Sir Samuel Baker had had such an unpredictable and hostile reception from the young chief, Kabba Rega. Baker was then in the employ of the Khedive of Egypt and had with him only a very small military force. He also had with him his attractive and spirited young second wife, Florence. By this time established as Lady Baker in British society, Florence von Sass was in fact a Hungarian girl whom Samuel Baker had bought on the spur of the moment at a slave auction in 1859 at the Turkish town of Vidin (on the Danube in what is now Bulgaria) and whom he had married surreptitiously on their return to England in 1865. Besides her good looks, she evidently also had a courageous and forceful character. She accompanied Samuel on all his subsequent travels, sharing all his hardships and also all his triumphs, to which she contributed in no small measure. The main objective of their visit to Bunyoro was to open up trade and bring the country under the jurisdiction of the Khedive but, under the influence of the powerful slave traders, Kabba Rega attempted a massacre. Samuel and Florence Baker were lucky to escape with their lives and made a hazardous and harrowing forced march to return northwards to the Nile.

Although Masindi had rather more facilities than in Kabba Rega's time, it was by no means a metropolis. However, it did have a garage which promised to obtain a spare windscreen and fit it for me on my return in two days' time and I set off, following more or less the same route taken by the Bakers.

From Masindi the road continued across the plateau and then down an escarpment, at the foot of which it entered the Murchison Falls National Park and thence, with a deteriorating surface, to Paraa on the banks of the Nile. The Bakers had taken nine days to cover this distance and it was mainly due to Samuel Baker's resourcefulness and determination that they survived, being constantly under attack from Kabba Rega's men and also having to contend with lack of food, exhaustion, and swamps, which necessitated wading through many miles of deep water and mud. I took only a couple of hours and the only hazard I encountered was tsetse flies. Through the open windscreen I acquired a collection of them in the car which soon made their presence felt. With a bite like a red-hot needle, they seem to be armour-plated and are almost impossible to swat (especially with one eye on the road). Even a direct hit seldom seemed to quieten them for long. Besides the tsetses I had also acquired a large collection of other insects which would have been the envy of any entomologist, and their crawling, fluttering and buzzing, sometimes within my clothing, became so distracting that I had to spend considerable time and effort ejecting them from the various places in which they had taken refuge or had become wedged.

At Paraa I renewed acquaintance with members of a friendly Indian family I had first met at Mweya who were waiting for the ferry across the river to Paraa Lodge on the northern bank. The Bakers had found this area devastated by slave raids and had had to make their own dug-outs before being able to embark. We found a small ferry waiting which could carry both cars and it was not long before we arrived on the northern shore. I found myself allotted a bedroom in a newish block overlooking the river. It was somewhere near here, on his outward journey, that Samuel Baker had had to wait for several weeks while seeking permission to cross south into Bunyoro and where he had entertained several local chiefs with an improvised band composed of those members of his entourage who could play instruments. He later used this band to great effect during his dealings with Kabba Rega in the period leading up to his escape. My bedroom suite had apparently been constructed for use by H.M. the Queen on her visit some years previously, but I doubt whether a band was in attendance. Whether Her Majesty had found it adequate, I do not know: it seemed very comfortable to me, but I felt I should have preferred the *makuti*-built rooms of Mweya. I found here, as at the Queen Elizabeth Park, that the park wardens and lodge manager mixed with the guests at the bar in the evenings and most people seemed to be enthusiastic naturalists.

Apart from the falls themselves, the main attractions of the Park were the launch trip upriver to the foot of the Falls, which provided excellent views of the huge Nile crocodiles sunning themselves on the sandy spits and beaches, and a visit to the area near the shores of Lake Albert which was frequented by great herds of elephants and plain's game. It was here, in the papyrus marsh fringing the lake, that I had my first view of a shoe-billed stork, an extraordinary grey-coloured creature with a massive, boat-like bill and just a hint of the air of an absent-minded professor. It stood motionless, only its massive head and neck above the vegetation, the tiny, curled feathers of its crest just ruffled by the breeze.

*The Murchison Falls, showing the footbridge.*

On the afternoon of my first day I visited the Falls by road. Named by Samuel Baker after Sir Roderick Murchison, the influential and long-serving President of the Royal Geographical Society in the mid nineteenth century, the Murchison Falls are a curious geographical feature, being not only falls but a narrow cleft, about 20 ft. wide, through which the whole river plunges with a mighty roar and rising clouds of spray. There was a small footbridge across this cleft, which I traversed rather gingerly and then climbed down a steep path to the foot of the falls where I found a pair of keen fishermen casting for Nile perch. The height difference from top to bottom of the Falls is not huge, perhaps about 100 ft., but the force of the boiling torrent is such that it is easy to see why the fish fauna below the falls differs from that above them. In particular, the large and voracious Nile perch does not occur naturally above the falls and used to be a special attraction to fishermen at Paraa and downstream. However, there are now many more perch in Lake Victoria than in the Nile.

In August 1954 Nile perch from Lake Albert were introduced into Lake Victoria with subsequently disastrous ecological results for the lake's interesting and valuable indigenous fish fauna. This was apparently sanctioned on his own initiative by the Senior Fisheries Officer of the Ugandan Government. Further introductions were made in the early 1960s with Nile perch from both Lake Albert and Lake Rudolf (now Lake Turkana). The main idea of the introductions was to utilise the numerous species of small fish (mostly *Haplochromis* spp.) which made up a large proportion of Lake Victoria's fish biomass, but which were economically of little value. These, it was thought, would be eaten by the Nile perch and thus converted into large and economically desirable fish. Although there were many warnings and much protracted argument over the proposal to introduce Nile perch to Lake Victoria, no decision was announced and the introduction did not become widely known for many years. However, once the fish had been introduced, there was no way of getting them out again. Unfortunately, the Nile perch liked their new environment and ate not only the *Haplochromis* species, but also almost everything else, including any small Nile perch which came within reach. They grew to enormous size (over 200 lbs), decimated the profitable fisheries based on the two indigenous species of tilapia (*Oreochromis* spp.), and eliminated many unique and interesting indigenous species of Cichlid fish. Much of the tilapia catch had been marketed as dried fish, but the Nile perch is oily and unsuitable for drying. It therefore had to be marketed fresh or frozen, which was difficult in the more remote areas and furthermore, being large, it damaged the nets and gear of the tilapia fishers. In addition to the Nile perch, Nile tilapia were also introduced into Lake Victoria in the 1950s and these tilapia ousted the remaining indigenous tilapia species. It was thought that eventually the Nile perch population would crash when its food supply of small fish ran out. However, the population seems to have stabilised at quite a high level by subsisting largely on a species of prawn which inhabits the lake bottom and which proliferated hugely when the prawn-eating haplochromids had been eliminated. Although it has been alleged that the introduction was to provide a sporting fish in Lake Victoria for the benefit of expatriate fishermen, in 1954 this would have been unlikely and has never been substantiated.

The Murchison Falls National Park has been renamed the Kabalega National Park, although for the present the Falls themselves seem to have retained their European name. This National Park and the animals it contained were virtually destroyed during Uganda's troubled years and is now unrecognisable as the Park I visited. Perhaps it is just as well that the name has changed.

Prudently but reluctantly, I made a reasonably prompt start on my last day, crossing on the first ferry and arriving in Masindi by mid morning. The ordered windscreen had not arrived, so I pressed straight on and arrived in Kampala three hours later. Coopers were efficient and prompt as usual and had the windscreen replaced within an hour. I knew this was going to be a long day if I was to reach Kibabet for the night as planned, so I left Kampala as soon as possible and crossed the Kenya border soon after dark. It then began to rain, the murram road became muddy and slow, and at one point I stopped to give a lift to someone who had run out of petrol (this ordinary action of simple humanity was quite safe then but to do so now, alone and after dark, would be insanely dangerous). Reaching Eldoret late in the evening, I then took a wrong turning and found myself in what seemed to be an extensive pine forest, with tall trunks stretching away into the gloom on either hand. Eventually, after about 10 miles, a lighted house appeared, the occupants of which directed me back onto the Nandi road and I arrived at Kibabet well before midnight, having travelled 456 miles in the day. Tony and Elaine were as hospitable as ever and incorporated me into their hectic social life which, on the second evening, involved a drinks party followed by a function at the club in aid of the League of African Women (although no African women seemed to be present and I later discovered that the title did not refer to those of African origin). A dance then started which was unexpectedly pleasant for me as, in contrast to Ceylon, several unattached girls participated and we continued until people began to drift away at about 4 a.m.

After two pleasant days I said goodbye to Tony and Elaine for the last time, and four hours' driving brought me again to Nairobi and the Norfolk Hotel. The car registration book had not arrived at Kibabet and I had an acrimonious confrontation the next morning with Mr Davis's Indian ADC, who stoutly maintained that he had indeed posted it to me there as promised. In any case, he now had not got it, and if it had not arrived it must be presumed lost. I felt I could not make too much fuss, as I was hoping that Davis's would buy the car back at a reasonable price. However, with an airy wave at the ranks of cars parked on his lot, Mr Davis said he already had six VW Beetles in stock and did not want any more. As a slight softening of his refusal he then suggested that I try some of the other dealers and that I might be able to arrange for a replacement registration book through the UK High Commission. This turned out to be a valuable piece of information and, after several visits and much form-filling, a replacement was eventually forthcoming. I hawked the car round the other dealers in central Nairobi, but none of them were interested and all maintained that business was slow and that they had a glut of cars in stock. At ABC Motors the manager was out and a very young Indian assistant was holding the fort. Evidently he was unable to take any decisions and all had to wait on the manager's return. As I was waiting for him, a young European came in and I heard him ask whether they had any VW Beetles in stock. Pricking up my ears, I could scarcely believe it when I heard the assistant say that they had none and then, indicating me, add naively that I had one to sell and would he like to deal direct with me? Well, I didn't care whether he wanted to deal with me, but I certainly wanted to deal with him, and we were soon in negotiation. Gerry Murdoch seemed a pleasant but cautious individual and insisted we take the car round to Coopers to have it checked over. As I was fairly confident it would be, the result was favourable and we soon agreed on £250 as a fair price and that I could keep the car until near my departure the following day. This was wonderful for me, as it meant that I could make last visits to the Nairobi National Park, to my kind friends the Bakers, and could also make another visit to satisfy my fascination with the drive-in cinema, all of which made the end of my stay in Nairobi pleasant and easy. The only thing which was not easy was to cram all my belongings, which somehow had unaccountably multiplied, into my suitcase and bag. In those days airlines were very fussy about excess baggage, which could be charged for at exorbitant rates, so I made sure that my suitcase was not overweight while putting heavy items into my cabin bag. After all, I reasoned, many people weighed considerably more than I did, so what difference would it make? At the airport I approached the check-in desk trying to swing my leaden bag in a light and airy way before placing it out of sight while my ticket was dealt with. However, it was not weighed, so all was well, and neither were there any customs or passport checks.

The overnight flight was routed via Entebbe, Khartoum, and Rome and at first there were many empty seats, but they soon filled up. Many people joined the flight at Entebbe, including a colonial administrator (as I took him to be) and his family, who came on board carrying pineapples and locally-woven baskets. They took the neighbouring seats to mine, which I felt was a bit of luck as the seat next to me was occupied by his very attractive daughter. However, my luck did not last. After attending to the stowage of their bags in the overhead lockers, the paterfamilias suddenly noticed my presence and, worse, that his daughter and I were actually in conversation. With some such remark as 'Hmm, we don't want any problems overnight', he made her change places and occupied the seat himself.

Morning sunshine on 17 December brought a wonderful view of Mont Blanc and other alpine peaks, gleaming in their best clothing of winter snow. Glaciers rolled down steep cirques and far below I could see dark shadows where alpine villages nestled in deep valleys. Then the clouds closed in and did not relent until we were over southern England. I had not been in England for eight years. This would be my first visit as an adult and I wondered what it would be like. It would certainly be strange to hear everyone speaking English. Suddenly the surprisingly green fields of Surrey appeared below and we landed at Heathrow, taking what seemed an interminable time to taxi back along the smooth runways. The B.O.A.C. terminal was a long, low, building and had the temporary air of a Nissen hut, as well it might, as it was destined soon to be replaced. I passed quickly through customs and emerged to be greeted by my aunt, who had kindly come to meet me. We left the airport to enter what seemed to me to be a maelstrom of traffic but which she seemed to find quite normal, and with this slight shock I was introduced to a winter's day in London.

# On furlough 14

Looking back on it, I now think that I wasted much of my precious long leave, although it did not seem so at the time. At first I felt London was an alien environment with which I was unaccustomed and it took me some time to feel at ease travelling about, visiting the great department stores, and getting used, not only to the way things were done, but to what it might be possible to do. In those days it was not as easy as it is now to arrange to share a flat or house for a few months so, as my kind uncle and aunt were willing to put up with me, seemingly without too much inconvenience to themselves, I based myself at their house in Hampstead Garden Suburb during the time I spent in England. I owe them a great debt of gratitude. No doubt it would have been much better for all concerned if I had made the effort to find accommodation of my own but I did not, partly because I valued the company of my uncle, aunt and cousin, and partly because I did not appreciate the possibilities.

One of my first actions was to collect my new car from the delivery depot in Wardour Street, Soho, W1. With the transport of the *Nandu* in mind, I had opted for a Vauxhall Victor estate model which had enough room to accommodate the boat in its folded state with the tailgate closed. Car manufacturers had only just discovered how to make windscreens and windows of curved glass and for this model they had used their new skills to the full. The windscreen was not only curved, it wrapped around the car on either side so much that it protruded into the door space and the front doors had to have corresponding notches to accommodate it. There was a bench-like front seat which stretched unbroken from one side of the car to the other, and the gear change was on the steering column. This I found quite convenient when I got used to it, although it was not very smooth and there were only three forward gears. Nevertheless, the car was considerably more powerful than the old Morris Minor, it seemed wonderfully modern and I was highly delighted with it.

Visiting Soho for the first time was quite an eye-opener for me, even though the sex industry was then only a mild premonition of what it later became. This was several years before the *Lady Chatterly* case liberalised journalism; four-letter words did not appear in everyday print and advertising for films and shows had to be relatively demure. Driving the car back to Hampstead was also my first experience of driving in London traffic, which I did not find as alarming as I had at first anticipated. Navigating, however, was a different matter and I found that I had inadvertently crossed Oxford Street several times without recognising it before I eventually found my way north.

The car conferred mobility and I contacted various friends and acquaintances. The M1 motorway had just been opened, although it started only on the northern fringe of London and ended well short of Birmingham. Nevertheless, it was the largest road I had ever seen and I tried it out at the start of a journey up to the Lake District. Traffic was so light that only an occasional vehicle was visible and I took great delight in clocking up 92 mph, which seemed a very great speed to me as in Ceylon 40 mph was dangerously fast on almost all roads. It was probably lucky that the traffic was no heavier as the car was completely without the safety features of today, such as seat belts, and had no trace of any padding over the steel surround of the dashboard.

When I contacted friends, I came up against an obvious but unforeseen problem in that most people were at work all day during the week and could socialise only in the evenings and at weekends. For someone who was not working, there did not seem to be a great deal to do in the winter and very little of interest in the way of natural history compared to Ceylon. The weather was cold, colder than I had experienced since I had been a small boy, and it took some getting used to. This was forcefully brought home to me when my aunt kindly put some of my clothes through the wash and hung them on the line in the garden. To my great astonishment she later came in holding my frozen pullover vertically above her head by the sleeves: it was stiff as a board. Starting from scratch, it was not easy to acquire a congenial social circle in the space of a few weeks and I started to find time hanging rather heavily on my hands. Shortly after my arrival, Christmas parties began to occur and invitations to my cousin, Cherry, often included me, so I soon met her circle of friends. As she was several years younger than me, her friends also tended to be younger and I found many were not yet out of school. Susan, however, was 18 and was doing a course at one of the London secretarial colleges. She was the daughter of friends of my uncle and aunt and lived not far away. I found her attractive as she was lively and had a slim figure and wavy brown hair. After we had met at one of the Christmas parties I asked her out and we became friendly, our evenings out becoming regular weekly occasions (as this was the most her parents seemed willing to permit). Usually we would visit the theatre or go for dinner in the West End, but she never seemed to be free at the weekends and I gathered that she was probably also seeing someone else. This didn't concern me much at first, as I felt I had arrived rather suddenly in her orbit and that she needed some time to sort out the situation. Meanwhile, I decided to try a skiing holiday and booked a fortnight in the Austrian Tyrol.

I chose Obergurgl, partly because it is the highest ski resort in the Austrian alps and partly because of its wonderful name. When I got there, I discovered that this derived from the suitably-named River Gurgl, which ran below the village, and that there were neighbouring villages named Untergurgl and Hochgurgl. Travel was by train - the 'Snowsports Special'- which departed from London, Victoria, in the evening. After crossing the Channel by ferry, we boarded another train at Calais in which couchette accommodation was provided. The end carriage was fitted out with a bar and disco, and many people hardly used their couchettes, except to recover from these attractions and for consumption of their duty-free purchases, although I got a few hours sleep. This seemed a good way of starting the holiday and of meeting the other members of one's group. Unfortunately, my group seemed to consist of older and duller people than some of the others and of course many people were going to other resorts, so this advantage was small. Nevertheless, I feel that it was a better and more convivial way to travel than the regimented and impersonal flights which have now taken its place.

By dawn we were well into alpine scenery which would have done credit to any Christmas card, with powdery icing over spruce and pine forests and deep snow by the side of the track. High above, the tops of the snowy crags were spot-lit in gold as the first rays of the sun caught their gleaming and precipitous slopes. Presently we arrived at the appointed station and were bussed up the Otz Tal valley to the village, where I was booked in at the Hotel Jenewein.

I found I was in fairyland. I had seen snow before of course, as a child at school in Derbyshire and, rather grimily, in London, but never like this. It lay in a smooth blanket more than two feet deep over the mountain slopes and in the village, where it caked the roofs and in the streets had been collected into huge heaps. It squeaked underfoot as I walked softly along the lanes where deep drifts obscured the ditches and hedges, and at the Hotel Edelweiss it had been compacted to make a counter for the Ice Bar on the terrace, where drinks were served at lunch time. What made the whole effect so special was the sunshine, which made each flake and grain sparkle with a whiteness such I had never seen. The warmth melted trickles of water from the roofs which at night quickly froze into long arrays of icicles hanging nearly to the ground like rope curtains. The snow lay so thick and heavy on the roofs that on several houses men were clearing it with long-handled shovels, throwing large lumps with careless abandon down into the street where they exploded in a burst of white spray. One had to keep a sharp watch out to avoid getting a shovel-full down the neck. More hazardous still was the snow blower, also new to me, of which the village possessed an early version. This was an attachment like a gigantic lawn-mower fitted on the front of a truck. It could chew its way through the heaviest snow, which it then blew out through two swivelling nozzles. The driver did not seem concerned as to where it went, so long as it was off the road, and when the deep hum of the machine drew near, people rushed to close their doors and window shutters to avoid the unpleasant experience of having their rooms forcefully filled with snow.

Fairyland was populated with pleasant, down-to-earth, Austrians and the largely British skiing visitors. The least fairy-like of these was my room-mate, Frank, who was middle-aged, slightly stout, and as bald as the onion dome of the village church. Fortunately, he was also amiable, a farmer who had come skiing alone, leaving his family at home near Braintree in Essex, where I later paid them a visit.

*The church, Obergurgl.*

I joined the ski school and kitted myself out with hired boots and skis. The ski hire man stood me against the skis and checked that I could just reach the points with up-stretched arms, this then being the accepted measure. As I am quite tall, this resulted in enormous skis which I found amazingly difficult to control. The beginners' class took a couple of days in the nursery area before our instructor, Hans, thought we could tackle the higher slopes and the ski lift to get us there. This first lift was a drag-lift of the anchor type, where one stood in pairs awaiting the drag 'anchor' as it came round on the overhead cable. Theoretically, one then pulled it down, placed a 'fluke' behind each posterior, and glided smoothly away. At first it seldom worked out like this. It took us several seconds to get the thing correctly into position and before we were ready it would jerk us away, clinging frantically to the anchor 'stem'. Inevitably one's skis then got inextricably entangled with one's partner's and we both ended up in a heap a few yards up the slope. It was almost worse later when we felt more confident than our ability warranted. We would glide nonchalantly away, chatting to one another and looking around at the wonderful scenery but half way up, just as we felt masters of our environment, disaster would strike. The path of the drag lift became worn into two pairs of tram-like grooves by the two sets of skis. However, these were not very deep and if one's attention wandered, one's skis were liable to do likewise. Either my right ski would slip out of its groove so that I was in danger of inadvertently doing the splits, or my left ski would sneak over into the right groove of my lift partner. This would interfere with the guidance systems of all our skis, which would instantly run amok and drag us off the anchor, forcing us to abort mission and abandon the lift in mid slope. Lying in a heap, trying to retrieve detached skis, we would hear anxious shouts from the next pair on the lift. If we failed to evacuate the track in time, this pair would then run over or into us, causing further disruption, until there could be a sizeable heap of struggling bodies. Even when one had cleared the track, one then had the ignominy of having to remove skis and plod up or down to the lift terminal through deep snow and bushes which seemed intent on tipping their burden into your boots.

*At the head of the Otz Tal valley, above Obergurgl.*

In those days Obergurgl was a delightful small alpine village, with a picturesque church, two or three hotels and a couple of ski lifts. The après ski entertainment was very simple, consisting of a few *bier-kellers* with discos, and a few small restaurants. The Hotel Edelweiss held 'tea-dances' in the afternoons to which one went in ski boots, straight from the slopes. These were possibly a left-over from the fashion for tea dances between the wars, but in fact it was fun and filled the hour or so from dark until dinner, to the accompaniment of creamy Austrian cakes and much *glühwein* served in grey pottery jugs with dark blue designs. Ski boots (which in those days were leather and not completely inflexible) were not very elegant or easy to dance in, but they certainly protected the girls' feet from their heavy-footed partners. The locals also put on an entertainment each week; the inevitable *Tyroler arbend*, consisting of folk dances, songs, and performances by the brass band. I much enjoyed this, as I like folk music, and I attended on each occasion.

I have always had a good sense of balance and I gradually became a more proficient skier. Every day Hans would lead us out in the morning and demonstrate some new technique which we would each try to learn, with more or less success. As time went on we were able to explore more of the countryside around the village and at the end of each day we would have an exhilarating run back. Hans would take up position at the front and remind us 'Bend zee knees and lean outvards. Remember, ze veight is on ze lower ski'. Then, with a final '*Sehr gut*, ok, follow me,' he would zoom away and we would follow him as best we could. By the end of the fortnight I felt reasonably confident on medium grade slopes and was thoroughly hooked on skiing.

Although I had got to know the other members of my rather small group, I had not met any particularly congenial people and relatively few girls of my own age. Joan was a dark-haired girl with bright eyes who was in my ski class and we became quite friendly, but I found she lacked much sense of humour and she was less than flirtatious. On our last evening we walked back from the bier-keller together and paused by the door of the village church. At the very least, I thought, a kiss might ensue, if not something more. The church was floodlit and every surface gleamed with sparkling powder snow. 'Oh', she said, 'Isn't it lovely? I really feel I'd like to go in and pray', and she started testing the door to see if it was open. This was about the last thing on my mind and I left her at the church while I gloomily returned to the Hotel Jenewein. When we said farewell at Victoria Station on our return, she asked for my phone number, but I felt fed up with her and declined to give it.

Back in London, I sought to pursue my various interests. I had read of the flocks of brent geese on the east coast and arranged to visit the bird reserve at Scolt Head in north Norfolk. I navigated north through the grey February countryside and eventually found Brancaster and the bed and breakfast accommodation I had booked (for which the charge was 18/6: about 93p). When I arrived at dusk the village seemed deserted; not a soul braved the freezing north-easterly which swept down the village street, and few lights were visible. My landlady, who did not normally take visitors in the winter but had made a special exception for me, seemed to think me a little strange in wanting to visit the area at this time of year. The following morning the warden of the reserve called for me and we embarked in his dinghy. The wind had abated only slightly and the grey scudding clouds complemented the dull green and choppy sea as we chugged down the channel. By the time we neared the point of the long sandy promontory both my eyes and nose were streaming and I was wet from the spray lifted from the waves and whipped over the boat by the wind. The cold had gripped my hands and feet and seemed intent on gripping other portions of my anatomy before very long. My interest in geese was rapidly waning and my sympathy with the landlady's views increased. Eventually we had good sightings of the dark geese, both on the water and overhead, but somehow they could not excite me like flamingos at Lake Manyara or the varied storks of the Ceylon lagoons.

In order to have access to darkroom facilities, and in hopes of meeting interesting people and perhaps learning new techniques, I joined The Camera Club. The Club premises were at 23 Manchester Square, in central London, which was not very convenient from Hampstead, but I spent several days there processing and printing my films of East Africa and Austria. The Club Handbook gave details of all the Club's activities and had a long list of female models 'available to members at modest rates'. This sounded interesting, but I knew nothing about this branch of photography, so

I attended a session or two on portrait and figure photography. The lecturer demonstrated various lighting techniques and poses for the model, but the class was large and seemed to me to be populated by middle-aged men of humourless demeanour. It was not much fun and my visits to the Club gradually became less frequent.

I visited various relatives and family friends, most of whom had not seen me since I was a child, if at all. This was not very rewarding and I was regarded as rather an oddity: a tea planter on leave? How fascinating! After the war and the slow recovery of the economy during the long post-war years, Britain was at last starting to brighten up. The last of the rationing had ended several years previously. New buildings were replacing the bombed sites in London which I remembered as a school boy and I felt people were more interested in what was going on in their own world rather than in some remote corner of the ex-empire. People were also becoming more prosperous; television aerials were sprouting from more and more roofs each day and the papers had stories of successful entrepreneurs who had struck it rich and of the increasingly lively life style of students and young people. Was I missing out on something?

Before leaving Ceylon I had been considering what I should do if my long leave did not produce a fiancée, or at least a serious girl friend. I could see very little chance of meeting anyone congenial in my remote corner of the planting world and in fact, as the older planters retired, the number of daughters and young female relations who came out for visits was diminishing. I certainly did not want to spend another four year tour without a female companion and five months in the UK was not a very long time in which to find one, especially as few might like the sound of life on remote estates. Also, living with my uncle and aunt, I did not get to meet very many girls on whom I might try to exercise such fascination as I could muster. I was turning over in my mind the possibility that there might be nothing for it but to leave planting and start again. But what could I do? My qualifications and experience fitted me only for tea planting and I felt no inclination to move to other tea planting areas in East Africa or New Guinea as some of my friends were beginning to consider doing, because I thought that in the long term these areas would probably suffer from the same problems as those in Ceylon. No, if I had to leave Ceylon, I would try to get better academic qualifications and that meant a university degree. My matriculation qualification from the University of Melbourne would not get me into a British university and, now that I had had a taste of life in England, I did not feel I wanted to go back to Melbourne, which in those days still seemed very cut off from Britain and Europe where the improving economy and social developments seemed so attractive. To get into a British university I would need several subjects at the General Certificate of Education Advanced Level, and the only way to get these quickly would be to attend a tutorial establishment. I therefore spent some time sifting through the merits of the various London tutorial colleges and visited one or two of them to get some idea of what they might be like. However, I still hoped that this course would not be necessary, so I made no firm arrangements.

I was still seeing Susan fairly regularly but, although friendly, our relationship did not seem to be developing. One evening I tried to encourage things by talking about the future and gently implied that our futures might perhaps develop together if she felt inclined. This evidently had the opposite effect: perhaps her relationship with her other boyfriend had come under strain or he had started to complain about her seeing me. In any event, she evidently decided that he was a better bet than a tea planter who was about to disappear back into the unknown whence he had so suddenly materialised. A few days later I received a 'Dear John' letter, ending our relationship. This upset me considerably at the time, but in reality our relationship had been very superficial and I had been naïve to think that it was anything more. After moping for a few days, I started to consider what other girls I knew who might be worth investigating. I had met Pam several times in Ceylon and had found her very attractive. She was a very pretty girl, with shoulder-length pale blonde hair, but she had been staying with her parents in the far distant Kotmale District and at the time I had met her she had also seemed to be involved with one of my planting acquaintances. However, I knew she was attending a nursery nurses' training college not far away, so I decided to contact her. She seemed surprised but pleased to hear from me and we arranged to go out one evening. However, I found her hard work. She chatted easily enough, but was decidedly cold and seemed to have a horror of physical contact. Even holding hands was *verboten* and a goodnight kiss out of the question. I saw her a few more times, but she did not seem to thaw and, as my leave by then was drawing to a close and I had to relinquish my car, I gave up asking her out.

The car had to be delivered to the shipping company in early April in order to arrive in Bombay by early May. I was due back on the estate in mid May and I planned to take a week driving down through southern India en route to Ceylon. Without a car, my movements were limited and I did not stray much outside the London area. I spent much time selecting and buying items to take back with me, such as a tape recorder (recorders were just then coming onto the market from many different manufacturers) and a tent. These would go out by sea direct to Colombo in my trunk. I also wanted to give my uncle and aunt a substantial present for their kindness and hospitality and decided on a set of jug and eight tumblers in high quality cut crystal, which I got from Selfridges.

Eventually the day for my departure arrived and my uncle, aunt and cousin delivered me to Heathrow to catch the Air India International overnight flight to Bombay. Besides my heavy suitcase, I was again encumbered with excessive hand baggage but there were no objections. The flight was full and I spent an uncomfortable night surrounded by bags and various parcels which I had arranged to be delivered, duty-free, direct to the aircraft and which would not fit into the lockers. After a couple of stops en route, we arrived the following day to the heat and blinding sunshine, the crowded streets and dense, honking traffic of Bombay.

Back at the Ambassador Hotel, my first inclination was to have a bath. The bathroom had an unusual water heating system. Fixed to the wall above the taps, there was a sort of electrical geyser which had various wires and pipes connected to it. The geyser's white casing was rather discoloured in the area from which most of the attached gubbins seemed to sprout and beside it was a switch labelled 'Hot Water'. Switching this on, I returned to the bedroom to undress. After a few moments I became aware of a hissing sound which rapidly increased to resemble a particularly active volcanic fumerole. Hastily returning to the bathroom, semi-clothed, I was just in time to see a blinding flash as the geyser exploded with a loud bang and clouds of steam. My attention was then drawn to little notice, higher up the wall, which gave instructions that the bath hot water tap should be opened before the geyser was switched on. Feeling somewhat shaken, but still wanting a bath, I dressed and went down to Reception to explain what had happened. The manager seemed not at all perturbed and shouted instructions to someone in the back regions of the hotel to repair the geyser. Evidently this type of mishap was not infrequent and the discoloured casing of the geyser was explained.

Eventually I got my bath and later I set off to visit the offices of the shipping agents and the West India Automobile Association. There was some good news and some bad news. The good news was that the car had actually arrived and was on the dockside; the bad news, conveyed by the friendly AA man with a broad smile, was that hitherto nobody had managed to clear a car through customs in less than a week. This was serious, as I had allowed only a week to travel south, including staying a couple of nights on the way with friends. Nothing could be done that day, as it was already late, but the AA man and I would start the clearance process first thing the following morning.

The clearance process was complicated and slow. Without the help of the AA it would have been well nigh impossible. The basic document was the Carnet, issued to me by the AA in London which, something like a passport, permitted me to take the car through countries which were not its final destination without paying duty. There ensued endless phone calls, filling in of countless forms, and visits to minor officials in the Customs and other Departments. Bureaucracy reaches a pinnacle of development and refinement in India, where the wielding of innumerable rubber stamps and the transfer of forms, duplicated in hazy print on faintly coloured paper of varying hues, is loved by all. However, the procedures are not arbitrary and there is a recognised system to deal with most things if only one can determine what it is and one does not die before completing it. Officials were invariably courteous and their first action was to try to get me to sit down, often proffering chairs and even cups of tea in dubious-looking cups. However, once seated, I would then be ignored and the tide of office life would swirl around me, with people of all kinds ebbing and flowing, each claiming the attention of the official for as long as possible. I thus soon discovered that Rule 1 was Never Sit Down. While I remained standing, whichever official I was dealing with seemed to feel a much greater obligation to progress my business. With the great assistance of the man from the AA, who guided me through the maze of offices and procedures and who knew many of the officials, I gradually began to see some progress and towards the end of the second day we actually received the last piece of paper with the last rubber stamp and the last signature which permitted me to remove the car from the Customs' clutches. As it was by then quite late I suggested to the AA man that perhaps it might be better if we collected the car the following morning, but he firmly vetoed the idea. 'No, no,' he said, 'We must be collecting it today. Otherwise, who can tell what may happen or be changing their minds?' So we set off for the docks.

In the docks work had largely finished for the day and we found the car looking rather forlorn and very grimy in the corner of a large godown. Apart from a few knocks, it seemed to be unscathed and none the worse for its sea voyage. It had been completely drained of petrol for shipment and none was available within the docks area, so the AA man and I pushed it half a mile or so, out through the dock gates and to the nearest filling station. I then delivered him back to the WIAA office with effusive thanks and he responded that in his experience clearance in two days was 'a record'.

Tired, hot, and grimy, but triumphantly on four wheels, I returned to the Ambassador for a bath. Clicking on the hot water switch, I began to undress in the bedroom when a hissing sound, this time accompanied by a low rumble, issued from the bathroom . . . . Hobbled by my shorts round my ankles, I made a rush for the bathroom and was just passing through the door in a more or less horizontal attitude when the geyser went through its now familiar performance with blinding flash, deafening bang and impenetrable clouds of steam. The manager again seemed unruffled and resigned to accept these occurrences as Acts of God. Accepting my apologies he again wheeled out the electrician and an hour later I was successfully bathed and clean.

Through the good offices of the man at the WIAA, who made the booking, I made a reservation for the car on the train ferry across the Palk Straits from India to Ceylon. There was no road connection to the ferry terminal on the Indian side at Dhanushkodi, which was situated on an island connected to the mainland only by the railway bridge. The car would have to be put on the train at the loading station further inland at Mandapam. I felt less than confident of this booking as it had had to be made by telephone, without any written confirmation and, to judge by the shouting that had gone on, the line had been anything but clear. However, there was nothing more that I could do.

The following day, with a full tank of petrol, I made an early start and navigated my way out of Bombay through endless wretched suburbs and shanty towns. Time was short if I was to catch the ferry on the appointed day and one of the aims of my journey was to stay a couple of nights with John, my erstwhile neighbour during Meeriabedde days who had been on Poonagalla Group. He had decided to leave Ceylon about a year before I went on furlough, had married his childhood sweetheart, Faye, and had returned to the land of his birth, where he felt that the government was more favourably disposed towards European planters. He had got a new planting post in the Chikmagalur District of Mysore State, (now Karnataka) on Karadykhan, a coffee estate in the foothills of the Western Ghats, the great mountain chain running down the western side of southern India.

A few miles out of Bombay on the Delhi road I turned off south-east into the dry hills around Poona. Names on the signposts seemed to read like a gazetteer of the Raj and as I arrived at strange places with familiar names I felt history weighing heavily upon me. From Poona I followed the main road south, to Kolhapur and Belgaum. The surface was reasonably good, varying between tarmac and concrete, and I made good progress, stopping only to buy a few mangoes and a drink in a wayside village. To be on the safe side, I avoided water or tea with milk and opted for a fizzy drink. As usual in southern India before the monsoon breaks in late May, it was very hot and I sat by the bar sipping my cool fizzy drink with relish. Gradually I became aware of activity in the room behind the bar, through the doorway to which I could see someone busy filling bottles from the grimy tap. The bottles must have had a measure of concentrate in them, for as they filled they turned a bright orange, - just the colour of my fizzy drink. I took another sip and watched with interest as the bottles were transferred to a machine and the operator then reached down to connect a cylinder and opened the valve. When the bottles were removed from the machine, they had been fitted with tops . . . just like my fizzy drink. Quietly I put down my half empty glass, paid for my drink, and returned to the car hoping that my last typhoid inoculation was still effective.

At Belgaum I stopped at the hotel for afternoon tea. This was served on the veranda by a waiter in an immaculate white starched uniform which on closer inspection revealed ragged and frayed cuffs and turn-ups. There was an aura of decayed gentility about the place, aided by the presence of two elderly European women who were also taking tea. The table linen was also frayed and starched, and the worn cane furniture glowed in the afternoon sun. Dark panelled walls were hung with faded photographs depicting groups of *pukka sahibs*, often in military or ICS uniform, with their memsahibs in the voluminous dresses of a bygone era. Altogether the place harked back to the lost days of the Raj in so faded a way that it seemed positively ghostly. I pressed on as quickly as possible and as dusk was falling I began to wonder if the next small town might have a hotel. It did not, but Davangere did have a Rest House to which I made my way.

The Rest House was typical of innumerable examples of its kind then to be found all over India and Ceylon and originally built to provide accommodation for government officials on tour. A white-washed building of bungalow style, it had a tiled roof, a wide veranda, and several bedrooms opening off a central dining room. The compound was devoid of any shade but the gravel had been swept clean of debris and the tracks of several mangy pie dogs lying by the steps could clearly be seen in the dust. Only one other car was visible and the place seemed to be devoid of any guests other than myself. However, when I eventually located the Rest House Keeper, he stoutly maintained that the Rest House accommodation was full and he had no provisions for a meal. This was a nuisance: it was too late to go on or to search in the dark town for somewhere to eat, and so I reluctantly decided to forego supper and sleep in the car.

Dawn was a relief and I emerged to stretch my cramped limbs, scratch my mosquito bites, and search for some breakfast. I felt much better after a brief wash under the tap. The Rest House Keeper admitted he actually did have tea, some bread and an egg, which I thereupon requested as breakfast, with instructions that it should be boiled for five minutes. I sat at one of the dining tables pleasantly anticipating my egg with bread and butter and, after what seemed an age, the Rest House Keeper appeared bearing a tray with the desired comestibles. Setting this before me, he hastily retired to the dim rear regions of the establishment while I inspected the meal. The egg was very small and suspiciously cool. There were two slices of rather dirty white bread of open texture, and a small pot of an oily substance which was certainly not butter but might have been ghee. I began to feel less than enthusiastic about the eating standards of the place but, determined to have my breakfast, I took the top off the egg. The contents was gelatinous and virtually raw, the white being grey and liberally sprinkled with dubious-looking black specks. I did not examine it further, but pushed it away and did the best I could with dry bread and black tea (since milk in these parts appeared to be unknown, which perhaps was just as well). It did not take me long to resume my journey.

From Davangere I diverged from the main road south and found my way to the District town of Chickmagalur, where John and Faye had arranged to meet me at the club. This had once been a rather imposing building with a pillared portico and a tiled roof, now partly shrouded in bouganvillea and various creepers. However, the walls had evidently not been painted for many years and many of the tiles were awry or broken. The garden also had an unkempt air and whoever looked after it was evidently losing a battle with the vigorous local vegetation, which had gained the upper hand. Inside, the club was rather dark and furnished with large, heavy furniture. At first it appeared deserted, but soon a movement attracted my attention and a very elderly European materialised from the gloom, clutching a newspaper. He seemed delighted to see me. My arrival was evidently the event of his week, and he welcomed me to Chickmagalur, going on to sketch out his personal history in increasing detail. I was not surprised to learn that he was a retired planter who had decided to stay on in Chickmagalur as he had no family back in Britain. I was somewhat relieved when John and Faye presently arrived and rescued me, and I followed them back to Karadykhan Estate.

Karadykhan was a coffee estate, originally opened up by a planter named Charles Crawford in the late 1880s. Charles and his two brothers had apparently started planting while still teenagers in 1887 when they joined Bruce Mockett, an old-timer who had opened many hundreds of acres of coffee and cardamom in these hills. When opening coffee estates in these parts it was not the practice to clear fell the native jungle, as was the case when opening for tea in Ceylon. Like tea, coffee is naturally a small tree of the forest understorey and here coffee estates were often started by replacing the undergrowth and smaller trees with coffee, leaving most of the larger trees *in situ*. It was doubtless cheaper to do this, although perhaps the yields of coffee were not as great as they might have been if they had had rather less shade. In fact Karadykhan was opened just at the time that coffee in Ceylon was in its final years of decline in the face of the onslaught of coffee leaf disease.

Curiously, the course of the disease was the reverse of the pattern followed by the blister blight of tea some 80 years later. The first recognised outbreak of coffee leaf disease, caused by the then unknown coffee rust fungus, was in Ceylon, whence it soon spread to southern India and eventually to all major coffee growing areas in Asia. It was first noticed in May 1869 on Galloola Estate in the Madulsima District, away on the extreme eastern side of the central hills. This was an unlikely location for a first landfall if the wind-borne spores had travelled direct from their native haunts on wild coffee in the Ethiopian highlands 3,000 miles to the west. However, it made its presence felt wherever it occurred and would have been difficult to overlook. As a young SD on Gallebodde Estate in the Narwalapitiya area, William Forsythe describes how the white drill suits which he and his fellow planters customarily wore were stained the 'colour of canaries' by the rust spores after walking through the infected coffee. Within five years of its first appearance it was present on every coffee estate in Ceylon and by 1871 it was well established in the coffee planting districts of south India.

Although the effect of coffee rust disease on the Ceylon and southern Indian coffee industries was catastrophic and was the indirect cause of tea drinking becoming a characteristic habit of the British, the devastation did not occur overnight. The damage was caused by its effect in defoliating the coffee trees so that, although they still produced flushes of new leaves, they gradually became debilitated and over a period of several years the crop produced dwindled to uneconomic levels. Presumably the decline in coffee production in Ceylon increased demand for coffee elsewhere and somehow the coffee rust did not wreak such havoc in the northern parts of the Indian coffee-growing area as it did further south. Perhaps the climate and the habit of growing coffee in less intensive and more natural shady conditions beneath native jungle trees were less favourable to the disease. Whatever was the reason, coffee survived on Karadykhan and other estates in the Chickmagalur and neighbouring districts. Small pockets of coffee survived even in the more severely affected areas (there were still six acres of coffee on Gallebodde Estate in 1959), but the general decline of coffee in India and Ceylon was irreversible and its centre of production shifted to South America.

Karadykhan bungalow was old fashioned, with a wide veranda in front, screened with a wooden trellis. The garden was shady; full of large trees and birds. John and Faye made me welcome

179

and John took me round the estate in a Jeep. I asked him how he was coping with the different crop and the different language of the area (Telagu).

'Well', he said, 'Telagu's not much different to Tamil, really. Almost like a dialect. For example, 'pig' is *hundi* instead of *pundi* in Tamil, and so on. So I soon got used to it. Then coffee is much simpler to deal with than tea: no regular plucking rounds and no complicated manufacturing process. There's just one harvest period, although you have to pick the trees two or three times. Then the ripe berries are taken to the mill and the red outer flesh is stripped off and washed away, leaving just the skin round the seed. This is fermented in heaps to remove the remaining mucilage and when it's washed and dried this inner skin becomes papery, - what's called 'parchment coffee'. The parchment coffee is then hulled and the seed - the coffee bean - becomes polished, in the same way as the grains of white rice. It's then dried again and bagged up, and that's it. Of course there's still weeding, pruning, manuring and general maintenance, - and spraying against the leaf rust disease, of course, which is important, - but it's a lot less hassle than tea. And you should see the place at blossom time, - it's beautiful, all the coffee trees covered in white, frothy blossom, with a wonderful scent that wafts over the whole place.'

I felt that Karadykhan was much more remote than most estates in Ceylon, - even Idulgashena. From what I had seen of it, the club did not seem as though it would provide much social life and I wondered how Faye would cope with the isolation in the years after the novelty of being newly-married had worn off. Anyway, I kept my doubts to myself, enjoying their company, the wonderful tree-covered landscape, and the partly familiar birds, many of which were the same or similar to those in Ceylon. Two days later I resumed my journey and a relatively short run of about 100 miles brought me again onto the main road at Mysore.

In Mysore I booked in at a small hotel not far from the great palace of the Maharaja of Mysore. It's gleaming dome, towers and pinnacles could be seen in the distance, beyond the ornate white walls which surrounded the grounds and which were a major feature of the locality. These were enhanced by lines of flamboyant trees, covered in orange-red blossom and with great feathery leaves which cast a welcome shade over the footway and the street vendors who displayed their wares below. The palace is not old, having been built to the design of a British architect at the turn of the nineteenth century to replace an earlier, wooden one, which apparently burnt down in 1897. Although I should have liked to visit it, I had to be at the car-loading railhead next day at the appointed time, so I set off southwards once more. The road led me up into the Nilgiri Hills, through Ootacamund and down again to the next large city of Coimbatore.

The Nilgiris or 'Blue Mountains' rise sharply from the plains to a high, rolling plateau at between about seven and eight thousand feet. Although they are linked to the Western Ghats by subsidiary ranges, they stand relatively isolated as a haven of cool and temperate climate amid the heat of the lowlands of southern India. As in Ceylon, coffee was the first plantation crop which, after the ravages of coffee rust, was replaced by even more extensive plantations of tea, and today the Nilgiris are regarded as the heartland of the planting industry in South India. However, they were opened up rather later than the Ceylon hills and were unknown to the British administration of Madras until 1812, when the Collector of Coimbatore sent two members of his staff, Keys and Macmahon, to investigate the mountains to the north of the town. Keys was the Assistant Revenue Surveyor and Macmahon his apprentice, so one can guess that the primary objective of their investigation was to assess what taxes could be raised in the area. However, as the indigenous inhabitants, the Todas, were simple and unsophisticated hill people, their report was probably not very optimistic. A later Collector of Coimbatore, John Sullivan, was the first to realise the potential of the Nilgiris as a refuge from the heat and fever of the plains and in 1819 he built a house for himself near what is now the town of Kotagiri. Sullivan must have been pleased with his first house because he built another in 1823 even higher up at Ootacamund. This started a trend and with more houses and a new road up from Coimbatore 'Ooty', as it is universally known, became the capital of the Nilgiris. It prided itself on its Britishness and many of the buildings and gardens would not have been out of place in Brighton, Cheltenham or, indeed, Edinburgh. The British Governors of the Madras Presidency soon took advantage of its attractions and the Duke of Buckingham when he was the incumbent, instituted the practice of moving the administration from Madras to Ootacamund during the heat of the summer months, just as the Viceroy and his staff moved from Delhi to Simla.

I arrived in Ooty early in the afternoon but, with 200 more miles to do that day, I felt I had no time to linger and pressed straight on. On the outskirts of the town were many small houses of European appearance and in front of one tiled cottage two elderly European women were chatting in the garden amidst a riot of hollyhocks, nasturtiums and geraniums. The road up on the northern side of the hills is steep and winding, but on the southern side the massif is much more precipitous and the road descends in a succession of looping hairpin bends, reminding me of Needwood on a larger scale. At one point I crossed the railway, a narrow-gauge line, built during the 1890s, which ascends from Mettupalayam to Ooty and is still in use. The rest of the day was occupied with a tedious drive over rather flat country and through the crowded streets of towns and villages, and I eventually arrived at the city of Madurai after dark.

The crossing from India to Ceylon is not at the southernmost tip of the Indian peninsula but is a considerable distance northwards on the eastern coast, where a promontory reaches out towards the end of the elongated island of Manaar on the Ceylon side. On the Indian side at the end of the promontory the island of Pamban is also detached from the mainland, with Dhanushkodi, the ferry terminal, at the far end. The water of the Palk Strait separating the two countries is shallow and a chain of reefs and sand banks, known as Adam's Bridge, connects Pamban and Manaar. As there was no road bridge, most passengers and goods had to travel by rail from the Indian mainland to Dhanushkodi. Entrainment was at the station of Mandapam, a few miles inland, and there I presented myself the following morning in good time to load the car before the scheduled time of the train's departure.

The stationmaster was polite but firm. 'No, Sir, we are absolutely not having any booking for your car on this train. ... No, no, there is no record of any booking from Bombay last week. No, I am sorry, bookings cannot be made on the day of departure, but must be made in advance. There is no spare flat car on the train. ... No, I am sorry.' There seemed little I could do and, even if he had not seemed such a pillar of integrity, I did not have enough cash on me to serve as an inducement to soften his stance. The trains did not run every day and the next one on which I could make a reservation was in three days' time. My gloomy premonitions in Bombay had materialised and I hoped that George Steuarts in Colombo would not be too upset at my delayed return. I sent them a telegram saying 'Unavoidably delayed Mandapam' and, at the stationmaster's suggestion, I booked in at the railway rest house in the neighbouring settlement of Mandapam Camp.

The next three days were probably the most boring of my life. There was virtually nothing to do: English language newspapers did not appear to exist in these parts, there were no shops, and the lengthy return journey to Madurai for the doubtful possibility of seeing an English film did not seem worth while. However, the rest house was clean, the cook was able to produce curry and tea and, as the local population were all Tamils, I could at least communicate with them easily. The monsoon had not yet broken, so it was hot at night and hotter by day. The surroundings of the rest house were devoid of trees of any kind and even the threadbare grass patches were brown and parched. I whiled away the time watching the few birds which frequented the area and the languid activity at the station when trains arrived. These were even fewer than the birds, so I did not get much entertainment.

At long last the three days were up, and I returned to Mandapam station. This time the stationmaster was co-operation itself, and the car was loaded from a ramp without any demur. Along with the other passengers I boarded one of the passenger coaches and the train moved off more or less on time. After a short distance of rather barren country, we clanked across the iron latticework of the bridge to Pamban Island and soon drew to a halt at the Dhanushkodi terminal where a ferry

181

was waiting. As far as I can remember, only the goods wagons were rolled onto the ship and all the passengers embarked on foot, leaving the coaches behind. The lower decks became crowded with people and their piles of baggage, this often consisting of stout bundles wrapped in cloth or bulging baskets with cloth covers over the top. The water was remarkably clear and in the bright sunlight numbers of edible-sized fish could be seen swimming beneath the ship. These attracted the attention of several fishermen amongst the passengers, who promptly produced lines and started to haul them on board, much to the satisfaction of all concerned. After some delay, the ship emitted several sonorous blasts on its siren and we slowly moved away from the pier. These days most travellers have to go by air, as the ferry service was discontinued in 1984.

I think the crossing took about a couple of hours. The ship was slow, but the distance was not very far and in mid afternoon the buildings and port installations of Talaimanaar came into view on the low and sandy shores of Manaar Island. There was a rush to disembark and secure the best seats in the waiting train, which was the overnight service to Colombo, while I waited anxiously to see my car reappear. Eventually the wagon with the car was rolled off and the car unloaded. At this point an unforeseen hitch occurred. The Carnet document permitted the car to enter countries into which it was not being permanently imported without being liable to tax. However, as the perspicacious Ceylon customs officer pointed out, this was not the case for Ceylon, where I was a returning resident. He therefore maintained that duty on the car should be paid before it could be released. This was quite a blow, as I had on me nothing like the amount of duty which would be due and I had visions of further delay while I obtained funds from Colombo. I explained the predicament to the customs officer and pleaded that I should be allowed to pay the duty in Colombo. Much to my surprise, he eventually agreed to this, probably partly because he had no suitable bonded store in which to keep the car and partly because he was not sure what the duty should be. Anyway, to my relief, the car was released and I set off as dusk was falling, arriving in Colombo late in the evening to be greeted by my parents and family at my sister and brother-in-law's house.

The next day I called at George Steuart & Co. to pay my respects and to offer my apologies for my late return. However, the directors did not seem unduly put out and appeared more interested in my unusual method of return than in reprimanding me for overstaying my leave. I lost no time in paying the duty on the car and returned to Idulgashena as soon as possible, spending one night at my parents' bungalow where I was reunited with a slightly fatter Fredo to our great mutual delight.

# Kahagalla                                                    **15**

---

Back at Idulgashena I found Carupiah waiting for me. Nobody had occupied the bungalow during my absence and I found he had already made it clean and tidy. The garden was also looking good, the lawn had been mown, red pelargoniums and pink begonias were in flower round the bungalow, pink and mauve petunias in the terraced beds, and the camellias up on the bank were in bloom. Work on the Division seemed to be back to normal and as I picked up the threads of daily work again I made no mention of the go-slow. In my absence the KP had reverted to doing the daily check-roll and Mr Meikle seemed quite happy to let this state of affairs continue.

On my first visit to the club I found that the District seemed little changed. Two or three PDs had moved or had gone on furlough and had been replaced by new people from other districts. There were one or two new faces among the young SDs on the tennis court and at the bar, while the greatest change among my closer friends was that Hans and Ingrid on Kinellan had produced a baby daughter. However, there had been a change on Needwood. Mr Meikle was still firmly in charge, down at Needwood Bungalow, but on Haldumulla Division Trevor La Brooy had been replaced by Ian Macdonald. I had grown used to being the youngest and most junior European planter in the District, so it felt rather novel to have someone junior to myself in the area, and even on the same estate. Ian was a cheerful and rather sporty type, and he was probably a year or two older than myself. He was sharing his bungalow with a lively brown-haired girl named Pat, who was in fact married to someone else at the time, and I soon became friendly with both of them.

This served to highlight the fact that I had returned to Ceylon without any female attachment. However, although I had been rather favourably impressed by life in England and had returned to Idulgashena with mixed feelings, it was good to be back in my own home once again with my books and woodwork workshop, so I resumed the former pattern of my life with visits to the Haldummulla and Bow Clubs on Sundays and Wednesdays, interspersed with occasional Sunday natural history excursions to the low country jungles near the south or east coasts. These were as enjoyable as ever, but my time in the UK seemed to have given me a stronger taste for social contact and I became quite reluctant to forego visiting the club on Sunday in favour of a solo expedition to the Bundala lagoons or to Arugam Bay. There was always the feeling that *this* Sunday an unattached girl might appear and my imagination would run away into a wonderful consequent romance. But no girls ever appeared, or at least extremely seldom, and those that did always seemed to be already attached. I resumed my various other interests, while during my long walks of inspection round the Division, I turned over in my mind the question of what I should do with my future.

Photography gave me a lot of pleasure. I had taken many hundreds of feet of cine film with the Bolex camera in East Africa and I had also taken a lot of black and white stills with the new Edixa Reflex. This kept me busy in the evenings editing and titling the cine film and making enlargements of the best of the stills. The results were pleasing and I had many requests to show the East African film at clubs, meetings of the Wildlife Protection Society, or when I was invited to dinner with friends on other estates. People were gratifyingly complimentary and I found there was quite a lot of spin-off from this exercise, culminating in an invitation to become a member of the Wild Life Protection Society's General Committee.

My friend, Ted Norris, a well-known naturalist and fellow member of the Ceylon Bird Club, was the principal activist in wild life conservation in the Island and had recently become President of the WLPS after serving the Society in many other posts. Ted had started planting in 1935 in the Kandy District, where his interest in natural history and especially ornithology had been much encouraged by W. W. A. Phillips, another planter and renowned zoologist who was the author of several books on Ceylon mammals and birds. Phillips had retired from Ceylon several years previously, but I had got to know him and his wife when they had returned to visit their daughter, Eileen, who had married another planter in the Bandarawela area, and I had visited them at their home near Bognor Regis when I had been on furlough. I warned Ted that, if elected, I might not be able to attend Committee meetings regularly, as meetings were almost always held in Colombo. This evidently did not dissuade the Committee and I was duly appointed. Although I did my best to participate in the activities of the Society and the General Committee by correspondence, as I feared, it proved very difficult for me to attend meetings and I do not think that I managed to attend a single meeting during the year that I was a Committee member.

I was able to make a greater contribution to the Ceylon Camera Club. This was expanding and was forming branches in various districts outside Colombo. Soon after I joined, a new branch was formed in Bandarawela and, to my surprise, I was elected as Branch Chairman. We held meetings at regular intervals at the Bow Club in Bandarawela which were usually well attended. I organised speakers on various topics and some competitions for colour slides and for black and white prints. People seemed to like these and Camera Club evenings became an enjoyable feature of the local social scene.

My thoughts during my perambulations round the Idulgashena *totum* did not quickly reach a conclusion. My favourable impressions of life in England discouraged me from contemplating a return to Australia, where I had no close family connections. At that time communications were slow, travel expensive, and Australia seemed a backwater very far removed from Europe. However, if I quit planting I was determined to acquire some qualifications, starting with GCE A-Levels. But the academic year started in September and I would need a full academic year, if not more, to acquire my A-Levels. My planting contract, such as it was, specified 'one month's notice on either side', but I knew that my employers would not take it kindly if I gave them the minimum amount of notice and, if I was to give much more, it would mean resigning almost immediately. I thought they might well withhold the meagre yearly bonus I was expecting and anyway probably they would not be willing to fund my passage back to the UK as I would not have more than a few months of my second tour to my credit. Pat, my kind neighbour on the next-door estate of Beauvais, had worked for The Gibson Estates himself in earlier years (in fact he had been a previous occupant of the Small Bungalow on Meeriabedde Lower Division) and told me that he had had his bonus withheld when he resigned to change companies. Also, it had been an enormous effort to learn Tamil; all that would be completely wasted if I left planting. The pay was reasonable, the accommodation good and the climate wonderful. Was it really necessary to make a new start? I certainly did not want to wait another four years before I had my next furlough, but many companies were now giving their managers three months leave every 21 months and perhaps The Gibson Estates could be persuaded to do likewise? I could not come to any firm decision and as the weeks went by the window of time for an amicable resignation gradually diminished.

Having returned to Ceylon in May, it was not so very long before the dry season returned and with it the prospect of the tennis meets at upcountry clubs which featured so largely in my sparse social life. However, apart from the local meets at the Haldummulla and Bow Clubs, which Mr Meikle expected me to attend, I could not really ask for leave to attend more than one or two further afield. I carefully needed to weigh the merits of the various possibilities (of which there were not many) before broaching the subject of leave when I had only relatively recently returned from furlough. Eventually I decided to opt for the meet at the Badulla Gymkhana Club. As this was the Uva Provincial club the meet was the biggest tennis event of the year in Uva. Championships of singles, doubles and mixed pairs would be played over the two days of the appointed weekend. The dance which took place on the Saturday evening was always well attended and would be sure to attract any unattached girls within Uva and, with any luck, some from Colombo or elsewhere as well. However, I thought it might also be possible to attend other tennis meets just for the evening dance and I decided to try this at the Dickson's Corner Club.

The Dickson's Corner Club was situated in the Udapussellawa District, which covered the range of hills forming the northern rim of the Uva Basin. These were clearly visible from Idulgashena, and ran more or less due east from Nuwara Eliya, ending with a saddle-backed mountain on the slopes of which was Kirklees Estate. To get there by the main road from Haputale one first had to pass through Bandarawela, ascend to Nuwara Eliya, take the Kandapola road, and then branch east to Udapussellawa, a journey of perhaps nearly three hours from Idulgashena. However, there was a short-cut which I knew through Kirklees Estate which would cut the journey time to not much more than two hours, which I felt was just possible.

One day I received a summons from Mr Meikle to meet him the next morning, as usual at the Idalgashinna level crossing, for a round of the Division. We set off up the railway line with Haggis and Fredo in front, turning off onto the cartroad at the top of Field Six and making our way gradually down towards the factory. The dry season was becoming established and, although the sky was overcast with a high thin cloud, the morning light was bright and the birds were calling in the trees above the railway. Growth of the tea was slowing down, we had had no rain to speak of for nearly a month and I was having to lengthen the plucking rounds and reduce the number of women in the plucking gangs. Mr Meikle had been silent for a while, but at length he spoke.

'Well, David,' he said, 'things seem to be looking ship-shape - I'm glad to see ye've got the weeds under control and the spraying rounds up to date. But ye'll not be seeing much more of Idulgashena, ye know.'

'Really, Sir?' I replied, somewhat taken aback and wondering what bombshell he was about to drop.

'Aye,' he said, 'I've decided to make a few changes in the organisation and I thought I'd tell ye now before ye learn it from those useless sods in Colombo.'

My mind started to race through all the possible scenarios I could envisage. Perhaps I was going to be sacked, and I wondered if the directors at George Steuarts had been more displeased with my late return from furlough that it had seemed. An old joke of an acquaintance of my father's came into my head: 'How much wood is in a Board?' Answer: 'The sackfull'. I wondered what was coming next.

'Ah . . .err . . . um . . . well', he said, 'I've decided to transfer you to Kahagalla in September as Assistant-in-Charge.'

I had never heard of anyone being 'assistant-in-charge' on any estate, but it sounded as if I would have more responsibility. I knew that Kahagalla was not large enough to have an SD and had always been a billet for a PD alone. Was it just a way of getting me to do a PD's job for an SD's salary?

'I see, Sir,' I said, 'what does that mean in terms of responsibility?'

'Just what it says,' he replied, curtly, 'I shall move to Netherbyres and become a full time VA, and you will be responsible for running Kahagalla under my supervision.'

So that was it. I wasn't going to escape Mr Meikle as yet. Netherbyres was the large bungalow on Kahagalla Estate which old Mr Gibson had built for himself when he was nearing retirement. After his death it had been let out to tenants, and I could see that it would make a good base for Mr Meikle. On the whole, the proposition seemed reasonably favourable. Kahagalla was an excellent and productive estate in a plum position and surely I would be given a pay rise for the additional responsibility. At least it seemed worth while to give it a try and enjoy the luxury of being near the clubs and other amenities. In a year's time I could think again and, if I decided on resignation, at least I would have just about earned a passage back to the UK. I was pleased to have reached a decision, and I felt able to give my full attention to Idulgashena while looking forward to my transfer to Kahagalla.

A notice announcing that the Dickson's Corner tennis meet would be held on the weekend of 3rd and 4th September had appeared in the *CPS Bulletin* for March 1960. As well as calling for entries to men's handicap singles, and to men's, ladies and mixed handicap doubles, it also said 'There will be a dance with band on the Saturday night and lunch and tea will be provided on both days.' The date was rather near to that of my transfer to Kahagalla, which was scheduled for 7th September. However, the dry weather meant that work would have to be cancelled on the Saturday, so I would not have to ask for any leave - or even make any mention of the matter to Mr Meikle.

I set off for the dance in good time as I was not very familiar with the Kirklees shortcut, and I was glad to be able to navigate it in daylight, taking good note of the way for my return journey in the dark small hours. The club was a small one, not much larger than the Haldummulla Club, and I found several acquaintances already ensconced at the bar.

The band started up and more people arrived, but very few young women were present and none were unattached. I then became aware that three girls had made their appearance. I recognised Pat, the brunette, who had been around for several years and was one of the three teachers from the Hill School in Nuwara Eliya who I had met at the Aislaby party before I had gone on furlough. The other two, who were both blondes, seemed unfamiliar. I quickly moved to make their acquaintance and found that indeed all three were Hill School teachers. Julia had recently arrived to replace Anne, who had completed her contract, and the other turned out to be Shirley, who had been at the Aislaby party but now had her blond hair cut much shorter. It curled round her ears to frame her face and I noticed with approval that she had an excellent figure. She also seemed much more confident and had no doubt become more used to the social scene and the ways of the local young planters. We danced together for much of the evening and found we had a lot to say. We both enjoyed the Scottish dances - played atrociously by the band with a monotonous, unvarying tune - and I carried her off the floor at the end of the last one. At the end of the evening we made a date for the Sunday of the following weekend.

I drove back down the Kirklees shortcut feeling elated and did not mind how long the journey home was. The bright moon was shining over the Uva basin and I could see the mountains above Idalgashinna clearly against the starry sky. I could hardly wait for the next weekend to come round, but I had much else to do. Nevertheless, my thoughts kept gravitating towards Nuwara Eliya.

My move to Kahagalla duly took place the following Wednesday. Carupiah and I had to pack up all my belongings and the bungalow had to be cleaned and made ready for the new occupant, whoever that might be (I had not been informed and, as when I had left Meeriabedde, there was to be no direct hand-over). Once again all my *sarmen* was loaded into the estate lorry and this time Fredo and I followed in the Vauxhall Victor. Of course I knew the Kahagalla bungalow from having visited it for Dickie Dickenson's record concert four years previously, and more recently I had passed it almost every week on my way to and from Bandarawela, although it was not quite visible from the road. Dickie was now retired, having departed without ceremony in his unobtrusive way a couple of years previously.

I knew that Kahagalla had always been a PD post and that it was considered a high quality property, so I felt quite elated as I turned up the short drive from the main road and pulled up outside the garage. Neither the bungalow nor the garden had changed in appearance since I had last seen them and both looked immaculately kept. From the front the bungalow appeared almost square, with a flight of steps leading up to the front door and with a bay window on one side. It faced approximately north-west, looking out across the dry hills of the central Uva Basin towards Diyatalawa and the more distant high mountains around Udapussellawa. The walls were covered in rough-cast plaster painted white, setting off the dark wooden window frames and the scarlet pelargoniums which occupied the beds at the foot of the walls. The most distinctive feature was the roof, which was unusually high and steep ('to shed all the snow' according to my friends) and covered with wooden shingles instead of corrugated iron or tiles.

Inside, the bungalow was rather dark. A gallery with several windows ran along the front, which reduced the light to the sitting-room and hallway, which lay behind. The main bedroom suite, with its bay window, was on the left and there were two other bedrooms on the other side of the bungalow, each with an attached bathroom. As this had been a PD billet, there were some soft furnishings which went with the bungalow and greatly helped to make it seem immediately habitable. These included curtains for most of the windows, a couple of Indian carpets and some coconut matting. It did not take very long to install my belongings and feel at home.

*Kahagalla Bungalow.*

As the hillside was rather steep at this point, the gardens above the drive were terraced, with a sloping lawn on the lower side. A large monkey-puzzle tree (*Arucaria*) rose on one side of the bungalow and a vegetable garden was situated at a higher level at the back. Two *totakarans* attended to the gardening, explaining why the gardens looked so well-kept, and I also inherited a houseboy named Ramanathan who became assistant to Carupiah.

The following Sunday I set off for Nuwara Eliya in high spirits, relishing the halving of the journey time as compared with that from Idulgashena. At this time, Shirley and several of her fellow teachers were occupying the headmaster's bungalow while he was away on long leave. This bungalow was higher up the hillside than the main school buildings and was reached by a long flight of steps. I left my car in the school forecourt, where I had so often played in my childhood, and saw Shirley coming down the steps to meet me. I do not remember what we did on this first date, but very probably we had a walk round the lake with other teachers or mutual friends, a visit to the golf club or one of the hotels for a drink and a snack, and later perhaps a visit to the cinema which showed English films. As far as I was concerned the day could go on for ever, but eventually I was back on the Bandarawela road en route to Kahagalla and the usual estate work of a Monday morning.

My Sunday visits to Nuwara Eliya to see Shirley became a regular feature of my life and I no longer attended the Sunday morning tennis gathering at the Haldummulla Club. There always seemed to be activities planned in which Shirley and I could participate and, if not, we were happy in each other's company. We joined other teachers for a picnic up on the approaches to the Horton Plains, made the 2,000 ft climb up the footpath to the top of Pidurutalagala (commonly known as Mt Pidro) which, at 8,281 ft, is the Country's highest mountain, and on one occasion we borrowed two retired race horses from the local stables and rode round the lake. I had not been on a horse for about ten years and felt less than confident as we set off. However, my mount was reasonably docile and by the time we passed by the race course I was feeling quite at ease in the saddle. This did not last long. My mount recognised the race course, which doubtless triggered his old training. Accelerating rapidly, he took off at a gallop which I could do nothing to restrain. Bushes and trees flashed by with me hauling on the reins and trying desperately to remain on board. Eventually we arrived back at the stables rather quicker than intended, but unscathed, - or almost. Later examination by Shirley revealed that I had sustained a certain amount of arse abrasion, which she seemed to find quite amusing and took it upon herself to apply appropriate treatment.

On another occasion we determined to climb Thotupolakanda (Mt. Thotupola). At 7,733 ft, this is the third highest mountain and is visible from Haputale as part of the ramparts of the Horton Plains. The one-inch ordnance survey sheet for Nuwara Eliya showed a footpath to the summit taking off from the track which climbed up the steep escarpment from Pattipola railway station to the Horton Plains. The whole Island was mapped on coloured sheets at this 1: 63,360 scale and these sheets were a tribute to the superb work of the Ceylon Survey Department during colonial times. Their accuracy and print quality was fully equal to those of the UK and few other tropical countries, save possibly India, possess maps which could rival them. The few recent revisions which have appeared look very poor in comparison and the Sinhala script used severely restricts their use. None are presently available.

Leaving the car at Pattipola station, we set off up the track. This was a rough cart track which had been cut into the mountainside through the jungle and scrub. It would probably have been passable, with some difficulty, to a jeep or Landrover if there had not been occasional barriers formed by fallen trees lying across the way. A lush growth of grass, ferns and shrubs clothed the banks and the surface of the track was eroded into deep ruts. After some careful scouting around and consultation of the map, we found the entrance to the summit footpath. This was considerably overgrown and we had to fight our way through a dense growth of *nillu* beneath the jungle trees.

There are many species of *nillu* (*Strobilanthes* spp.), which are shrubby but not particularly woody plants, many with showy purple or mauve flowers. They grow commonly in the high montaine forests and have the curious habit of flowering synchronously over wide areas at intervals of about 12 years. The plants die after flowering and the abundant seed gives rise to a new growth. It also attracts large numbers of seed-eating birds, such as jungle fowl and spurfowl, and small rodents.

This year was not a flowering year on Thotupola, so only a few occasional flowers were visible as we clambered upwards.

Occasionally we had to cross small streams with delightfully clear water tinkling between rocks and small pools, from which we drank. Not surprisingly, as few people except the odd hunter would use it, the path sometimes became indistinct and we were in doubt as to how we should proceed.

*Shirley.*

However, we usually solved this problem by choosing the way which seemed to lead most directly uphill. The vegetation also became thicker and often I needed to cut a way through, using the heavy Malay parang, or jungle knife, which I had brought with me. After about an hour or two the jungle suddenly thinned and we emerged onto the summit. A small area on the immediate summit had evidently been cleared, perhaps by surveyors. There was no cairn, but a tall and weather-beaten pole had been erected with a cross-piece tied to it about 10 ft up. The view was magnificent, encompassing

189

the whole of the Uva Basin, Hakgalla mountain to the north, and the high points around the Horton Plains to the south and south-west. However, we did not stay very long and soon began to retrace our steps, looking for trampled vegetation and the branches I had cut on the way up.

The midday sun and the climb had made us hot and we paused by one of the streams to have a drink and catch our breath. I sat on a boulder while Shirley sat slightly lower down on a flat stone in the path. We somehow got onto the subject of birthdays. I had had mine not very long before, when I had turned 23. 'When is yours?' I asked. She paused a moment, 'April 14th' she replied. This was still some way off, but of course I could not help wondering. Another pause. She did not volunteer anything more, so I decided to ask: 'How many will that be?' 'Twenty six'. So that was it: two and a bit years older than me. It did not seem to matter very much. I gently gripped her shoulders and pulled her back to lean against my knees. 'I wish you didn't have such a long journey up to Nuwara Eliya', she said. 'It wastes so much of the day before we can get out.' I thought about this. 'Well', I said, 'why don't you come down to Kahagalla on a Saturday and stay the night? You could come by train. Then we could do a day trip down to the jungle near Tissa or Arugam Bay on the Sunday.' Had I gone too far? Would she think I had other things in mind? 'That's a good idea', she said, 'I'd love to.' So we fixed a date several weeks ahead and after a while we continued our return journey.

Kahagalla had been one of the first estates established in the Haputale area and had originally been opened into coffee. It is shown (as 'Kohagalle') as a coffee estate on the map in the second volume of Sir James Emerson Tennent's work, *Ceylon*, published in 1859. The only other coffee estate in the area at that time was Haputale Estate (shown as 'Happootella'). Presumably they had both been replanted in tea during the decline of coffee in the 1880s. Out of a total area of 545 acres, 501 acres were now excellent tea. The remaining 44 acres were almost entirely occupied by the factory, the labour lines and other estate buildings of one kind or another. The only other area which was uncultivated was a few acres adjacent to the Haputale-Bandarawela road, where the tea had been abandoned to protect the springs and stream from which the estate derived much of its water supply. Here the tea had grown into trees 20 ft high and the old giant albizzia shade trees had become enormous. They were much beloved by the wild bees and in the swarming season it was often possible to see 20 or 30 swarms hanging in black amorphous masses beneath the high branches.

The Haputale-Bandarawela road bisected the estate and passed below my bungalow but above the factory, stores and muster ground. Above the bungalow (at 4,700 ft. elevation) the tea ran up the hillside to adjoin the jungle covering the upper slopes of the mountain, which had been left intact and was still government land (or 'Crown' land, as old-timers referred to it). Below the factory the estate cart road wound down the slopes and eventually, at the very bottom of the estate, it crossed the railway line between Diyatalawa and Bandarawela. There were a couple of short lengths of tunnel on the railway at this point, through which I occasionally walked on my way to various tea fields on the lowest part of the estate. They were not long enough to become very dark and were occupied by the little edible-nest swiftlets, who glued their nests to the rock near the tunnel roof. At this point it was not very far to the tiny estate of Arcadia.

Arcadia was little larger than a smallholding, being only 30 acres of tea. It had no factory of its own and the harvested leaf was processed at Kahagalla. It was owned by an absentee Ceylonese landlord and was run by a Head Kangany who, by arrangement with George Steuarts, was supervised by the superintendent of Kahagalla, who also had to approve all financial expenditure and deal with the monthly paying of the labour force. I inherited this arrangement, for which I received an extra Rs50 per month. Although I judged that this covered little more than a day of my time, I visited the property at least once a week and rather enjoyed the extra responsibility. There was no road exit from the bottom of Kahagalla and to reach Arcadia one had to go up the main road towards Haputale and then branch right, down the road towards Diyatalawa. This road traversed the dry patana grasslands, rather like chalk downs, which, in April, were dotted with the yellow blooms of the daffodil orchid (*Ipsea speciosa*) emerging amongst the grass.

The size and seniority of the Kahagalla job, combined with the responsibility for Arcadia, justified the provision of a motorbike for the use of the superintendent. In my time this was a BSA 250, in reasonable condition, which resided in the bungalow garage. I had never ridden a motorbike before although, illogically, my car driving licence entitled me to do so. However, after a few minutes instruction from the estate mechanic, I got the hang of the accelerator, clutch, and the foot gear change, and was soon enjoying zooming around the estate on this machine. It was a wonderful novelty to have a means of transport provided free by the estate and I found it great fun for visiting, not only Arcadia, but also the clubs in Bandarawela and Haputale and for making other short journeys. So long as the weather was dry, it was warm enough to ride the machine comfortably without any protective clothing, and nobody ever thought of wearing a helmet. However, although the motorbike could negotiate many of the minor paths through the tea, there was a disadvantage in that everyone on the estate could hear where I was. I therefore used it only for reaching general areas of the estate and then continued my tours of inspection on foot.

The substantial pay rise which I had hoped for on appointment to Kahagalla did not materialise. My salary was increased by a small amount and with the additional allowance for Arcadia it totalled Rs1,030 per month. This was still less than £1,000 per year at the fixed current rate of exchange (Rs13.50 to £1), and I got no car allowance as the motorbike was provided. Nevertheless I felt quite well off. My daily routine changed slightly in that although I still spent all morning in the field, the afternoon was largely spent attending to office work in the little office building near the bungalow. This comprised just two rooms with a veranda along the front. There was an office for me with a wall safe and a desk, and a room for the Head Clerk and the two assistant clerks. Most of the work involved signing orders, drafting estimates, attending to correspondence, making minor payments and dealing with requests from the labourers, who now came to see me at this office in the same way as they had done to my bungalow office on Idulgashena. I also had to deal with disputes which could not be settled by the Head Kangany. This was done by holding an inquiry, usually with the aid of the Head Clerk, who acted as a witness to what was said and also helped in various other ways, such as with elucidation of traditions or estate customs with which I was not familiar or with understanding rapid and complicated narratives or statements from the opposing protagonists. I had been given no training or advice on how to handle such inquiries and I did not enjoy these sessions, which I found stressful and I worried that I might not come to the right conclusion or take the most appropriate action. However, I tried to apply simple common sense and this seemed to work.

Mr Meikle retained control of estate finances and I was not a signatory for the Kahagalla bank account. I did not see much of him but he would accompany me round the estate about once a fortnight, and occasionally I would be summoned to Netherbyres to receive instructions or to explain something which he had noticed on the estate. One day we were making a tour of inspection down by the railway. The government of Mrs Sirimivo Bandaranaike, newly elected with a large majority, seemed to be becoming increasingly nationalistic and we were discussing the possibility that the estates might be nationalised. This had been frequently mooted in government circles and, rather to my surprise, Mr Meikle was taking a pessimistic view.

'Aye, David,' he said, 'It's all verra different now to what it was like when I was your age. We could actually get things done in those days whereas now we get so tied up by red tape we can't move. And I don't know what the future holds for young chaps like you; - in my day we could look to the future with fair confidence, but now in your place I'd really be wondering if I should chuck it in.'

I had not heard Mr Meikle talk in such terms before and felt rather taken aback. Was he trying to tell me I had no future here? Of course I had been wondering this myself, but I did not want to divulge this to him just yet, so decided to make a noncommittal reply.

'Well, Sir,' I said, 'Prospects don't seem very promising just at present, but I feel I should see how things go for a while.'

We dropped the subject as we entered one of the short tunnels and turned to other matters as we emerged into the sunshine once again.

As on Idulgashena, it appeared that I was not expected to concern myself with tea manufacture. This was supposed to be supervised by Mr Meikle through the Head Teamaker, although Mr Meikle's visits to the factory were not very frequent. However, I received the reports on samples of our tea from the agents in Colombo before passing them on to Mr Meikle and I made inspections of the factory to try and ensure that no obvious rackets were being operated. A great many years later I discovered that shortly before this, perhaps while I was away on furlough, Mr Meikle had been summoned to Colombo to explain why Needwood was producing only 50% BOP and BOPF instead of about 70%, as it should have done. Apparently he had been unable to give a satisfactory explanation, responding with much pompous bluster, and had been hauled over the coals by the young head of the Tea Department, Tony Peries, in the presence of the George Steuarts senior partner, A. D. McLeod. Apparently the Needwood teamaker had been falsifying the outturn because he had been too scared to inform Mr Meikle himself that the standard of plucking was unsatisfactory. It would have been doubly galling to Mr Meikle to be reprimanded by a Ceylonese – and a young one at that. Apparently it was concluded that Mr Meikle had been spending too much time on his VA activities (for which he was paid separately) and not enough on running Needwood. Probably, therefore, it was this that precipitated his move to full-time VA work from Netherbyres and, in turn, my own move to Kahagalla. It was also no wonder that he had made no attempt to teach me anything about tea manufacture or factory management, but then he had never made any effort to teach me anything. However, it was clear that I would need to have a good understanding of both if ever I was to become a PD. I knew that the Ceylon Planters' Society held an examination in tea manufacture, so I purchased the monograph on *Tea production in Ceylon* published by the Tea Research Institute. After reading this through and making a few notes I entered and successfully passed the examination.

I also decided to learn Sinhala, the language of the majority of the Ceylon population. If it was to become the only national language, as the government proposed, it seemed to me essential to have good knowledge of Sinhala if I was to remain in Ceylon in the future. I made some enquiries through the Head Clerk and eventually arranged for a Buddhist priest to come and give me lessons once a week. I found these hard going (as I do with all languages) and my efforts were not helped by the fact that I had little opportunity to practice the language on the estate. There were virtually no Sinhalese labourers on Kahagalla, but a few of the skilled artisans, such as the *baas* (carpenter) and the blacksmith were Sinhalese. I made a point of speaking to these people as much as possible in their own language and I was also able to practice my conversation with villagers I met on my excursions to the Wirawila and Hambantota area. After about six months I felt I should attempt the Ceylon Planters' Society junior Sinhala exam. As for the Tamil exam, but feeling much less confident, I made my way over to the Queens Hotel in Kandy. It was not a success and I just failed to reach the pass mark. However, I received no encouragement or reward for passing these exams, so my success or failure made no difference to me except for my personal satisfaction or disappointment.

A few weeks after our ascent of Thotupolla, the weekend for Shirley's much-anticipated visit to me at Kahagalla eventually arrived. I had thought of little else during this time and had instructed Carupiah to prepare a bedroom for her, the one which opened into the closed veranda. She was coming by train from Nanuoya and at about four o'clock on the Saturday afternoon I was waiting on the platform as the Udarata Menike drew in to Haputale Station. Anxiously I scanned the first class carriages and to my delight saw her alight from one near the front of the train, her fair hair shining in the sun. We hurried to meet each other and I kissed her, which I think was the first time I had actually done so. Carrying her case, I led her to the car and we drove back to Kahagalla. That evening I had my first experience of dining with my girl friend in my own bungalow, which we both seemed to find novel and enjoyable. As usual, there was a bright fire burning in the sitting-room fireplace and, after Carupiah and the kitchen coolie had performed the 'goodnight ceremony' and retired, we sat on the floor to enjoy its warmth. Our conversation became more sporadic as my arm slid around her shoulders and we started to kiss more seriously. Time seemed to pass unaccountably quickly, yet we seemed to be suspended in each other's consciousness. I felt a breath on the back of my neck and looked up to see Fredo gazing down at us with an expression of mild curiosity. We sat up and eventually parted to go to our separate rooms, as neither of us was really ready or prepared to spend the night together – a much bigger step then than it is considered to be now.

The following morning we were up early and after a quick breakfast we were on the road as the pale light of dawn chased the darkness from the hills above the Haputale Pass. By mid morning we were at the coast at Bundala, where I happily showed Shirley the birds on the lagoons and the crocodiles on the sand banks. We swam in the sea and later made our way to the Tissa Rest House for lunch. I had brought the *Nandu* with us, as in its folded condition it fitted easily into the back of the Vauxhall Victor estate. Assembling it on the grass between the Rest House and Tissa Wewa, I launched it on the waters of the tank and we embarked. The outrigger kept the craft very stable and we soon covered the few hundred yards separating the heronry island from the shore. The birds were in the early stages of nesting and, making as little disturbance as possible, we walked through the undergrowth to examine the eggs and young of the herons, egrets, and cormorants. After an hour or so, dripping with sweat and somewhat bemused by the noise and stench of the colony, we left it in peace and returned to the Rest House for a cup of tea. On our way home, I discovered that Shirley wanted to learn to drive, so we had an impromptu lesson on a remote stretch of road, which gave wonderful opportunities for hand-holding and other pleasurable exercises. The three hour drive back to Kahagalla had never seemed so short. However, Shirley had to be back for the night, so we paused only to collect her case before continuing on for another hour to Nuwara Eliya, where I delivered her to the school and was back at Kahagalla by midnight. This proved to be the first of several memorable weekend visits as our relationship developed, interspersed with my regular Sunday visits to her in Nuwara Eliya.

In the early days of my relationship with Shirley I was rather uneasy as to what she might expect of me. As the product of a single-sex education environment and having had very little contact with girls of my own age during my teenage years, I felt at a disadvantage in knowing how to behave. How sexually forward would she expect me to be? Was I perhaps too diffident, and was that the reason that Susan had got fed up with me? I did not want Shirley to be disappointed in me. In those days there was no such thing as television in Ceylon and, compared with today, sexual sequences in films and even books were very inexplicit in character. Even in England the idea of sex manuals being sold in high street shops was unthinkable and would have created uproar. In libraries anything of an explicit character (books by Frank Harris, for example) was held on closed shelves and had to be specially requested (which was not made easy and sometimes necessitated braving the disapproval of the library staff). Nevertheless, I felt I needed some guidance and determined to have a look for a suitable book when next I was in Colombo. H. W. Cave's bookshop certainly did not have any section marked 'personal relationships', but it did have a very small medical section in which I found a book entitled *Ideal marriage*. This was in no way comparable to the manuals now available and the author had to be at pains to make clear that his information was directed solely to married couples. However, it was some help and I later discovered that it was famous as a pioneering work in this field.

With *Ideal marriage* furtively concealed in my bungalow for careful study, I felt more confident in embarking on a normal relationship with my girlfriend.

I had now been a member of the Ceylon Bird Club for a couple of years and I found the notes from members extremely interesting. These were collated and circulated by the secretary each month and gave a good picture of the birds and other wild life seen by members in the vicinity of their homes and on visits elsewhere. However, it was evident that some members were much more objective in their observations than others, while much irrelevant and sometimes fanciful information tended to creep into some of the reports. Soon after my move to Kahagalla I received a letter from the secretary, a clergyman stationed up north in the Jaffna peninsula, to say that he was finding it difficult to devote enough time to producing the monthly Notes and asking if I would be willing to take over the secretaryship. I looked upon this as a great compliment and felt that I could considerably improve the format and timeliness of the Notes, so I accepted. I then set about putting some improvements into practice. First I purchased a cheap, hand-operated cyclostyle duplicator with some of the meagre Club funds I had received. I then had some headed, lightweight paper printed and set to work in the evenings editing the contributions I received from other members. I cut stencils on my portable typewriter and found that I could produce duplicated pages with roller and ink fairly quickly, once I had got the hang of the duplicator. The result looked a great improvement over previous editions and members seemed pleased with the Notes, which I made a point of posting on the same date each month. I also felt that the information we collected should be more widely shared and more permanently recorded, so I started to send half yearly summaries of the more interesting observations for publication in *Loris*.

The stencils had to be typed carefully, as corrections and alterations had to be done with some luridly pink coloured fluid, rather like nail polish, which was a great nuisance. Gradually, I became a fast and accurate touch-typist, reaching speeds of 35 words per minute without mistake. I also often had to correct grammar and shorten the more rambling contributions. Therefore, although I did not realise it at the time, these activities gave me useful skills in editing and keyboard operation which stood me in good stead in later life.

Besides being so conveniently situated for the clubs at Bandarawela and Haputale, Kahagalla was also near the armed services playing fields at Diyatalawa. Many of the young SDs roundabout were keen rugby players and some played for the Uva Province team. Although I had not played rugby since the age of 13 and did not really wish to play regularly, I was nevertheless co-opted for weekly practices at these playing fields. I was happy to participate for the social contact and I regularly met David, who was acting on Glenanore, Mervyn from Dyraaba, Karl from Nayabedde, and John from Dambatenne. We ran about, practiced catching, kicking and line-outs, and generally enjoyed ourselves for an hour before the light faded and we retired to our respective bungalows.

Of course the rugby eventually caught up with me and one weekend when the Uva team was desperately short of players I found I could not really refuse to play in a match. This was against the Kelani Valley side, down in the south-west low country at Avissawella, half way between Ratnapura and Colombo. The Kelani Ganga was the river which entered the sea at Colombo and the valley was one of the principal rubber-growing districts, although some tea and other crops such as coconuts, cocoa, and spices were also grown. The Kelani Valley Club was one of the oldest of planters' clubs, having been established in 1883. It was a typical building of the Ceylon low country, with wide verandas surrounding open-plan lounge and dining areas and facing over the rugby pitch. Someone lent me an Uva rugby shirt of black and white stripes and on the appointed Saturday I travelled to Avissawella to join the rest of the team. Being tall but thin, I was not of typical rugby build and was assigned to a position somewhere in the three quarters line. Unused to rugby tactics and not liking the look of the large and gorilla-like members of the opposing team, I decided that my best plan was to keep as low a profile as possible. This seemed to be confirmed by our captain and his final piece of advice was 'Now, David, if you get the ball and have any difficulty, just fall on it'.

The game commenced and I managed to avoid coming to grips with the ball quite successfully for some time, while making a great show of running about and seeming to support the rest of my team. Suddenly I found the ball arcing into the air in a trajectory which seemed designed to deliver it into my hands. Sure enough, it hit the ground just in front of me and, as luck would have it, the ball did not kink to either side. I caught it and was immediately set upon by several of the opposing primates. Doing as I was told, I fell on the ball and almost instantly was at the bottom of a struggling heap of bodies. Somehow or other I managed to get rid of the ball from under me and later learned that one of our number had whipped it out of the mêlée and scored a try. Afterwards everyone was most congratulatory and I almost came to believe that our winning score was due to my efforts.

*An Uva vs Dimbula rugby match at the Uva Club, Badulla, 1961. The Uva team wear black and white banded jerseys with the 'Uva Goose' emblem of the 'merrie men of Uva'.*

As usual there was a party and dance in the evening after the match. I did not know many people and, also as usual, there were no European girls present. I did not want to stay late as I was driving back to Kahagalla in order to see Shirley on the Sunday, but I joined the rest of the team in the bar. The atmosphere became jollier as the evening progressed and someone started up a rugby song. These were many and various and one did not need to play rugby to hear them fairly regularly. Some, such as *Eskimo Nell* and the *Ball of Kirriemuir* were obviously imported from Britain, but there were also planters' songs of Ceylon origin, including *The peeley by the store* and *The girl from Kotmale*, although these tended to be less well known. There was even a *Kelani Valley Song* which had a chorus:

He's a man from the Kelani Valley,
A man of superior worth,
A far better jat than the usual lot

Who swagger about on the earth.
The world would be Hades without him,
In Heaven he'll sit with the great,
When he's not buzzing round
He'll always be found
On a Kelani Valley estate.

Some songs, such as *I don't want to join the army*, obviously had their origins in the army rather than the rugby scrum.  Most were more or less scurrilous and had catchy tunes.  This one went with a swing in 3/3 time:

There once was a bold caballero,
An exceedingly bold caballero,
Who had a large ell - an eltomarel - an elto-marelto-marino.

He went to a low-down casino,
An exceedingly low-down casino,
Where he played merry hell with his eltomarel - his elto-marelto-marino.

The caballero saga went on for some time and chronicled the details of his sexual exploits, which eventually came to an untimely end owing to his having upset the locals:

They left him a little stumpeno,
An exceedingly little stumpeno, - . . .
Which does just as well as his eltomarel - his elto-marelto-marino!

The next song was the ever-popular *Harlot of Jerusalem*.  This had a chorus and innumerable verses, of which most people could only remember a few, especially at this stage in the evening. However, if enough people remembered different verses, it could go on for a long time.  This seemed a suitable moment at which to depart, so I collected my bag and was walking out of the club just as the song reached the point at which Cathusel decides to get rid of her client:

Cathusel was an artful tart,
She crossed her legs and blew a fart
That sent him soaring like a dart
High above Jerusalem.

Hey ho Cathusalem, Cathusalem, Cathusalem,
Hey ho Cathusalem, the Harlot of Jerusalem.

The warm darkness of the humid low country enveloped me as I crossed over the lawn to the car park.  The song had gathered momentum and as I got into the car I could hear a lusty chorus being beaten out on the bar counter:

He went soaring out to sea,
Rotating gyroscopically,
He caught his balls upon a tree
Which grew outside Jerusalem

Hey ho Cathusalem, Cathusalem, Cathusalem,
Hey ho Cathusalem, the Harlot of Jerusalem.

It was a good two hours drive back to Kahagalla and I wanted to be up in good time the following day.

Rugby matches were always major social events and could only be held at the largest clubs as these were the only ones with rugby pitches. One of the largest events of the upcountry social calendar was the England vs Scotland match, between teams composed of members deriving from each country. It was always held at the Darrawella Club in the Dickoya District, the centre of the largest concentration of tea estates in the Island and a long way from Haputale, so I did not attend every year. The Club was actually adjacent to Darrawella Estate, where my father had been PD shortly after the war and I could well remember my mother trying to teach me the piano on the old instrument in the Club house. The England-Scotland match was followed by a supper dance and, in the last few years, this had been preceded by a play put on by a group of people from Colombo. The play was always in rhyming couplets and included several songs to tunes from well-known musicals. It was usually a libellous farce and was written each year largely by my brother-in-law, Alan, and his elder brother, Dennis, who worked together in Colombo in their father's firm, A. F. Jones & Co. Ltd. The one which I remember best was parody of planting life called *Trouble in the tea, or dirty deeds on Doublebedde*.

The plot was fairly simple: Mrs Hardup has mortgaged Doublebedde Estate to the villainous Silas Smith of Colombo who, for nefarious reasons, wishes to marry his frightful son, Brucellosis (Bruce for short), to Mrs Hardup's nubile daughter, Virginia, who is in love with the handsome SD, John Goodroll. One of the principal characters was the appu, played by a European member of the group, liberally covered with cocoa and with an outrageous chee-chee accent. In Scene One Virginia is explaining how her family has come to such a low ebb:

V:     'And then, when things were just about as bad as they could be,
        Grandmama got blister blight and typhoid took the tea.
        - At least, I think that's how it was – it doesn't sound quite right-
        Maybe grandmamma got typhoid and the tea got blister blight.
        At any rate, poor grandmamma eventually died
        And grandpapa, who was distraught, committed suicide.
        So thus it was, oh fateful day, when they were R.I.P.
        Poor mother found herself alone – alone, that is, with me . . .
        Alone because my poor papa had died some years before.
        Apparently, so mother says, 'twas alcohol for sure.
        'A great mistake', she always says, 'to wed a man who drinks'.'
Appu  (aside): 'Lady make mistake all right, but not what Missy thinks.'

The electricity has been cut off (one could tell that this had been written by a 'Colombo wallah') and the fan doesn't work:

V:     'They must have cut the current off – oh dear, what shall we do?
Appu:  'Lady hasn't paid the bill since 1952.'
V:     'We owe you three years' wages, Kumaranasavan.'
Appu:  'I not wanting money, Missy, - I very humble man –
      (aside) But Lady doing cook's book, - I making what I can!'

The labour force has gone on strike and in the third scene Mrs H and John G are discussing what to do and decide to interview the Union representatives:

John G: 'Appu!'
Appu:   'Master, here I am!'
John G: 'All right, we'll see those guys.'
Appu:   'Come on in you fellows – huh? And you! Do up your flies!
        Left right! Left right!  And wiping feet when coming in this house!'
John G: 'All right, then, Appu – you can go –
                (*Exit* Appu)
                (to Union reps) now tell us – what's the grouse?'

The audience was in fits at the exaggerated antics of the appu, who emphasised all the traits which appus were popularly supposed to have.  Of course all was made to come right in the end, mainly by the expedient of having a rich American relation buy up Ceylon in its entirety, and there was always a song to finish with:

Hiram:  'I've just gone and bought Lanka –
        I guess that means I've bought you.
        I've bought Ceylon,
        I've got Sir John,
        And Bandaranaike too.'

John G: 'Now I'm so glad you've bought Lanka,
        That must include this estate.
        I'll get my pay
        From the USA
        Now Lanka's the forty –ninth state.'

Hiram:  'I'd like to take you all with me,
        But I ain't going away, -
        Don't give a damn
        For Uncle Sam –
        In Lanka I'm going to stay!'

All this was rapturously received and the audience was delighted with the political references. As the applause died down the band struck up and curry and rice was served from the kitchens.

# Departure                                                    16

---

The hill station of Nuwara Eliya was first established in 1829, during the governorship of Sir Edward Barnes, who intended it as a sanatorium for the armed forces. Before this the area was apparently uninhabited, although it was frequented by occasional hunters and about 1610 had served as a refuge from the Portuguese for the Kandyan king of the time. The road from Kandy took two years to construct, which seems remarkably fast, considering the obstacles which had to be overcome. The final stage rises in several hairpin bends up the Ramboda Pass to an elevation of about 6,600 ft before descending 400 ft to the level floor of the valley in which the town stands. The road was continued on eastwards, down the Hakgalla Pass, to Badulla in the 1830s. In 1874 a later governor, Sir William Gregory, directed the building of a barrage across the Nanu Oya at the point where it flows out of the valley and so formed the lake which bears his name. Jungle-covered mountains rise above the town and on the northern side these culminate in Ceylon's highest mountain, Pidurutalagala, at 8,282 ft.

As a young man, Samuel Baker was a convalescent in Nuwara Eliya in 1847 when the town was no more than a village of about 20 thatched cottages of very English appearance, having gardens containing roses and many other European flowers and fruits. He was so taken with the place that in 1848 he returned with his young wife, Henrietta, their family and a party of English artisans to establish an agricultural settlement a couple of miles out of the village on the Badulla road. His brothers, John and Valentine, accompanied him and, all told, there were 18 adults in the party, for which Samuel chartered a ship for the voyage out from England. In fact this was also an experiment in social engineering, as he intended that the settlement should contain a spectrum of social classes with his brothers and himself, naturally, at the top. The experiment did not long survive his departure in 1855, although some of the settlers stayed on for many years. Today little tangible remains to show where the settlement once existed. However, the locality still bears the name 'Baker's Farm', the brewery which Baker established was the forerunner of the major brewery which still operates in Nuwara Eliya, and the practice of growing European vegetables, which he introduced, has flourished to such an extent that every scrap of cultivatable ground for miles around is now covered with them.

Sam Baker was a large and physically powerful man whose main interest was in hunting. He seems to have spent most of his time out with his hounds in pursuit of sambur, the 'elk' of Baker's writing and of the Elk Plains above the Kande Ela reservoir. Sambur were by no means his only quarry and he was only too happy to shoot or knife anything which gave his hounds a good run. In those days there was a very large population of elephants in the highland jungles as well as in the lowlands and Sam was ready to shoot these as often as he could, although tusks are not found on female Ceylon elephants and on very few of the males. However, one must remember that elephants were then a major hazard for many activities and that their numbers were so great that nobody foresaw the threat of their extinction which exists today. Elephants did a lot of damage, to roads, water channels and other installations, and especially to villagers' crops, which could be wiped out overnight with very serious consequences for the owners. The government placed a bounty on killing elephants and in 1855 Baker wrote 'The Government reward for the destruction of elephants in Ceylon was formerly ten shillings per tail; it is now reduced to seven shillings in some districts, and is altogether abolished in others, as the number killed was so great that the Government imagine they cannot afford the annual outlay.' Samuel Baker was but one of numerous 'sportsmen' who enthusiastically embraced elephant shooting, which became a favourite pastime of army officers, planters and government officials of all kinds. It was also quite profitable, as ten shillings was a substantial sum at the time. Many could boast of having shot over a hundred elephants, but it was generally acknowledged that the record was held by Major Rogers with a tally of at least 1,500. Rogers was a real Pooh-Bah, as he held the position of Government Agent (the senior administrative officer) in Uva Province as well as being a District Judge and local Commandant of the armed forces. According to Sir James Emerson Tennent, his purchase of promotion from subaltern to Major was financed, at least in part, by the elephant bounty. His hunting activities were brought to a sudden and spectacular end when he was struck dead by lightening at the Haputale Rest House on 8th June 1845. Many years later a new rest house was built near the railway station, and when I was on Kahagalla the old rest house building had become the post office, situated above the road as one came into the town from the Bandarawela side.

*Nuwara Eliya, 1988: the bus station and the two-storey covered market, with the colonial pillar box in the foreground at the foot of the steps to the post office. Pidurutalagala (Mt Pidro) is directly above the market, with the communications mast just visible.*

On Sundays I would set off soon after breakfast to see Shirley in Nuwara Eliya. Usually I went in the car but sometimes, if it was fine and dry, I used the estate motorbike. This did the journey considerably more quickly and also saved on petrol. Nobody wore helmets and only a light wind-cheater jacket was necessary for warmth. From Bandarawela I took the road through the little town of Welimada and wound up the Hakgalla Pass, past Baker's Farm, and at the end of Lake Gregory I branched right on the road which skirted the northern shore of the lake to reach the Hill School. The buildings were near the shore, overlooking a bay. When I had been a schoolboy there the circuit run round the lake (about four miles) was a regular feature of life for the older boys. At this elevation the competitive run was quite taxing for children aged 13 or younger, and several parents, including mine, objected, so in later years the event was discontinued as a regular exercise.

I soon got to know the other teachers at the school, with whom Shirley and I would often make excursions for the day, perhaps to the Horton Plains or up Mt Pidro, before gathering for drinks at the Nuwara Eliya Golf Club in the evening. Chris, who taught Latin and French, was an unusual character and had an unconventional view of life. He had a small car of venerable age which antedated the invention of the winking light direction indicator. Instead it had 'trafficators' of the kind which flipped out of the door pillar like a little arm to indicate which way the driver was turning. However, these were both loose, and when the car went over a bump they would both flip out and back as though the car was raising its arms in excitement.

Chris also had a fund of anecdotes, one of which dated from his undergraduate days. Apparently he had had digs just opposite a 'request' bus stop. He had also acquired a rather superior catapult, for which he found that grapes were excellent ammunition and with these he became a very accurate shot. On summer evenings when he had the window open, he would apparently amuse himself by targeting the palms of waiting bus passengers as they raised their hands to flag down a bus. This caused most satisfactory surprise, shock and consternation on the part of the bus passengers, who apparently never discovered whence the grapes had come.

One of the major events of the Hill School year was a reunion dinner and dance for former pupils of both the Hill School (the 'Old Hillocks') and those of its predecessor, Haddon Hill (the 'Old Haddocks'). Although the south-west monsoon was at its height, this was always held in August, when sons and daughters who were out for the summer vacation were likely to be available, and the dinner was preceded by a hockey match on the school playing field between the Old Hillocks and the current staff and pupils. The dinner dance was always held at the Grand Hotel, a huge colonial pile in mock Tudor style, the nucleus of which had been Sir Edward Barnes's cottage. It had huge rooms and endless dark corridors, with various dark-panelled lounges, function rooms and a vast billiard room. I well remembered being taken there by my parents on the Sundays when they would come to take me out of school for the day and, armed with our picnic, we often took refuge in the billiard room from the wet and cold monsoon weather. Usually I was asked to play hockey for the Old Hillocks team, and I would be pleased to participate as there would always be several girls present, many of whom I would know from our mutual school days.

The dinner dance was a formal evening dress affair, with dinner jackets and black ties for the men and evening gowns for the girls. A band would play and the dance floor in the centre of the huge dining room would soon be full of couples. For the SDs among the Old Hillocks this was a rare and welcome opportunity for a bit of smooching with any young woman one could induce to be one's partner. As the evening wore on those who had struck lucky would disappear into the dark corridors, or even into one or other of the bedrooms, before Auld Lang Syne would be struck up by the band at the end of the evening. We would then emerge into the wet or foggy night to find our motorbikes or cars and start what for many of us would be a long journey back to a lonely and remote bungalow. On one such occasion I took the Badulla road and ran into impenetrably thick mist as I skirted the lake. The grass verge by the edge of the road was only just visible and of course there was no road lighting so I had to creep slowly along with my head out of the window, trying to remember all the small turnings which took off to left and right, which might indicate where I had got to. In this I was not entirely successful and I found myself driving onto a slatted landing stage, from which I hastily had to reverse. After a long time driving at a slow walking pace through what seemed to be a thick bed of cotton wool, I suddenly emerged from the mist to find myself at the head of the Hakgalla Pass. The view was crystal clear in the brilliant light of a full moon and I could easily see the dark outlines of Namunukula mountain and the hills of Dambatenne the opposite side of the Uva Basin. Thick mist filled the deeper valleys from which the lower hills protruded as dark islands in a silver-white sea. As I descended, I dipped in and out of mist as I wound my way back through Welimada and Bandarawela.

Now that I had better things to do on Sundays, I seldom attended the Haldummulla Club at Haputale. However, I was still a regular at the Bow Club in Bandarawela on Wednesday afternoons. The Bow Club still operated under its antiquated rule disqualifying non-Europeans from becoming members and must have been the last club in the Island to do so. However, this was being challenged. A general meeting was called to discuss the proposal to abolish the rule and admit members of any ethnic origin. I made a point of attending this meeting and found a large proportion of the membership present. Many members spoke convincingly in favour of repealing the rule, while an approximately equal number spoke against. Mr Meikle was prominent among these, the general thrust of his argument being that he would not feel able to relax fully and 'let his hair down' if non-Europeans were present, as he would feel that in such company Europeans should maintain proper and decorous behaviour. There did not seem to be any rapprochement between the two points of view and at the end of the meeting a vote was taken. The result was a narrow majority in favour of maintaining the status quo.

I was surprised at this result and felt very disheartened. Irrespective of what they might think, it seemed to me that those intent on continuing to refuse admission to Ceylonese were not only burying their heads in the sand, but had sealed the fate of the club. The current government was making increasingly nationalistic and anti-European noises, as the move to eliminate English as a national language had shown, and to maintain colonial attitudes was simply an act of self-destruction. I gave more thought to this as I walked round the estate and in the evenings when I sat alone reading, listening to music or editing the Bird Club Notes. Was there really no future for European planters, and what should I do? Could I see myself still living my rather monotonous and lonely planting life in ten years' time? The answer was decidedly 'no'. I certainly felt that I could not do another four-year tour of duty before my next home leave. I had probed Mr Meikle on this point some time previously and he had not been sympathetic, pointing out that when *he* had started he had had to do *five* years before he had got his furlough, like my father. However, one of the directors of the Gibson Estates was soon due to come out from London for a visit and I determined to ask him if my tours of duty could be shortened to 21 months or two years, as was now becoming increasingly common with quite a number of the better planting companies.

The director duly arrived and Mr Meikle arranged a cocktail party in his honour at Netherbyres for all the senior Gibson Estates staff. During the course of the evening, and with some trepidation, I managed to buttonhole the director and asked him if the Board would consider reducing the length of tours of duty for European staff. He seemed to take this as a personal affront. Without making any effort to enquire into my reasons or circumstances, a frown came over his face and he curtly replied 'You should not be asking me this, Ebbels, you must approach your senior manager.' and with that he turned away.

This rebuff more or less made my decision for me. In any case, for some time I had felt that planting was not really holding my interest. Although I liked the agricultural aspects of the job, these were largely routine, especially for an SD, while much of my time was spent on labour relations and dealing with disputes, which I did not relish. After careful thought I had to admit that I could not see myself continuing as a planter in the longer term. So, despite all the effort I had made in becoming a planter and in learning Tamil, there was no other conclusion to be reached than to resign.

I did not do so immediately, but I decided to take Mr Meikle into my confidence. A month or two after the director had departed I was at Netherbyres on a routine visit. After we had finished the business in hand, I reminded Mr Meikle of our conversation by the railway line and said I was seriously thinking of resigning but would like his opinion as to how this would be viewed by George Steuarts and the Gibson Estates directors. Would they be likely to dock my bonus for the year (due about July) or would adequate notice improve their attitude on this and as regards my passage back to the UK (bearing in mind that I had been recruited in Ceylon)? To my surprise, he was unusually forthcoming and advised me that so long as I gave adequate notice – of several months – I was unlikely to have my bonus docked and that my passage would also be more likely to be granted.

Meanwhile, life continued much as usual. The teachers at the Hill School, of course, were free during the school holidays and spent some of this time touring the sights of Ceylon in the venerable school minibus, which they could hire together with its driver, George. In this way they managed to see much more of the Island during their three-year contracts than I had done during the whole of my life. I envied them their trips to the ancient ruined cities at Anuradhapura and Polonnaruwa, the magnificent rock fortress palace of Sigiriya, and the beautiful beaches at Kalkudah on the east coast or Bentota on the west. Sometimes they went further afield, and Shirley told me of her intention to revisit Kashmir for pony trekking, which she had done the previous year. I was sad that I should not see her for six weeks or so, but said that if she would get me a piece of Kashmiri walnut, I would make her a bowl. I had set up my wood-turning apparatus at Kahagalla in what had been a large chicken house, up in the vegetable garden, and had continued to turn bowls and platters of such suitable woods as I could find. The six weeks seemed to pass infinitely slowly, but eventually she returned after a wonderful holiday with a lovely piece of walnut, from which I fashioned two bowls.

I resumed my regular visits to see Shirley in Nuwara Eliya with renewed enthusiasm, which seemed to be reciprocated. The weather was often wet, and on such days we sometimes drove around a circuit, down towards Nanuoya and then up through Mahagastotte Estate, past Ambawela, where the green fields and Friesian cows of the government dairy farm looked ridiculously English, down through Warwick Estate to the Hakgalla road and back to Nuwara Eliya past Baker's Farm. The road through Warwick Estate was very little frequented and there were numerous places where, in stopping to admire the view, a canoodle could be had. Some time after she had returned from Kashmir, Shirley again came to stay at Kahagalla one weekend. We had become very close and I had told her of my decision to resign. Her own contract was also due to end soon, so both of us were looking towards the future and wondering what it might hold. Eventually I found the courage to ask her if she thought that, after our return to England, we might become engaged. She did not say 'no'.

My parents were at that time on Midford Group in the Lower Dickoya district. This was quite a long journey from Kahagalla, so I did not see them very often. However, if there was a possibility that Shirley and I would get engaged to be married in the not-too-distant future, I felt I should make an effort to introduce her to them before I left Ceylon. So it was arranged. One Sunday I set off early, collected Shirley from Nuwara Eliya, and we motored down through Nanuoya, Talawakele, Hatton and Dickoya to Midford. The bungalow had a lovely view, overlooking the small reservoir which fed a hydroelectric power station at the little local town of Norton Bridge. After drinks in the garden we had an excellent curry lunch, prepared by my parents' long-serving and capable appu, Mutthu. As in most planters' bungalows, lunch on Sunday was always a curry, which my father liked to be reasonably hot and spicy. Although the rest of the family used soup plates, curry was always served for my father in a specially large, bowl-shaped dish which had been given to him many years previously. In this there would accumulate quite a large mound of curry and rice when all the numerous curries and sambols had been sampled, and my father would then set to and work his way through it in his slow and methodical way. By the time he was nearing the end, he would be sporting copious drops of perspiration on his bald pate, which he would dab from time to time with a folded hanky. Shirley made quite a hit with my parents and, indeed, with my grandmother, so I felt that the effort had been well worth while. We retraced our way back to Nuwara Eliya and by the time I got home to Kahagalla I felt it had been a very long day indeed.

I sent in my letter of resignation to George Steuarts in June, to take effect as from the 1st September 1961, and started seriously to think about what I might do next. I activated the contingency plans I had made to study for my A-Levels on my return to London and wondered which university and what course I should try for. Something in the agricultural science area seemed to fit my interests and hold the possibility of future employment. I thought of *The advance of the fungi*, the book on Mr Meikle's shelves which I had read while I was at Needwood, of which I now had my own copy. Perhaps there would be openings in the field of plant pathology? But my main concern was to find a new home for Fredo. Mervyn had moved from Dyraaba to Henfold, an estate in the Dimbula District, but when I contacted him, he readily agreed to take Fredo on, which was a considerable weight off my mind.

After a week or two, one of the directors of George Steuarts replied to my letter, accepting my resignation and saying that I would be eligible for a first class passage by sea back to England. This was encouraging, and I booked a passage on the MV *Oriana* requesting, as everyone did, that my cabin should be on the starboard side, thus maintaining the long tradition of POSH travel (Port Out and Starboard Home). In fact this could be no small matter because cabins were not then air conditioned and on the side of the ship facing south and west they could get roasting hot during the warmer months and at almost any season during the days in the Red Sea. The *Oriana* was one of the newest and largest of the P&O-Orient Line passenger liners, being just under 42,000 tons and had been in service for less than a year since her maiden voyage in December 1960. She was due to sail from Colombo on 14th September and arrive at Southampton 12 days later.

As a final farewell to the wild life of Ceylon and the jungles of the low country where I had spent so many happy hours, Shirley and I accepted an invitation from Ted and Patsy Norris to join them and my sister for a weekend in August in Yala Block II. This was the part of the national park to the east of the Menik Ganga which was not normally open to casual visitors and it was a significant privilege to be able to visit it. For the last time I was again in camp on the east bank of the river, but several miles below the site north of Kataragama where I had camped for the first time in 1956. We had a memorable two days, spent on game viewing drives in areas I had not before visited, or enjoying

*Shirley and Ted Norris, Yala Block II, August 1961.*

the beautiful surroundings of our camp beneath the giant *kumbuck* trees. All too soon, Shirley had to return to the Hill School and I to Kahagalla.

As passengers (especially first class) could take with them a considerable quantity of baggage free of charge, there would be no problem in taking with me all the belongings which I wanted to keep. As for the rest, I began to give these away or sell them off as fast as possible. The *Nandu* I gave to the Hill School, where the children used it on the lake at weekends. The car, of course, was the major item for sale, but I needed to keep it right up to the day of sailing, as it would have been extremely awkward to be without transport. The Government had recently introduced a 100% rate of tax on new private cars, all of which were imported, so theoretically I thought this would push up the second hand price. However, when I came to advertise the car, I found that people were not sufficiently prosperous to be able or willing to pay a good price for what I considered a very desirable vehicle. Although I advertised the car in several places, there were no takers locally except at a much reduced price, so eventually I came to an arrangement with the Vauxhall agents in Colombo to leave the car with them for sale after I had left the Island. This eventually worked reasonably well, although the agents took a hefty cut of the sale price.

The date of my departure drew steadily nearer. Again, nobody was appointed as my successor before my departure, so there would be no hand-over. Also, I had been on Kahagalla only a short time; just a few days short of a year, so naturally the labour force and junior staff felt that a farewell ceremony was not appropriate. Eventually, all my belongings had been either sold, given away to Carupiah or the other bungalow staff, or packed into trunks, cases or *momi* chests - the tea chests made not of plywood but of *Albizzia* wood, which were rather more robust. I paid off Carupiah and gave him a gratuity of, I think, a month's wages for each year of his service with me, as was the custom. His family home was on Attampettia Estate near Bandarawela, so he would go there until he found a new post as an appu, for which I gave him a glowing reference.

Towards the end of August I took Fredo over to his new home with Mervyn on Henfold. He seemed completely unconcerned and quite at home as soon as we entered the door. I took care to leave just as he was given his dinner. Back at Kahagalla the bungalow seemed very empty. The day before my departure I went up to Netherbyres and took my leave of Mr Meikle. I cannot say that I did this with any affection for him, but we had a chat and he wished me well for the future, saying that he understood my reasons for going and that I could well be right. The appointed day was bright and fine, as usual for a September morning in Haputale. The barbets were making their wok-wok-wok calls from the taller trees while the bulbuls were chirruping in the undergrowth. The car was packed to capacity. Taking a last look around, I made my farewells to the assembled *totakarans* and bungalow staff with the customary placing together of my hands and fingers followed by a little bow. Getting into the car, I let in the clutch and moved off down the drive.

I spent a couple of nights with my parents at Midford and then travelled down to Colombo, where I stayed with my sister and brother-in-law, who now had a small son, Kenneth. There were many arrangements and formalities with the bank, income tax office, and other matters to complete during the next few days. There were to be changes too at the Hill School. One of Shirley's colleagues, Julia, was to marry one of my planting friends, John, in Colombo just after I was due to leave the Island. Shirley had therefore arranged to come down to Colombo both to see me off and to attend the wedding. The day before my ship was due to sail I picked her up from the friends' house where she was staying and we motored down the coast road to find a quiet beach for a swim and a picnic.

The road south from Colombo hugs the coast tightly all the way, although the railway line manages to squeeze in between the road and the sea. But the trains are infrequent and do not spoil the canopy of coconut palms which covers the land, nor the golden sands of the beaches. We made slow progress, as the road is not wide and many of the numerous villages and towns have coalesced to form almost continuous shops and houses. The traffic could also be heavy, with a mixture of cars, lorries, bicycles, bullock carts, pie dogs and cows, let alone large numbers of people of many kinds, all vying for use of the meagre road. Eventually we came to the town of Beruwela, which was the site of the first Moorish settlement in the Island in about 1024. In those days the place was known as Barberyn, and there is still an ancient mosque in the town. However, the name Barberyn is now reserved for the tiny island which sits a little to the south of the town, about half a mile off shore, on which stands a lighthouse and little else except for coconut palms. We made our way to the beach, from which Barberyn Island looked most enticing and just the place for our picnic, but how could we get there? Fishing is a major activity in all the coastal villages and towns of Ceylon and Beruwela was no exception. The beach was lined with fishing boats, which were almost exclusively outrigger canoes, so we sought one of the owners.

Here on the west coast these outrigger craft were of a distinctive design peculiar to Ceylon, on which many writers have remarked. Essentially, they were elaborations of a simple dugout, for the base of the hull was a heavy log hollowed out to provide space and buoyancy. However, the sides were made rather straighter than those of a simple canoe and were extended upwards by two or three planks, attached horizontally to the dugout base and fastened edge to edge partially by sewing with coir cord and partially by metal pins. This gave a narrow hull about a foot in width in which the occupants could place their legs and catch, but not much else. The prow and stern were not sharpened but were flat planks, sloping gracefully down to the base, so that in side view the hull was an elongated inverted trapeze. Perhaps the most distinctive feature was the double mast. Rising from a single point, the two tall upright spars supported from their tips the upper corners of a huge oblong sail. One of the lower corners was tethered by a foresheet, while the other was attached to the rope which served as the mainsheet. Two or three narrow and uncomfortable thwarts across the hull provided rigidity and somewhere to sit, while a large oar served as a rudder. To complete the vessel and, indeed, to enable it to remain upright, there was a slim outrigger consisting of a single log attached to the hull by two curved wooden stays made from branches of suitable shape.

These boats were remarkably seaworthy and swift, slicing through the water under the billowing power of the brown or white sails but, having no keels, could not make much headway to windward. Normally they simply ran before the wind, catching the offshore breeze in the evenings and coming home with the onshore wind at dawn. The largest of them traveled considerable distances out to sea and might be away, out of sight of land, for several days at a time, but more usually their trips lasted no more than overnight. It was a fine sight to see the fleet sail at sunset and later, in the dark of the evening, the lanterns on the boats decorated the inky horizon with a chain of dancing lights. These formed an ever changing constellation, the few pressure lanterns forming the brighter stars, which faded only with the growing light of dawn. Most of the fishing was done with hand lines for seer and mullet, but the pressure lights were used by some to entice shoals of sprats within distance of the netting scoops.

In the early morning sunshine, the outrigger canoes, or catamarans as we called them, would fly in one by one over the waves to crunch home on the sand as the sail was released. The tired crews timed their leaps into the surf so that they could run the vessel as far up the beach as possible with the wave they were riding. When the wave retreated, leaving the catamaran beached on the newly washed sand, the crew put their backs to the outrigger supports to hump it inch by inch up the beach. At first they would time their push to catch the buoyancy afforded by succeeding waves but later, beyond the reach of the tide, progress was by muscle power alone, the heaves of tired backs synchronized to a chant, often with caller and chorus, much like a sea shanty.

The arrival of the boats was always greeted by an excited crowd of villagers and fish merchants, some with bicycles and one or two with ancient vans. Amid much shouting and bargaining the catch would be hauled out from the bottom of the catamarans, some fish still alive and flapping from the water sloshing in the bilges of the hull. All would eventually be disposed of, the magnificent six-foot seer being bought by merchants for sale in the larger towns or upcountry, while the smaller butter fish, pomfreit and sprats were taken in ones and twos by the village populace and the local rest house keeper. Finally, the beach would be left to the hot mid morning sun and the fishermen to tidy their sails, nets and lines before making their way home for food and sleep.

Many fishing villages also had communal seine nets which were operated from the sandy beaches. The coiled net would be loaded into one of the largest outrigger canoes or, more usually, into a much wider, flat-bottomed craft without an outrigger. This would be paddled in a wide semi-circle while the net was paid out over the side. Back at the beach, gangs of villagers would take the ropes connected to the two ends of the net and begin to haul it in, again to much chanting and response. As the net closed in, fish would start to jump over the top, which was marked by a row of floats, but only a few got away. A loud cheer always greeted the appearance of the bulging pod at the end of the net and a crowd would form to see what had been caught that day. Besides the pelagic fish there would usually also be many other kinds, including a ray or two, perhaps a type of dogfish, a few squid and octopus, and numerous prawns and small fry.

It did not take us very long to find one of the fishermen who, for a few rupees, was willing to take us out the island. His canoe was one of the smaller ones and either did not have a sail or perhaps the masts had been removed for some reason. The journey by paddle power took about half an hour, and after making sure our fisherman would come back for us later in the day, we jumped ashore on the rocks as there seemed to be no beach. The tidal range on the Ceylon coasts is small, so there was no problem with outgoing or incoming tide, but time seemed to pass all too quickly and before long our boatman hove into sight to collect us for the return trip. Sadly, we drove back to Colombo and after a meal we parked and sat facing the sea on the Galle Face Green, as so many couples have done before and since. Shirley was not coming to see me off on board, so at long last we said our goodbyes and I dropped her back at the house where she was staying.

The following day the *Oriana* appeared in port, huge and gleaming in the combination of ochre and white paint which characterised ships of the Orient Line. Ships of the P & O fleet were pure white. Because of her size, she could not come alongside the wharf but anchored out in the harbour, where she towered over all the other ships in port. Passengers were ferried to and fro in launches from the covered jetty at the passenger terminal. This was immediately opposite the solid and sober Grand Oriental Hotel, always known as the G.O.H., which had been the first or last place of call in Ceylon for innumerable travelers during the past century. Like the P & O liners, the G.O.H. was also painted white, although this had not been done for many years and it was starting to look distinctly tatty. Inside, one entered a central foyer paved in a mosaic of black and white tiles with cane tables and chairs for the taking of tea, coffee, fresh lime squash, or something stronger. There were also large, potted, fan-leaf palms, making this the archetypal palm court. I well remembered as a child in the 1940s hearing the small 'palm-court' orchestra of a couple of violins, a piano and a double-base playing typical 'palm-court' music in this appropriate setting. It was in the palm court here in December 1904 that Leonard Woolf's beloved dog, Charles, was violently sick on the floor through over-excitement at their reunion after their long sea voyages on different ships. In those days the palm court was open to the sky and not closed within the hotel as it is now. Apparently the crows, which were just as numerous then, flew down and consumed the vomit with alacrity while nobody took the slightest notice. Beyond the palm court was a huge dining room, while up on the fourth floor was a lounge from which one could get a magnificent view of the harbour and all that went on there. I had arranged to meet my parents and Alan, my brother-in-law, in the palm court before going on board. We did not have a meal, but had afternoon tea and then walked across the street to the passenger terminal to present my 'steamer' ticket and passport to the authorities before climbing into the little launch and motoring out to the ship.

As usual with most liners leaving Colombo, the *Oriana* was due to sail in the evening at 6 p.m. This gave me and my little entourage plenty of time to find my cabin, in which my trunk and suitcase had already been placed, and to unpack some of the clothes I would need for the voyage. On sea voyages like this, luggage was divided into three classes and marked with appropriate labels. Items were marked 'Cabin' (where space was of course very limited), 'Baggage Room, wanted on voyage' (which were stored in the baggage room, accessible during certain hours of the day), and 'Hold', which went into the bowels of the ship and could not normally be accessed during the voyage. Many cabins were 'inside' ones without any porthole or window, which relied entirely on a supply of fresh air from a vent in the ceiling. These could get very claustrophobic and hot. However, my single birth cabin was a good one, on a deck well above the waterline and with a porthole. It had a hanging cupboard, a few drawers and a washbasin, but no toilet, for which one had to go along the corridor. The stewards, mainly Lascars from north-west India, were busy delivering luggage and other items, such as bouquets of flowers, to the cabins. I had no bouquets, but there was a little parcel from my sister, which proved to be a copy of John Still's *Jungle tide*, inscribed 'To remind you of all our expeditions'. I still have it.

People much enjoyed going on board the great liners to see off friends and relatives, or as guests of the officers, to enjoy the relatively luxurious surroundings – especially in the first class areas – and to have drinks or tea in the public rooms. Everyone who was not sailing with the ship was required to leave for shore half an hour before the time of sailing although many people, my father included, delayed their departure until the last possible minute, which always used to agitate me. Sometimes somebody would cut things a little too fine and on arrival at the gangway would find that it was being lifted and the ship already starting to get under way. In these cases the pilot cutter had been known to remove involuntary stowaways. The friends, relatives and other guests who came on board for one reason or another were usually so numerous that in port the ship would seem very crowded indeed and one could not tell how full the ship really was until after sailing.

A loud blast on the ship's siren signaled 5.30 p.m. and about 20 minutes later I bade a sad farewell to my parents and brother-in-law before they departed down the gangway. This was soon hauled up and almost simultaneously the faint murmur of the engines increased to an all-pervading throb as, almost imperceptibly at first, the ship started to move forward. Soon we were passing through the harbour entrance and from the lounge I could see the lights at the ends of the harbour moles pass by the windows. I went out on deck and leaned on the rail to watch the old Clock Tower at the head of Chatham Street and the other familiar and fondly-remembered buildings of Colombo Fort become smaller and the blue shapes of the central mountains, which were visible in the far distance, become fainter. As dusk closed in, the lights of Colombo and the built-up parts of the west coast came on, twinkling occasionally as passing traffic or our changing position momentarily obscured individual lights. Would I ever see this land again? I wondered how things would work out and what the future would hold. But I had laid my plans and was determined to stick to them. Meanwhile there was much else to think about and I was starting to feel hungry. In first class one was expected to dress for dinner, which I knew was at 7.30. I turned and went down to my cabin to change.

# Epilogue

---

I pushed up the shutter on the cabin window and let in a flood of sunlight. The plane was now losing height rapidly and out of the window a sea of palm trees stretched to the blue ocean somewhere near Negumbo. Sitting beside me, Shirley determinedly avoided looking out of the window until we were firmly on the tarmac at Katunayake Airport, just north of Colombo. Soon we were in the airport terminal and after collecting our cases we were collected ourselves by the tour rep and ushered out into the heavy heat of the morning and onto the tour bus. So this was what it was like to be a tourist in Sri Lanka instead of a resident in Ceylon.

Our three children were by now more or less grown up, the two girls away at university and Tim, in the lower sixth at school, able to look after himself for a while. As a slightly belated silver wedding holiday, we had booked a fortnight in January 1988 at one of the tour company's cheap hotels on the coast at Mt Lavinia. However, secretly we intended to make our own tour upcountry, for which we had arranged to hire a car and driver for 10 days. We planned to use the coastal hotel only for a few nights at the beginning and end of our stay.

The old inter-racial conflict between the Tamils in the plains of the North and East and the majority Sinhalese in the rest of the Island, of which I had witnessed the beginnings in 1958, had developed into a full-blown civil war which had been raging, on and off, since the mid 1970s. Originally, the main point of contention had been the position of Sinhala, which had been made the exclusive national language and had even been used for the new national name, Sri Lanka, since 1972. Added to this were measures to virtually establish Buddhism as the state religion and to reduce the (formerly disproportionate) numbers of Tamils gaining places at the national universities. Feeling that they and their Hindu religion were being excluded from participation in national life, these legislative measures had alienated the Tamils. Furthermore, it had provoked them to take up armed revolt in favour of an independent state in their home areas, for which they adopted the old name of Eelam, which had been used in the sixteenth century. The government had replied with heavy-handed and sometimes undisciplined force, exacerbating an already explosive situation. Caught in the middle of this, the Tamils on the estates (who had severed links with their Indian origins but had virtually no contacts with the Tamils of northern Sri Lanka) kept their heads down and continued to produce the commodities which were the mainstays of the economy. Although Tamil had subsequently been raised to parity with Sinhala in the Tamil areas, this was too little too late, and fighting had continued. Attacks in Colombo had halted the developing tourist industry from time to time, but a recent lull in the fighting (which was usually confined to the northern and eastern areas) had encouraged tourism to resume and we had felt confident enough to organise a visit.

The tour bus joined the dense stream of traffic on the main Colombo road; no dual carriageway here, but a milling mass of hire cars, three wheeler taxis, trucks and buses with poorly tuned diesel engines belching black fumes, mixed with cars ancient and modern, pedestrians, street hawkers and the odd bullock cart. One did not need to read the statistics to realise that the population had more than doubled while we had been away. But although its volume was greater, the traffic seemed much the same as it always had been, and the roadside shops sold the same goods and repair services. As we neared Colombo and crossed the old iron Victoria Bridge over the Kelani Ganga we began to see greater changes. Tower blocks of offices and hotels were evident in the city centre where the old clock tower cum lighthouse, formerly the tallest building, was now dwarfed in its niche at the top of Chatham Street. The Galle Face Green was unchanged and brown after a spell of dry weather, but the Galle Face Hotel itself was no longer its familiar brick red. It was now an anaemic cream colour and was cowering below the massive bulk of a new hotel where the old Colombo Club had been. Many new tourist hotels had also been built down the west and south-west coasts, and even the famous Mt Lavinia Hotel, seven miles south of Colombo, had had a monstrous new wing rammed onto the old building which had formerly been the governor's residence. Arriving at our hotel, we were just unpacking when the lights went out. This, apparently, was now a frequent occurrence and the manager quickly appeared with hurricane lamps and candles. The power cut was only about half an hour, but was by no means the only one during our stay.

The following morning the car and driver we had hired appeared punctually. Mr G, our driver, was most obliging in every way and was delighted to hear of our interest in every aspect of Sri Lanka. Setting off for Kandy, we found the road wider and busier than it used to be, but there were still bunches of bananas hanging from the eaves of the caddies and fruit bats (the 'flying foxes') hanging in the trees by the bridge at Mawanella where I had seen them as a child. Driving through the lush, green countryside of south-west Sri Lanka is rather like travelling through a botanical garden or tropical glasshouse, and I took great pleasure in looking at the wonderful diversity of vegetation with the eye of a trained plant scientist rather than that of an enthusiastic young planter. I had indeed followed the interest sparked in me by E. C. Large whose book I had found on Lesley Meikle's bookshelf and I had become a plant pathologist. At first this had taken me back to East Africa to work on cotton diseases and later I had joined the Plant Pathology Laboratory of the UK Ministry of Agriculture. This was where E. C. Large himself had worked and although he had by then retired, I made his acquaintance and was able to tell him of the influence his book had had on my life.

There is nothing quite as green as young rice, and the road was frequently bordered by terraced paddy fields which surrounded each village and ran a little way up the sides of the hills. Among the thatched or cadjan-roofed houses stood tall and thin arecanut palms, each with bunches of orange fruits below a topknot of dark green, feathery leaves. Many houses were almost obscured by bushy mango and breadfruit trees, while the occasional jak tree could be picked out at a glance by the huge jak fruits hanging from its trunk. Away from the coast, coconut palms were only occasionally a feature of the landscape, but most of the caddies sold the ready-husked nuts and also bunches of golden king coconuts or *kurumbu*, which supplied the refreshing coconut juice drink. In colonial times many roads had been lined with rain trees whose massive umbrella-shaped forms frequently met overhead to form a canopy over the road. Most of these had now gone, either chopped down for firewood or become top-heavy with their huge horizontal branches and fallen. But some remained to grace the countryside with their feathery foliage and to shade passing travellers.

In Kandy the Queens Hotel looked well kept and virtually unchanged. I could easily imagine my mother descending the wide staircase in her evening gown to attend a dinner dance. We noticed that, whereas in the past the waiters and other staff in hotels had been fairly evenly split between Sinhalese and Tamils, there were now very few of the latter in evidence. There also appeared to be a decline in the ability of people to make themselves understood in all three main languages of the Island, which had formerly been a prerequisite for any post dealing with the general public. This was no doubt due to the lack of emphasis in schools on teaching languages other than the mother tongue, which appeared not only to be divisive in social contact within Sri Lanka but also handicapped those seeking employment in the global market through a lack of good English – perhaps the principal benefit bequeathed by Britain to all former colonial territories. Our driver, although fluent in English, was evidently unable to speak even a smattering of Tamil, and it was I who had to ask for directions from Tamil estate labourers when he was unsure of the way on unfamiliar estate roads.

We did not stay long in Kandy, but continued on into the planting districts. Here the country had not changed at all and the twists and turns of the road, even the rocks by the roadside, were still just as they had been 30 years before. The neatly painted signs with the well-remembered names were still in evidence at the entrances to estates, and the tea looked lush and well cared for, much of it showing evidence of having been replanted with high-yielding clones. But these were no longer privately owned. The long-threatened nationalisation of estates eventually occurred in 1973, when the last few remaining expatriate planters left. Not all estates were nationalised; those smaller than a certain size or which were in very poor condition were omitted, as apparently were properties belonging to several influential people. However, the foreign-owned estates were taken into government possession (with some non-cash compensation) and were grouped into two organisations for management purposes. This, in fact, permitted some much-needed rationalisation to be carried out. Small estates were amalgamated with larger ones, small factories closed, and tea on poor land was abandoned or sold off. However, although agriculturally the estates seemed to prosper, administratively the two government companies got into difficulties of one kind or another. Ten years later, by the end of the 1990s, Thatcherism had penetrated even to Sri Lanka and government policy had changed so much that estates were being sold back again into private ownership.

We arrived in Nuwara Eliya to find it scarcely changed. Lake Gregory had shrunk considerably, partly through silting up and partly from encroachment by the numerous polythene tunnels of a carnation-growing enterprise, which was apparently commercially very successful. The eucalyptus trees which had stood around the shores had all disappeared. The Golf Club and course looked well-kept, but the race course appeared dilapidated and the grandstand in disrepair. The town streets were still lined in places with the old cupressus trees and the Grand Hotel retained the same furniture and appearance, both inside and out, as it had done 50 years previously. The Hill School had long since ceased to function. The school had moved for a few years to Colombo before closing completely, while its old buildings in Nuwara Eliya had become the headquarters and barracks of an Army regiment, with a smart sentry stationed in a sentry box at the end of the drive. Our kind driver carefully explained our identity and asked permission for us to visit the buildings. To our surprise, this was granted, and we were ushered in to meet the commanding officer, whose office turned out to be Shirley's old classroom with the blackboard still in place. He took us on a conducted tour of part of the ground floor, but we were not permitted upstairs.

Travelling on to Bandarawela, we stayed in the old Bandarawela Hotel, completely unchanged. The town had expanded considerably and was much more populous with some new buildings, but the little branch of Millers opposite the hotel was still there, although with little to sell. Nearby the Bandarawela Tennis Club appeared to be thriving. Next door, however, the Bow Club premises were now the local offices of the Ministry of Education and when I climbed to the top floor of the new hotel opposite, I could see that the old tennis courts were now an orderly vegetable garden.

The next day we drove past Kahagalla to Haputale, down the Haputale Pass and then eastwards to Meeriabedde and Koslanda. The estate road turning up to the left just before Koslanda village was just the same as it had been when I first used it on my way from Needwood on 1st August 1956. Few of the flowering trees were left, however, and they had not been replaced. We soon came to Koslanda factory, but Meeriabedde factory was nowhere to be found. Thinking we had missed it somehow, we turned back and I found the superintendent of Koslanda estate in his office. Courteous and helpful, he explained that Meeriabedde had been split up on nationalisation, some of the worst areas of tea had been abandoned or sold off as smallholdings while the remainder of the Lower Division had been amalgamated with Koslanda and Meeriabedde factory had been demolished. However, he said we were welcome to drive on and have a look at the small bungalow. This we did, arriving in the bungalow yard to be surrounded by small children and the various women of the house. It seemed that the bungalow was now the residence of the KP and word was sent to fetch him from the field. Meanwhile we were ushered into the bungalow, Shirley was taken off to be entertained in the gloomy and grimy kitchen and I was taken into the sittingroom. Most of the garden was now given over to vegetable growing and little was left of the fine lawn which old Paliniandy had levelled so laboriously. The KP then arrived to greet me effusively and offer tea and biscuits while we chatted.

On another day we drove from Bandarawela to Poonagalla and down the road through the estate to Koslanda village, stopping en route to search for the entrance to the path to the Poonagalla rock pool. We failed to find it on this occasion, but on a later visit we realised that what had been patana grassland was now a tall eucalyptus plantation and through this we eventually found our way down to the pool. The tree under which we used to sit had gone, but nothing else had changed, there was no visible development. The old metal ladder which the Coombs had fixed to the rock for people to climb out of the pool was still in place.

Also on a later visit, we took the train from Haputale to Idalgashinna. Although the condition of the roads in Sri Lanka had not changed very much, the railway was showing serious signs of geriatric disintegration. The tracks supported a plentiful growth of weeds and the worn rails were visibly buckled. Trains on the upcountry line not only appeared to have the very same rolling stock as they had had 30 years before, but evidently no refurbishment had been done either and everywhere the lack of even minimum investment or upkeep was all too apparent. Windows and seats were dirty and worn, doors were missing and, although the pace was painfully slow, one wondered how the train managed to keep going at all. We got into conversation with a young man and his girl friend, who were evidently out for a day trip from Badulla or Bandarawela.

'Yes', he agreed, 'the view here is amazing and the line is a wonderful feat of engineering – it was built in British days, you know. I am sure we could not do it now.'

We found that when Needwood had been nationalised, Idulgashena had been incorporated as a Division into Beauvais, - a very logical move. At long last the cart road had been cut through to join the two estates and the SD on Idulgashena reported to the Superintendent of Beauvais. In fact at the time of our visit, he was doing just that, and although we waited for some time at the unchanged and well-remembered bungalow, he did not appear and we had to depart without making his acquaintance. We were told that Needwood Division had already been sold back into private hands.

We found the countryside little changed in the lowland areas around Wirawila and Tissamaharama. However, the villages were more populous and there was now little undisturbed jungle adjacent to the Wellawaya-Hambantota road, where habitation had spread in a ribbon along the roadside. Extensive new settlements had also followed the creation of major new tanks. The largest of these was the Uda Walawe tank on the Walawe Oya, which also formed the major feature of a new national park. I could remember the preliminary observations being made for this reservoir by Canadian surveyors during my time on Meeriabedde. The old rain trees still lined the road along the bund of Tissa Wewa, but the heronry on the island was gone: evidently there was now too much disturbance. The old rest house was only recognisable by its location and the pillars outside what is now the dining-room. The garden was largely occupied by a swimming pool, while large blocks of rooms and other extensions had changed its appearance to that of a hotel. Nevertheless, a large troop of wanderoos, the grey langurs, often still visited the garden and climbed the buildings.

Returning to Colombo along the coast road, we passed many large hotels set pressing on the beaches and surrounded by the former coconut groves. Garishly dressed tourists could be seen along the roadside purchasing tourist tat from stalls which had sprung up to supply demand. But on the inland side of the road and along the small roads through the non-coastal villages, no changes were apparent.

In many ways, change has been more marked in East Africa. I had worked in Tanzania as a cotton pathologist for six years in the late 1960s and early 1970s, when we had lived on a government agricultural research station at Ukiriguru, just south of the port of Mwanza on Lake Victoria. Visits in 1994 and 1999 emphasised the population explosion which had taken place. Shanty towns now covered the hills around Mwanza which before had supported grassland or scrub. Several large and luxurious lodges now perched along the rim of the Ngorongoro crater and the Lake Manyara Hotel had long ago arisen on the site where I had slept in the tented camp. Although animals were plentiful in the protected areas, we found the Athi Plains criss-crossed with wire fences and the few wild animals we saw seemed no longer to belong in what had become a managed environment. In Nairobi the crowded pavements seethed with humanity and constant vigilance was needed to repel hassle from those wanting to sell safaris or artefacts. On the outskirts of the city, shanty towns stretched as far as the eye could see and lack of maintenance was painfully apparent on roads, streets, and those buildings not directly concerned with the tourist trade. One day we took an excursion to Lake Naivasha in a tour minibus with an exuberant driver. At one point near Naivasha town the main road consisted of so many moon-like craters and holes as to render it impassable and our driver left the road and traversed the rutted verges for a mile or so.

'Sorry, my friends,' he apologised, waving an arm with an expensive-looking wrist watch at the road, 'this road was built by the British, so it is very old.' This he apparently regarded as a perfectly reasonable explanation for the condition of the road.

This book is not a history and I am not qualified to analyse the economic and social progress of Sri Lanka since I knew it 40 years ago. However, one cannot help asking oneself whether the average man or woman in the street, on the estates, or in the villages, is now much better off and happier than they were in my time or, indeed, during colonial days. The people I saw in the central and south-west areas of the Island are certainly better dressed and shod than they were 40 years ago, which must reflect some increase in prosperity, although the improvement did not seem great. Also, the eventual acceptance of the estate Tamil population as citizens must have given them new confidence and, to some extent, wider opportunities. But the civil war and its consequences showed a catastrophic decline in ethnic social harmony since colonial days. In the areas administered by the national government there is no doubt a positive feeling that the people can control their own destiny in a more or less democratic way. But is this adequate compensation for lack of peace and harmony, and what about those in areas not nationally administered?

On the 26th December 2004 a huge tsunami struck the eastern, southern and south-western shores of Sri Lanka and other shores all around the Bay of Bengal. A narrow, densely populated littoral strip was devastated and 30,000 people in Sri Lanka were killed while hundreds of thousands were rendered homeless. Sri Lanka is not accustomed to such major natural calamities. The Island is blessed with a balmy climate and fertile land and severe excesses or deficiencies of meteorological factors are rare. Tropical cyclones are almost unknown, while severe earthquakes have not been recorded within historical times, during which natural disasters have mainly taken the form of occasional floods on a localised scale. The unprecedented scale of the tsunami disaster has had a profound effect on the economy and also on the 'peace process' for settling the inter-racial conflict, which had seemed to be developing in a promising way and had resulted in a cease fire for three years before the tsunami occurred.  Disputes about the distribution of the massive amounts of aid which were proffered by governments and NGOs now threaten to escalate into renewed conflict.  One can only hope that polarised positions can be moderated into a compromise solution as, in the longer term and in today's global society, compromise is the only way forward.

# Bibliography

These are the principal works I have referred to while writing this book.

Anon. *Ferguson's Ceylon Directory.* The Ceylon Observer, Colombo, Sri Lanka. Annually from 1858.

Anon. *Handbook for the Ceylon traveller.* 2nd ed. Studio Times Ltd., Colombo, Sri Lanka. 1983.

Baker, Samuel W. *Eight years in Ceylon.* New ed. Longmans, Green & Co., London, UK. 1891.

Forrest, D. M. *A hundred years of Ceylon tea, 1867-1967.* Chatto and Windus, London, UK. 1967.

Goldschmidt, Tijs. *Darwin's dreampond: drama in Lake Victoria.* The MIT Press, Cambridge, Mass., USA. 1996.

Grzimek, Bernhard and Grzimek, Michael. *Serengeti shall not die.* Collins Fontana Books, London, UK. 1964.

Hall, Richard *Lovers on the Nile.* Collins, London, UK. 1980.

Henry, G. M. *A guide to the birds of Ceylon.* Oxford University Press, London, UK. 1955.

Hutchinson, Mrs. J. A. Kilimanjaro. *Tanganyika Notes and Records,* No.64, March 1965.

Huxley, Elspeth. *Out in the midday sun.* Penguin Books, London, UK. 1987.

Keegel, E. L. *Tea manufacture in Ceylon.* Monographs on tea production in Ceylon, No.4, 2nd ed. (rev.), 179 pp. The Tea Research Institute of Ceylon. 1958.

Lewis, Frederick. *Sixty four years in Ceylon.* 1926. Reprint by Navrang, New Delhi, India, 1993.

Mason, Phillip. *The men who ruled India.* Jonathan Cape, London, UK. 1980.

Moxham, Roy. *Tea; addiction, exploitation and empire.* Constable & Robinson Ltd., London, UK. 2003.

Muthiah, S. *A planting century. The first hundred years of The United Planters' Association of Southern India, 1893-1993.* Affiliated East-West Press Private Ltd., New Delhi, India. 1993.

Niven, Christine; Noble, John; Forsyth, Susan and Wheeler, Tony. *Sri Lanka, a Lonely Planet travel survival kit.* Lonely Planet Publications, Hawthorn, Victoria, Australia. 6th edn., 1996.

Osmaston, H. A. and Pasteur, D. *Guide to the Ruwenzori, the Mountains of the Moon.* West Col Productions, Goring-on-Thames, UK. 1972.

Perera, G. F. *The Ceylon railway. The story of its inception and progress.* The Ceylon Observer, Colombo, Ceylon. 1925.

Peries, Tony. *George Steuart & Co. Ltd., 1952-1973. A personal odyssey.* Wasala Publications, Nugegoda, Sri Lanka. 2003.

Salkeld, Audrey. *Kilimanjaro: to the roof of Africa.* National Geographic Society, Washington, D.C., USA. 2002.

Skinner, Thomas. *Fifty years in Ceylon.* W. H. Allen & Co. Ltd., London. 1891. Reprint by Asian Educational Services, New Delhi, India, 1995.

Smith, Anthony. *The Great Rift, Africa's changing valley.* BBC Books, London, UK. 1992.

Stephen, Leslie, and Lee, Sidney (eds.). *The dictionary of national biography, from the earliest times to 1900.* 21 vols & Supplement. Oxford University Press, UK. 1963-65.

Tennent, James Emerson. *Ceylon. An account of the island, physical, historical and topographical, with notices of its natural history, antiquities and productions.* Vols. I and II. Longman, Green, Longman, and Roberts, London, UK. 2nd ed., 1859. Reprint by Asian Educational Services, New Delhi, India, 1996.

Williams, Harry. *Ceylon, pearl of the East.* Robert Hale Ltd., London, UK.1950.

Woolf, Leonard. *An autobiography, 1: 1880-1911.* Oxford University Press, Oxford, UK. 1980.

Printed in the United States
By Bookmasters